Burt Franklin: Research & Source Work Series #173
(Selected Essays in Literature & Criticism #4)

THEORIES OF STYLE IN LITERATURE

THEORIES OF STYLE

WITH ESPECIAL REFERENCE TO PROSE COMPOSITION

ESSAYS, EXCERPTS, AND TRANSLATIONS

LANE COOPER

Quare non ut intellegere possit, sed ne omnino possit non intellegere, curandum.

— QUINTILIAN, *Institutio Oratoria*, VIII. 2.

Burt Franklin: Research & Source Works Series #173
(*Selected Essays in Literature & Criticism #4*)

BURT FRANKLIN
New York, N.Y.
1968

Published By
BURT FRANKLIN
235 East 44th St.
New York, N. Y. 10017

ORIGINALLY PUBLISHED
LONDON: 1907

Reprinted 1968

This work has been reprinted on
long- life paper.

Printed in U. S. A.

PREFACE

THIS volume, the editor imagines, may prove serviceable to teachers of English in more than one way.

From its origin — and apart from the style of the editor's translations — it may be regarded first of all as a body of literary models to be used in illustration of some good handbook on English prose composition, by classes in what is technically known as Exposition, *i.e.* written explanation. The editor's conception of such a volume of models arose partly from his belief — which needs no discussion here — that of the three generally recognized Forms of Prose Writing, namely, Description, Narration, and Exposition, only Exposition can be advantageously taught as a practical art by the average instructor in English to the average class; partly from his objection to certain books of "standard" selections, which professed rhetoricians have seen fit to compile for similar purposes of illustration in the classroom. In his opinion these compilations suffer from one fairly obvious defect.

As a rule, they seem to lack a fundamental principle which every teacher of thinking and writing is supposed to demand of every book, and to inculcate in the mind of every pupil. They seem lacking in unity. The several selections in a typical volume, if they happen to be complete in themselves, and if they are really taken from *standard* authors, have otherwise a purely formal bond of similarity: they are merely samples of one or other of the three kinds of writing that com-

prise all literature. Diversity of authorship, of course, is
inevitable in an anthology. Whether the *substance* of any
book employed in the teaching of composition should be so
heterogeneous as of itself to produce no definite and lasting
impression on the plastic mind, merits serious consideration.
Perhaps it is a question to be decided by experience. So far
as the writer's observation goes, the typical book of illustrative
excerpts, drawn from many authors, and dealing with widely
diverse topics, is not a ready instrument for coördinating the
processes of the average undergraduate brain. Hurrying,
within the space of a college term, from some popular account
of a glacier through eighteen other disconnected and often
fragmentary discussions, and ending, let us say, with a chapter from Darwin's *Descent of Man*, the student of such a collection will hardly observe along the route much more of the
method of exposition than can be totally dissociated from a
well-earned grasp of any one subject.

In brief, the present volume owes its origin to a conviction
that the link between substance and form, between knowledge
and expression, ought never to be broken; and that before an
underclassman is urged to write a composition, he ought to
begin systematic thinking in a field where his teacher is qualified to judge of his manner of discussion, through a critical
acquaintance with the matter discussed. A specialist in
English need not be thoroughly versed in Darwinism; he
can scarcely be expected to show much familiarity with the
theory of glacial action; he may properly be supposed to know
something about the mechanism of style, and to have made
some study of the evolution of types in literature. Hence arose
in my mind the idea of an orderly collection of essays on style,
with especial reference to prose composition; a body of
expository writing, for the most part by masters of expression,
at once illustrating and reiterating the salient principles of the

text-book * which it may accompany; a group of stimulating and, on the whole, mutually corroborative selections, representing not too many literary types for easy comprehension of their structure, and printed as far as possible without curtailment.

The material of the volume has been chosen, however, with a view to possible applications other than the one just outlined, though not, it is hoped, inconsistent with it. For example, aside from the question of models for practical criticism and imitation, the selections offer some opportunity 'for a purely theoretical investigation of at least two closely allied literary species, the *essay* and the *address* on *style*. Facilities for the study of specific types in prose are as yet not too abundant. In addition to its use in the classroom, the volume may likewise serve as a work of outside reference, since, although it makes no pretence to inclusiveness, it aims to bring together a considerable number of historic utterances on style, not all of which are very accessible elsewhere. By supplying an adequate historic background for the more recent treatises, it has, I think, a substantial advantage over the collection of nineteenth-century essays on style edited by Professor W. T. Brewster of Columbia.

In the actual employment of material like this, every teacher, of course, will pursue to a certain extent his own method, in accordance with his personal leanings and the constitution of his classes. In general, — even with not very advanced students, — the writer inclines to a practice somewhat as follows. Some text-book having afforded a preliminary knowledge of the main forms of prose composition at a given meeting let the class be ready to discuss the substance and the form of one of the earlier selections, say that from Wackernagel, with suffi-

---

* For example, Professor J. M. Hart's *Essentials of Prose Composition*, Philadelphia, 1902.

cient free play of opinion; each individual, however, basing
his share in the discussion upon a thorough written analysis
of the whole selection. In the case of immature students
these analyses would afterward be subject to the instructor's
private supervision. At the next meeting let each member
of the class be prepared with a paper — also accompanied by
an outline — expanding some special topic in that selection,
or elaborating some point raised in the discussion. When one
has read, the others should feel encouraged to question and
comment. The instructor may or may not pass final judgment on a paper. He is a moderator, whose function is to
stimulate his class to mental self-activity, and quietly to mould
it into a living, intelligent, social unit. This function he can
best perform with groups of not more than fifteen pupils —
preferably of ten or twelve; and, if he has tact, with much
younger minds than are usually drilled in anything approach-
ing a "seminary" course. Each student should preserve
his own papers, properly revised, for special conference from
time to time with the instructor. The net amount of writing
expected of an underclassman per week should be far less
than is customary in some of the "theme" courses at our
American universities; the amount of time spent in the preparation and revision of any one theme, far greater. The student who cannot be sufficiently interested in his English to
plan a composition twice, and to rewrite it thrice, should not,
under ordinary circumstances, hope to master even the rudi-
ments of plain exposition.

Save for the introductory translation from Wackernagel,
the order of the selections is roughly chronological; but it
need not be followed. The excerpt from Aristotle might be
read before that from Plato. Lewes or Thoreau might be
kept until the close of the term. Manifestly, Wackernagel,
Aristotle, Plato, and Longinus are inserted as standards by

which to measure the remaining authors, and should be taken up before Swift, Buffon, and the rest.

In the process of comparing one selection with another, students should cultivate the habit of marginal cross-reference; for the various authors may be made, so to speak, to annotate and reënforce one another on essential points. A few parallels are indicated in the Notes: enough, it is hoped, to suggest to a reader the possibility of his discovering many more by himself. A complete critical apparatus has not been attempted, the editor having desired throughout to suppress adventitious matter, so as to include a greater number of masterpieces, and thus to increase the general field of comparison. However, he hopes that the remarks preceding and following the several selections will be of some utility to students or to teachers.

In the introductory notes teachers will not overlook certain references that would enable classes inadequately furnished with copies of this book, but near a good library, to find many of the selections in a variety of sources.

As a general introduction to the volume, the editor offers, not, of course, his own theory of style — nobody would want that — but a theory, or the skeleton thereof, by an established modern authority, Wackernagel, with whom the editor feels himself essentially in agreement. The Introduction, then, amounts merely to an extra selection taken out of chronological order, and placed for the sake of prominence at the beginning.

In concluding the Preface, the editor desires to acknowledge, very gratefully, his indebtedness to others whose good-will has made the collection possible: to the late and lamented M. Brunetière and to Mr. Harrison for permission to use their articles here reprinted; to Mr. Saunders and Bishop Welldon for sections from their translations of Schopenhauer and Aristotle respectively; to Mr. Havell for his version of Longinus; to the publishers of material here included, and not otherwise in the copyright of Messrs. Macmillan; these last obligations are specifically noted in the proper places. To the series of essays on style edited by Professor Fred N. Scott (Boston, Allyn & Bacon) such a compilation is necessarily indebted. That series, and the *Methods and Materials of Literary Criticism*, by Professors Gayley and Scott (Boston, Ginn & Co.), ought to be owned by every teacher who would use the present volume most intelligently. Finally, the editor owes his thanks to Professor Louis Bevier of Rutgers College, for looking over the translations from Wackernagel and Goethe; to Professors O. G. Guerlac and W. Strunk, Jr., of Cornell, for glancing through those from Buffon and Voltaire; to Professor J. L. Haney of the Central High School, Philadelphia, for valuable suggestions touching the Bibliography; and to Mr. A. W. Craver and Mr. A. H. Gilbert for their assistance in reading proof. All other debts are, he hopes, properly recognized where they occur.

BIBLIOGRAPHY

[The following titles represent such books and articles dealing with style, especially prose style, as the editor has noted in compiling the present volume. References which, in his opinion, cannot safely be disregarded by anyone who wishes to go more deeply into the subject, are indicated by asterisks. Certain titles included above, in the Table of Contents, are not repeated here; a few additional references, on the style of individual authors, will be found in subsequent introductions and notes to the several selections.]

1. ACADEMY. **The Proper Prose Style.** (Vol. 57, p. 576.)
2. ACADEMY. **Studies in Contemporary Style.** (Vol. 57, pp. 379, 767.)
3. ACADEMY. **Excess of Style.** (Vol. 58, p. 15.)
4. ACADEMY. **Literary Style.** (Vol. 59, p. 223.)
·5. ACADEMY. **Style of Modern Journalists.** (Vol. 60, p. 231.)
6. ACADEMY. **The Glittering Style.** (Vol. 61, p. 243.) (Same article: *Living Age*, Nov. 16, 1901, Vol. 231. pp. 458–461.)
7. ALBALAT, A. **L'Art d'écrire.** Paris, Colin, 7ᵉ éd., 1901. (Reviewed in *Nation*, May 18, 1899, Vol. 68, pp. 381–382; *Athenæum*, Feb. 4, 1899, — 1899, Vol. I, p. 145.)
8. ALBALAT, A. **La Formation du style par l'assimilation des auteurs.** Paris, Colin, 1901. (Reviewed in *Nation*, Oct. 17, 1901, Vol. 73, pp. 308–309; *Athenæum*, Oct. 12, 1901, — 1901, Vol. 2, p. 491.)
9. * ARISTOTLE. **Poetics, Chapters XIX–XXII.** (Butcher, S. H., *Aristotle's Theory of Poetry and Fine Art*, London, Macmillan, 1898, pp. 69–87.)
10. ARNOLD, M. (See COOK, No. 39.)
11. * ATHENÆUM. **Review of Symons, A., Studies in Prose and Verse.** (April 22, 1905 ; 1905, Vol. I, pp. 487–488.) (Contains a noteworthy description of the subjective side of *style*.)
12. BAIN, A. **English Composition and Rhetoric.** New York, Appleton, 1879, etc. (*Part I* [pp. 20–152] is on *style*.)
13. BAIN, A. **On Teaching English.** New York, 1887. (Deals chiefly with *style* [esp. pp. 41–206] ; not a well-organized book.)
14. BAINTON, G. [Ed.] **The Art of Authorship . . . Advice to Young Beginners, personally contributed by Leading Authors of the Day** [etc.]. London, Clarke, 1890. (See *Spectator*, May 17, 1890.)
15. BALDWIN, C. S. **How to Write. A Handbook based on the English Bible.** New York, Macmillan, 1905. (Reviewed in *Literary Digest*, July 15, 1905, Vol. 31, pp. 79–80.)

16. * BECKER, K. F. Der deutsche Stil. Prag, Tempsky, *3. Aufl.*, 1883.

17. BIRD, F. M. Paralyzers of Style. *Lippincott's Magazine.* (Feb., 1896; Vol. 57, pp. 280–284.)

18. BLAIR, H. Lectures on Rhetoric and Belles Lettres. Edinburgh, 1783. (*Lectures XVIII–XXIV* treat of *style.*)

19. * BOECKH, A. Encyclopädie und Methodologie der philologischen Wissenschaften. Leipzig, Teubner, 1886. (For *style*, see pp. 124–140; 245–248; 810–816.)

20. BOURGET, P. Essais de psychologie contemporaine. Paris, Lemerre, 4ᵉ *éd*, 1885. (Pp. 156–173: *Gustave Flaubert, III, Théories d art.*)

21. BOURGET, P. Nouveaux Essais de psychologie contemporaine. Paris, Lemerre, 1886. (Pp. 180–198: *MM. Edmond et Jules de Goncourt, III, Questions de style.*)

22. BREWSTER, W. T. [Ed.] Representative Essays on the Theory of Style. New York, Macmillan, 1905. (Introduction, pp. ix–xxvii. Contains essays on *style* by De Quincey, Spencer, Stevenson, Pater, and Harrison, and selections from Newman and Lewes.)

23. BREWSTER, W. T., and G. R. CARPENTER. Studies in Structure and Style (Based on Seven Modern Essays). New York, Macmillan, 1896.

24. BROCKHAUS. Conversations-Lexicon. 1898. (Vol. 15, p. 359, *Stil.*)

25. * BRUNETIÈRE, F. Style (en littérature). *La Grande Encyclopédie.* (Vol. 30, pp. 558–562.)

26. BUCK, W. J. Style in English. *Writer.* (Vol. 11, p. 30.)

27. BULWER LYTTON, E. Caxtoniana. New York, Harper, 1864. (*Chapter VIII: On Rhythm in English Prose as conducive to Precision and Clearness,* pp. 79–81. *Chapter IX: On Style and Diction,* pp. 83–101.)

28. BURROUGHS, J. Style and " The Stylist." *Critic.* (Dec., 1898; Vol. 33, pp. 464–465.)

29. BURROUGHS, J. The Vital Touch in Literature. *Atlantic Monthly.* (March, 1899; Vol. 83, pp. 399–406.)

30. CAMPBELL, G. The Philosophy of Rhetoric. New York, Harper, 1846, etc. (*Parts II* and *III* treat of *style.*)

31. CHAIGNET, A. La rhétorique et son histoire. Paris, Bouillon et Vieweg, 1888. (Pp. 413–539: *Théorie du style.*)

32. CHAMBERS'S JOURNAL. Style. (May 24, 1845; Vol. 3, pp. 321–322.)

33. CHRISTIAN MONTHLY SPECTATOR. **Essay and Oratorical Style.** (Vol. 4, p. 356.)

34. * CICERO. **On Oratory and Orators** [etc.], Translated [etc.] by J. S. Watson. London, Bohn, 1855. (For *style*, see Index.)

35. * COLERIDGE, S. T. **Biographia Literaria, Chapter XX.** *Coleridge's Works*, ed. Shedd. New York, Harper, 1884. (Vol. 3, pp. 443–460 : " The Neutral Style, or That Common to Prose and Poetry," etc.)

36. CONDILLAC, E. B. Œuvres. Paris, 1798. (Vol. 7, pp. 337–423 : *Traité de l'art d'écrire*. Pp. 429–443, a separate treatise : *Dissertation sur l'harmonie du style.*)

37. CONSTABLE, J. **Reflections on Accuracy of Style.** London, 1734.

38. * COOK, A. S. **The Bible and English Prose Style.** Boston, Heath, 1892.

39. * COOK, A. S. **The Touchstones of Poetry. Selected from the Writings of Matthew Arnold and John Ruskin.** Privately printed [San Francisco] [1887].

40. CRAWSHAW, W. H. **The Interpretation of Literature.** New York, Macmillan, 1896.

41. * DEMETRIUS. **On Style,** ed. W. Rhys Roberts. Cambridge University Press, 1902.

42. DENNIS, J. **Style.** *Time.* (Vol. 13, p. 71.)

43. * DE QUINCEY, T. **Essays on Style, Rhetoric, and Language,** ed. F. N. Scott. Boston, Allyn & Bacon, 1893.

44. DIDEROT, D. **Thoughts on Art and Style,** selected and translated by Beatrix Tollemache. London, Rivingtons, 1904. (Reviewed in *Nation*, Oct. 6, 1904, Vol. 79, p. 279.)

45. * DIONYSIUS OF HALICARNASSUS. **The Three Literary Letters,** ed., with English translation [etc.], by W. Rhys Roberts. Cambridge University Press, 1901.

46. DRAKE, N. **Essays, Biographical, Critical, and Historical.** London, 1814. (Vol. 2, pp. 1–116: *On the Progress and Merits of English Style.*)

47. DUBLIN UNIVERSITY MAGAZINE. **On Style.** By "A Student of Pascal." (Aug., 1865 ; Vol. 66, pp. 178–179.)

48. DUBLIN UNIVERSITY MAGAZINE. **The Cutting Style of Writing.** (April, 1872 ; Vol. 79, pp. 415–425.)

49. * EARLE, J. **English Prose : Its Elements, History, and Usage.** London, Smith, Elder, 1890. (*Passim* and *Chapter IX : Style.*)

50. EDINBURGH REVIEW. **Some Tendencies of Prose Style.** (Oct., 1899; Vol. 190, pp. 356–376.) (A review of Craik's *English Prose*, Raleigh's *Style*, and Henley and Whibley's *English Prose.*)

51. ELLWANGER, W. D. **Religious Helps to forming Style.** *Critic.* (Vol. 43, p. 406–410.)

52. *ELSTER, E. **Prinzipien der Litteraturwissenschaft.** Halle, Niemeyer, 1897. (*5. Kapitel: Sprachstil,* pp. 414–487.)

53. *ELZE, K. **Grundriss der englischen Philologie.** Halle, Niemeyer, 1887. (Pp. 322–339: *Stilistik.*)

54. FAGUET, É. **Les Corrections de Flaubert.** *Revue politique et littéraire.* (*3 juin,* 1899; Vol. 63, pp. 695–697.)

55. FISHER, E. **Style.** *Universalist Quarterly Review.* (Vol. 11, p. 194.)

56. FORSYTH, W. **Literary Style.** *Fraser's Magazine.* (Vol. 55, pp. 249, 424.)

57. FORSYTH, W. **Essays, Critical and Narrative.** London, Longmans, 1874. (P. 162.)

58. *F[OWLER], H. W. and F. G. F. **The King's English.** Oxford, Clarendon Press, 1906.

59. *Gayley, C. M., and F. N. SCOTT. **Methods and Materials of Literary Criticism.** Boston, Ginn, 1899. (An indispensable work. For *style,* see Index.)

60. GENUNG, J. F. **The Practical Elements of Rhetoric.** Boston, Ginn, 1902. (*Style* and *Style in General,* pp. 11–27; in detail, pp. 28–210.)

61. *GERBER, G. **Die Sprache als Kunst.** Berlin, Gaertner, *2. Aufl.,* 1885.

62. GUMMERE, F. B. **A Handbook of Poetics.** Boston, Ginn, 1888. (*Part II, Style,* pp. 83–118.)

63. HARPER'S MONTHLY. [**Individuality of Style.**] *Editor's Study.* (Dec., 1904; Vol. 110, pp. 162–164.)

64. HART, J. S. **A Manual of Composition and Rhetoric.** Revised Edition, by J. M. Hart, Philadelphia, Eldredge, 1897. (*Part I, Style.*)

65. HARTMANN, E. VON, **Æsthetik.** Leipzig, Friedrich, 1886. (For *style,* see Vol. 2, pp. 139–143; 554–556.)

66. *HARTOG, P. J. **The Teaching of Style in English and French Schools.** *Fortnightly Review.* (June, 1902; Vol. 77, pp. 1050–1063.)

67. HASTINGS, T. S. **Oratorical and Rhetorical Style.** *Presbyterian Review.* (Vol. 10, p. 210.)

68. *HENDRICKSON, G. L. **The Peripatetic Mean of Style and the Three Stylistic Characters.** *American Journal of Philology.* (Vol. 25, pp. 125–146.)

69. *HENDRICKSON, G. L. The Origin and Meaning of the Ancient Characters of Style. *American Journal of Philology.* (Vol. 26, pp. 249–290.)

70. HEYDRICK, B. A. Qualities of Style. *Chautauquan.* (April, 1903; Vol. 37, pp. 43–46.)

71. HOME, H., LORD KAMES. Elements of Criticism (1762). New York, 1854. (Esp. pp. 235 ff.)

72. HOSMER, J. K. Perspicuity the Prime Requisite of Style. *Western.* (Vol. 4, p. 223.)

73. HUNT, T. W. Studies in Literature and Style. New York, Armstrong, 1890. (Cf. *Modern Language Notes,* June, 1890, Vol. 5, pp. 179–181.)

74. JAMES, H. The Question of our Speech. *Booklover's Magazine.* (Aug. 6, 1905; Vol. 6, pp. 199–210.)

75. *JESPERSEN, O. Growth and Structure of the English Language. Leipzig, Teubner, 1905. (Pp. 1–17 characterize the general *style* of English.)

76. *JONSON, B. Timber, ed. F. E. Schelling. Boston, Ginn, 1892. (Pp. 54–72 deal with prose *style* and the art of writing.)

77. *JOUBERT, J. Pensées. Paris, 1880. (Pp. 273–300.)

78. KAMES. (See HOME, No. 71.)

79. KEARY, C. F. What is Style? *Independent Review.* (Dec., 1904; Vol. 4, p. 363.) (Same article: *Eclectic Magazine,* March, 1905, Vol. 144, pp. 393–399; *Living Age,* Jan. 21, 1905, Vol. 244, pp. 149–155. Cf. *Literary Digest,* Feb. 11, 1905, Vol. 30, p. 202.)

80. KELLOGG, M. D. A Study in Style. *Education.* (Sept., 1900; Vol. 21, pp. 50–53.)

81. * KING'S ENGLISH, THE. (See FOWLER, No. 58.)

82. * KÖNIG, E. Stilistik, Rhetorik, Poetik in Bezug auf die biblische Litteratur. Komparativisch dargestellt. Leipzig, Dieterich, 1900.

83. KÖRTING, G. Encyklopädie und Methodologie der englischen Philologie. Heilbronn, Henninger, 1888. (*Der Stil im Englischen,* pp. 357–362.)

84. KÖRTING, G. Encyklopädie und Methodologie der romanischen Philologie. Heilbronn, Henninger, 1884–1886. (*2. Theil,* pp. 296–311, *Die Stylistik; 3. Theil,* pp. 257–278, *Satzbau,* etc.)

85. LA BRUYÈRE, J. DE, Caractères. I. Des Ouvrages de l'esprit. *Œuvres.* Paris, Hachette, 1865. (Vol. 1, pp. 113–150.)

86. LA HARPE, J. F. DE, Cours de Littérature. Paris, 1826. (See Index, Vol. 18, under *Style.*)

LAMB, L. A. A Standard Newspaper Style. *Writer.* (Vol. 3, p. 13.)

88. LANSON, G.　**Conseils sur l'Art d'écrire.**　Paris, Hachette, 5e *éd.*, 1903.

89. LANSON, G.　**L'Art de la prose, I.**　*Les Annales politiques et littéraires.*　(26 *mars*, 1905.)　(The introductory article in a series on masters of French prose.)

90. LEGGE, A. O.　**Style.**　*Manchester Quarterly.*　(Vol. 2, p. 37.)

91. LEISURE HOUR.　**Peculiarities of Style.**　(Vol. 9, p. 621.)

92. *LEWES, G. H.　**The Principles of Success in Literature,** ed. F. N. Scott.　Boston, Allyn & Bacon, 1892.

93. *LIERS, H.　**Zur Geschichte der Stilarten.** *Neue Jahrbücher für Philologie und Paedagogik.*　(1887; Vol. 135, pp. 681–717.)

94. LIVING AGE.　[?] **Excellence of Simplicity.**　(Sept. 30, 1905; Vol. 246, pp. 877–880.)

95. LITERATURE [N.Y.].　**Departure of English Prose from Classical Standards.**　(Nov. 17, 1899; Vol. 5, pp. 433–434.)

96. LOISE, F.　**Traité de littérature : Les lois du style.**　Bruxelles, Vromant, 1887.

97. LOGAN, J. D.　**Postulates of a Psychology of Prose Style.** *Education.*　(Dec., 1901 ; Vol. 22, pp. 193–201.)

98. LONG, G.　**An Old Man's Thoughts about Many Things.**　London, Bell and Daldy, 2 ed., 1872.　(*Of Style*, pp. 92–161.)

99. *LONGINUS.　**On the Sublime,** ed. W. Rhys Roberts.　Cambridge University Press, 1899.

100. *LUTOSŁAWSKI, W.　**The Origin and Growth of Plato's Logic.**　New York, Longmans, 1897.　(*Chapter III*, pp. 64–193 : *The Style of Plato.*　Very important for the bearing on stylometry.)

101. LYTTON, E. B.　(See BULWER, No. 27.)

102. LYTTON, E. R.　**Le Style c'est l'homme.** *Fortnightly Review.*　(June 1, 1884; Vol. 41, pp. 712–723.)　(Same article : *Eclectic Magazine,* Aug., 1884, Vol. 103, pp. 145–153.)

103 MALLOCK, W. H.　**Style c'est l'homme.** *New Review.*　(April, 1892 ; Vol. 6, pp. 441–454.)　(Same article : *Eclectic Magazine,* Vol. 118, pp. 793 ff. ; *Living Age,* Vol. 193, pp. 643 ff.)

104. MARMONTEL, J. F.　**Élémens de littérature.**　Paris, 1787.　(Vol. 6, pp. 189 ff.)

105. MARCOU, P. B.　**Two Points in French Style.** *American Journal of Philology.*　(1885 ; Vol. 6, pp. 344–348.)

106. MATHER, F. J., JR.　**Wanted — a Style for the Times.** *Nation.*　(Sept. 4, 1902 ; Vol. 75, pp. 185–186.)

107. MERWIN, H. C.　**Style in Judicial Opinions.** *Green Bag.*　(Dec., 1897 ; Vol. 9, pp. 521–525 ; Jan., 1898 ; Vol. 10, pp. 7–11.)

108. MINTO, W. **A Manual of English Prose Literature** . . . **designed mainly to show Characteristics of Style.** Edinburgh and London, 1881 ; Boston, Ginn, 1901. (Esp. Introduction, pp. 1–28.)

109. MOORE, C. L. **On Style in Literature.** *Dial* [Chicago]. (Sept. 16, 1905; Vol. 39, pp. 156–159.)

110. *MORLEY, J. **Studies in Literature.** London, Macmillan, 1904. (*On the Study of Literature*, pp. 189–228 ; esp. pp. 221 ff.)

111. NATION. **Style and Statecraft.** (Dec. 3, 1903 ; Vol.. 77, pp. 440–441.)

112. *NEWMAN, J. H. **The Idea of a University** [etc.]. London, Longmans, 1889. (*Part II, Lecture II*, pp. 268–293, *Literature.*)

113. *NORDEN, E. **Die Antike Kunstprosa.** Leipzig, Teubner, 1898. (See Index, under *Stil.*)

114. NORTH BRITISH REVIEW. **Modern Style.** (Feb., 1857 ; Vol. 26, pp. 339–375.) (Review of Trench's *English, Past and Present*, and *On the Study of Words.*)

115. O'BRIEN, R. L. **Machinery and English Style.** *Atlantic Monthly.* (Oct., 1904 ; Vol. 94, pp. 464–472.)

116. PAGE, W. H. **An Intimate View of Publishing.** *World's Work.* (Sept., 1902 ; Vol. 4, pp. 2561 ff. — esp. p. 2562.) (See *Nation*, Sept. 4, 1902 ; Vol. 75, pp. 185–186.)

117. PAGET, V. ["VERNON LEE."] **Studies in Literary Psychology. I. The Syntax of De Quincy** [*sic*]. **II. The Rhetoric of Landor. III. Carlyle and the Present Tense.** *Contemporary Review.* (Nov., Dec., 1903 ; March, 1904. Vol. 84, pp. 713–723, 856–864 ; Vol. 85, pp. 386–392.) (See *Nation*, Dec. 3, 1903, Vol. 77, pp. 440–441.)

118. PEABODY, A. P. **Style.** *Harvard Magazine.* (Vol. 6, p. 1.)

119. PEARSON, C. H. **Reviews and Critical Essays.** London, Methuen, 1896. (*V. The Grand Style*, pp. 89–98.)

120. PELLISSIER, G. **Études de littérature et de morale contemporaines.** Paris, Cornély, 1905. (Reviewed in *Nation*, June 1, 1905, Vol. 80, p. 436.)

121. PHELPS, A. **English Style in Public Discourse.** New York, Scribner's, 1883.

122. PLUMBE, G. E. **Style in Composition.** *University Quarterly.* (July, 1861 ; Vol. 4, pp. 94–98.)

123. *QUINTILIAN. **Institutes of Oratory,** translated [etc.] by J. S. Watson. London, Bell, 1875. (For *style*, see Vol. 2, Index.)

124. RALEIGH, W. **Style.** London, Arnold, 1897. (See *Academy*, Nov. 13, 1897; Vol. 52, pp. 404–405, 433–434.)

125. RENTON, W. **The Logic of Style.** London, Longmans, 1874.

126. ROBERTSON, J. M. **Essays towards a Critical Method.** London, Unwin, 1889. (Pp. 64–104; see also Index.)

127. * RUSKIN, J. Fiction — Fair and Foul, III. *Nineteenth Century.* (Sept., 1880; Vol. 8, esp. pp. 400–403.) (Cf. above, COOK, No. 39.)

128. * RUSKIN, J. **Modern Painters.** New York, Wiley, 1884. (Vol. 3, pp. 1–43.)

129. SAINTSBURY, G. **Specimens of English Prose Style from Malory to Macaulay.** London, Kegan Paul, 1886. (Introductory essay on *English Prose Style*, pp. xv–xlv; an interesting, not always safe, historical sketch, written with little attention to form. See *Athenæum*, 1885, Vol. 2, pp. 725–726; *Spectator*, Vol. 59, pp. 199–200; *Saturday Review*, Vol. 61, p. 23.)

130. * SCHOPENHAUER, A. **Parerga und Paralipomena.** Leipzig, Brockhaus, 1888. (Vol. 2, pp. 536–581; see Saunders' free translation, mentioned below, p. 251.)

131. SHEDD, W. G. T. **Fundamental Properties of Style.** *American Presbyterian Review.* (Vol. 13, p. 561.)

132. SHEDD, W. G. T. **Relation of Style to Thought.** *Bibliotheca Sacra.* (Vol. 8, p. 491.)

133. * SMITH, G. G. [Ed.] **Elizabethan Critical Essays.** Oxford, Clarendon Press, 1904. (See Index, under *Style.*)

134. SOUTHERN LITERARY MESSENGER. **Innovations in Style.** (1838; Vol. 4, p. 322. See *The Southern Literary Messenger*, by B. M. Minor, New York, Neale, 1905, pp. 68–69.)

135. SPECTATOR. **Literary Style.** (Oct. 1, 1892; Vol. 69, pp. 445–446.)

136. SPECTATOR. **The Art of Authorship.** (May 17, 1890; Vol. 64, pp. 689–690.) (Review of Bainton; see above, No. 14.)

137. SPECTATOR. **The Technique of Style.** (Sept. 16, 1905; Vol. 95, pp. 382–383.) (A comment on Stevenson's well-known essay.)

138. STANLEY, H. M. **Essays on Literary Art.** London, Sonnenschein, 1897. (*XI. The Secret of Style*, pp. 127–164.)

139. * STEINTHAL, H. **Zur Stylistik.** *Zeitschrift für Völkerpsychologie.* (1866; Vol. 4, pp. 465–480.)

140. * STEVENSON, R. L. **Essays in the Art of Writing.** London, Chatto & Windus, 1905. (Reviewed in *Athenæum*, 1905,

Vol. 1, p. 464; *Spectator*, Sept. 16, 1905, Vol. 95, pp. 382–383.)

141. SUTTON, W. **Charm of Style.** *Irish Monthly.* (Vol. 12, p. 32.)

142. *SYMONDS, J. A. **Essays, Speculative and Suggestive.** New York, Scribner's, 1894. (Pp. 139 ff. — esp. pp. 145–146; *Notes on Style*, pp. 181–254.)

143. TEACHENOR, R. B. **Style.** *Writer.* (Vol. 3, p. 13.)

144. TRUEBA, A. DE, **El Estilo es el Hombre.** [A Story.] (In *Coleccion de Autores Españoles* ; Vol. 18, *Cuentos Campesinos.* Leipzio, Brockhaus, 1865. Pp. 233–265.) (The story is translated by T. F. Crane, *Cornell Review*, Nov., Dec., 1878, Vol. 6, pp. 68–79, 122–134.)

145. VÉRON, E. **L'Esthétique.** Paris, Reinwald, 1878. (*Part I, Chap. VIII, Le Style*, pp. 153–177.) (English translation by W. H. Armstrong, London, Chapman, 1879.)

146. VOSSLER, K. **Benvenuto Cellini's Stil in seiner Vita, Versuch einer psychologischen Stilbetrachtung.** *Beiträge zur romanischen Philologie. Festgabe für Gustav Gröber.* Halle, Niemeyer, 1899. (Pp. 414–451.)

147. VOSSLER, K. **Die philosophischen Grundlagen zum " süssen neuen Stil " des Guido Guinicelli, Guido Cavalcanti und Dante Alighieri.** Heidelberg, Winter, 1904.

148. VOSSLER, K. **Stil, Rhythmus und Reim in ihrer Wechselwirkung bei Petrarca und Leopardi.** *Miscellanea di Studi Critici edita in onore di Arturo Graf.* Bergamo, Istituto Italiano d' Arti Grafiche, 1903. (Pp. 453–481.)

149. * WACKERNAGEL, W. **Poetik, Rhetorik und Stilistik.** *2. Aufl.*, Halle, 1888.

150. WALLACE, B. J. **The Volcanic Style in Writing.** *American Presbyterian Review.* (Vol. 4, p. 135.)

151. WESTERN. **French Style.** (Vol. 2, p. 581.)

152. WHATELY, R. **Elements of Rhetoric** (1828). New York, 1833, etc. (*Part III, Of Style.*)

153. WHEELER, D. H. **Conditions of Style.** *Methodist Review.* (Nov., 1893; Vol. 53, pp. 910–914.)

154. WHELPLEY, J. D. **On Style.** *American Whig Review.* (Oct., 1845 ; Vol. 2, pp. 338–364.)

155. WHIBLEY, C. **Language and Style.** *Fortnightly Review.* (Jan. 1899 ; Vol. 71, pp. 100–109.) (A review of M. Bréal's *Essai de Sémantique.*)

156. WHITE, R. G. **Words and their Uses.** New York, Sheldon, 1872. (*Chapter IV, Style*, pp. 63–79.)

157. WISEMAN, N. **Gossip on Style.** *Monitor.* (Vol. I, p. 217.)

158. * WRIGHT, T. H. **Style.** *Macmillan's Magazine.* (Nov., 1877;
Vol. 37, pp. 78–84.) (On Spencer's *Philosophy of Style.*)

159. WOODS, M. L. **English Style and Some French Novels.** *Nineteenth Century.* (Dec., 1903 ; Vol. 54, pp. 1026–1034.)

160. ZANELLA, E. **Lingua e stile: conversazioni letterarie.** Roma,
Tipografia alle Terme diocleziane, 1886.

*   *   *   *   *   *   *

ADDENDA

161. ALDEN, H. M. **Notes on Style.** *Current Literature.* (July,
1901 ; Vol. 31, pp. 53–54.)

162. BOOTH, D. **Essay on Style:** a supplement to **The Principles of
English Composition.** London, 1833.

163. BROCK, A. C. **Language and Thought.** *Living Age.* (May 21,
1904; Vol. 241, pp. 497–499.)

164. FELTON, H. **Dissertation on Reading the Classics and Forming a
Just Style.** London, 1713.

165. "LEE, VERNON." (See PAGET, No. 117.)

166. NATION. **Lafcadio Hearn on Style.** (Dec. 6, 1906; Vol. 83,
pp. 478–479.)

167. PALLAVICINO, S. **Trattato dello Stile e del Dialogo.** Roma, 1662.
(Modena, 1819.)

168. * PASCAL, B. **Pensées** (1670). Nouvelle Édition . . . par Léon
Brunschvicg. Paris, Hachette, 1904.

169. * SIEVERS, E. **Ueber Sprachmelodisches in der deutschen Dichtung.** *Annalen der Naturphilosophie.* (Vol. I, pp. 76–94.)
(Note the further investigation promised at the end of the article, p. 94.)

170. TYTLER, A. F., LORD WOODHOUSELEE. **Essay on the Principles
of Translation** (1791). Lately reissued in Everyman's Library, London, Dent.

CONTENTS

THEORIES OF STYLE IN LITERATURE

I. INTRODUCTION

WILHELM WACKERNAGEL (1806–1869)

Selections from Poetics, Rhetoric, and the Theory of Style
(1836–1837)

[Translated from *Poetik, Rhetorik und Stilistik, Academische Vorle-sungen*, herausgegeben von Ludwig Sieber, 2. Auflage, Halle, 1888. (Pp. 309–316 ; 409–421.)

KARL HEINRICH WILHELM WACKERNAGEL, a gifted scholar and man of letters, trained in exacter studies under the phi-lologist Lachmann, but of broader development and more artistic bent than his master, is better known for his *History of German Literature* than for his lectures on literary theory in general. However, these lectures, first given (1836–1837) early in his long career as professor at the University of Basel, Switzerland, and frequently revised by him for sub-sequent delivery, — though not for other publication, — are by no means the least of his many contributions to scholar-ship. Based not only upon a wide scholarly acquaintance with ancient and modern literatures and literary theory, but also upon the intuitions and experience of one who was himself a talented writer, — for Wackernagel was no mere abstract pedant, — his treatment of *Poetics, Rhetoric, and the Theory of Style* may count as one of the most consistent and acceptable attempts in recent times to systematize a body of knowledge which is usually considered piecemeal

B   I

and without correlation. If this seem sweeping praise, at all events the work deserves to be better known, for example among our rhetoricians; and there might be advantage in presenting certain portions of it merely as evidence that the Germans have not after all been wholly inattentive to literary form. "Since Heine," says Mr. Frederic Harrison, playfully, "Germans . . . have no style at all."

Wackernagel's style is that of the effective university lecturer, clear, logical, full of matter, with obvious transitions and not too condensed; repeating under varying form what is essential, yet with less concealment of the repetition than is usual in a page meant simply for the eye of a reader. We must bear in mind that the selections are from a posthumous work, not prepared for the press by its own author. Finally, it would be unfair to judge the merits of the original on the strength of a translation.

An account of Wackernagel's life, of his early struggles, his rapid rise as a teacher, his powerful influence on his pupils, his rich and varied scholarship, and his ventures in the field of original poetry, will be found in an article by Edw. Schröder in the *Allgemeine deutsche Biographie*, Vol. 40.]

[On the Distinction between Rhetoric and the Theory of Style]

Rhetoric has long been a word of quite indefinite and variable meaning, its signification being now extremely limited and again improperly extended.[1]

Inasmuch as ῥήτωρ meant to them an orator and a teacher of oratory, the ancients understood by *rhetoric* simply the art and theory of persuasive speaking; so Aristotle considered it;[2] and he, as he was the father of poetics, may likewise be called the father of rhetoric. Corresponding, then, to the aim of a complete and exhaustive discipline for orators, the ancients included in the subject not merely all that concerns the orator as such, but also, *necessarily*, much that the art of the orator has in common with that of the master of prose in general, and even with that of the poet; all manner of things, in fact, that condition the presentation of thought through the medium of words.

Under rhetoric, accordingly, they taught not merely how to construct a "speech" and what means further the specific ends of oratory, but they gave directions also about propriety and beauty of expression, about the formation of periods, about euphony in word grouping, about embellishment with metaphors and tropes; in short, about an endless variety of matters that pertain quite as much to a philosophic treatise, to a historical narrative, and to an epic, lyric, or dramatic poem, as to an oration. Under rhetoric they included also the theory of style, though not as if the *rhetor* alone made use of it, but because it was common property. If, for example, they had been led to put together a treatise on the art of writing history, they would have introduced their theory of style into this in just the same way. Similarly, Aristotle has several sections on style in his *Poetics*.[3]

In more recent times this coupling of the theory of style with rhetoric, though perfectly justified by the aim of the Greek and Latin text-books where it was originally met with, has given rise to error in two directions. On the one hand, because the laws and rules of style have an application also to poetry, the word *rhetoric* has been stretched so as actually and expressly to include the theory of poetical discourse as well as prose; so that in this case rhetoric is made equivalent to the whole art of language, in the broadest sense; that is, the art of poetical as well as prose representation, not merely the art of prose in oratory. On the other hand, the term has been restricted properly enough by some to the art of expression in prose; yet in this case the rules of style, being carried over *en masse*, have been treated as if they all counted only for prose; although very many of

them are valid only in poetry and have absolutely no application to prose. This second conception of rhetoric is the
one generally current; it is to be found not simply in text-
books that deal with rhetoric exclusively, but also in such as
deal with rhetoric and poetics together; where, accordingly,
the simple fact of juxtaposition might have brought to the
authors' notice what a serious blunder it was to subordinate
the doctrine of style in general to the specific theory of prose.
How thorough and widespread the confusion thus wrought
in the latter can be readily seen by a glance at the table of
contents in any ordinary text-book on rhetoric, where head-
ings relative to the theory of prose in particular and others
bearing on style in general follow one another in the most
variegated sort of cross-division.

In our present treatment we shall understand by rhetoric
something more than the pure theory of oratory; not more,
however, than the theory of prose. In fact, as poetics is
the theory of poetry, so we may consider rhetoric as equivalent to the theory of prose. It is true, such extension and
definition of the word are not entirely sanctioned on grounds
of etymology; still, since tradition offers no other term that
corresponds exactly, herein we must follow in a certain
measure the authority and procedure of the modern text-
books. But all that lies outside the realm of prose as such,
in the region where prose and poetry meet; that is to say,
all that lies in the field of style — all rules which both forms
of expression have in common: this will be treated separately
under the head of *Stylistics*.[4]

On Prose in General

Prose is the direct, as it were the polar, opposite of poetry.
It is the expression in language of mental perceptions whose
basis is in the intellect and whose object-matter is truth:

that intellect which in the productions of poetry stands, so to speak, in the background, and that truth which is acceptable to poetry only in so far as it is beautiful. Prose is the form in which the intellect as the organ of scientific curiosity records and presents its experiences and opinions — its knowledge; to the end that through this reproduction the intellect becoming active in another person may arrive at the same knowledge. In so far the common characteristic of prose is instruction; by nature prose is didactic. Poetry directs itself toward what is good and what is true only in so far as this is beautiful; hence, without the coöperation of feeling and imagination even didactic poetry can have no existence. Prose, on the contrary, needs no such coöperation and mediation. It proceeds simply and directly from intellect to intellect. Nor is that which the intellect recognizes as true, necessarily beautiful and good; where, however, it is beautiful and good, it is not made the object of the intellect's contemplation on that account, but above all because it is true.

Prose, then, the language of the intellect, is a representation of what is good and beautiful in so far as this is true, and of what is true even when that is not good or beautiful. Consequently, the language of prose does not require the same beauty of form as the language of poetry. Only in poetry, only where some perception of the beautiful as such is to be represented, must the law of beauty dominate the language — the law which demands unity in multiplicity; there, and only there, exists the need of rhythmical ordering of discourse in verses and of uniting these verses in strophes. The intellect, on the other hand, so far as concerns form of presentation, asks simply for intelligibility — for clearness; it wishes no more; it lays stress on beauty of language only as this may promote clearness and lighten the task of understanding. The language of the intellect will, indeed, if cultured, never leave euphony out of consideration, yet only because an intimate relation between the soul and the senses renders the intellect more ready to reproduce in itself any proffered knowledge when such knowledge is presented in a way that pleases the senses. Only within these narrow limitations is it proper in connection with prose to speak of artistic treatment or of the art of eloquence.[5] To that supreme richness of euphony which is peculiar to the language of poetry, and the cause of which lies deeper than a mere flattery of the senses, the language of the intellect does not attain. This language is just what it is called, *prosa, oratio prosa*, i.e. *prorsa — proversa;* that is, it moves straight forward, without repetition of similar rhythmical arrangement, without any noticeable return of the language upon itself: whereas poetical language is called *oratio versa.* Opposed to " linkèd " language, to *oratio alligata metris (oratio ligata* is an unclassical expression), stands that which is unfettered, *soluta;* this and no other form is the demand of the intellect, where the intellect speaks and speaks to its like; and this form in turn demands and endures no content other than an intellectual. In purely intellectual didactic poems the poetical form is no less a defect than is the prose form in a drama: in both cases the incongruity destroys that interdependence which ought always to exist between form and matter.

So much on prose in general and on the difference between it and poetry. It is in order now to speak of the age and origin of prose. This will furnish opportunity for enumerating and describing the main varieties of prose language.

In all ages and among all peoples prose as a literary form is a later development than poetry.[6] Outside of literature, of course, prose is older,[7] since without doubt prose conversation must originally have preceded the composition of verses. Considered, however, as a form of representation consciously adapted to literary ends, prose may count as the younger sister or, better, the daughter of poetry, for in all cases centuries must go by before a literary prose is attained; there are in existence peoples of ancient origin that possess none yet. A literary prose arises first at the point where a nation passes out of the stage of naïve simplicity into the more conscious life of an artificial civilization. Up to this point the whole literature is poetical: history is known only in the saga; that is, there is no prying into the events of the past for the naked and unadorned truth; there is retained of those events only the poetically garbed idea in its living beauty; the saga, imaginative in its very nature, assumes also an imaginative outer form, as ballad or as song. During this stage what Tacitus says of the ancient Germans holds good for all races: "Their traditional songs are their one and only species of record and chronicle."[8] The intellect itself continues more or less submerged in poetry; its instruction is given such a relation to imagination and feeling as to border on poetical vision. This we have already at some length shown to be the case with the didactic epic and the didactic lyric.[9] In these, even where the attempt is essentially unsuccessful, the particular doctrine inculcated must put up with at least the external semblance of poetry; so little suspicion is there as yet of any other form of exposition. At this stage even legal maxims, for example, are put in meter, and always with a certain poetical coloring in the diction. We have frequent testimony concerning the existence of such saws among Hellenic and Celtic tribes; and instances enough are preserved for us in the case of the Germans.

Little by little, however, the crucial point approaches, and at length the intellect comes to a consciousness of its right and property in literature. Growing displeased with what fancy has made out of history, it finally rejects fancy altogether, and will set to work with no coadjutor but pure memory. Concerning itself with truth alone, it disdains no detail of history whatsoever. Accordingly, materials are amassed, and, with the necessity of a more convenient and less artificial form of expression, comes the discovery that such a form is likewise more appropriate. Thus, then, out of epic poetry is developed one main variety of prose, namely, *narrative* or *historical*. Similarly, in didactic poetry it becomes gradually more and more evident how unsuitable, and how cramping to the matter, are the poetical point of view and outer form in the majority of cases — how much more briefly one thing might be stated, how much more exactly another amplified, how much more clearly and intelligibly both might be expressed, if only the prose form were chosen. As social life and political organization grow more and more complex, as, perhaps, moral corruption becomes greater and greater, the few old maxims in metrical garb no longer suffice; there is need of a greater number, more carefully elaborated: and so to didactic poetry is added *didactic prose*.

Besides all this, one external circumstance must not be overlooked, since it has everywhere contributed to support and hasten the evolution of prose, both historical and didactic. The art of writing, which the present age of advanced civilization is continually spreading, was in earlier times, even when well known, much less confidently relied on. Hence it was necessary in the case of narratives and teachings, the preservation of which was desirable, to intrust them to the more easily remembered form of poetry. On the other hand, by a natural reaction, writing tended not to come into vogue, simply because there was another satisfactory way of preserving everything. In a higher stage of culture we find a corresponding relation of action and reaction between writing and prose: writing, on account of its greater convenience, making prose possible, because the preservation of the latter cannot be so safely left to the unaided memory; again, prose once in existence, the need of employing the pen increases.

Historical or narrative, and didactic or expository, these are the two chief varieties into which this second form of representation[10] through the medium of language is to be divided. The origin and goal of both varieties is the intellect; the aim of both, the production and reproduction of a knowledge of the true. To what extent, however, the two other faculties of the soul, namely, imagination and feeling, play a part in prose, and what activity can properly be allotted them, may be considered to better advantage in a closer examination of the two varieties in question. To this survey we shall now proceed. [See Wackernagel, pp. 316 ff.]

Stylistics

Without repeating what has been said[11] (pp. 3–4) concerning the usual confusion of rhetoric and the theory of style, we may call attention again to an observation that obtruded itself when we began the discussion of poetics. It can never be the aim of a theory of poetry or rhetoric to turn a student of that theory or the reader of a text-book into a poet or an orator. The teacher, or the writer of the text-book, if wise and conscientious, will attempt to consider poetry and prose simply as they exist for us in literature, from the standpoint of the laws that govern them; to bring these laws into clearer view, and thereby to facilitate our appreciation, to increase our enjoyment, and to make our judgment more sharp and sure. If, then, among the hearers or readers there be any one on whom God has bestowed the gift of poetry or eloquence, to such a one the theoretical instruction will be of double value, for he will have also a practical advantage from it; such a one the teacher of poetics or of rhetoric will help to develop. But to make a poet or an orator of a man who is not one to begin with, is impossible for the teacher or anybody else.

With the theory of style the case is similar. It is true, this theory does not concern itself with matters so profound as do poetics and rhetoric. Its object is the surface of linguistic expression; not the idea, not the material, but simply the outer form — the choice of words, the construction of sentences. And external things like these, one might suppose, could well be taught, so as to be learned once for all. Yet style, to tell the truth, is no mere mechanical handicraft: the linguistic forms with which the art of style has to do are conditioned in the most necessary way by matter and meaning. Style is no lifeless mask laid upon the substance of thought: it is the living play of the countenance, the play of living feature, produced by the expressive soul within. Or, again, it is simply an investiture of the substance, a drapery; yet the folds of the drapery are caused by the posture of the limbs that the drapery veils, and it is the soul, once more, that alone has given the limbs such and such movement and position. Accordingly, in a discussion of the theory of style we must neither promise nor expect more than in a treatment of poetics or rhetoric. With reference to style, also, the aim can be only a theoretical explanation of literary material already existent; nor can the theorist propose to do more than awaken a reasonable and conscious appreciation in the student and educate his power of criticism. So far as concerns actual practice he can wish to further only the rare individual who, having a rich fund of beautiful ideas, possesses also an inborn sense for the beauty of external form. For everyone else all rules have only a negative value. They can teach us what not to do — never positively what to do.

With these few words by way of introduction we can now go on to the main discussion.

1. On Style in General

As is well known, the word *style* has its origin in Greek, passing thence into Latin, and through the latter coming at length to us. The Greek original signifies a uniform rectilinear body of greater length than thickness: στῦλος means a wooden pile, a stone pillar, finally, a metallic graver for writing and drawing. In meaning, as well as by derivation, it corresponds to our [German] word *Stiel.* The Latins adopted it chiefly in the latter signification of *graver;* their language wanting the sound of upsilon, they spelled the word *stilus.* With them, not with the Greeks, the literal meaning was developed figuratively, and by *style* was signified, first, what we also express metaphorically by the word *hand,* and the Latins at times by *manus* — that is, a characteristic way of making letters; second, still more figuratively, a characteristic manner of dressing thought in words; one finds the usage as early as Terence,[12] Cicero,[13] and others. We have a similar way of referring to " a clever pen," or in the art of painting to " a delicate brush " or " the brush of Apelles." It is in the latter, metaphorical sense that we are in the habit of using the word *style,* or, since we have borrowed it from the Romans, *stile.* However, we have made its application wider than the literal signification warrants. Throughout the entire range of art — painting, sculpture, music, etc. — we speak of style, wherever an inner peculiarity shows itself in the outward representation through characteristic marks. Thus we speak, for example, of the Romance style in architecture, or of the style of Raphael or Sebastian Bach. And the artists in general and without further qualification say, for instance, of an ordinary vessel, " It has style," [14] if the thing answer its purpose, and be beautiful, and at the same time show a certain distinctive peculiarity of form. In particular, however, we employ the word *style* with regard to expression in language, whether prose or poetical. The term *manner of writing* is synonymous; synonymous, yet not equivalent: *style* one may say under all circumstances, but not under all circumstances *manner of writing*. With reference to an essay one may speak of the author's *manner of writing* as well as of the *style;* with reference to a sermon or song it is not proper to speak of the *manner of writing* even when the thing lies written before us and is actually neither spoken nor sung. Where it is a question of reproduction or appreciation, the sermon must be considered as spoken, the song as sung.

If, then, the word *style* is to be defined more sharply with particular reference to representation in language, this can be done about as follows: Style is the mode of representation in language, conditioned partly by the psychological peculiarities of the one who represents, partly by the matter and purpose of what is represented. This definition is neither too broad nor too restricted. It is broad enough to include the various applications of the word reasonably possible within the range of literature, whether one has in mind, say, dramatic style in general, or the dramatic style of the Greeks, or, again, the style of a single dramatist like Æschylus. It is not, however, so elastic as a rather commonly accepted definition which makes an altogether arbitrary distinction between style and manner of writing, and for the sake of this distinction includes in the conception of style matters that belong by right to poetics, rhetoric, or even logic. According to the distinction in question, style is the way in which a person shapes, arranges, and puts down his *thoughts* for the attainment of a specific end; whereas manner of writing, being the way in which he selects and combines *words*, considered purely as audible elements of expression, concerns only the relation borne by the discourse to the demands of euphony and, possibly, sentence structure. All this, however, gives more to style and less to manner of writing than is allowable.

Our definition, proposed above, will find its best justification as we amplify further. In that definition we have affirmed that the mode of representation is conditioned partly by the psychological peculiarities of the one who represents, partly by the matter and purpose of what is represented; that is, to put it in other words and more briefly, style has a *subjective*[15] and an *objective* side. For example, let us take Herder's academic address[16] on geography. Here the style, the mode of representation, is on the one hand conditioned objectively by matter and purpose: by the matter, that is, first by the ruling idea of the theme, namely, the utility and attractiveness of geographical studies, and secondly by the substance as a whole, the entire material of thought with which the one main idea surrounds itself; by the purpose, in so far as the attempt is made to win over the audience, and just that sort of an audience — scholars and teachers and their assembled friends — to the recognition and support of this idea, and in so far as the particular thoughts that are here brought together have been ordered in accordance with this purpose for an address, and, specifically, for an address given before a school. Objectively considered, therefore, the whole has the style of an academic address on geography. To a certain extent, then, this address has something in common with every other address ever given, or ever to be given, on the like theme before such an audience. What distinguishes it from every other and makes it Herder's address is the subjective side of the style, the mode in which Herder alone, just because he had his particular mind and training, and lived in a particular age, put his thoughts into language — his mode of clothing and embellishing his ideas and of ordering, separating, and uniting his words.[17]

Necessarily, of course, both sides always belong together: they are not and must not be disjoined, for they are one and the same thing — the outer form of language, merely viewed from different standpoints; and, in a healthy and well-conceived composition, it is impossible that either should exist alone. A composition that has only objectivity of style — unfortunately there are too many such — if one can succeed in reading it, makes the same unsatisfactory impression as lack of character makes everywhere. Both sides must be present, both in the right organic relation; now more of the one, now more of the other, the excess or diminution being conditioned at every instant by the content, according as that is of a more subjective or more objective nature. Simply on this depends the greater or lesser subjectivity or objectivity of the outer expression, that is to say, of the style. In the epic poet, since his very point of view demands the utmost objectivity, since he does not draw his idea and material from within, but takes them into himself entirely from without, the outer representation also — the style — will be found praiseworthy when the subjective element is reduced to a minimum; for this element could show itself extensively only in case the poet had been unduly subjective in his point of view. On the other hand, no one will censure the lyric poet if in his songs it be hard to discover the general style of all lyric poetry — that is, the objective side — in the presence of the peculiarities of his individual lyric strain. The more individual, the more akin to his innermost temperament, or in other words the more truly lyric, his conceptions, just so much more of the subjective may he, nay, must he, give to the outward expression of his conceptions.

But the art of observing measure and limit in this matter is bestowed only on a few elect. In point of style, writers but seldom display the right natural and artistic relation between subjectivity and objectivity. The large majority border on colorless lack of character. Others, however, whether through vanity or through a vivacity of spirit which they cannot control, are driven to the opposite extreme, where their subjectivity preponderates to excess. Such disproportion in the blending of style causes what we call mannerism; just as we speak of mannerism in painting and sculpture the moment we meet, in line and composition, elements that have no foundation in the object represented, that are really foreign to it, having their origin purely in the temper, caprice, and acquired habit of the artist. They betray mannerism, therefore, who subordinate the object to their own subjective natures, where they should rather subordinate their own natures to the object: for example, among the Greeks, Æschylus — whose *mannerism* Aristophanes ridicules in the *Frogs* — in contrast to the true *style* of Sophocles, and the *lack of character* in Euripides; among the Latins, Tacitus; among the mediæval German poets, Wolfram von Eschenbach; among the prose writers of recent times, Johannes von Müller and Jean Paul. I have intentionally taken examples where mannerism is simply a result of overmastering spiritual potency in the author, and a result unconscious, for the most part, to the producer; writers who in other respects belong among the first in all ages, and who, each in his own field, would easily be the very first, could they have kept free from the reproach of mannerism. A peculiar and distinctive manner is, indeed, the mark of an unusual author. Those of a lower order go to no such lengths; their mental individuality is too trivial to preponderate so and make itself count for so much in the expression. If men of insignificant caliber have a manner, they have it rather from imitation of other, greater minds. In that case the defect is double: for if the mannerism of the original was, after all, made possible only by derangement of a proper organic relation, it at least proceeded from a living organism; in the imitation, however, the mannerism sinks to a purely mechanical artifice, a mere externality, without any inner principle of life. The style of Johannes von Müller, which, for all its warmth, is somewhat inflexible and harsh, may now and then be cumbersome and disturbing, since it is not directly conditioned by the matter; being, in fact, manneristic, it often hampers rather than furthers the intended conception. Nevertheless, considered purely from the subjective side and given its due value from that standpoint, it is the unconstrained, inevitable expression of a spirit nourished on the historians of antiquity and matured among mediæval and native annalists. But when we come to the imitators of Johannes von Müller, who, owing to their lack of character, artistic or otherwise, are unable to achieve a style — not to speak of a manner — of their own; when we come, for example, to Zschokke and King Ludwig of Bavaria, and watch them copying the laconic sentences of Johannes von Müller, his abruptly finished clauses, his inversions, his archaic turns, and the like, we are aware, so to speak, of a something that apes the gestures of a man, yet apes them unsuccessfully, because it is unconscious of any underlying reason and purpose for its action. As the saying goes in *Wallenstein's Lager*, they have caught from their leader only his trick of hawking and spitting.

It is of the subjective side of style that Buffon's well-known dictum holds: The style is the man; " le style c'est l'homme." [18] The subjective side is the individual physiognomy, whereby a poet or historian, however strong the family likeness, is distinguishable from the other poets or historians of his time. Upon it first of all, accordingly, grammatical and æsthetic criticism must fasten their glance, where there is question of estimating a particular author, or of comparing and distinguishing several. Hence, to recognize the subjective side is a service the greater, the more objective a work is in its own nature — that is to say, the more the stylistic utterance of the writer's subjectivity is repressed. For example, you cannot claim that only a dull eye would fail to see in the *Iliad* and the *Niebelungenlied* that these poems are the product of a number of different, and stylistically different, authors; for the individual authors were all such good, *i.e.* such objective, epic poets, that the subjective side of their styles is necessarily hidden from ordinary observation. On the contrary, you cannot help praising the keen eye of Wolf and Lachmann, since, in spite of all difficulties, they perceived the separate individualities of style, and thus recognized and demonstrated the originally composite character of these heroic poems.

In such fashion what is subjective in style becomes the object of a criticism of individual authors and works. Naturally, however, the general theory of style cannot enter very deeply into that. Its business is rather the discovery and explanation of universal laws: those laws that govern the expression in language not merely of one author, indeed, not merely of one people or one age, but of all authors and peoples in all ages. These universal laws, however, lie on the objective side: in a region where style is conditioned, not by the changing personality of the individual who represents, but by something everywhere of similar value — by the content and purpose of what is represented; they relate to the action of motives which each individual shares with all others. Accordingly, though in the further course of discussion we may be led to touch, incidentally, upon this or that question of pure subjectivity, as a whole and essentially we can treat only of that element in style which is objective.

Were we indeed to touch immediately on one or two topics

c

of such incidental sort, we might call attention to a passage (paragraph 76) in Jean Paul's *Introduction to Æsthetics*, where in his own individual style he briefly characterizes the individual styles of a number of other authors; the passage may serve as a pattern of the way to deal with these matters. In a similar passage in the *De Oratore*, Cicero gives an estimate of various Greek and Roman writers, including himself: unquestionably he is cooler and clearer here than Jean Paul; whether he is as strikingly vivid one may be inclined to doubt.

Looked at from the objective side, — for this is our concern henceforth, — style, or the mode of representation in language, is conditioned, as we have said, by the content and purpose of the matter represented. Content and purpose can vary, however, accordingly as this or that function of the soul is preponderantly active during the creation of the content, and, correspondingly, as the particular function is called into activity in the re-creation of that content, which is the first purpose of all representation. Now there are three functions here to be considered: *intellect, imagination,* and *feeling.* As it is either the experiences and judgments of the intellect, or the conceptions of the imagination, or the impulses of the feelings, that make up the content of what is represented in language; so also in the representation is involved the purpose that this intelligible knowledge, or these images of the phantasy, or these movements of the feelings, shall in similar wise be awakened and called forth in the hearer or reader, and be reproduced in his soul just as they have arisen in the soul of the producing author. Hence arises first a threefold distinction between a *style of the intellect*, a *style of the imagination*, and a *style of the feelings*. But therewith is indicated only what function of the soul in any given case is active, here in the author, there in the reader; not, however, the nature of the representation which lies, so to speak, between these two persons — not what the character of the style must be in each case in order to serve as intermediary between creation and re-creation.[19]   Yet with respect also to this the distinctions and nomenclature arise readily and spontaneously. Where creations of the intellect are to be represented for the purpose of intelligible reproduction,[20] the demand laid upon the representation will be for sharp definiteness and easy comprehension, in a word, for clearness.[21]   Where creation and reproduction are alike the business of the imagination — that is, of the function of the soul which contemplates the idea under the forms of actual reality — a corresponding sensuousness and vividness are proper to the style; here the representation must be *vivid*.   Finally, where the sensibilities or sympathies of the creator are to work correspondingly upon the reproducer, where lighter or graver impulses of joy or sorrow are to be reflected in the soul of the latter, there the representation which is to bring about such effect must bear the impress of agitated feeling; it must be *impassioned*.   Herewith, then, we should have three main varieties, and three chief characteristics, of style: the style of the *intellect*, whose characteristic is *clearness;* the style of the *imagination*, whose characteristic is *vividness;* the style of the *emotions*, whose characteristic is *passion*.

The question immediately arises how such triple division of the kinds and characteristics of style can be made to harmonize with our previous dual division of all linguistic expression into *poetry* and *prose*.[22] This question is easily answered in the following way: The underlying basis, the beginning and the end of all poetry, is imagination; the function of poetry is to *image* ideas in the forms of actually existing reality.   This is the exclusive character of the eldest species of poetry, namely, the epic; and similarly a sensuous and animated imaging is the essential thing in the highest stage of development to which poetry can attain, that is, in the drama. At the same time the style of poetry in general, and of the epic and the drama in particular, is precisely that style of the imagination, that same sensuous mode of representation already mentioned. On the other hand, as a direct opposite to poetry, stands prose, a thing in its essential nature as unsensuous and abstract, as poetry is instinct with pure concrete sensuousness; prose directs itself toward the true, whereas poetry leans toward the beautiful; prose aims to bring new knowledge to the intellect — its first and last purpose is to instruct. Instructiveness is its general characteristic, even though a further division has to distinguish between prose in a narrower sense, and narration. Accordingly, since prose is the form for intellectual instruction, as didactic and narrative composition it appropriates the style of the intellect, and lays paramount claim to clearness of presentation.

But as the field of poetry is not exhausted by the epic and the drama, neither is that of prose by didactic writing and narration. In either field there remains still another species; and to these two supplementary species of poetry and prose, respectively, falls the third variety of style, the impassioned style of the emotions. We refer, among the species of poetry, to the lyric; among the species of prose, to the oration. In the lyric we find poetry overstepping the bounds of her wonted realm — released from the world of external reality: here the poet draws the material for the embodiment of his idea out of his own emotions; it is his own inner impulses and passions that the lyric poet represents. And the relation borne by lyric to the other forms of poetry is paralleled by that borne by oratory to the other forms of prose. To be sure, the primary affair of the orator, as of other makers of prose, is to instruct his audience; he also, just as the didactic essayist, must establish convincingly some definite proposition. Nevertheless didactic exposition is not the orator's peculiar and final aim: it is rather a means to an end; he convinces merely in order to persuade. The goal toward which all his instruction tends is simply the arousing of a sentiment, and by and with this latter a determination of his audience's will. Since, therefore, to awaken sentiment is the chief and continual business of the orator as of the lyric poet, the style which is peculiar to both can be none other than the style of the feelings, that is, the mode of representation which is impassioned.

[1] Compare Hart's *Essentials of Prose Composition,* p. 163.

[2] Theoretically, Aristotle's conception is somewhat broader: "Rhetoric may be defined as a faculty of discovering all the possible means of persuasion in any subject" (*The Rhetoric of Aristotle,* Welldon's translation, p. 10). Practically, Wackernagel is justified in citing Aristotle; compare *Rhetoric,* Book III, at the beginning (below, p. 53).

[3] See below, p. 59.

[4] The term *stylistic,* or *stylistics,* is rare in English; in general it may be replaced by *theory of style.*

[5] Compare Stevenson's essay, sections 3, 4 (below, pp. 373–384).

[6] Note Mr. Harrison's remarks on the same head (below, p. 444).

[7] The translation at this point condenses the original slightly.

[8] Tacitus, *Germania 2: Carmina antiqua unum apud illos memoriæ et annalium genus.*

[9] Wackernagel, *Poetik,* etc., pp. 131, 201.

[10] The first, of course, is poetry.

[11] Wackernagel, p. 309.

[12] "*Andria, prol.* 12 (*Menandri Andria et Perinthia*): *dissimili oratione sunt factæ ac stilo; (oratione et scriptura, Phorm. prol.* 5)." [Note in Wackernagel.]

[13] "*Brutus,* 26, 100: *unus sonus est totius orationis et stilus;* (ibid. 25, 96)." [Note in Wackernagel.] Compare *Correspondence of Cicero,* ed. Tyrrell and Purser, Vol. 5, p. 170 (DCLXVIII. 2).

[14] Compare Brunetière, below, p. 418.

[15] The average student is advised to look up the meaning of the words *objective, objectivity, subjective, subjectivity,* in Funk and Wagnalls's *Standard Dictionary.*

[16] Mentioned previously by Wackernagel, *Poetik,* etc., p. 363.

[17] Here, Wackernagel's analysis is inadequate. He fails to recognize that the individual or subjective element in style is conditioned externally in three

important ways, and that the objective side, correspondingly, presents three phases that must be carefully distinguished.   The individual style varies, first (I), with (*a*) the race, (*b*) nation, (*c*) dialect, or literary school, and (*d*) family, to which the individual writer belongs.   Could we imagine Herder as born (*d*) in some other family than his own, or (*c*) in Bavaria instead of East Prussia, or (*b*) in France instead of Germany, or (*a*) in Asia instead of Europe, we might suppose his initial tendencies in expression to be unchanged, but the resultant style of what he wrote would be in each case entirely different.   We have, then, to distinguish, objectively, (I) between racial style, national style, style of the dialect or school, and style of the family. This, we observe, is largely a geographical or spatial distinction.   Next (II), there is a distinction that is essentially temporal — a variation of style according to historical periods.   Had Herder lived in Luther's time, or in the present, his style, though retaining, of course, certain traits discoverable in his national literature throughout all its history, would necessarily betray the German idiom either of our or of Luther's day.   Finally (III), the individual style varies objectively with the literary genus or variety of production which the writer attempts.   In the drama, or another form of imaginative production, Herder's style, though still preserving the marks of (I) his race, nation, etc., and (II) of his period, would not be the same as in his address on geography, which is mainly scientific and intellectual.   Wackernagel lays undue emphasis upon this third condition, as if it alone were external, and includes *race, age*, etc., as belonging altogether to Herder's own personality.   Strictly considered, the individual style is the residuum or kernel obtained when we strip from an author everything that is not peculiar to him alone — everything which he has in common with others: the idiom of his language, and of the particular period in that language during which he lives, and the qualities of style which inhere "objectively" in the forms of literature that he essays.

[18] Observe the customary misquotation; compare below, p. 179.

[19] The student will do well to reread this statement attentively.

[20] *I.e.* in another intellect.

[21] Compare the ideal of Quintilian, given as the motto of this volume.

[22] Wackernagel, *Poetik*, etc., p. 11.

II

PLATO (B.C. 428–347)

From the Phædrus

[From *The Dialogues of Plato*, translated into English by B. Jowett, M.A., Oxford, The Clarendon Press; New York, Macmillan, 1892, Vol. 1 (pp. 466–489).

THE *Phædrus* is one of several Platonic dialogues in which fundamental questions about literature are discussed. Others are the *Ion*, *Republic*, and *Symposium;* in connection with rhetoric, more especially the *Gorgias*. The *Phædrus* was probably composed after the *Symposium*, when Plato was upwards of forty years old, an influential university teacher — we may call him so, although of his activities as a lecturer little is definitely known — and an assured master of the imaginative literary form in which his doctrines are preserved for us. Regarding this dialogue form, as opposed to the strict prose of an academic lecturer, we must always remember that it does not necessarily transmit to us in a given case Plato's actual, so to speak, *scientific*, opinion on any problem. Thus in the *Phædrus*, we must observe, the discussion of " the rules of writing and speech " represents first of all, not Plato's own theory, but a theory which Plato's imagination puts into the mouth of Socrates; even though Grote in this particular instance holds that " the theory of rhetoric . . . is far more Platonic than Socratic " (*Plato*, etc., 1875, Vol. 2, p. 245). Were it true, as some have maintained, that the *Phædrus* constituted Plato's inaugural address at the opening of his school (see Hirzel, *Der Dialog*, Vol. 1, p. 245), we should still expect a less poetical treatment of the theory in his everyday instruction.

Neither the matter nor the manner of Plato's dialogue is a thing to be disposed of in a cursory note. Plato's style is well handled by M. Alfred Croiset in the incomparable *Histoire de la Littérature Grecque* of MM. A. and M. Croiset

(Vol. 4, pp. 315–324).   It is treated exhaustively by Wincenty Lutosławski in Chapter III of his *Origin and Growth of Plato's Logic* (1897, pp. 64–193).   A good analysis of the substance of the *Phædrus* is given in Jowett's Introduction.

The English version of Plato by the Master of Balliol, though not unblemished in point of minute scholarship, has become almost a recognized classic on account of the translator's style.   A brief estimate of this, and a comparison of the third with the first edition, may be consulted in the *Nation* for July 7, 1892 (Vol. 55, p. 15); Professor Thomas D. Seymour has a more extended criticism of *The New Edition of Jowett's Plato* in the *Educational Review*, Vol. 4 (1892), pp. 270–276.

The scene of the Dialogue is: " Under a plane-tree, by the banks of the Ilissus."]

Socrates.   A lover of music like yourself ought surely to have heard the story of the grasshoppers, who are said to have been human beings in an age before the Muses.   And when the Muses came and song appeared they were ravished with delight; and singing always, never thought of eating and drinking, until at last in their forgetfulness they died. And now they live again in the grasshoppers; and this is the return which the Muses make to them — they neither hunger, nor thirst, but from the hour of their birth are always singing, and never eating or drinking; and when they die they go and inform the Muses in heaven who honors them on earth.   They win the love of Terpsichore for the dancers by their report of them: of Erato for the lovers, and of the other Muses for those who do them honor, according to the several ways of honoring them; — of Calliope the eldest Muse and of Urania who is next to her, for the philosophers, of whose music the grasshoppers make report to them; for these are the Muses who are chiefly concerned with heaven and thought, divine as well as human, and they have the sweetest utterance. For many reasons, then, we ought always to talk and not to sleep at mid-day.

Phædrus. Let us talk.

Soc. Shall we discuss the rules of writing and speech as we were proposing?

Phædr. Very good.

Soc. In good speaking should not the mind of the speaker know the truth of the matter about which he is going to speak?

Phædr. And yet, Socrates, I have heard that he who would be an orator has nothing to do with true justice, but only with that which is likely to be approved by the many who sit in judgment; nor with the truly good or honorable, but only with opinion about them, and that from opinion comes persuasion, and not from the truth.

Soc. The words of the wise are not to be set aside; for there is probably something in them; and therefore the meaning of this saying is not hastily to be dismissed.

Phædr. Very true.

Soc. Let us put the matter thus: — Suppose that I persuaded you to buy a horse and go to the wars. Neither of us knew what a horse was like, but I knew that you believed a horse to be of tame animals the one which has the longest ears.

Phædr. That would be ridiculous.

Soc. There is something more ridiculous coming: — Suppose, further, that in sober earnest I, having persuaded you of this, went and composed a speech in honor of an ass, whom I entitled a horse, beginning: ' A noble animal and a most useful possession, especially in war, and you may get on his back and fight, and he will carry baggage or anything.'

Phædr. How ridiculous!

Soc. Ridiculous! Yes; but is not even a ridiculous friend better than a cunning enemy?

Phædr.   Certainly.

Soc.   And when the orator instead of putting an ass in the place of a horse, puts good for evil, being himself as ignorant of their true nature as the city on which he imposes is ignorant; and having studied the notions of the multitude, falsely persuades them not about ' the shadow of an ass,' which he confounds with a horse, but about good which he confounds with evil, — what will be the harvest which rhetoric will be likely to gather after the sowing of that seed?

Phædr.   The reverse of good.

Soc.   But perhaps rhetoric has been getting too roughly handled by us, and she might answer: What amazing nonsense you are talking !   As if I forced any man to learn to speak in ignorance of the truth !   Whatever my advice may be worth, I should have told him to arrive at the truth first, and then come to me.   At the same time I boldly assert that mere knowledge of the truth will not give you the art of persuasion.

Phædr.   There is reason in the lady's defence of herself.

Soc.   Quite true; if only the other arguments which remain to be brought up bear her witness that she is an art at all. But I seem to hear them arraying themselves on the opposite side, declaring that she speaks falsely, and that rhetoric is a mere routine and trick, not an art.   Lo ! a Spartan appears, and says that there never is nor ever will be a real art of speaking which is divorced from the truth.

Phædr.   And what are these arguments, Socrates ?   Bring them out that we may examine them.

Soc.   Come out, fair children, and convince Phædrus, who is the father of similar beauties, that he will never be able to speak about anything as he ought to speak unless he have a knowledge of philosophy.   And let Phædrus answer you.

Phædr.   Put the question.

Soc. Is not rhetoric, taken generally, a universal art of enchanting the mind by arguments;[1] which is practised not only in courts and public assemblies, but in private houses also, having to do with all matters, great as well as small, good and bad alike, and is in all equally right, and equally to be esteemed — that is what you have heard?

Phædr. Nay, not exactly that; I should say rather that I have heard the art confined to speaking and writing in law-suits, and to speaking in public assemblies — not extended farther.

Soc. Then I suppose that you have only heard of the rhetoric of Nestor and Odysseus, which they composed in their leisure hours when at Troy, and never of the rhetoric of Palamedes?

Phædr. No more than of Nestor and Odysseus, unless Gorgias is your Nestor, and Thrasymachus or Theodorus your Odysseus.

Soc. Perhaps that is my meaning. But let us leave them. And do you tell me, instead, what are plaintiff and defendant doing in a law-court — are they not contending?

Phædr. Exactly so.

Soc. About the just and unjust — that is the matter in dispute?

Phædr. Yes.

Soc. And a professor of the art will make the same thing appear to the same persons to be at one time just, at another time, if he is so inclined, to be unjust?

Phædr. Exactly.

Soc. And when he speaks in the assembly, he will make the same things seem good to the city at one time, and at another time the reverse of good?

Phædr. That is true.

Soc. Have we not heard of the Eleatic Palamedes (Zeno),

who has an art of speaking by which he makes the same things appear to his hearers like and unlike, one and many, at rest and in motion?

Phædr. Very true.

Soc. The art of disputation, then, is not confined to the courts and the assembly, but is one and the same in every use of language; this is the art, if there be such an art, which is able to find a likeness of everything to which a likeness can be found, and draws into the light of day the likenesses and disguises which are used by others?

Phædr. How do you mean?

Soc. Let me put the matter thus: When will there be more chance of deception — when the difference is large or small?

Phædr. When the difference is small.

Soc. And you will be less likely to be discovered in passing by degrees into the other extreme than when you go all at once?

Phædr. Of course.

Soc. He, then, who would deceive others, and not be deceived, must exactly know the real likenesses and differences of things?

Phædr. He must.

Soc. And if he is ignorant of the true nature of any subject, how can he detect the greater or less degree of likeness in other things to that of which by the hypothesis he is ignorant?

Phædr. He cannot.

Soc. And when men are deceived and their notions are at variance with realities, it is clear that the error slips in through resemblances?

Phædr. Yes, that is the way.

Soc. Then he who would be a master of the art must understand the real nature of everything; or he will never know either how to make the gradual departure from truth

into the opposite of truth which is effected by the help of resemblances, or how to avoid it ?

Phædr. He will not.

Soc. He then, who being ignorant of the truth aims at
appearances, will only attain an art of rhetoric which is ridiculous and is not an art at all ?

Phædr. That may be expected.

Soc. Shall I propose that we look for examples of art
and want of art, according to our notion of them, in the speech
of Lysias which you have in your hand, and in my own speech ?

Phædr. Nothing could be better; and indeed I think that
our previous argument has been too abstract and wanting in
illustrations.

Soc. Yes; and the two speeches happen to afford a very
good example of the way in which the speaker who knows the
truth may, without any serious purpose, steal away the hearts
of his hearers. This piece of good-fortune I attribute to the
local deities; and, perhaps, the prophets of the Muses who
are singing over our heads may have imparted their inspiration to me. For I do not imagine that I have any rhetorical
art of my own.

Phædr. Granted; if you will only please to get on.

Soc. Suppose that you read me the first words of Lysias'
speech.

Phædr. ' You know how matters stand with me, and how,
as I conceive, they might be arranged for our common interest; and I maintain that I ought not to fail in my suit, because
I am not your lover. For lovers repent — '

Soc. Enough:—Now, shall I point out the rhetorical
error of those words ?

Phædr. Yes.

Soc. Every one is aware that about some things we are
agreed, whereas about other things we differ.

Phædr. I think that I understand you; but will you explain yourself?

Soc. When any one speaks of iron and silver, is not the same thing present in the minds of all?

Phædr. Certainly.

Soc. But when any one speaks of justice and goodness we part company and are at odds with one another and with ourselves?

Phædr. Precisely.

Soc. Then in some things we agree, but not in others?

Phædr. That is true.

Soc. In which are we more likely to be deceived, and in which has rhetoric the greater power?

Phædr. Clearly, in the uncertain class.

Soc. Then the rhetorician ought to make a regular division, and acquire a distinct notion of both classes, as well of that in which the many err, as of that in which they do not err?

Phædr. He who made such a distinction would have an excellent principle.

Soc. Yes; and in the next place he must have a keen eye for the observation of particulars in speaking, and not make a mistake about the class to which they are to be referred.

Phædr. Certainly.

Soc. Now to which class does love belong — to the debatable or to the undisputed class?

Phædr. To the debatable, clearly; for if not, do you think that love would have allowed you to say as you did, that he is an evil both to the lover and the beloved, and also the greatest possible good?

Soc. Capital. But will you tell me whether I defined love at the beginning of my speech? for, having been in an ecstasy, I cannot well remember.

Phædr. Yes, indeed; that you did, and no mistake.

Soc. Then I perceive that the Nymphs of Achelous and Pan the son of Hermes, who inspired me, were far better rhetoricians than Lysias the son of Cephalus. Alas ! how inferior to them he is ! But perhaps I am mistaken; and Lysias at the commencement of his lover's speech did insist on our supposing love to be something or other which he fancied him to be, and according to this model he fashioned and framed the remainder of his discourse. Suppose we read his beginning over again:

Phædr. If you please; but you will not find what you want.

Soc. Read, that I may have his exact words.

Phædr. ' You know how matters stand with me, and how, as I conceive, they might be arranged for our common interest; and I maintain I ought not to fail in my suit because I am not your lover, for lovers repent of the kindnesses which they have shown, when their love is over.'

Soc. Here he appears to have done just the reverse of what he ought; for he has begun at the end, and is swimming on his back through the flood to the place of starting. His address to the fair youth begins where the lover would have ended. Am I not right, sweet Phædrus ?

Phædr. Yes, indeed, Socrates; he does begin at the end.

Soc. Then as to the other topics — are they not thrown down anyhow? Is there any principle in them? Why should the next topic follow next in order, or any other topic? I cannot help fancying in my ignorance that he wrote off boldly just what came into his head, but I dare say that you would recognize a rhetorical necessity in the succession of the several parts of the composition?

Phædr. You have too good an opinion of me if you think that I have any such insight into his principles of composition.

Soc. At any rate, you will allow that every discourse ought to be a living creature, having a body of its own and a head and feet; there should be a middle, beginning, and end, adapted to one another and to the whole? [2]

Phædr. Certainly.

Soc. Can this be said of the discourse of Lysias? See whether you can find any more connection in his words than in the epitaph which is said by some to have been inscribed on the grave of Midas the Phrygian.

Phædr. What is there remarkable in the epitaph?

Soc. It is as follows: —

> 'I am a maiden of bronze and lie on the tomb of Midas;
> So long as water flows and tall trees grow,
> So long here on this spot by his sad tomb abiding,
> I shall declare to passers-by that Midas sleeps below.'

Now in this rhyme whether a line comes first or comes last, as you will perceive, makes no difference.

Phædr. You are making fun of that oration of ours.

Soc. Well, I will say no more about your friend's speech lest I should give offence to you; although I think that it might furnish many other examples of what a man ought rather to avoid. But I will proceed to the other speech, which, as I think, is also suggestive to students of rhetoric.

Phædr. In what way?

Soc. The two speeches, as you may remember, were unlike; the one argued that the lover and the other that the non-lover ought to be accepted.

Phædr. And right manfully.

Soc. You should rather say 'madly'; and madness was the argument of them, for, as I said, 'love is a madness.'

Phædr. Yes.

Soc. And of madness there were two kinds; one produced by human infirmity, the other was a divine release of the soul from the yoke of custom and convention.

Phædr. True.

Soc. The divine madness was subdivided into four kinds: prophetic, initiatory, poetic, erotic, having four gods presiding over them; the first was the inspiration of Apollo, the second that of Dionysus, the third that of the Muses, the fourth that of Aphrodite and Eros. In the description of the last kind of madness, which was also said to be the best, we spoke of the affection of love in a figure, into which we introduced a tolerably credible and possibly true though partly erring myth, which was also a hymn in honor of Love, who is your lord and also mine, Phædrus, and the guardian of fair children, and to him we sung the hymn in measured and solemn strain.

Phædr. I know that I had great pleasure in listening to you.

Soc. Let us take this instance and note how the transition was made from blame to praise.

Phædr. What do you mean?

Soc. I mean to say that the composition was mostly playful. Yet in these chance fancies of the hour were involved two principles of which we should be too glad to have a clearer description if art could give us one.

Phædr. What are they?

Soc. First, the comprehension of scattered particulars in one idea; as in our definition of love, which whether true or false certainly gave clearness and consistency to the discourse, the speaker should define his several notions and so make his meaning clear.

Phædr. What is the other principle, Socrates?

Soc. The second principle is that of division into species according to the natural formation, where the joint is, not breaking any part as a bad carver might. Just as our two discourses, alike assumed, first of all, a single form of unrea-

D

son; and then, as the body which from being one becomes double and may be divided into a left side and a right side, each having parts right and left of the same name — after this manner the speaker proceeded to divide the parts of the left side and did not desist until he found in them an evil or left-handed love which he justly reviled; and the other discourse leading us to the madness which lay on the right side, found another love, also having the same name, but divine, which the speaker held up before us and applauded and affirmed to be the author of the greatest benefits.

Phædr. Most true.

Soc. I am myself a great lover of these processes of division and generalization;[3] they help me to speak and to think. And if I find any man who is able to see ' a One and Many ' in nature, him I follow, and ' walk in his footsteps as if he were a god.' And those who have this art, I have hitherto been in the habit of calling dialecticians; but God knows whether the name is right or not. And I should like to know what name you would give to your or to Lysias' disciples, and whether this may not be that famous art of rhetoric which Thrasymachus and others teach and practise? Skilful speakers they are, and impart their skill to any who is willing to make kings of them and to bring gifts to them.

Phædr. Yes, they are royal men; but their art is not the same with the art of those whom you call, and rightly, in my opinion, dialecticians: — Still we are in the dark about rhetoric.

Soc. What do you mean? The remains of it, if there be anything remaining which can be brought under rules of art, must be a fine thing; and, at any rate, is not to be despised by you and me. But how much is left?

Phædr. There is a great deal surely to be found in books of rhetoric?

Soc. Yes; thank you for reminding me: — There is the exordium, showing how the speech should begin, if I remember rightly; that is what you mean — the niceties of the art?

Phædr. Yes.

Soc. Then follows the statement of facts, and upon that witnesses; thirdly, proofs; fourthly, probabilities are to come; the great Byzantian word-maker also speaks, if I am not mistaken, of confirmation and further confirmation.

Phædr. You mean the excellent Theodorus.

Soc. Yes; and he tells how refutation or further refutation is to be managed, whether in accusation or defence. I ought also to mention the illustrious Parian, Evenus, who first invented insinuations and indirect praises; and also indirect censures, which according to some he put into verse to help the memory. But shall I ' to dumb forgetfulness consign ' Tisias and Gorgias, who are not ignorant that probability is superior to truth, and who by force of argument make the little appear great and the great little, disguise the new in old fashions and the old in new fashions, and have discovered forms for everything, either short or going on to infinity. I remember Prodicus laughing when I told him of this; he said that he had himself discovered the true rule of art, which was to be neither long nor short, but of a convenient length.

Phædr. Well done, Prodicus !

Soc. Then there is Hippias the Elean stranger, who probably agrees with him.

Phædr. Yes.

Soc. And there is also Polus, who has treasuries of diplasiology, and gnomology, and eikonology, and who teaches in them the names of which Licymnius made him a present; they were to give a polish.

Phædr. Had not Protagoras something of the same sort?

Soc. Yes, rules of correct diction and many other fine precepts; for the ' sorrows of a poor old man,' or any other pathetic case, no one is better than the Chalcedonian giant; he can put a whole company of people into a passion and out of one again by his mighty magic, and is first-rate at inventing or disposing of any sort of calumny on any grounds or none. All of them agree in asserting that a speech should end in a recapitulation, though they do not all agree to use the same word.

Phædr. You mean that there should be a summing up of the arguments in order to remind the hearers of them.

Soc. I have now said all that I have to say of the art of rhetoric : have you anything to add ?

Phædr. Not much; nothing very important.

Soc. Leave the unimportant and let us bring the really important question into the light of day, which is: What power has this art of rhetoric, and when ?

Phædr. A very great power in public meetings.

Soc. It has. But I should like to know whether you have the same feeling as I have about the rhetoricians? To me there seem to be a great many holes in their web.

Phædr. Give an example.

Soc. I will. Suppose a person to come to your friend Eryximachus, or to his father Acumenus, and to say to him: ' I know how to apply drugs which shall have either a heating or a cooling effect, and I can give a vomit and also a purge, and all that sort of thing; and knowing all this, as I do, I claim to be a physician and to make physicians by imparting this knowledge to others,' — what do you suppose that they would say ?

Phædr. They would be sure to ask him whether he knew ' to whom ' he would give his medicines, and ' when,' and ' how much.'

Soc. And suppose that he were to reply: 'No; I know nothing of all that; I expect the patient who consults me to be able to do these things for himself'?

Phædr. They would say in reply that he is a madman or a pedant who fancies that he is a physician because he has read something in a book, or has stumbled on a prescription or two, although he has no real understanding of the art of medicine.

Soc. And suppose a person were to come to Sophocles or Euripides and say that he knows how to make a very long speech about a small matter, and a short speech about a great matter, and also a sorrowful speech, or a terrible, or threatening speech, or any other kind of speech, and in teaching this fancies that he is teaching the art of tragedy —?

Phædr. They too would surely laugh at him if he fancies that tragedy is anything but the arranging of these elements in a manner which will be suitable to one another and to the whole.

Soc. But I do not suppose that they would be rude or abusive to him: Would they not treat him as a musician would a man who thinks that he is a harmonist because he knows how to pitch the highest and lowest note; happening to meet such an one he would not say to him savagely, ' Fool, you are mad !' But like a musician, in a gentle and harmonious tone of voice, he would answer: 'My good friend, he who would be a harmonist must certainly know this, and yet he may understand nothing of harmony if he has not got beyond your stage of knowledge, for you only know the preliminaries of harmony and not harmony itself.'

Phædr. Very true.

Soc. And will not Sophocles say to the display of the would-be tragedian, that this is not tragedy but the preliminaries of tragedy? and will not Acumenus say the same of medicine to the would-be physician?

Phædr. Quite true.

Soc. And if Adrastus the mellifluous or Pericles heard of these wonderful arts, brachylogies and eikonologies and all the hard names which we have been endeavoring to draw into the light of day, what would they say? Instead of losing temper and applying uncomplimentary epithets, as you and I have been doing, to the authors of such an imaginary art, their superior wisdom would rather censure us, as well as them. 'Have a little patience, Phædrus and Socrates,' they would say; ' you should not be in such a passion with those who from some want of dialectical skill are unable to define the nature of rhetoric, and consequently suppose that they have found the art in the preliminary conditions of it, and when these have been taught by them to others, fancy that the whole art of rhetoric has been taught by them; but as to using the several instruments of the art effectively, or making the composition a whole, — an application of it such as this is they consider to be an easy thing which their disciples may make for themselves.'

Phædr. I quite admit, Socrates, that the art of rhetoric which these men teach and that of which they write is such as you describe — there I agree with you. But I still want to know where and how the true art of rhetoric and persuasion is to be acquired.

Soc. The perfection which is required of the finished orator is, or rather must be, like the perfection of anything else, partly given by nature, but may also be assisted by art. If you have the natural power and add to it knowledge and practice, you will be a distinguished speaker; if you fall short in either of these, you will be to that extent defective. But the art, as far as there is an art, of rhetoric does not lie in the direction of Lysias or Thrasymachus.

Phædr. In what direction then?

Soc. I conceive Pericles to have been the most accomplished of rhetoricians.

Phædr. What of that?

Soc. All the great arts require discussion and high speculation about the truths of nature; hence come loftiness of thought and completeness of execution. And this, as I conceive, was the quality which, in addition to his natural gifts, Pericles acquired from his intercourse with Anaxagoras whom he happened to know. He was thus imbued with the higher philosophy, and attained the knowledge of Mind and the negative of Mind, which were favorite themes of Anaxagoras, and applied what suited his purpose to the art of speaking.

Phædr. Explain.

Soc. Rhetoric is like medicine.

Phædr. How so?

Soc. Why, because medicine has to define the nature of the body and rhetoric of the soul — if we would proceed, not empirically but scientifically, in the one case to impart health and strength by giving medicine and food, in the other to implant the conviction or virtue which you desire, by the right application of words and training.

Phædr. There, Socrates, I suspect that you are right.

Soc. And do you think that you can know the nature of the soul intelligently without knowing the nature of the whole?

Phædr. Hippocrates the Asclepiad says that the nature even of the body can only be understood as a whole.

Soc. Yes, friend, and he was right: — still, we ought not to be content with the name of Hippocrates, but to examine and see whether his argument agrees with his conception of nature.

Phædr. I agree.

Soc. Then consider what truth as well as Hippocrates says about this or about any other nature. Ought we not to consider first whether that which we wish to learn and to teach is a simple or multiform thing, and if simple, then to inquire what power it has of acting or being acted upon in relation to other things, and if multiform, then to number the forms; and see first in the case of one of them, and then in the case of all of them, what is that power of acting or being acted upon which makes each and all of them to be what they are?

Phædr. You may very likely be right, Socrates.

Soc. The method which proceeds without analysis is like the groping of a blind man. Yet, surely, he who is an artist ought not to admit of a comparison with the blind, or deaf. The rhetorician, who teaches his pupil to speak scientifically, will particularly set forth the nature of that being to which he addresses his speeches; and this I conceive to be the soul.

Phædr. Certainly.

Soc. His whole effort is directed to the soul; for in that he seeks to produce conviction.

Phædr. Yes.

Soc. Then clearly, Thrasymachus or any one else who teaches rhetoric in earnest will give an exact description of the nature of the soul; which will enable us to see whether she be single and same, or, like the body, multiform. That is what we should call showing the nature of the soul.

Phædr. Exactly.

Soc. He will explain, secondly, the mode in which she acts or is acted upon.

Phædr. True.

Soc. Thirdly, having classified men and speeches, and their kinds and affections, and adapted them to one another, he will tell the reasons of his arrangement, and show why one soul is persuaded by a particular form of argument, and another not.

Phædr. You have hit upon a very good way.

Soc. Yes, that is the true and only way in which any subject can be set forth or treated by rules of art, whether in speaking or writing. But the writers of the present day, at whose feet you have sat, craftily conceal the nature of the soul which they know quite well. Nor, until they adopt our method of reading and writing, can we admit that they write by rules of art?

Phædr. What is our method?

Soc. I cannot give you the exact details; but I should like to tell you generally, as far as is in my power, how a man ought to proceed according to rules of art.

Phædr. Let me hear.

Soc. Oratory is the art of enchanting the soul, and therefore he who would be an orator has to learn the differences of human souls — they are so many and of such a nature, and from them come the differences between man and man. Having proceeded thus far in his analysis, he will next divide speeches into their different classes: — ' Such and such persons,' he will say, ' are affected by this or that kind of speech in this or that way,' and he will tell you why. The pupil must have a good theoretical notion of them first, and then he must have experience of them in actual life, and be able to follow them with all his senses about him, or he will never get beyond the precepts of his masters. But when he understands what persons are persuaded by what arguments, and sees the person about whom he was speaking in the abstract actually before him, and knows that it is he, and can say to himself, ' This is the man or this is the character who ought to have a certain argument applied to him in order to convince him of a certain opinion; ' — he who knows all this, and knows also when he should speak and when he should refrain, and when he should use pithy sayings, pathetic appeals, sensational effects, and all the other modes of speech which he has learned; — when, I say, he knows the times and seasons of all these things, then, and not till then, he is a perfect master of his art; but if he fail in any of these points, whether in speaking or teaching or writing them, and yet declares that he speaks by rules of art, he who says ' I don't believe you ' has the better of him.   Well, the teacher will say, is this, Phædrus and Socrates, your account of the so-called art of rhetoric, or am I to look for another ?

Phædr.   He must take this, Socrates, for there is no possibility of another, and yet the creation of such an art is not easy.

Soc.   Very true; and therefore let us consider this matter in every light, and see whether we cannot find a shorter and easier road; there is no use in taking a long rough roundabout way if there be a shorter and easier one.   And I wish that you would try and remember whether you have heard from Lysias or any one else anything which might be of service to us.

Phædr.   If trying would avail, then I might; but at the moment I can think of nothing.

Soc.   Suppose I tell you something which somebody who knows told me.

Phædr.   Certainly.

Soc.   May not ' the wolf,' as the proverb says, ' claim a hearing ' ?

Phædr.   Do you say what can be said for him.

Soc.   He will argue that there is no use in putting a solemn face on these matters, or in going round and round, until you arrive at first principles; for, as I said at first, when the question is of justice and good, or is a question in which men are concerned who are just and good, either by nature or habit, he who would be a skilful rhetorician has no need of truth — for that in courts of law men literally care nothing about truth, but only about conviction: and this is based on probability, to which he who would be a skilful orator should therefore give his whole attention. And they say also that there are cases in which the actual facts, if they are improbable, ought to be withheld, and only the probabilities should be told either in accusation or defence, and that always in speaking, the orator should keep probability in view, and say goodby to the truth. And the observance of this principle throughout a speech furnishes the whole art.

Phædr. That is what the professors of rhetoric do actually say, Socrates. I have not forgotten that we have quite briefly touched upon this matter already; with them the point is all-important.

Soc. I dare say that you are familiar with Tisias. Does he not define probability to be that which the many think?

Phædr. Certainly, he does.

Soc. I believe that he has a clever and ingenious case of this sort: — He supposes a feeble and valiant man to have assaulted a strong and cowardly one, and to have robbed him of his coat or of something or other; he is brought into court, and then Tisias says that both parties should tell lies: the coward should say that he was assaulted by more men than one; the other should prove that they were alone, and should argue thus: ' How could a weak man like me have assaulted a strong man like him? ' The complainant will not like to confess his own cowardice, and will therefore invent some other lie which his adversary will thus gain an opportunity of refuting. And there are other devices of the same kind which have a place in the system. Am I not right, Phædrus?

Phædr. Certainly.

Soc. Bless me, what a wonderfully mysterious art is this which Tisias or some other gentleman, in whatever name or country he rejoices, has discovered. Shall we say a word to him or not?

Phædr. What shall we say to him?

Soc. 'Let us tell him that, before he appeared, you and I were saying that the probability of which he speaks was engendered in the minds of the many by the likeness of the truth, and we had just been affirming that he who knew the truth would always know best how to discover the resemblances of the truth. If he has anything else to say about the art of speaking we should like to hear him; but if not, we are satisfied with our own view, that unless a man estimates the various characters of his hearers and is able to divide all things into classes and to comprehend them under single ideas, he will never be a skilful rhetorician even within the limits of human power. And this skill he will not attain without a great deal of trouble, which a good man ought to undergo, not for the sake of speaking and acting before men, but in order that he may be able to say what is acceptable to God and always to act acceptably to Him as far as in him lies; for there is a saying of wiser men than ourselves, that a man of sense should not try to please his fellow-servants (at least this should not be his first object) but his good and noble masters; and therefore if the way is long and circuitous, marvel not at this, for, where the end is great, there we may take the longer road, but not for lesser ends such as yours. Truly, the argument may say, Tisias, that if you do not mind going so far, rhetoric has a fair beginning here.

Phædr. I think, Socrates, that this is admirable, if only practicable.

Soc. But even to fail in an honorable object is honorable.

Phædr. True.

Soc. Enough appears to have been said by us of a true and false art of speaking.

Phædr. Certainly.

Soc. But there is something yet to be said of propriety and impropriety of writing.

Phædr. Yes.

Soc. Do you know how you can speak or act about rhetoric in a manner which will be acceptable to God?

Phædr. No, indeed. Do you?

Soc. I have heard a tradition of the ancients, whether true or not they only know; although if we had found the truth ourselves, do you think that we should care much about the opinions of men?

Phædr. Your question needs no answer; but I wish that you would tell me what you say that you have heard.

Soc. At the Egyptian city of Naucratis, there was a famous old god, whose name was Theuth; the bird which is called the Ibis is sacred to him, and he was the inventor of many arts, such as arithmetic and calculation and geometry and astronomy and draughts and dice, but his great discovery was the use of letters. Now in those days the god Thamus was the king of the whole country of Egypt; and he dwelt in that great city of Upper Egypt which the Hellenes call Egyptian Thebes, and the god himself is called by them Ammon. To him came Theuth and showed his inventions, desiring that the other Egyptians might be allowed to have the benefit of them; he enumerated them, and Thamus inquired about their several uses, and praised some of them and censured others, as he approved or disapproved of them. It would take a long time to repeat all that Thamus said to Theuth in praise or blame of the various arts. But when they came to letters, This, said Theuth, will make the Egyptians wiser and give them better memories; it is a specific both for the memory and for the wit. Thamus replied: O most ingenious Theuth, the parent or inventor of an art is not always the best judge of the utility or inutility of his own inventions to the users of them. And in this instance, you who are the father of letters, from a paternal love of your own children have been led to attribute to them a quality which they cannot have; for this discovery of yours will create forgetfulness in the learners' souls, because they will not use their memories; they will trust to the external written characters and not remember of themselves.[5] The specific which you have discovered is an aid not to memory, but to reminiscence, and you give your disciples not truth, but only the semblance of truth; they will be hearers of many things and will have learned nothing; they will appear to be omniscient and will generally know nothing; they will be tiresome company, having the show of wisdom without the reality.

Phædr. Yes, Socrates, you can easily invent tales of Egypt, or of any other country.

Soc. There was a tradition in the temple of Dodona that oaks first gave prophetic utterances. The men of old, unlike in their simplicity to young philosophy, deemed that if they heard the truth even from ' oak or rock,' it was enough for them; whereas you seem to consider not whether a thing is or is not true, but who the speaker is and from what country the tale comes.

Phædr. I acknowledge the justice of your rebuke; and I think that the Theban is right in his view about letters.

Soc. He would be a very simple person, and quite a stranger to the oracles of Thamus or Ammon, who should leave in writing or receive in writing any art under the idea that the written word would be intelligible or certain; or who deemed that writing was at all better than knowledge and recollection of the same matters?

Phædr. That is most true.

Soc. I cannot help feeling, Phædrus, that writing is unfortunately like painting; for the creations of the painter have the attitude of life, and yet if you ask them a question they preserve a solemn silence. And the same may be said of speeches. You would imagine that they had intelligence, but if you want to know anything and put a question to one of them, the speaker always gives one unvarying answer. And when they have been once written down they are tumbled about anywhere among those who may or may not understand them, and know not to whom they should reply, to whom not: and, if they are maltreated or abused, they have no parent to protect them; and they cannot protect or defend themselves.

Phædr. That again is most true.

Soc. Is there not another kind of word or speech far better than this, and having far greater power — a son of the same family, but lawfully begotten?

Phædr. Whom do you mean, and what is his origin?

Soc. I mean an intelligent word graven in the soul of the learner, which can defend itself, and knows when to speak and when to be silent.

Phædr. You mean the living word of knowledge which has a soul, and of which the written word is properly no more than an image?

Soc. Yes, of course that is what I mean. And now may I be allowed to ask you a question: Would a husbandman, who is a man of sense, take the seeds, which he values and which he wishes to bear fruit, and in sober seriousness plant them during the heat of summer, in some garden of Adonis, that he may rejoice when he sees them in eight days appearing in beauty? at least he would do so, if at all, only for the sake of amusement and pastime. But when he is in earnest he sows in fitting soil, and practises husbandry, and is satisfied if in eight months the seeds which he has sown arrive at perfection?

Phædr. Yes, Socrates, that will be his way when he is in earnest; he will do the other, as you say, only in play.

Soc. And can we suppose that he who knows the just and good and honorable has less understanding, than the husbandman, about his own seeds?

Phædr. Certainly not.

Soc. Then he will not seriously incline to ' write ' his thoughts ' in water ' with pen and ink, sowing words which can neither speak for themselves nor teach the truth adequately to others?

Phædr. No, that is not likely.

Soc. No, that is not likely — in the garden of letters he will sow and plant, but only for the sake of recreation and amusement; he will write them down as memorials to be treasured against the forgetfulness of old age, by himself, or by any other old man who is treading the same path. He will rejoice in beholding their tender growth; and while others are refreshing their souls with banqueting and the like, this will be the pastime in which his days are spent.

Phædr. A pastime, Socrates, as noble as the other is ignoble, the pastime of a man who can be amused by serious talk, and can discourse merrily about justice and the like.

Soc. True, Phædrus. But nobler far is the serious pursuit of the dialectician, who, finding a congenial soul, by the help of science sows and plants therein words which are able to help themselves and him who planted them, and are not unfruitful, but have in them a seed which others brought up in different soils render immortal, making the possessors of it happy to the utmost extent of human happiness.

Phædr. Far nobler, certainly.

Soc. And now, Phædrus, having agreed upon the premises we may decide about the conclusion.

Phædr. About what conclusion?

Soc. About Lysias, whom we censured, and his art of writing, and his discourses, and the rhetorical skill or want of skill which was shown in them — these are the questions which we sought to determine, and they brought us to this point. And I think that we are now pretty well informed about the nature of art and its opposite.

Phædr. Yes, I think with you; but I wish that you would repeat what was said.

Soc. ⁶ Until a man knows the truth of the several particulars of which he is writing or speaking, and is able to define them as they are, and having defined them again to divide them until they can be no longer divided, and until in like manner he is able to discern the nature of the soul, and discover the different modes of discourse which are adapted to different natures, and to arrange and dispose them in such a way that the simple form of speech may be addressed to the simpler nature, and the complex and composite to the more complex nature — until he has accomplished all this, he will be unable to handle arguments according to rules of art, as far as their nature allows them to be subjected to art, either for the purpose of teaching or persuading; — such is the view which is implied in the whole preceding argument.

Phædr. Yes, that was our view, certainly.

Soc. Secondly, as to the censure which was passed on the speaking or writing of discourses, and how they might be rightly or wrongly censured — did not our previous argument show — ?

Phædr. Show what ?

Soc. That whether Lysias or any other writer that ever was or will be, whether private man or statesman, proposes

E

laws and so becomes the author of a political treatise, fancying that there is any great certainty and clearness in his performance, the fact of his so writing is only a disgrace to him,
whatever men may say.   For not to know the nature of justice
and injustice, and good and evil, and not to be able to distinguish the dream from the reality, cannot in truth be otherwise
than disgraceful to him, even though he have the applause
of the whole world.

Phædr. Certainly.

Soc. But he who thinks that in the written word there is
necessarily much which is not serious, and that neither poetry
nor prose, spoken or written, is of any great value, if, like the
compositions of the rhapsodes, they are only recited in order
to be believed, and not with any view to criticism or instruction; and who thinks that even the best of writings are but a
reminiscence of what we know, and that only in principles of
justice and goodness and nobility taught and communicated
orally for the sake of instruction and graven in the soul, which
is the true way of writing, is there clearness and perfection
and seriousness, and that such principles are a man's own
and his legitimate offspring; — being, in the first place, the
word which he finds in his own bosom; secondly, the breth-
ren and descendants and relations of his idea which have been
duly implanted by him in the souls of others; — and who cares
for them and no others — this is the right sort of man; and
you and I, Phædrus, would pray that we may become like
him.

Phædr. That is most assuredly my desire and prayer.

Soc. And now the play is played out; and of rhetoric
enough. Go and tell Lysias that to the fountain and school
of the Nymphs we went down, and were bidden by them to
convey a message to him and to other composers of speeches
— to Homer and other writers of poems, whether set to music

or not; and to Solon and others who have composed writings in the form of political discourses which they would term laws — to all of them we are to say that if their compositions are based on knowledge of the truth, and they can defend or prove them, when they are put to the test, by spoken arguments, which leave their writings poor in comparison of them, then they are to be called, not only poets, orators, legislators, but are worthy of a higher name, befitting the serious pursuit of their life.

Phædr. What name would you assign to them?

Soc. Wise, I may not call them; for that is a great name which belongs to God alone, — lovers of wisdom or philosophers is their modest and befitting title.

Phædr. Very suitable.

Soc. And he who cannot rise above his own compilations and compositions, which he has been long patching and piecing, adding some and taking away some, may be justly called poet or speech-maker or law-maker.

Phædr. Certainly.

Soc. Now go and tell this to your companion.

---

[1] Compare Aristotle's definition, below, p. 52.

[2] This and the preceding speech by Socrates have a highly instructive parallel in Aristotle's *Poetics*, Chapters vii, viii (Butcher's translation, pp. 31–35).

[3] These processes, the student will remember, and the art of illustrating abstractions, mentioned above, p. 29, are essential to all clear explanation.

[4] Notice this recapitulation, and observe with what skill it is introduced.

[5] Compare Wackernagel, above, pp. 8–9

[6] Again note the method of recapitulation.

III

ARISTOTLE (B.C. 384–322)

Rhetoric, Book III, Chapters I–XII

[From *The* Rhetoric *of Aristotle,* translated, etc., by J. E. C. Welldon, M.A. (London and New York, Macmillan, 1886, pp. 224–274).

Bishop Welldon's excellent version, entire, should be in the hands of every teacher of rhetoric who lacks an easy reading knowledge of the original Greek. Directly or indirectly, Aristotle's *Rhetoric,* itself a final product and perfected summary of prior Grecian theory, is the foundation of almost all that is good in subsequent text-books on the same subject. The majority of these might well be discarded in its favor. Unfortunately, it is often absent from the libraries of many whose collections of handbooks on composition, and the like, are extensive. It is not, of course, specifically a theory of composition, but a treatise upon " a faculty of discovering all the possible means of persuasion in any subject " (Welldon's translation, p. 10), and, practically, a manual for the public speaker. However, on account of the close relation between oratory and written prose in origin and development, much of Aristotle's treatise is of immediate interest to the teacher of prose composition. This seems particularly true of Book III, Chapters I–XII, where the discussion of style is taken up. The student should try to discover just what portions of that discussion *are* applicable to the art of written exposition and persuasion. He is urged also to replace Aristotle's illustrations, as far as possible, by familiar examples from his own reading. His success in this would be a fair measure of his care in grasping Aristotle's thought.

Aristotle's style received generous praise in antiquity for its ease and grace (" *eloquendi suavitate* " — Quintilian, *Inst. Orat.* X, I, 84), its " sweetness, abundance, and variety " (Cicero, see Grote, *Aristotle,* 1872, Vol. 1, pp. 43 ff.); qualities characteristic rather of literary works now lost than of his scientific works that have come down to us. The student should not lose sight of the question to what species of composition the *Rhetoric* belongs and what style would be appropriate thereto. Like the preceding selection from Wackernagel, and like the larger part of Aristotle's extant writings, this is probably a more or less expanded form of the lecture notes used by a scientific teacher in addressing an audience of younger men.

Most of the translator's foot-notes are included.]

Book III

There being three proper subjects of systematic treatment in Rhetoric, viz. (1) the possible sources of proofs, (2) style, and (3) the right ordering of the parts of the CHAP. I. speech, the first of these has been already dis- The three subjects of a cussed. We have ascertained the number of the rhetorical sources of proofs, which are three, the nature of treatise. these sources, and the reason why they are not more numerous, viz. that persuasion is invariably effected either by producing a certain emotion in the audience itself or by inspiring the audience with a certain conception of the character of the speaker or *thirdly* by positive demonstration. The sources from which enthymemes are to be Style. derived have also been stated; for these are both special and common topics of enthymemes. We have next to discuss the question of style, as it is not enough to know what to say but is necessary also to know how to say it,[1] and *the art of saying things* is largely influential in imparting a certain color to the speech.

The first point which was naturally the subject of investigation is that which is first in the natural order, viz. the sources from which facts themselves derive their persuasiveness, the second is the disposition *or setting out* of the facts by the style, and the third, which has never yet been attempted, although it has the greatest weight, is the art of *declamation. *Nor*

Declamation.
is it surprising that declamation should have been neglected; for it has only lately been introduced into the tragic art and rhapsody, as poets were themselves originally the declaimers of their own tragedies. It is clear then that there is such a thing as an art of declamation in Rhetoric as well as in Poetry; and indeed it has been systematically treated by Glaucon of Teos among others. †The art consists in understanding (1) the proper use of the voice for the expression of the several emotions, i.e. when it should be loud or low or intermediate, (2) the proper use of the accents, ‡i.e. when the tone should be acute or grave or intermediate, and (3) the rhythms suitable to each emotion. For there are three things which are matters of such investigations, viz. magnitude *or volume of sound*, harmony, and rhythm. It is people who are careful about these that generally carry off the prizes in the *dramatic and rhapsodical* competitions, and as in such competitions the influence of the declaimers *or actors* is greater nowadays than that of the poets, so is it also in political competitions owing to the depraved character of our polities. But up to the present time no scientific treatise upon declamation has been composed; for it was not till a late date that the art of style itself made any progress, and *declamation* is still popu-

---

* Aristotle uses ὑπόκρισις in a limited sense, confining it, as he says below, to the management of the voice and especially excluding delivery or gesticulation, which is treated as a part of ὑπόκρισις by Longinus and as a part of *actio* by Cicero and Quintilian.

† Reading αὕτη.

‡ The "intermediate" or "middle" accent is the circumflex, which may be regarded as a combination of the others. It is clear that each accent marks a particular *tone* of voice, and that the rhetorical harmony (ἁρμονία) consists in a due variation of the tones.

larly considered, and indeed is rightly supposed, to be something vulgar. Still as the entire study of Rhetoric has regard to appearance, it is necessary to pay due attention to declamation, not that it is right to do so but because it is inevitable. Strict justice indeed, if applicable to Rhetoric, would confine itself to seeking such a delivery as would cause neither pain nor pleasure. For the right condition is that the battle should be fought out on the facts of the case alone; and therefore everything outside the *direct* proof is *really* superfluous, although extraneous matters are highly effective, as has been said, owing to the depraved character of the audience. Nevertheless attention to style is in some slight degree necessary in every kind of instruction, as the manner of stating a fact has some effect upon the lucidity of the explanation. Still the difference is not so great *as is supposed;* these tricks of style are all merely pretentious and are assumed for the sake of gratifying the audience, and accordingly nobody teaches geometry after this fashion.

The art of declamation, when it comes into vogue, will produce the same effects as the histrionic art; and there are some writers, e.g. Thrasymachus in his *Rules of Pathos* (ἔλεοι), who have in a slight measure attempted to treat it. The truth is that a capacity for *declaiming or* acting is a natural gift, comparatively free from artistic regulations, although it may be reduced to an art in its application to style. Hence it is that people who possess this faculty, *viz. the faculty of a histrionic style*, are the winners of prizes in their day, as are also rhetorical actors; for ˙*in written speeches the style is more effective than the thought.

The art of rhetorical declamation.

The origin *of this style* was due, as is natural, to the poets.

* The reference is to the epideictic style of orators, in which the speeches were more usually written than delivered.

For not only are all names imitations, but there was the *human* voice, which is the most imitative of all our members,
History of style. ready to their use. Thus it was that the various arts, rhapsody, the histrionic art, and others, as I need not say, were composed. And it was because the poets were thought, despite the simplicity of their sentiments, to have acquired their reputation by their style that *prose* style assumed at first a poetical form, as e.g. * the style of Gorgias. Nay even at the present time it is the opinion of most uneducated people that a poetical style is the finest. This however is an erroneous idea, the styles of prose and of poetry being distinct,[2] as is shown by the fact that the writers of tragedies themselves have ceased to use *the poetical style* as once they did, and that, as they passed from the tetrameter to the iambic measure as being the metre which bears the closest resemblance to prose, so too they have abandoned all such words as depart from the usage of *ordinary* conversation and were employed as ornaments by earlier dramatic writers and are still so employed by the writers of hexameter verse. It is absurd then to imitate those who themselves no longer employ their old style.

It clearly results from all this that we should be wrong in entering upon a minute discussion of all the possible points of style, and that we must confine ourselves to those of *rhetorical* style, which is now under our consideration. The other *or poetical* style has been discussed in my treatise on *Poetry.*[3]

We may rest content then with our study of that question, and may take it as settled that one virtue of style is perspicuity. There is an evidence of this in the fact that our speech, unless it makes its meaning clear, will fail to

---

* Dr. Thompson has excellently shown the poetical nature of Gorgias's style in the Appendix to his edition of Plato's *Gorgias*, pp. 175 sqq.

perform its proper function.* Again, style should be neither mean nor exaggerated, but appropriate; for a poetical style, although possibly not mean, is still not appropriate to prose. Among nouns and verbs, while per- spicuity is produced by such as are proper *or usual*, a character which is not mean but ornate is the result of the various other kinds of nouns enumerated in my † treatise on *Poetry*. The reason is that such variation im- parts greater dignity to style; for people have the same feeling about style as about foreigners in comparison with their fellow-citizens, *i.e. they admire most what they know least.* Hence it is proper to invest the language with a foreign air, as we all admire anything which is out of the way, and there is a certain pleasure in the object of wonder. It is true that in metrical compositions there are many means of producing this effect, and means which are suitable in such compositions, as the subjects of the story, whether persons or things, are further removed *from common life.* But in prose these means must be used much more sparingly, as the theme *of a prose composition* is less elevated. For in poetry itself there would be a breach of propriety, if the fine language were used by a slave or a mere infant or on a subject of extremely small importance. It is rather in a *due* contraction and exaggera- tion that propriety consists even in poetry. Hence it is necessary to disguise the means employed, and to avoid the appearance of speaking not naturally, but artificially. For naturalness is persuasive, and artificiality the reverse; for people take offence at an artificial speaker, as if he were prac- tising a design upon them, in the same way as they take of- fence at mixed wines. *The difference is much the same* as

CHAP. II. Virtues or graces of style.

---

* The sentence σημεῖον γὰρ ὅτι ὁ λόγος . . . τὸ ἑαυτοῦ ἔργον is parenthetical and should be marked off from the context by colons.

† *Poetic*, ch. 21.

between the voice of *Theodorus and those of all the other actors; for, while his appears to be the speaker's own voice, theirs have the appearance of being assumed. But the deception *which we have in view* is successfully effected, if words are chosen from ordinary parlance and combined, as is the practice of Euripides and indeed is the practice of which he was the first to set an example.

Nouns and verbs being the component parts of the speech and the nouns being of all the various kinds which have been considered in my †treatise on *Poetry*, it is only seldom and in few places that we must make use of ‡rare or foreign words, §compound words or words *specially* invented *for the occasion*. The question where they should be used we will discuss at a later time; the reason for using them but rarely has been already stated, viz. that they constitute too wide a departure from propriety. It is only the ‖ proper and the special name of a thing and the metaphor that are suited to the style of prose composition. We may infer this from the fact that these alone are of univeisal use, as every one in conversation uses metaphors and the special or proper names of things. It is clear therefore that successful composition will have an air of novelty without betraying its art and a character of lucidity, and these, as we have seen, are the virtues of

Words.

---

* Theodorus was a famous tragic actor, of whom a story is told in the *Politics* IV (VII), p. 129, ll. 8 sqq. [p. 220 of Welldon's Translation].

† *Poetic*, ch. 21.

‡ Although in the *Poetic*, ch. 21, p. 172, l. 19, Aristotle says λέγω δὲ κύριον μὲν ᾧ χρῶνται ἕκαστοι γλῶτταν δὲ ᾧ ἕτεροι, it is clear that in the *Rhetoric* he includes rare and obsolete as well as foreign words under the general term γλῶτται.

§ That διπλᾶ ὀνόματα are "compound words" is clear from ch. 3 in init., p. 116, ll. 4 sqq. Cp. *Poetic*, ch. 21, p. 172, ll. 11–14.

‖ There seems to be practically no difference in meaning between "proper" and "special" names; they are the names employed in ordinary speech.

rhetorical speech. Among nouns, while it is *homonymous nouns, *i.e. words which have several meanings,* that are serviceable to a sophist, as being the instruments of logical deception, it is synonyms which are serviceable to a poet. As an instance of proper and synonymous words I may mention e.g. "going" and "proceeding"; for these are both proper and also synonymous.

The nature of these several terms, the number of kinds of † metaphor, and the extreme importance of metaphor, both in poetry and in prose, are matters which have been discussed, as we said, in the ‡ treatise on *Poetry.* But they deserve the § more diligent attention in prose in proportion as prose is dependent upon a smaller number of aids than metrical composition. Perspicuity, too, pleasure, and an air of strangeness are in an especial sense conveyed   Metaphors. by means of metaphor, and for his metaphors a speaker must depend upon his own originality. The epithets and metaphors used must alike be appropriate, and the appropriateness will arise from ‖ proportion *or analogy;* otherwise there will be a glaring impropriety, as the contrariety of contraries is rendered most evident by juxtaposition. It is our business on the contrary to consider, as a scarlet robe is becoming to a young man, what it is that is

---

* Aristotle's own definitions of a "homonym" and a "synonym" will explain his meaning here: ὁμώνυμα λέγεται ὧν ὄνομα μόνον κοινόν, ὁ δὲ κατὰ τοὔνομα λόγος τῆς οὐσίας ἕτερος . . . συνώνυμα δὲ λέγεται ὧν τό τε ὄνομα κοινὸν καὶ ὁ κατὰ τοὔνομα λόγος τῆς οὐσίας ὁ αὐτός. Κατηγορίαι ι.

† Retaining μεταφοράς.

‡ There is no discussion of synonyms in the *Poetic,* perhaps, as Schmidt suggests, because the book in its present form is more or less imperfect.

§ Reading τοσούτῳ.

‖ Proportion or analogy (τὸ ἀνάλογον) in the choice of epithets implies that they agree in meaning with the words to which they belong, and in the choice of metaphors that there is no incongruity or confusion in the transference of ideas. See Mr. Cope's note.

becoming to an old man; for the same dress is not appropriate to both. Again, if it is your wish to adorn a subject,

Propriety in the use of metaphors.

the proper means is to borrow your metaphor from things superior to it which fall under the same genus; if to disparage it, from such things as are inferior. An instance of this, as contraries fall under the same genus, is to describe one who begs as a suppliant and to describe one who prays as a beggar, *praying and begging* being both forms of request. It was thus that Iphicrates called Callias a *mendicant priest instead of a torchbearer in the Mysteries, and Callias replied that he could never have been initiated or he would not have made such a mistake. The fact is that both are offices of divine worship, but the one is an honorable office and the other an ignoble one. Again, while somebody calls actors mere † parasites of Dionysus, they call themselves artists; both these terms are metaphorical, but one is defamatory and the other the contrary. Again, pirates nowadays style themselves purveyors; and by the same rule one may describe crime as error, error as crime, and stealing as either taking or plundering. Such a phrase as that of Telephus in Euripides

" Lord of the oar and setting forth to Mysia "

is a breach of propriety, as the word " lording " is too pom-

---

* The δᾳδουχία was a high hereditary office in the ritual of the Eleusinian Demeter. A μηταγύρτης, on the other hand, was no better than a begging friar who collected alms at the festival of Cybele or some other deity. See Lobeck, *Aglaophamus*, p. 629.

† "Parasites of Dionysus," i.e. hangers-on of the god who was the presiding deity of the drama. It is to be noticed that the Aristotelian use of μεταφορά is considerably wider than that of "metaphor" in English. Any transference of a word from its proper or ordinary application to another would be a μεταφορά, whether it involved a comparison or not. See the definition given in *Poetic*, ch. 21, p. 172, ll. 22–25, and the illustrations of it which follow; also Mr. Cope's *Introduction*, Appendix B to Book iii.

pous for the subject, and accordingly the * deception is unsuccessful. A mistake may be made too in the mere syllables
of a word, if they are not significant of sweetness in a voice.
It is thus that Dionysius the †Brazen in his elegies calls poetry
"Calliope's screeching," as both *poetry and screeching* are
voices *or sounds;* but his metaphor is only a sorry one, as
the sounds of screeching, *unlike poetical sounds,* possess no
meaning. Again, the metaphors should not be far-fetched,
but derived from cognate and homogeneous subjects, giving
a name to something which before was nameless, and mani-
festing their cognate character as soon as they are uttered.
There is a metaphor of this kind in the popular enigma

‡ "A man on a man gluing bronze by the aid of fire I discovered,"

for the particular process was nameless, but, as both processes
are kinds of application, *the author of the enigma* described
the application of the cupping-glass as gluing. It is generally
possible in fact to derive good metaphors from well-constructed
enigmas; for as every metaphor conveys an enigma, it is clear
that a metaphor *derived from a good enigma* is a good one.
Again, a metaphor should be derived from something beautiful, and the beauty of a noun, as Licymnius says, and similarly its ugliness, resides either in the sound or in the sense.
There is a third point to be observed in regard to metaphors,
which upsets the sophistical theory. For it is not true, as
Bryson said, that there is no such thing as the use of foul lan-

---

* "The deception," i.e. the concealment of art which the speaker or writer
has in view. See p. 113, ll. 11 and 24.

† Dionÿsius, an Athenian rhetorician of the fifth century B.C., is said by
Athenæus (*Deipn.* xv. p. 669 D) to have received the name or nickname of
"the Brazen," as having first suggested the use of bronze money.

‡ Athenæus (*Deipn.* x. p. 452 C.) gives the second line of the enigma or
riddle thus:

οὕτω συγκόλλως ὥστε σύναιμα ποιεῖν.

guage, because, whether you say one thing or another, your meaning is the same. For one word is more properly applicable to a thing than another and more closely assimilated to it and more akin to it, as setting the thing itself more vividly before our eyes. Nor again is it * under the same conditions that a word signifies this or that, and hence on this ground alone we must regard one word as being fairer or fouler than another; for although both words signify the fairness or foulness of a thing, it is not *merely* in respect of its fairness or foulness that they signify it, or, if so, at least they signify it in different degrees. The sources from which meta-

Sources of metaphors. phors should be derived are such things as are beautiful either in sound or in suggestiveness or in *the vividness with which they appeal to* the eye or any other sense. Again, one form of expression is preferable to another e.g. " rosy-fingered dawn " to " purple-fingered," while " red-fingered " is worst of all. In regard to † epithets

Epithets. again, the applications of them may be derived from a low or foul *aspect of things*, as *when Orestes is called* a matricide, or from the higher aspect, as *when he is called* the avenger of his father. *There is a similar instance in the story of* Simonides who, when the victor in the mule-race offered him only a poor fee, refused to compose *an ode*, pretending to be shocked at the idea of composing it on "semi-asses," but on receipt of a proper fee wrote *the ode beginning*

" Hail! daughters of storm-footed mares,"

although they were equally daughters of the asses. The same

---

* The difference seems to be that, although two words or expressions may have practically the same meaning, yet one may suggest widely different associations from the other.

† Aristotle uses ἐπίθετον to denote any word or words describing or characterizing a "proper noun," not merely a single adjective, as the English "epithet."

result may be attained by the use of diminutives. * By a diminutive I mean that which diminishes either the good or the evil of a word, and I may cite as instances the banter of Aristophanes in the *Babylonians* where he substitutes " gold-let " (χρυσιδάριον) for gold, " tunickin " (ἱματιδάριον) for tunic, " wee little censure " (λοιδορημάτιον) for censure, and " sickiness " (νοσημάτιον) for *sickness*. But in the use both of epithets and of diminutives it is necessary to be cautious and never to lose sight of the mean.

Faults of taste occur in four points of style. Firstly, in the use of compound words, such as Lycophron's " many-visaged heaven," " vast-crested earth," and "narrow-passaged strand," or Gorgias's ex-pressions, " a beggar-witted toady," or "forsworn and †forever-sworn." There are instances too in Alcidamas, e.g. "his soul with passion teeming and his face fire-painted seeming," or " he thought their zeal would prove end-executing," or " his words' persuasiveness he made end-executing," or " steel-gray the ocean's basement "; for all these are terms which, as being compound, have a certain poetical character. A second cause of faults of taste is the use of rare words, as when Lycophron called Xerxes " a vasty man," and Sciron " a man of bale," or when Alcidamas said " baubles in poetry," " the retchlessness of his nature," and ‡ " whetted with his mind's unadulterated ire." A third fault lies in the misuse of epithets, i.e. in making them either long or unseasonable or very numerous. For if in

CHAP. III.
Faults of taste
(τὰ ψυχρά).

---

* ὑποκορισμός may properly be rendered in this place by the neutral word "diminutive," but it would not ordinarily include such diminutives as are of a depreciatory or censorious character.

† It is apparently the compound κατευορκήσαντας which is objection-able, as the simpler form εὐορκήσαντας would express the meaning.

‡ The γλῶττα here, as Mr. Cope says, is the word τεθηγμένον, which is rare and generally poetical in its usage.

poetry it is proper to speak e.g. of " white milk," such epithets in prose are in any case inappropriate, and, if there are too many of them, they expose *the art of the style* and show it to be *simple* poetry. I do not say that epithets should not be used, as they are means of diversifying the ordinary style and giving the language a certain air of strangeness. But it is important to keep the mean ever in view, as *exaggeration* is worse in its effect than carelessness; for while in the latter there is only the absence of a merit, in the former there is a positive defect. Hence the epithets of Alcidamas appear tasteless, being so numerous and prolix and obtrusive as to be used not like a seasoning of the meat so much as like the meat itself. He says e.g. not " sweat " *simply* but " the damp sweat," not " to the Isthmian games " but "to the general assembly of the Isthmian games," not " laws " but " laws the sovereigns of states," not "by running " but " with the impulse of his soul at a run," not " a museum " but " a museum of all Nature that he had inherited." Again, *he says* " the thought of his soul sullen-visaged," " artificer " not "of favor " but " of universal favor," " steward of the pleasure of his audience," " con-cealed " not "with boughs " but " with the boughs of the wood," " he clothed " not " his body " but " his body's shame," "his soul's ambition counterfeit " (ἀντίμιμος) — a word which is at the same time a compound and an epithet, so that *the prose* is converted into poetry — and " the excess of his villainy so abnormal." The consequence is that this poetical diction by its impropriety is a source of absurdity and tastelessness as well as of obscurity from its verbiage; for any speaker who accumulates words, where the audience is already cognizant of the subject on which he is speaking, involves it in an obscurity which is fatal to distinctness. People *for the most part* only use compound words when what they want to express is destitute of a name and the word they use is easily compounded, as e.g. pastime (χρονοτριβεῖν); if this is overdone, the effect is wholly poetical. Hence it is that compound words are eminently serviceable to dithyrambic poets, whose style is noisy; rare words to epic poets, as epic poetry is a stately and austere *style of composition;* and metaphors to iambic writers, for the iambic is now the vehicle *of tragic poetry,* as I have remarked. There is a fourth and last fault of taste which is shown in the use of metaphors; for metaphors too may be inappropriate, whether from their absurdity — for they are used by comic as well as by tragic poets — or from an excess of dignity and tragic effect, or again they may be obscure, if they are far-fetched. Take e.g. such expressions as Gorgias's, " a business green and raw " (*a case of obscurity*), or " you sowed in shame and reaped in misery," which is too poetical, or Alcidamas's description of philosophy as " an outpost against the laws," and of the *Odyssey* as " a fair mirror of human life," or his *phrase* " importing no such bauble into poetry," all which for the reasons stated fail in persuasiveness. Gorgias's address to the swallow, when she dropped her leavings on his head, is in the best style of tragic diction, " For shame," he said, " Philomela." The point is that it was not a shame to a bird to have behaved so, but it was to a maiden. It was a happy thought then in his censure to speak of her as she was rather than as she is.

The simile too is a metaphor, the difference between them being only slight. Thus when *Homer* says of Achilles that * " he rushed on like a lion," it is a CHAP. IV. Similes. simile; but when he says that " he rushed on, a very lion," it is a metaphor, for here, as valor is an attribute common to both, he transfers to Achilles the

---

* The words quoted are not found in the existing poems of Homer, but for the simile see *Iliad,* xx. 164.

F

metaphorical appellation of " a lion." The simile is useful in prose as well as in poetry, although it should not be employed except sparingly, as it has a poetical character. The use of similes must be much the same as that of metaphors; for they are metaphors, but with the difference already stated.

An instance of a simile is e.g. that which Androtion applied to Idrieus when he said that he resembled curs which have been just unchained; for they fly at you and bite you, and so Idrieus was vicious when just unchained. Another is Theodamas's comparison of * Archidamus to Euxenus *minus* his knowledge of geometry; which is a † proportional simile, for *vice versa* Euxenus will be Archidamus *plus* his geometrical knowledge. Another is the expression in the ‡ *Republic* of Plato that people who despoil the dead are like curs that bite the stones thrown at them without touching the thrower. Or § Plato's comparison of the commons to a ship's captain who is strong but a little deaf. Or the ‖ simile which he applies to poets' verses, that they are like blooming faces without beauty; for such faces, when the bloom has faded from them, and poets' verses, when they are broken up, both entirely lose their former appearance. Or the similes of Pericles about the Samians, that they are like children which take their sop but cry while taking it, or about the Bœotians, that they are like their own holm-oaks, for, as these are cut to pieces by axes made of their own wood, so are the Bœotians cut to pieces by civil war. Again, there is ¶ Demosthenes's

---

* Euxenus and Archidamus are unknown, except from this passage.

† The "proportional" or "reciprocal" metaphor is illustrated in the *Poetic*, ch. 21, p. 173, ll. 1 sqq. See *infra*, l. 29, p. 132, l. 3.

‡ *Republic*, v. p. 469 D.E.   § *Republic*, VI. p. 488 A.

‖ *Republic*, X. p. 601 B.

¶ It is doubtful whether this is the great orator or not; his name has been mentioned, but not any passage of his speeches, p. 106, l. 28.

comparison of the commons to seasick passengers on board ship; or Democrates's of the orators to nurses who swallow the bonbon themselves, while they slobber the children with kisses; or Antisthenes's of Cephisodotus the thin to frankincense, as giving pleasure only by wasting away. For these may all be expressed either as similes or as metaphors, so that such as are popular, when expressed as metaphors, will be always convertible into similes, and the similes, if the explanatory words are omitted, into metaphors. But the proportional metaphor should be always transferable reciprocally and to either of the two congeners; e.g. if the goblet is the shield of Dionysus, then the shield may be properly called the goblet of Ares. *Similes and metaphors.*

Such then being the component elements of the speech, the basis of style is purity of language. But purity of language falls under five heads; and of these the first is *the proper use of* connecting words or clauses, i.e. when they are made to correspond in the natural relation of priority or posteriority to one another, as some of them require, e.g. as μὲν and ἐγὼ μεν require δέ and ὁ δέ *as correlatives.* But the correspondence should take place before the audience has had time to forget *the first of the* words or clauses, and the two should not be too widely separated, nor should another such word or clause be introduced before the one required as a correlative to the first, as such a construction is generally inappropriate. *Take e.g. the sentence* " But I, as soon as he told it me — for Cleon came to me with prayers and expostulations — set out with them in my company." In cases like this there are sometimes a number of connecting words or clauses prematurely introduced before the one which is required *as a correlative.* But if the clauses intervening between *the protasis and* the verb " set out " are numerous, *the sentence is* Chap. V. Style continued. Purity of language.

rendered unintelligible. A second point of purity of style consists in calling things by their own proper names rather than by *general or* class-names.[4] A third consists in the avoidance of ambiguous terms, but this only if your purpose is not opposed *to perspicuity.* People use ambiguous terms when they have nothing to say but make a pretence of saying something, and, if this is their object, they express themselves ambiguously in poetry, as e.g. Empedocles; for the length of their circumlocution imposes upon their audience and affects it as common people are affected in the presence of soothsayers; for they signify their assent to *such* ambiguous phrases *as*

> "If Crœsus pass the Halys, he shall whelm
> A mighty empire."

Again, it is because there is less opportunity of error *in generalities* that soothsayers express themselves in general terms of their subject; for as in the * game of " odd and even" you have a better chance of being right if you say simply " odd " or " even " than if you specify the number of things held in the hand, so too *in prophecy you have a better chance if you say* that a thing will be than if you say when it will be, and this is the reason why soothsayers never go so far as to specify the date of an event. All these *circumlocutions, ambiguities, and the like* must be classed together *as so many faults,* and must therefore be avoided, unless you have some such object as I have suggested. A fourth point is to observe Protagoras's classification of nouns generically as masculine, feminine, and neuter; for it is important that the genders

---

* The Greek game known as ἀρτιασμός is briefly described by Becker, *Charicles,* Excursus III to Scene VI; *Gallus,* Excursus II to Scene X. It was played by two persons, of whom one would hold in his hand a number of counters and the other would guess whether the number was odd or even, or more accurately what the number was.

should be properly assigned, *as e.g. ἢ δ' ἐλθοῦσα καὶ διαλεχ-
θεῖσα ᾤχετο. A fifth is the correct expression *of number, i.e.*
many, few, or unity, as e.g. οἲ δ' ἐλθόντες ἔτυπτόν με.

It is a general rule that the composition should be such as
is easy to read and — which is the same thing — easy to deliver. But this will not be the case where there are many
connecting words or clauses or where the punctuation is difficult, as in the writings of Heracleitus.
It is no easy task to punctuate his writings, from the difficulty
of determining to which of two words, the preceding or the
following, a particular word *in his sentences* belongs. There is
an example of this difficulty at the beginning of his book,
where he says, "Although this divine reason exists for ever men
are born into the world without understanding"; it is impossible
to tell to which of the words "exists" or "are born" the words
"for ever" should be joined by punctuation. Again, you are
guilty of a solecism, if in writing two words in a
single phrase you fail to assign to them a word
appropriate to both. Thus *if you take e.g. the word* "sound"
or "color," the participle "seeing" does not apply to both
alike, but "perceiving" does. And you become obscure,
if in seeking to introduce a number of details
in the middle *of a sentence* you do not complete the sense before you mention them, as *e.g. if you say*
"I meant, after discussing with him this, that, and the other,
to proceed" rather than "I meant to proceed after discussing
with him, and then this, that, and the other occurred."

We will pass now to dignity of style. The following are the

> Punctuation.

> Zeugma.

> Parenthesis.

---

* The point of the illustration is the agreement of the feminine participles
with the preceding feminine relative. But Mr. Cope is, I think, right in
arguing that the "classes" of Protagoras were not the same as the ordinary
genders of classical grammar but composed (1) male agents, (2) female
agents, (3) all inanimate or inactive things.

causes which contribute to it. *Firstly*, to use a definition instead of the simple name of a thing, *to say* e.g. not "a circle" but "a plane figure which is at all points equidistant from the centre." (If brevity is the object, the contrary should be the rule, viz. the substitution of the simple name for the definition.) *Secondly*, where the subject is one that is foul or indecorous, if the foulness lies in the definition, to use the name, and if in the name, to use the definition. *Thirdly*, to employ metaphors and epithets as means of elucidating the subject, being on your guard at the same time against a poetical style. *Fourthly*, to put the plural for the singular, as the poets do when they say e.g.

CHAP. VI.
Dignity.

"Unto Achæan harbors,"

when there is only one harbor, or

"Lo! here the manifold tablet-leaves,"

meaning a single leaf. *Fifthly*, * not to combine *two cases by a single article but* to give each case its own article, as in τῆς γυναικὸς τῆς ἡμετέρας. (But here again for brevity's sake the contrary τῆς ἡμετέρας γυναικός.) *Sixthly*, to use connecting particles or, if for brevity's sake you omit the connecting particle, to preserve the connection, *saying* e.g. πορευθεὶς καὶ διαλεχθείς or πορευθεὶς διελέχθην, not πορευθεὶς διαλεχθείς. Another useful practice is Antimachus's device of describing a thing by attributes it does not possess, as he does in the case of Teumessus *in the* † *lines beginning*

"There is a low and wind-swept crest,"

for there is no limit to this method of amplification. This

---

* The instance given shows that Victorius, whom Mr. Cope follows, is right in understanding the rule to mean *non copulare vincireque uno articulo duos casus, sed utrique suum assignare.*

† The quotation is from the *Thebais* of Antimachus, an epic poem on the theme of the ἑπτὰ ἐπὶ Θήβας. Teumessus was a hut or village in Bœotia.

mode of treatment by negation is one that is applicable indifferently to things both good and bad, as occasion may require. It is the source of the epithets which poets use, *such as*
" stringless, lyreless music "; for they add privative epithets,
as these are popular in proportional metaphors, *as e.g. in
calling the trumpet-blast " a lyreless music."

The conditions of propriety in a speech are that the style
should be emotional and ethical, and *at the same
time* proportionate to the subject-matter. By a   CHAP. VII.
proportionate style I mean that the manner of   Propriety.
the composition should not be slovenly if the subject is
pompous, or dignified if it is humble; and that there
should be no ornamental epithets attached to unimportant
words; otherwise *the composition* has the air of a comedy,
like † Cleophon's poetry, which contains some expressions
as *ridiculous as* ‡ it would be to say e.g. " a sovereign
fig." The means of expressing emotion, if the matter
is an insult, is the language of anger; if it is impiety
or foulness, that of indignation and of a shrinking from the
very mention of such a thing; if it is something laudable,
that of admiration; if something pitiable, that of depression,
and so on. This appropriateness of language is one means of
giving an air of probability to the case, as the minds of the
audience draw a wrong inference of the speaker's truthfulness
from the similarity of their own feelings in similar circumstances, and are thus led to suppose that the facts are as he
represents them, § even if this is not really so. It should be

---

* The "proportional" metaphor has been already illustrated; see marginal reference. Here the "proportion" would apparently be this:
     Trumpet: trumpet-blast :: lyre : music of lyre (μέλος).

† A tragic poet whose name occurs more than once in the *Poetic*.

‡ Omitting ἄν or perhaps better εἰ before εἴπειεν.

§ There is no good reason for omitting the clause εἰ καὶ μὴ οὕτως ἔχει, ὡς
ὁ λέγων.

added that a listener is always in sympathy with an emotional speaker, even though what he says is wholly worthless.[5] This is the reason why a good many speakers try to overwhelm the audience by their clamor. This method of proof depending on *external* signs is ethical, as the appropriate characteristics are assigned to any particular class or moral state. I understand under " class " the different periods of life, boyhood, manhood, and old age, *the sexes*, male and female, or nationalities such as the Lacedæmonian or Thessalian; and under " moral states " such as determine the character of a person's life, as it is not every such state which influences the characters of lives. If then the words which the speaker uses are also appropriate to the moral state, he will produce this ethical effect; for there will be a difference both in the language and in the pronunciation of a clown and an educated person. Another means of moving an audience is the trick which is used *ad nauseam* by speech writers, viz. *the introduction of such phrases as* " Who is not aware? ", " Everybody is aware," where a listener is shamed into an admission of the fact for the sake of participating in the knowledge which everybody else *is said to possess.*

The question of opportuneness or inopportuneness in the use of any rhetorical device is one that belongs

Opportune-ness.

equally to all the species of Rhetoric. There is one remedy for exaggeration of every sort in the popular rule, that a speaker should * anticipate censure by pronouncing it on himself, as *the exaggeration* is then regarded as correct, since the speaker is aware of what he is doing. Let me add the rule of not employing simultaneously all the different means of proportion *or correspondence*, as this is one way to deceive the audience. What I mean is e.g. if the words used are harsh in sound, not to

* Reading προεπιπλήττειν.

carry the harshness into the voice and countenance and the other appropriate *means of expression ;* for the result of so doing is that the nature of each becomes conspicuous, whereas, if you use some and omit others, although you equally make use of art, you succeed in escaping detection.

It is a *general* result *of these considerations* that, if a tender subject is expressed in harsh language or a harsh subject in tender language, there is a certain loss of persuasiveness. The multiplication of compound words or epithets and the use of strange words are most appropriate to the language of emotion; for a person in a state of passion may be pardoned, if he speaks of an evil as " heaven-high " or " colossal." *The same excuse holds good* when the speaker has mastered his audience and has roused them to enthusiasm by praise or blame or passion or devotion, as * Isocrates e.g. does in his panegyrical speech, where he says at the end " sentence and sense " (φήμη καὶ γνώμη), and again " seeing that they brooked it " (οἵτινες ἔτλησαν). For this is the language of enthusiasm and is consequently acceptable to an audience in a state of enthusiasm. It is suitable to poetry for the same reason, as poetry is inspired. It must be used thus or else ironically, as by Gorgias and in the † *Phædrus* of Plato.

The structure of the style should be neither metrical nor wholly unrhythmical. If it is the former, it lacks persuasiveness from its appearance of artificiality, and at the same time diverts the minds of the audience from the subject by fixing their attention upon

CHAP. VIII. Structure of the style.

---

* Of the expressions cited from Isocrates, the first is a misquotation; and as the point seems to consist in the jingle of words, the original φήμην δὲ καὶ μνήμην καὶ δόξαν (*Paneg.* § 220) would be more appropriate. In the second (*Paneg.* § 110, not at the end of the speech), it is the poetical word ἔτλησαν which gives it color, although the mss. of Isocrates have ἐτόλμησαν.

† See e.g. *Phædrus*, pp. 238 D., 241 E.

the return of the similar cadence, so that they anticipate its coming as children anticipate the answer to the herald's summons, " Whom chooses the freedman for his attorney?" *and the answer is* * "Cleon." If on the other hand the composition is wholly unrhythmical, it has no definiteness, whereas it ought to be definitely limited, although not by metre, as what is indefinite is disagreeable and incapable

Rhythm.
of being known. It is † number which is the defining *or limiting* principle of all things, and the number of the structure of style is rhythm, of which metres are so many sections. Hence a prose composition should have rhythm but not metre, or it will be a poem. But the rhythm should not be elaborately finished, or in other words it should not be carried too far.

I pass now to the three kinds of rhythm. The heroic rhythm is too dignified, and is deficient in conversational

Kinds of rhythm.
harmony. The iambic rhythm on the other hand is the very diction of ordinary life, and is therefore of all metres the most frequent in conversation; but it is deficient in dignity and impressiveness. The trochaic rhythm approximates too much to broad comedy, as appears in *trochaic* tetrameters; for the tetrameter is a tripping rhythm (τροχερὸς ῥυθμός). There remains the pæan, which has been used by prose writers from Thrasymachus downwards, although they did not understand the

---

* It was part of Cleon's policy to pose as the champion of those who, like freedmen, could not appear for themselves in Court, and the children, whether in Aristotle's own day or later, seem to have caught up his invariable name.

† This is the well-known Pythagorean principle; see Ritter and Preller, *Historia Philosophiæ Græcæ et Romanæ*, §§ 52 sqq. Aristotle, in applying it to style, means that words which are themselves formless and incoherent are reduced to order by number, i.e. by rhythm. There is a very similar remark relating to music in Plato, *Philebus*, p. 26 A.

definition of it. *The pæan is the third rhythm, and is closely connected with the preceding ones, having in itself the ratio of 3 to 2, while they have the ratios of 1 to 1 and 2 to 1 respectively. The ratio of 3 to 2 is connected with both of these, *and is in fact the mean between them;* and this is the ratio of the pæan.

While the other rhythms should be discarded, partly for the reasons which have been already given and partly because of their metrical character, the pæan should be adopted *in prose compositions,* as it is the only one of the rhythms named which cannot form a regular metre and is therefore the most likely to escape detection. It is the fashion — a wrong fashion, as I think — at the present time to use the same pæan both at the beginning and † at the end of sentences. There are two opposite kinds of pæan, of which one is suitable to the beginning of a sentence and in fact is so employed; it is the one beginning with a long syllable and ending with three short ones, *as in*

Δαλογενὲς εἴτε Λυκίαν,

or   χρυσεοκόμα Ἑκατε παῖ Διός.

The other, which is opposite to it, has three short syllables at the beginning and the long syllable at the end, as

μετὰ δὲ γᾶν ὕδατά τ' ὠκεανὸν ἠφάνισε νύξ.

This is the pæan which *properly* terminates a sentence; for the short syllable from its incompleteness has a mutilated

---

* It is clear, on the principle of a long syllable being equivalent to two short ones, that the parts of the spondee (‿ ‿) or the dactyl (‿ ◡ ◡), which are the admissible feet in hexameter verse, have the ratio of 1 to 1, those of the iambus (◡ ‿) or the trochee (‿ ◡) have the ratio of 2 to 1, and those of the pæan (‿ ◡ ◡ ◡ or ◡ ◡ ◡ ‿) have the ratio of 3 to 2.

† It is very doubtful whether the words καὶ τελευτῶντες need be inserted in the text; Mr. Cope justly says Aristotle would be likely to let them be mentally understood.

effect, whereas the sentence should be cut off by the *final* long syllable, and its end be marked not by the scribe nor by the * marginal annotation but by the *natural* rhythm.

So much for the proof that the style should be rhythmical and for the nature and structure of the rhythms which make it so.

The style must be either jointed, i.e. united only by its connecting particles, after the manner of *modern* dithyrambic

CHAP. IX.
Two kinds
of style.

(1) jointed,

preludes, or compact, like the antistrophes of the ancient poets. The jointed style is the original one, *as in* † *Herodotus, e.g.* "The following is a statement of the researches of Herodotus of Thurii"; it was formerly universal but is now confined to a few writers. By a "jointed style" I mean one which has no end in itself except the completion of the subject under discussion. It is disagreeable from its *endlessness or* indefiniteness, as everybody likes to have the end clearly in view. This is the reason why *people in a race* do not gasp and faint until they reach the goal; for while they have the finishing-point before their eyes, they are insensible of fatigue. The compact style on the other hand is the

(2) periodic.

periodic; and I mean by a " period " a sentence having a beginning and an end in itself, and a magnitude which admits of being easily comprehended at a glance. Such a style is agreeable and can be easily ‡ learnt. It is agreeable, as being the opposite of the

---

* The "marginal annotation" (Gk. παραγραφή, Lat. *interductus librarii*) would answer to the modern full-stop.

† The opening passage of Herodotus's History, Ἡροδότου Θουρίου ἥδ' ἱστορίης ἀπόδειξις, is cited as a case of writing where there is no attempt to build up a sentence of parts subordinated to each other, but the sentence is a simple clause or consists of clauses which are merely pieced or jointed by connecting particles.

‡ It is to be remembered that the Greek and Roman orators were in the habit of getting their speeches by heart; hence the importance of μνήμη or *memoria* in a treatise on Rhetoric.

indefinite style and because the hearer is constantly imagining himself to have got hold of something from constantly finding a definite conclusion *of the sentence,* whereas *in the other style* there is something disagreeable in having nothing to look forward to or accomplish. It is easily learnt too, as being easily recollected, and this because a periodic style can be numbered, and number is the easiest thing in the world to recollect. It is thus that everybody recollects * verses better than irregular *or prose* compositions, as they contain number and are measured by it. But the period should be completed by the sense as well as by the rhythm and not be abruptly broken off like the iambics of † Sophocles

"This land is Calydon of Pelops' soil,"

for a wholly erroneous supposition is rendered possible by such a division, as e.g. in the instance quoted, that Calydon is in Peloponnesus.

A period may be (1) divided into members *or clauses,* (2) simple. If it is the former, it should be complete in itself, properly divided and capable of being easily pronounced at a single breath, not so however at the *arbitrary* division *of the speaker* but as a whole. A member *or clause* is one of the two parts of a period. A simple period on the other hand is a period consisting of a single member.

Periods.

The members *or clauses* and the periods themselves should

---

* The reason alleged depends in part upon the etymological connection of μέτρα with μετρεῖσθαι.

† The line belongs really to the *Meleager* of Euripides, not to any play of Sophocles. It is objectionable in Aristotle's view, because the rhythmical pause comes after χθονός but the pause in the sense after γαία, the words Πελοπείας χθονός being connected with the next line

ἐν ἀντιπόρθμοις πέδι' ἔχουσ' εὐδαίμονα.

be neither truncated nor too long. If they are too short, they often make a hearer stumble; for if, while he is hurrying on to *the completion of* the measure *or rhythm*, of which he has a definite notion in his mind, he is suddenly pulled up by a pause on the part of the speaker, there will necessarily follow a sort of stumble in consequence of the sudden check. If on the other hand they are too long, they produce in the hearer a feeling of being left behind, as when people who are taking a walk do not turn back until they have passed the usual limit; for they too leave their fellow-walkers behind. Similarly periods of undue length become *actual* speeches and resemble a dithyrambic prelude *in their discursiveness*. The result is what Democritus of Chios quoted as a taunt against Melanippides for writing dithyrambic preludes instead of regular *stanzas or* antistrophes:

> *"A man worketh ill to himself in working ill to his neighbor,
>   And there is nought to its author so ill as a — long-winded prelude";

for a similar taunt may be suitably applied to the patrons of long-winded clauses. Periods in which the clauses are too short are not periods at all; hence *such a period* drags the audience with it headlong.

The *periodic* style, which is divided into clauses, is of two kinds, according as the clauses are simply divided, as in the sentence † " I have often wondered at those who convened the public assemblies and instituted the gymnastic games," or opposed, where in each of the two clauses either one of two contraries is placed beside the other, or the two contraries

The periodic style.

Antithesis.

* The second line is a parody of Hesiod's

ἡ δὲ κακὴ βουλὴ τῷ βουλεύσαντι κακίστη.

Ἔργα κ. Ἡμέραι, 263.

† A quotation from Isocrates, *Paneg.* § 1.

are connected together by the same word, as * " Both parties they helped, those who stayed behind and those who went with them; for the latter they won a new land larger than that which they possessed at home; and to the former they left sufficient in that which was theirs at home." Here the words " staying behind " and " going with them," the ideas " sufficient " and " larger," are contrasted. *Another instance* is † " to those who wanted money and to those who desired enjoyment," where *sensual* enjoyment is opposed to the acquisition *of money*. Again, " It often happens in these cases that the wise are unfortunate and the fools are successful "; or " They were immediately presented with the prize of valor and not long afterwards acquired the empire of the sea "; or " To sail through the mainland and march through the ocean, by bridging the Hellespont and digging through Athos "; or " Citizens by nature but divested by law of their citizenship "; or " Some of them had a miserable end, and others a shameful deliverance "; or " In private life using foreigners as domestic servants and in public life suffering many of the allies to be slaves "; or " Either to bring them alive or to leave them dead." Another instance is, the remark which somebody made about Pitholaus and Lycophron in the Court of Law, " These fellows, who when at home used to sell you, now that they have come here, have purchased you." All these are instances of an antithetical style. The agreeableness of such a style lies in the fact that contraries are so easily known, especially when they are set in juxtaposition, and that it *is a style which* has a resemblance to a syllogism, the

* *Paneg.* § 37; but the words are not quoted exactly. The connection (ἐπίζευξις) lies in the verb ὤνησαν, which governs both τοὺς ὑπομείναντας and τοὺς ἀκολουθήσαντας; the juxtaposition of opposites is explained in the text.

† The following quotations are all taken (although sometimes inexactly) from the same panegyrical oration of Isocrates. Mr. Cope gives the references.

refutative syllogism being a bringing together of opposites. Such then is the explanation of antithesis.   * Parisosis is the equality of the members *or clauses*, paromoiosis the similarity of the extremities, i.e. either the beginnings or the ends of the sentences. When it is at the beginning, *the similarity is* always one of *whole* words, when at the end, it is one of the final syllables, as of *different* inflections of the same word or *a repetition of* the same word. †

Parisosis.

Paromoiosis.

But the same sentence may combine all these points, being at once a case of antithesis, of balance of clauses (parisosis), and of similarity of terminations.

The beginnings of periods have been pretty fully enumerated in the ‡ Theodectea.

There are not only true but false antitheses, as in § Epicharmus.

Having discussed and determined these points, we have next to consider the sources of clever and popular sayings. The invention of such sayings is the work of natural ability or of long practice; but the explanation of them belongs to

---

* It is, I fear, impossible to help importing Aristotle's own terms into English.

† Aristotle in the text cites the following instances: (1) of initial paromoiosis, ἀγρὸν γὰρ ἔλαβεν ἀργὸν παρ' αὐτοῦ and δωρητοί τ' ἐπέλοντο παράρρητοί τ' ἐπέεσσιν, (2) of final paromoiosis ᾠήθησαν αὐτὸν παιδίον τετοκέναι, ἀλλ' αὐτοῦ αἴτιον γεγονέναι, and ἐν πλείσταις δὲ φροντίσι καὶ ἐν ἐλαχίσταις ἐλπίσιν, (3) of varied inflection ἄξιος δὲ σταθῆναι χαλκοῦς, οὐκ ἄξιος ὢν χαλκοῦ, (4) of repetition σὺ δ' αὐτὸν καὶ ζῶντα ἔλεγες κακῶς καὶ νῦν γράφεις κακῶς, (5) of syllabic parallelism τί ἂν ἔπαθες δεινόν, εἰ ἄνδρ' εἶδες ἀργόν;

‡ Upon the Aristotelian *Theodectea*, see Mr. Cope's *Introduction*, pp. 55 sqq.

§ The line quoted is

τόκα μὲν ἐν τήνων ἐγὼν ἦν, τόκα δὲ παρὰ τήνοις ἐγών,

where there is no true antithesis between τόκα μὲν and τόκα δὲ or between ἐν τήνων and παρὰ τήνοις.

the present treatise. Let us enter then upon a complete enumeration of them. We may start with the assumption that learning without trouble is naturally agree- able to everybody, and that, as names *or words* possess a certain significance, those which impart instruction to us are most agreeable. Now rare words are unintelligible to us, and the proper *or ordinary* names of things we know already. It is metaphor which is in the highest degree instructive; for when e.g. * Homer calls old age " the sere, the yellow leaf," he imparts instruction and knowledge through the medium of the genus, as both old age and the sere leaf are withered. The similes of poetry again produce the same effect, and hence a simile, if it is well constructed, shows cleverness. For the simile, as has been already said, is a metaphor with a difference only in the mode of statement. Hence it is less agreeable, being couched in longer terms; also it does not *directly* say that one thing is another, and, as this is not said, it is not looked for by the minds *of the audience, and accordingly there is no oppor- tunity of instruction.* It follows in regard to enthymemes as in regard to style that they are clever, if they convey to us rapid instruction. And hence it is that the enthymemes which are popular are not such as are superficial, i.e. such as are perspicuous to everybody and need no research, nor such as are un- intelligible when stated, but those which are either appre- hended at the moment of delivery, even though there was no previously existing knowledge of them, or which are followed at little interval by the minds of the audience. For what is virtually instruction, whether immediate or subsequent, takes

Chap. X.
Clever say-
ings
(τὰ ἀστεῖα).

Metaphor
and simile.

p. 65.

Enthy-
memes.

---

* *Odyssey*, XIV. 214. The "sere leaf" will perhaps represent Homer's καλάμη, although it is used in a somewhat different train of thought.

G

place in these cases, but not otherwise. These being then the species of enthymemes which are popular, if considered relatively to the meaning they convey, relatively to style they may be considered in respect either of their structure or of the *single* words *employed in them.* Enthymemes are popular from their structure, if it is antithetical, as e.g. *in * Isocrates,* " considering the peace which all the world enjoyed as a war against their own private interests," where there is an antithesis between war and peace; and from their single words, if the words are such as contain a metaphor, and this a metaphor which is neither far-fetched nor superficial (for in the former case it is difficult to comprehend at a glance, and in the latter it leaves no impression), or again, if they vividly represent *the subject* to the eye, as it is desirable that the things should be seen in actual performance and not merely in intention. There are then these three objects to be ever kept in view, viz. metaphor, antithesis, and vividness of representation.

†Metaphors are of four kinds, and of these the proportional are the most popular. An instance of a proportional metaphor is the saying of Pericles, that " the blotting out of the youth who had perished in the war from the state was like the taking of the spring out of the year." Another is the saying of Leptines about the Lacedæmonians, that he "would not have *the Athenians* look on quietly, when Greece had lost one of her eyes." Again, Cephisodotus expressed his indignation at the eagerness of Chares for the audit of his accounts in the Olynthiac war, by saying that he had ‡ " driven the people into a choking fit by trying to get his accounts audited." The same Cephisodotus in one of his exhortations to the Athe-

Metaphors.

---

* *Phil.* § 82.

† The four kinds of metaphor are enumerated in the definition given in the *Poetic*, ch. 21, p. 172, §§ 22–25.   ‡ Reading ἀγαγόντα.

nians told them they ought to " march to Eubœa * with the decree of Miltiades for their commissariat." Again, Iphicrates showed his indignation at the truce which the Athenians had made with Epidaurus and the maritime states by saying that they had " stripped themselves of their journey-money for the war." Pitholaus called the † Paralian trireme the " people's bludgeon " and Sestos a ‡ " corn-stall of the Piræus." Pericles exhorted the Athenians to sweep away Ægina, that "eyesore of the Piræus." Mœrocles said he was every whit as virtuous as a certain respectable citizen whom he named, as the respectable citizen " got 33 per cent for his roguery and he himself got only 10 per cent." There is an instance too in the iambic line of Anaxandrides in pleading the cause of *somebody's* daughters who had been a very long time in getting married :

§ " The ladies' marriage-day is overdue."

Similarly Polyeuctus made the remark about a certain paralytic person named Speusippus that he could not keep himself quiet, " although Fortune had set him fast in the pillory of disease." Cephisodotus again called the triremes ‖ " painted millstones," and the Cynic *Diogenes* called the

---

* This difficult expression seems to mean that the Athenians were to march without any regard to the commissariat, but in the spirit of the resolution which Miltiades proposed at the crisis of the first Persian War. It is the use of ἐπισιτίζεσθαι in conjunction with such a word as ψήφισμα, which is in Aristotle's language "metaphorical."

† The Paralus or State galley, as being used in carrying prisoners of state, might be called the people's bludgeon or weapon against their enemies.

‡ It is clear that Sestos must have been an emporium of the corn which was exported from the coasts of the Euxine Sea to Greece.

§ The point lies in the legal term ὑπερήμερος, which is strictly applicable to somebody who has failed to pay a fine imposed upon him within the time prescribed.

‖ It must have been the grinding exactions in which the triremes were employed against the subject States of Athens that gave this name its appropriateness.

wine-shops the "Athenian * public messes." Æsion said
that *the Athenians* had " drained their whole city into Sicily "
(which is a metaphor and a metaphor of a vivid kind);
and again " so that Greece cried aloud " (which is also
in some sense a vivid metaphor). I may instance too
the advice of Cephisodotus *to the Athenians* to beware
of converting many of their † mob-*meetings into* assemblies;
or the address of ‡ Isocrates to those "who flock together at the general festivals." Another example is the
one in the § Funeral Oration, that "Greece might well
have her hair cut off at the tomb of those who had
perished at Salamis, as her liberty was buried in the
tomb with their valor;" for had he only said that she
"might well weep for the valor that lay buried with
them," *his expression* would have been a metaphor and a
vivid one, but the addition of the words "her liberty
with their valor " contains a sort of antithesis. Similarly
Iphicrates said, "The course of my argument runs through
the heart of Chares's conduct " ; this is a ‖ proportional
metaphor, and the phrase "through the heart " sets
the thing vividly before our eyes. Again, the phrase " to
invite dangers to the help of dangers " is a vivid
metaphor. The same is true of the phrase used by

---

* φιδίτια was the Spartan term for the συσσίτια which were so characteristic a feature of the Lycurgean legislation. See *Politics*, ii. ch. 9.

† The word συνδρομὰς is substituted for συγκλήτους (ἐκκλησίας) "extraordinary assemblies."

‡ *Phil.* § 14.   It is the strange use of συντρέχοντας, as of συνδρομὰς in
the last example, that makes the "metaphor."

§ The Funeral Oration, which seems to be here ascribed to Isocrates, is
usually regarded as the composition of Lysias, although its genuineness has
been much disputed.

‖ The "proportion" may perhaps be expressed thus:

A road : a country :: the speech : Chares's conduct.

* Lycoleon in behalf of Chabrias, " not awed even by that symbol of his supplication, the bronze image," which was a metaphor at the time when it was used, although not a permanent one, as it is only in the hour of his peril that the statue can be said to supplicate, but a vivid metaphor, *arising from* † the supposed animation of the inanimate memorial of the services he had rendered to the State. Or again " practising in every way meanness of spirit " is a metaphor, as practising is a species of increasing. Or *the saying* that " God lit up the light of reason in the soul," both light and reason being means of illumination. Or again ‡ " we are not putting an end to the wars but only putting them off," *which is a metaphor*, as postponement and such a peace as is described are both merely means of delay. Or again, if we say that § " the treaty is a very far finer trophy than those won in war; for that is commemorative of a trifling success and a single chance, whereas the treaty commemorates *the issue of* a whole war "; for both are signals of victory. Or *lastly if we say* that States ‖ " pay a heavy reckoning in the censure of mankind "; for the *audit or* reckoning is a sort of legal damage.

---

* A statue of Chabrias with his shield resting on his knee and his spear advanced, had been erected in honor of his victory over Agesilaus, B.C. 378. Twelve years later, when Chabrias himself was standing his trial, his advocate Lycoleon must have pointed to this statue.

† Reading τὸ ἄψυχον δὲ.

‡ Isocrates, *Paneg.* § 200. The "metaphor" is, I think, the use of ἀναβάλλεσθαι, as a peace would properly be said not to "postpone" but to "terminate" a war.

§ *Ibid.* § 211.

‖ The word εὔθυνα, meaning properly the audit, to which officers of State were called to submit at the expiration of their term of office, is applied metaphorically to the audit which states or nations undergo at the bar of history.

A reference to the *Poetic*, ch. 21, is necessary for the understanding of the "metaphors" cited in the present chapter.

It has been stated then that the sources of clever sayings are proportional metaphor and *vivid or* ocular representation

Chap. XI.

of the facts; but we have still to say what we understand by such representation and what are the means of producing it.

I mean that expressions represent a thing to the eye, when they show it in a state of activity.   For instance; to de-

Vividness.

scribe a good man as * "square" is a metaphor, as a good man and a square are both perfect *of their kind;* but it does not signify a state of activity.   On the other hand such a phrase as † "with his vigor all in bloom" or ‡ " thee like as sacred kine that roam at large" or in the § line

"Then the Greeks bounding forwards,"

the expression " bounding " is energetic as well as metaphorical.   It is the same in Homer's favorite treatment of inanimate objects as animate by the use of metaphor.   But it is always by representing things as in action that he wins applause, as e.g.

‖ " Down down again to the valley the shameless boulder came bounding,"
or
¶ " the arrow flew,"
or ** the arrow
" yearning for its mark,"
or †† the spears
" stood fixed in earth all panting to taste blood,"
or
‡‡ " through the breast
The point sped quivering,"

* Perhaps "an all-round man" would better give the idea in English.
† Isocrates, *Phil.* § 12.
‡ *Ibid.* §. 150.
§ Euripides, *Iphig. in Aul.* 80.
‖ *Odyssey,* xi. 598.
¶ *Iliad,* xiii. 587.
** *Ibid.* iv. 126.
†† *Ibid.* xi. 573.
‡‡ *Ibid.* xv. 542.

for in all these instances the living character of the expressions invests the objects with an appearance of activity, shamelessness, quivering eagerness, and the like being so many forms of activity. These expressions Homer applied to the objects by means of proportional metaphor; for * as the stone is to Sisyphus, so is a shameless person to the victim of his shamelessness. But in his most approved similes too he treats inanimate things in the same way, *e.g. in the line* "*Waves that are* arched, foam-crested, some foremost, others pursuing"; for he represents them all as moving and living, and activity is a form of motion.

It is proper to derive metaphors, as has been said before, from objects which are closely related to *the thing itself* but which are not *immediately* obvious. Similarly in philosophy it is a mark of sagacity to discern resemblances even in things which are widely different, as when Archytas said that an arbitrator and an altar were identical; for both are refuges of the injured; or if one should say that an anchor and a hook were identical; for they are both the same kind of thing, only they differ *in position*, † one being above and the other below. The ‡ equalization of states in regard to things very dissimilar, *as e.g.* equality in area and in prerogatives, would be another case.

Sources of metaphor. p. 60.

While metaphor is a very frequent instrument of clever sayings, another or an additional instrument is deception, as people are more clearly conscious of having learnt some-

* It is certainly noticeable that Aristotle understands Homer's ἀναιδής as an epithet of a stone to mean literally "shameless."

† The meaning is that an anchor holds fast something which is above it, and a hook something which is below it.

‡ The cleverness or originality lies, I think, in the comparison of things so different as superficial area and political privilege (or perhaps military strength).

thing from their sense of surprise *at the way in which the sentence ends*, and their soul seems to say, "Quite true, and I had missed the point." Again, the characteristic of clever apophthegms is that the speaker means something more than he says, as e.g. the apophthegm of Stesichorus that the cicalas will have to sing to themselves on the ground. This too is the reason of the pleasure afforded by clever riddles; they are instructive and metaphorical in their expression. And the same is true of what Theodorus calls "novel phrases," i.e. phrases in which *the sequel* is unexpected and not, as he expresses it, " according to previous expectation," but such as comic writers use when they alter the forms of words. The effect of jokes depending upon changes of letters is the same; they deceive the expectation. *Nor are these jokes found only in prose*, they occur also in verses, where *the conclusion is* not such as the audience had expected, e.g.

Deception (παρα προσδοκίαν).

> And as he walked, beneath his feet
> Were — chilblains,

whereas the audience expected *the writer* to say " sandals." But *in all such cases* the point must be clear at the moment of making a joke. A play upon the letters of a word arises not from using it in its direct meaning but from giving the meaning a new turn.*

A proper enunciation is requisite in all such sayings. Take

---

* Aristotle illustrates the "literal joke" by two expressions which would be untranslatable, even if it were possible to be sure of their meaning. The first of them (for the σε of l. 33 should be omitted) may apparently be pronounced either as θράττει " it confounds you" or as Θρᾷττ' εἶ "you are a Thracian slave girl." "This is amusing (he says) when its point is understood, for if you do not know the person to be a Thracian, it will seem silly." The second, βούλει αὐτὸν πέρσαι, has never been explained. "Both (he adds) need a proper enunciation."

e.g. the remark that Athens did not find the *rule of the sea a rule of misery, as it was a source of profit to her, or as † Isocrates put it, that the rule of the sea was a rule of misery to the state. For in both these cases there is something said which one would not have expected to be said, and *yet* it is recognized as true; for there is no cleverness in calling the rule a rule *in the second example*, but the word " rule " is employed in different senses, and *in the first example* it is not " rule" in the sense in which it has been used before, but " rule " in a different sense which is contradicted. But in all these cases the merit consists in the proper application of the term employed, *i.e. in the appropriateness of it to the thing described*, whether it is employed in a *double-entendre* or in a metaphor. Such an expression e.g. as "Mr. ‡ Bearable unbearable " is a contradiction only of the *double-entendre ;* but it is appropriate enough, if the person in question is a bore. So too the line

Clever sayings as ornaments of style.

§ " You should not be more stranger than a stranger,"

or in other words, not stranger than you are bound to be, which is the same thing. Or again, " A stranger must not always be a stranger "; for here too there is change of signification. The same is the case in the much lauded line of Anaxandrides

" 'Tis well to die ere meriting the death ";

* ἀρχή has the meaning first of "empire" and then of "beginning" in this expression.

† The passage which Aristotle has in mind is apparently either *Phil.* § 69, or *de Pace*, § 125.

‡ Plainly Ἀνάσχετος is a proper name, which lends itself to a play upon its meaning.

§ Vahlen's reading of the line :

οὐκ ἂν γένοιο μᾶλλον ἢ ξένος ξένος,

gives the best sense and is supported by the context.

for this is equivalent to saying, " 'Tis a worthy thing to die unworthily " or * " to die not being worthy of death " or " doing nothing worthy of death." The species of style is the same in all these instances; but the more concisely and antithetically it is expressed, the' more popular is the saying. The reason of this is that its instructiveness is enhanced by the antithesis and accelerated by the conciseness of its terms. But there should always be the additional element of some personal appositeness or propriety of expression, if what is said is to be true and not superficial. For truth and depth are not always combined, as e.g. *in the phrases* " One should die void of offence " or " A worthy man should wed a worthy wife," where there is no point at all. It is only when you combine the two *that you make a pointed phrase*, e.g. "It is a worthy thing to die unworthily." But the greater the number of such elements in a sentence, the more cleverly pointed it appears, as e.g. if its words convey a metaphor, and a metaphor of a particular kind, *i.e. a proportional metaphor*, an antithesis, a *parisosis or* balance of clauses and a vividness of action.

Successful similes too, as has been said above, are always in a certain sense popular metaphors, being invariably composed of two terms, like the proportional metaphor. For instance, the shield, as we say, is Ares's goblet, and a bow a stringless lyre. Such a form of expression is not a † simple one; but to call the bow a lyre or the shield a goblet is so.

Similes.
p. 67.

A simile is formed e.g. by the comparison of a flute player to a monkey or of a ‡ shortsighted person to a lamp with

---

* The clause is probably spurious.

† It is "not simple" because *e.g.* the comparison is not merely between shield and goblet but between the shield and Ares on the one hand and Dionysus and the goblet on the other.   ‡ Omitting εἰς.

water dripping upon it, as both * keep shrinking. A successful simile is one which is *virtually* a metaphor. For we may
compare the shield to " Ares's goblet " or the ruin to a " tatter
of a house " ; or we may describe † Niceratus as a " Phil-
octetes stung by Pratys," using the simile of Thrasymachus
when he saw Niceratus after his defeat by Pratys in the
rhapsody with his hair still dishevelled and his face unwashed.
It is here that poets are most loudly condemned for failure
and most warmly applauded for success, when *they so form
their simile that* the two members of it correspond, as e.g.

or
> " Like parsley curled his legs he bears "
>
> " Just as ‡ Philammon tilting at the quintain."

These expressions and all others like them are similes; and
that similes are metaphors is a truth which has been already
stated more than once.

Proverbs again are metaphors from one species to another,
e.g. when somebody has invited a person's help
in the hope of gaining by it and has afterwards   Proverbs.
found it to be a source of injury, § " 'Tis as the Carpathian
says of the hare "; for they are both the victims of this fate.

The sources of clever sayings and the reasons of their
cleverness have now been pretty fully discussed.

All approved hyperboles are also metaphors, as when it is
said of a man whose face is bruised, " You might
have taken him for a basket of mulberries." For   Hyperboles.
a bruise *like a mulberry* is something purple; but it is the

---

* The winking of the shortsighted person and the sputtering of the lamp
are both describable by the verb συνάγεσθαι.

† Niceratus seems to have engaged in a rhapsodical contest with Pratys.

‡ Philammon was a celebrated athlete.

§ It is supposed that some Carpathian had brought some hares or rabbits
into his island and that they had multiplied and devoured all his crops.

number of the bruises supposed which makes the hyberbole. But there are other phrases resembling those given above which are hyperboles with only a difference of expression, as if you change

> " Just as Philammon tilting at the quintain "

to " You would have thought he was Philammon fighting with the quintain " or

> " Like parsley curled his legs he bears "

to " You might have thought he had not legs but parsley; they were so curly."

There is a character of juvenility in hyperboles as showing vehemence. Hence people generally employ them in moments of passion, *as in the * lines*

> • " Not tho' he gave me gifts
> As many as the sand-grains or the dust."
>
> .   .   .   .   .   .
>
> " But Agamemnon's daughter wed I not,
> Tho' Aphrodite's beauty were her own
> And all Athene's art."

This is a favorite figure of the Attic orators. But, *as being juvenile,* it is unbecoming to elder people.

It must not be forgotten that every kind of Rhetoric has its own appropriate style. For there is a difference between the literary and controversial styles and CHAP. XII. *in the controversial style* between the political Propriety. and forensic styles. But the orator should be familiar with both; for the one (the controversial style) implies a power of expressing oneself in pure and accurate Greek, and the other (the literary style) a deliverance from

* *Iliad,* ix. 385 sqq.

the necessity of holding one's tongue, if one has anything that he wishes to impart to the world, as is the case of those who have no skill in composition.

It is the literary style which is the most finished and the controversial which is the best suited to declamation. Controversial oratory again is of two kinds, ethical and emotional. This is the reason why actors are fond of such dramas and poets of such *dramatis personæ* as lend themselves to the treatment of character or emotion. But it is poets who write to be read whose works are in everybody's hands, such as Chæremon who is as finished as a * professional speechwriter and Licymnius among the dithyrambic poets. Also a comparison of the speeches of literary men and those of rhetoricians shows that the former are found in actual contests to be meagre, and the latter, although highly commended, to be inartistic, when taken in the hands *and closely studied*. The reason is that they are adapted to an actual contest; hence the speeches which are intended to be declaimed, when the declamation is removed, appear ridiculous, as failing to discharge their proper function. Thus the use of asyndeta and the frequent repetition of the same word are rightly reprobated in the literary style, but are actually sought by orators in the controversial style for their dramatic effect. † (But in such repetitions there must be some variety *of expression*, which paves the way, if I may so speak, for declamation, *as e.g. in the words* " Here is he who robbed you;

Literary and controversial styles.

---

* The term λογογράφος is fully discussed by Mr. Cope in his note on ii. ch. 11, § 7. It means here not so much one who composed speeches to be delivered by others in a Court of Law as one who wrote panegyrical or epideictic speeches, meaning them not to be delivered at all but to be read and studied at home.

† The sentences placed in brackets contain remarks which are rather incidental than necessary to the subject of the chapter.

here is he who cheated you; here is he who at the last essayed to betray you." We may instance too the * trick of the actor Philemon in Anaxandrides's play *The Old Man's Dotage* at the passage *beginning* " Rhadamanthys and Palamedes," or his repetition of the personal pronoun in the prologue of the *Devotees;* for unless such passages are dramatically declaimed, the case is like that of † a man who has swallowed a poker. And the same is true of asyndeta, e.g. " I came, I met, I implored "; it is necessary to declaim the words dramatically and not to utter them, as if they were all one thing, with the same character and intonation. There is this especial property also in asyndeta, that they make it possible to present an appearance of saying several things in the time which would otherwise be required for saying one. For the effect of the connecting particle is to convert several things into one; hence, if the connecting particle is taken away, the consequence will clearly be the opposite effect of converting a single thing into several. The asyndeton is thus a means of amplification. *Take for instance* the words " I came, I conversed, I entreated "; the audience seems to survey several things, as many things in fact as the speaker mentioned. And this is Homer's purpose *in the reiteration of the name Nireus in the successive* ‡ *lines*

> " Nireus of Syme,
> " Nireus Aglaia's son,
> " Nireus the fairest man,"

for as a person of whom several things are said will necessarily

---

* The allusion is admittedly obscure; but it seems most probable that these were well-known passages in which the art of the actor Philemon had emphasized slight varieties of expression, where several similar clauses occurred together.

† " The porter who carried the beam" was a typical Greek instance of stiffness like "the man who has swallowed a poker" in English.

‡ *Iliad*, ii. 671–673.

be mentioned several times, it follows that, if a person is mentioned several times, it seems as if several things had been said of him. So that Homer by a single mention of Nireus exaggerated his importance through this fallacy and makes him famous, although he never alludes to him again.)

The style of political oratory is precisely similar to scene-painting. For the greater the crowd, the more distant is the view: hence it is that in both a finished style appears superfluous and unsuccessful. The forensic   Political rhetoric. style on the other hand is more finished, especially when addressed to a single judge; for he is least subject to rhetorical influences, as he can take a more comprehensive view of what is germane to the case or alien to it and, as there is no actual contest, is not prejudiced in his judgment. Accordingly it is not the same orators who succeed in all the different styles of Rhetoric; but, where there is most opportunity for declamation, there is the least possibility of finish. And this is the case where voice, and especially where a loud voice, is required.

The epideictic style is best suited to literary purposes, as its proper function is to be read; and next to it the forensic style. It is superfluous to add such distinctions   Epideictic as that the style should be pleasant and stately; and forensic we might as well say that it must be chastened rhetoric. and liberal and characterized by any other ethical virtue. For it is clear that the * qualities enumerated above will render it pleasant, if we have been right in our definition of virtue of style. What *other* reason is there why it should be clear and not commonplace but appropriate? For it will not be clear, if it is prolix or too concise. But it is

* Purity, propriety, vividness, rhythm, and the like, as Mr. Cop justly says.

evident that it is the intermediate style which is the appropriate one. Pleasantness will result from the elements above enumerated, if successfully combined, viz. familiar and foreign words, rhythm, and the persuasiveness which is the outcome of propriety.

We have now concluded our remarks upon style whether as belonging equally to all kinds of Rhetoric or as peculiar to the several kinds; it remains to consider arrangement.

[1] Compare Voltaire, below, p. 184.
[2] Compare Pater, below, pp. 387 ff.
[3] Compare Wackernagel, above, p. 3.
[4] Compare Buffon, below, p. 176, and Brunetière, below, p. 424.
[5] Compare Buffon, below, pp. 170-171.

IV

LONGINUS

On the Sublime (First Century A.D.)

[From *Longinus On the Sublime,* translated into English by H. L. Havell, with an Introduction by Andrew Lang (London and New York, Macmillan, 1890, pp. 1–86).

We give Mr. Havell's translation entire, with his foot-notes; for lack of space other annotation must be restricted. By far the best commentary on Longinus is to be found in the admirable edition of the treatise *On the Sublime* by Professor W. Rhys Roberts (Cambridge University Press, 1899). Students of English are referred particularly to Professor Roberts's remarks on the "Contents and Character of the Treatise" (pp. 23–37). It is to be regretted that his translation is not accessible in separate and cheaper form. Mr. A. O. Prickard's excellent version (Oxford, Clarendon Press, 1906) is accompanied by a valuable Introduction.

This celebrated and inspiring epistle, long attributed mistakenly to an author of the third century A.D., but in all likelihood by an unidentified writer of the first, may be not improperly described as an essay on style — "the grand style," as Matthew Arnold would say. Although it continues the tradition of earlier works on rhetoric, rather than poetics, it has a bearing on both subjects. It might not, in fact, wholly escape Wackernagel's censure of theories that fail to differentiate carefully between style in prose and style in verse (cf. above, pp. 3–4). The student would derive benefit in trying either to defend or to convict the treatise on this charge.]

I

The treatise of Cæcilius on the Sublime, when, as you remember, my dear Terentian, we examined it together, seemed to us to be beneath the dignity of the whole subject, to fail entirely in seizing the salient points, and to offer little profit

H

(which should be the principal aim of every writer) for the trouble of its perusal. There are two things essential to a technical treatise: the first is to define the subject; the second (I mean second in order, as it is by much the first in importance) to point out how and by what methods we may become masters of it ourselves. And yet Cæcilius, while wasting his efforts in a thousand illustrations of the nature of the Sublime, as though here we were quite in the dark, somehow passes by as immaterial the question how we might be able to exalt our own genius to a certain degree of progress in sublimity. However, perhaps it would be fairer to commend this writer's intelligence and zeal in themselves, instead of blaming him for his omissions. And since you have bidden me also to put together, if only for your entertainment, a few notes on the subject of the Sublime, let me see if there is anything in my speculations which promises advantage to men of affairs. In you, dear friend — such is my confidence in your abilities, and such the part which becomes you — I look for a sympathizing and discerning * critic of the several parts of my treatise. For that was a just remark of his who pronounced that the points in which we resemble the divine nature are benevolence and love of truth.

As I am addressing a person so accomplished in literature, I need only state, without enlarging further on the matter, that the Sublime, wherever it occurs, consists in a certain loftiness and excellence of language, and that it is by this, and this only, that the greatest poets and prose-writers have gained eminence, and won themselves a lasting place in the Temple of Fame. A lofty passage does not convince the reason of the reader, but takes him out of himself. That which is admirable ever confounds our judgment, and eclipses that which is merely reasonable or agreeable. To believe or

* Reading φιλοφρονέστατα καὶ ἀληθέστατα.

not is usually in our own power; but the Sublime, acting with
an imperious and irresistible force, sways every reader whether
he will or no. Skill in invention, lucid arrangement and
disposition of facts, are appreciated not by one passage, or by
two, but gradually manifest themselves in the general structure of a work; but a sublime thought, if happily timed,
illumines * an entire subject with the vividness of a lightning-
flash, and exhibits the whole power of the orator in a moment
of time. Your own experience, I am sure, my dearest Terentian, would enable you to illustrate these and similar
points of doctrine.

II

The first question which presents itself for solution is
whether there is any art which can teach sublimity or loftiness
in writing. For some hold generally that there is mere
delusion in attempting to reduce such subjects to technical
rules. "The Sublime," they tell us, " is born in a man, and
not to be acquired by instruction; genius is the only master
who can teach it. The vigorous products of nature " (such
is their view) " are weakened and in every respect debased,
when robbed of their flesh and blood by frigid technicalities."
But I maintain that the truth can be shown to stand otherwise in this matter. Let us look at the case in this way;
Nature in her loftier and more passionate moods, while de-
testing all appearance of restraint, is not wont to show herself
utterly wayward and reckless; and though in all cases the
vital informing principle is derived from her, yet to determine
the right degree and the right moment, and to contribute
the precision of practice and experience, is the peculiar province of scientific method. The great passions, when left
to their own blind and rash impulses without the control

* Reading διεφώτισεν.

of reason, are in the same danger as a ship let drive at random without ballast. Often they need the spur, but sometimes also the curb. The remark of Demosthenes with regard to human life in general, — that the greatest of all blessings is to be fortunate, but next to that and equal in importance is to be well advised, — for good fortune is utterly ruined by the absence of good counsel, — may be applied to literature, if we substitute genius for fortune, and art for counsel. Then, again (and this is the most important point of all), a writer can only learn from art when he is to abandon himself to the direction of his genius.*

These are the considerations which I submit to the unfavorable critic of such useful studies. Perhaps they may induce him to alter his opinion as to the vanity and idleness of our present investigations.

III

> . . . "And let them check the stove's long tongues of fire:
> For if I see one tenant of the hearth,
> I'll thrust within one curling torrent flame,
> And bring that roof in ashes to the ground:
> But now not yet is sung my noble lay." †

Such phrases cease to be tragic, and become burlesque, — I mean phrases like " curling torrent flames " and " vomiting to heaven," and representing Boreas as a piper, and so on. Such expressions, and such images, produce an effect of confusion and obscurity, not of energy; and if each separately be examined under the light of criticism, what seemed terrible gradually sinks into absurdity. Since then, even in

---

* Literally, "But the most important point of all is that the actual fact that there are some parts of literature which are in the power of natural genius alone, must be learnt from no other source than from art."

† Æschylus in his lost *Orithyia*.

tragedy, where the natural dignity of the subject makes a swelling diction allowable, we cannot pardon a tasteless grandiloquence, how much more incongruous must it seem in sober prose! Hence we laugh at those fine words of Gorgias of Leontini, such as " Xerxes the Persian Zeus " and " vultures, those living tombs," and at certain conceits of Callisthenes which are high-flown rather than sublime, and at some in Cleitarchus more ludicrous still — a writer whose frothy style tempts us to travesty Sophocles and say, " He blows a little pipe, and blows it ill." The same faults may be observed in Amphicrates and Hegesias and Matris, who in their frequent moments (as they think) of inspiration, instead of playing the genius are simply playing the fool.

Speaking generally, it would seem that bombast is one of the hardest things to avoid in writing. For all those writers who are ambitious of a lofty style, through dread of being convicted of feebleness and poverty of language, slide by a natural gradation into the opposite extreme. " Who fails in great endeavor, nobly fails," is their creed. Now bulk, when hollow and affected, is always objectionable, whether in material bodies or in writings, and in danger of producing on us an impression of littleness: " nothing," it is said, " is drier than a man with the dropsy."

The characteristic, then, of bombast is that it transcends the Sublime: but there is another fault diametrically opposed to grandeur: this is called puerility, and it is the failing of feeble and narrow minds, — indeed, the most ignoble of all vices in writing. By puerility we mean a pedantic habit of mind, which by over-elaboration ends in frigidity. Slips of this sort are made by those who, aiming at brilliancy, polish, and especially attractiveness, are landed in paltriness and silly affectation. Closely associated with this is a third sort of vice, in dealing with the passions, which Theodorus used to call false sentiment, meaning by that an ill-timed and empty display of emotion, where no emotion is called for, or of greater emotion than the situation warrants. Thus we often see an author hurried by the tumult of his mind into tedious displays of mere personal feeling which has no connection with the subject. Yet how justly ridiculous must an author appear, whose most violent transports leave his readers quite cold ! However, I will dismiss this subject, as I intend to devote a separate work to the treatment of the pathetic in writing.

IV

The last of the faults which I mentioned is frequently observed in Timæus — I mean the fault of frigidity. In other respects he is an able writer, and sometimes not unsuccessful in the loftier style; a man of wide knowledge, and full of ingenuity; a most bitter critic of the failings of others — but unhappily blind to his own. In his eagerness to be always striking out new thoughts he frequently falls into the most childish absurdities. I will only instance one or two passages, as most of them have been pointed out by Cæcilius. Wishing to say something very fine about Alexander the Great he speaks of him as a man " who annexed the whole of Asia in fewer years than Isocrates spent in writing his panegyric oration in which he urges the Greeks to make war on Persia." How strange is the comparison of the " great Emathian conqueror " with an Athenian rhetorician ! By this mode of reasoning it is plain that the Spartans were very inferior to Isocrates in courage, since it took them thirty years to conquer Messene, while he finished the composition of this harangue in ten. Observe, too, his language on the Athenians taken in Sicily. "They paid the penalty for their impious outrage on Hermes in mutilating his statues; and the chief agent in their destruction was one who was descended on his father's side from the injured deity — Hermocrates, son of Hermon." I wonder, my dearest Terentian, how he omitted to say of the tyrant Dionysius that for his impiety towards Zeus and Herakles he was deprived of his power by Dion and Herakleides. Yet why speak of Timæus, when even men like Xenophon and Plato — the very demigods of literature — though they had sat at the feet of Socrates, sometimes forgot themselves in the pursuit of such paltry conceits. The former, in his account of the Spartan Polity, has these words: "Their voice you would no more hear than if they were of marble, their gaze is as immovable as if they were cast in bronze; you would deem them more modest than the very maidens in their eyes."* To speak of the pupils of the eye as "modest maidens" was a piece of absurdity becoming Amphicrates † rather than Xenophon. And then what a strange delusion to suppose that modesty is always without exception expressed in the eye ! whereas it is commonly said that there is nothing by which an impudent fellow betrays his character so much as by the expression of his eyes. Thus Achilles addresses Agamemnon in the *Iliad* as "drunkard, with eye of dog." ‡ Timæus, however, with that want of judgment which characterizes plagiarists, could not leave to Xenophon the possession of even this piece of frigidity. In relating how Agathocles carried off his cousin, who was wedded to another man, from the festival of the unveiling, he asks, "Who could have done such a deed, unless he had harlots instead of maidens in his eyes?" And Plato himself, elsewhere so supreme a master of style, meaning to describe certain recording tablets, says, "They shall write, and deposit in the temples memorials of cypress wood"; § and

---

* *Xen. de Rep. Laced.* 3, 5.   ‡ *Il.* i. 225.
† C. iii. section 2.   § *Plat. de Legg.* v. 741, C.

again, "Then concerning walls, Megillus, I give my vote with
Sparta that we should let them lie asleep within the ground,
and not awaken them." * And Herodotus falls pretty much
under the same censure, when he speaks of beautiful women
as "tortures to the eye," † though here there is some excuse,
as the speakers in this passage are drunken barbarians.
Still, even from dramatic motives, such errors in taste should
not be permitted to deface the pages of an immortal work.

V

Now all these glaring improprieties of language may
be traced to one common root — the pursuit of novelty in
thought.[1] It is this that has turned the brain of nearly all
the learned world of to-day. Human blessings and human
ills commonly flow from the same source: and, to apply
this principle to literature, those ornaments of style, those
sublime and delightful images, which contribute to success,
are the foundation and the origin, not only of excellence,
but also of failure. It is thus with the figures called transitions, and hyperboles, and the use of plurals for singulars.
I shall show presently the dangers which they seem to involve. Our next task, therefore, must be to propose and to
settle the question how we may avoid the faults of style related to sublimity.

VI

Our best hope of doing this will be first of all to grasp some
definite theory and criterion of the true Sublime. Nevertheless this is a hard matter; for a just judgment of style is
the final fruit of long experience; still, I believe that the way
I shall indicate will enable us to distinguish between the
true and false Sublime, so far as it can be done by rule.

* *Ib.* vi. 778, D.   † v. 18.

VII

It is proper to observe that in human life nothing is truly great which is despised by all elevated minds. For example, no man of sense can regard wealth, honor, glory, and power, or any of those things which are surrounded by a great external parade of pomp and circumstance, as the highest blessings, seeing that merely to despise such things is a blessing of no common order: certainly those who possess them are admired much less than those who, having the opportunity to acquire them, through greatness of soul neglect it. Now let us apply this principle to the Sublime in poetry or in prose; let us ask in all cases, is it merely a specious sublimity? is this gorgeous exterior a mere false and clumsy pageant, which if laid open will be found to conceal nothing but emptiness? for if so, a noble mind will scorn instead of admiring it. It is natural to us to feel our souls lifted up by the true Sublime, and conceiving a sort of generous exultation to be filled with joy and pride, as though we had ourselves originated the ideas which we read. If then any work, on being repeatedly submitted to the judgment of an acute and cultivated critic, fails to dispose his mind to lofty ideas; if the thoughts which it suggests do not extend beyond what is actually expressed; and if, the longer you read it, the less you think of it, — there can be here no true sublimity, when the effect is not sustained beyond the mere act of perusal. But when a passage is pregnant in suggestion, when it is hard, nay impossible, to distract the attention from it, and when it takes a strong and lasting hold on the memory, then we may be sure that we have lighted on the true Sublime. In general we may regard those words as truly noble and sublime which always please and please all readers. For when the same book always produces the same impression on all who read it, whatever be the difference in their pursuits, their manner of life, their aspirations, their ages, or their language, such a harmony of opposites gives irresistible authority to their favorable verdict.

VIII

I shall now proceed to enumerate the five principal sources, as we may call them, from which almost all sublimity is derived, assuming, of course, the preliminary gift on which all these five sources depend, namely, command of language. The first and the most important is (1) grandeur of thought, as I have pointed out elsewhere in my work on Xenophon. The second is (2) a vigorous and spirited treatment of the passions. These two conditions of sublimity depend mainly on natural endowments, whereas those which follow derive assistance from Art. The third is (3) a certain artifice in the employment of figures, which are of two kinds, figures of thought and figures of speech. The fourth is (4) dignified expression, which is subdivided into (a) the proper choice of words, and (b) the use of metaphors and other ornaments of diction. The fifth cause of sublimity, which embraces all those preceding, is (5) majesty and elevation of structure. Let us consider what is involved in each of these five forms separately.

I must first, however, remark that some of these five divisions are omitted by Cæcilius; for instance, he says nothing about the passions. Now if he made this omission from a belief that the Sublime and the Pathetic are one and the same thing, holding them to be always coexistent and interdependent, he is in error. Some passions are found which, so far from being lofty, are actually low, such as pity, grief, fear; and conversely, sublimity is often not in the least affecting, as we may see (among innumerable other instances) in those bold expressions of our great poet on the sons of Aloëus —

> "Highly they raged
> To pile huge Ossa on the Olympian peak,
> And Pelion with all his waving trees
> On Ossa's crest to raise, and climb the sky;"

and the yet more tremendous climax —

> "And now had they accomplished it."

And in orators, in all passages dealing with panegyric, and in all the more imposing and declamatory places, dignity and sublimity play an indispensable part; but pathos is mostly absent. Hence the most pathetic orators have usually but little skill in panegyric, and conversely those who are powerful in panegyric generally fail in pathos. If, on the other hand, Cæcilius supposed that pathos never contributes to sublimity, and this is why he thought it alien to the subject, he is entirely deceived. For I would confidently pronounce that nothing is so conducive to sublimity as an appropriate display of genuine passion, which bursts out with a kind of " fine madness " and divine inspiration, and falls on our ears like the voice of a god.

IX

I have already said that of all these five conditions of the Sublime the most important is the first, that is, a certain lofty cast of mind.[2] Therefore, although this is a faculty rather natural than acquired, nevertheless it will be well for us in this instance also to train up our souls to sublimity, and make them as it were ever big with noble thoughts. How, it may be asked, is this to be done? I have hinted elsewhere in my writings that sublimity is, so to say, the image of greatness of soul. Hence a thought in its naked simplicity, even though unuttered, is sometimes admirable by the sheer force of its sublimity; for instance, the silence of Ajax in the eleventh *Odyssey* * is great, and grander than anything he could have said. It is absolutely essential, then, first of all to settle the question whence this grandeur of conception arises; and the answer is that true eloquence can be found only in those whose spirit is generous and aspiring. For those whose whole lives are wasted in paltry and illiberal thoughts and habits cannot possibly produce any work worthy of the lasting reverence of mankind. It is only natural that their words should be full of sublimity whose thoughts are full of majesty. Hence sublime thoughts belong properly to the loftiest minds. Such was the reply of Alexander to his general Parmenio, when the latter had observed, " Were I Alexander, I should have been satisfied "; " And I, were I Parmenio . . ."

The distance between heaven and earth † — a measure, one might say, not less appropriate to Homer's genius than to the stature of his discord. How different is that touch of Hesiod's in his description of sorrow — if the *Shield* is really one of his works: " rheum from her nostrils flowed "‡ — an image not terrible, but disgusting. Now consider how Homer gives dignity to his divine persons —

> " As far as lies his airy ken, who sits
> On some tall crag, and scans the wine-dark sea:
> So far extends the heavenly coursers' stride." §

He measures their speed by the extent of the whole world — a grand comparison, which might reasonably lead us to remark that if the divine steeds were to take two such leaps in succession, they would find no room in the world for another. Sublime also are the images in the Battle of the Gods —

* *Od.* xi. 543.   ‡ *Scut. Herc.* 267.
† *Il.* iv. 442.   § *Il.* v. 770.

> "A trumpet sound
> Rang through the air, and shook the Olympian height;
> Then terror seized the monarch of the dead,
> And springing from his throne he cried aloud
> With fearful voice, lest the earth, rent asunder
> By Neptune's mighty arm, forthwith reveal
> To mortal and immortal eyes those halls
> So drear and dank, which e'en the gods abhor." *

Earth rent from its foundations! Tartarus itself laid bare! The whole world torn asunder and turned upside down! Why, my dear friend, this is a perfect hurly-burly, in which the whole universe, heaven and hell, mortals and immortals, share the conflict and the peril. A terrible picture, certainly, but (unless perhaps it is to be taken allegorically) downright impious, and overstepping the bounds of decency. It seems to me that the strange medley of wounds, quarrels, revenges, tears, bonds, and other woes which make up the Homeric tradition of the gods was designed by its author to degrade his deities, as far as possible, into men, and exalt his men into deities—or rather, his gods are worse off than his human characters, since we, when we are unhappy, have a haven from ills in death, while the gods, according to him, not only live forever, but live forever in misery. Far to be preferred to this description of the Battle of the Gods are those passages which exhibit the divine nature in its true light, as something spotless, great, and pure, as, for instance, a passage which has often been handled by my predecessors, the lines on Poseidon:—

> "Mountain and wood and solitary peak,
> The ships Achaian, and the towers of Troy,
> Trembled beneath the god's immortal feet.
> Over the waves he rode, and round him played,
> Lured from the deeps, the ocean's monstrous brood,
> With uncouth gambols welcoming their lord:
> The charmèd billows parted: on they flew." †

* *Il.* xxi. 388; xx. 61.   † *Il.* xiii. 18; xx. 60; xiii. 19, 27.

And thus also the lawgiver of the Jews, no ordinary man, having formed an adequate conception of the Supreme Being, gave it adequate expression in the opening words of his "Laws": "God said " — what? — " let there be light, and there was light: let there be land, and there was."

I trust you will not think me tedious if I quote yet one more passage from our great poet (referring this time to human characters) in illustration of the manner in which he leads us with him to heroic heights. A sudden and baffling darkness as of night has overspread the ranks of his warring Greeks. Then Ajax in sore perplexity cries aloud —

> " Almighty Sire,
> Only from darkness save Achaia's sons;
> No more I ask, but give us back the day;
> Grant but our sight, and slay us, if thou wilt." *

The feelings are just what we should look for in Ajax. He does not, you observe, ask for his life — such a request would have been unworthy of his heroic soul — but finding himself paralyzed by darkness, and prohibited from employing his valor in any noble action, he chafes because his arms are idle, and prays for a speedy return of light. "At least," he thinks, "I shall find a warrior's grave, even though Zeus himself should fight against me." In such passages the mind of the poet is swept along in the whirlwind of the struggle, and, in his own words, he

> " Like the fierce war-god, raves, or wasting fire
> Through the deep thickets on a mountain-side;
> His lips drop foam." †

But there is another and a very interesting aspect of Homer's mind. When we turn to the *Odyssey* we find occasion to observe that a great poetical genius in the decline of power

* *Il.* xvii. 645.   † *Il.* xv. 605.

which comes with old age naturally leans towards the fabulous. For it is evident that this work was composed after the *Iliad*, in proof of which we may mention, among many other indications, the introduction in the *Odyssey* of the sequel to the story of his heroes' adventures at Troy, as so many additional episodes in the Trojan war, and especially the tribute of sorrow and mourning which is paid in that poem to departed heroes, as if in fulfilment of some previous design. The *Odyssey* is, in fact, a sort of epilogue to the *Iliad* —

> "There warrior Ajax lies, Achilles there,
> And there Patroclus, godlike counsellor;
> There lies my own dear son." *

And for the same reason, I imagine, whereas in the *Iliad*, which was written when his genius was in its prime, the whole structure of the poem is founded on action and struggle, in the *Odyssey* he generally prefers the narrative style, which is proper to old age. Hence Homer in his *Odyssey* may be compared to the setting sun: he is still as great as ever, but he has lost his fervent heat. The strain is now pitched to a lower key than in the "Tale of Troy divine": we begin to miss that high and equable sublimity which never flags or sinks, that continuous current of moving incidents, those rapid transitions, that force of eloquence, that opulence of imagery which is ever true to Nature. Like the sea when it retires upon itself and leaves its shores waste and bare, henceforth the tide of sublimity begins to ebb, and draws us away into the dim region of myth and legend. In saying this I am not forgetting the fine storm-pieces in the *Odyssey*, the story of the Cyclops,† and other striking passages. It is Homer grown old I am discussing, but still it is Homer. Yet in every one of these passages the mythical predominates over the real.

* *Od.* iii. 109. † *Od.* ix. 182.

My purpose in making this digression was, as I said, to point out into what trifles the second childhood of genius is too apt to be betrayed; such, I mean, as the bag in which the winds are confined,* the tale of Odysseus's comrades being changed by Circe into swine † ("whimpering porkers" Zoïlus called them), and how Zeus was fed like a nestling by the doves,‡ and how Odysseus passed ten nights on the shipwreck without food, § and the improbable incidents in the slaying of the suitors.‖ When Homer nods like this, we must be content to say that he dreams as Zeus might dream.   Another reason for these remarks on the *Odyssey* is that I wished to make you understand that great poets and prose-writers, after they have lost their power of depicting the passions, turn naturally to the delineation of character.   Such, for instance, is the lifelike and characteristic picture of the palace of Odysseus, which may be called a sort of comedy of manners.

X

Let us now consider whether there is anything further which conduces to the Sublime in writing. It is a law of Nature that in all things there are certain constituent parts, coexistent with their substance. It necessarily follows, therefore, that one cause of sublimity is the choice of the most striking circumstances involved in whatever we are describing, and, further, the power of afterwards combining them into one animate whole. The reader is attracted partly by the selection of the incidents, partly by the skill which has welded them together. For instance, Sappho, in dealing with the passionate manifestations attending on the frenzy of lovers, always chooses her strokes from the signs which she

* *Od.* x. 17.   † *Od.* x. 237.   ‡ *Od.* xii. 62.
§ *Od.* xii. 447.   ‖ *Od.* xxii. *passim.*

has observed to be actually exhibited in such cases. But her peculiar excellence lies in the felicity with which she chooses and unites together the most striking and powerful features.

> "I deem that man divinely blest
> Who sits, and, gazing on thy face,
> Hears thee discourse with eloquent lips,
> And marks thy lovely smile.
> This, this it is that made my heart
> So wildly flutter in my breast;
> Whene'er I look on thee, my voice
> Falters, and faints, and fails;
> My tongue's benumbed; a subtle fire
> Through all my body inly steals;
> Mine eyes in darkness reel and swim;
> Strange murmurs drown my ears;
> With dewy damps my limbs are chilled
> An icy shiver shakes my frame;
> Paler than ashes grows my cheek;
> And Death seems nigh at hand."

Is it not wonderful how at the same moment soul, body, ears, tongue, eyes, color, all fail her, and are lost to her as completely as if they were not her own? Observe too how her sensations contradict one another — she freezes, she burns, she raves, she reasons, and all at the same instant. And this description is designed to show that she is assailed, not by any particular emotion, but by a tumult of different emotions. All these tokens belong to the passion of love; but it is in the choice, as I said, of the most striking features, and in the combination of them into one picture, that the perfection of this Ode of Sappho's lies. Similarly Homer in his descriptions of tempests always picks out the most terrific circumstances. The poet of the " Arimaspeia " intended the following lines to be grand —

> "Herein I find a wonder passing strange,
> That men should make their dwelling on the deep,

I

> Who far from land essaying bold to range
>   With anxious heart their toilsome vigils keep;
>   Their eyes are fixed on heaven's starry steep;
> The ravening billows hunger for their lives;
>   And oft each shivering wretch, constrained to weep,
> With suppliant hands to move heaven's pity strives,
> While many a direful qualm his very vitals rives."

All must see that there is more of ornament than of terror in the description. Now let us turn to Homer. One passage will suffice to show the contrast.

> " On them he leaped, as leaps a raging wave,
>   Child of the winds, under the darkening clouds,
>   On a swift ship, and buries her in foam;
>   Then cracks the sail beneath the roaring blast,
>   And quakes the breathless seamen's shuddering heart
>   In terror dire: death lours on every wave." *

Aratus has tried to give a new turn to this last thought —

> " But one frail timber shields them from their doom," †—

banishing by this feeble piece of subtlety all the terror from his description; setting limits, moreover, to the peril described by saying " shields them "; for so long as it shields them it matters not whether the " timber " be " frail " or stout. But Homer does not set any fixed limit to the danger, but gives us a vivid picture of men a thousand times on the brink of destruction, every wave threatening them with instant death. Moreover, by his bold and forcible combination of prepositions of opposite meaning he tortures his language to imitate the agony of the scene, the constraint which is put on the words accurately reflecting the anxiety of the sailors' minds, and the diction being stamped, as it were, with the peculiar terror of the situation. Similarly Archilochus in his description of the shipwreck, and simi-

---

* *Il.* xv. 624.   † *Phænomena*, 299.

larly Demosthenes when he describes how the news came of the taking of Elatea * — " It was evening," etc. Each of these authors fastidiously rejects whatever is not essential to the subject, and in putting together the most vivid features is careful to guard against the interposition of anything frivolous, unbecoming, or tiresome. Such blemishes mar the general effect, and give a patched and gaping appearance to the edifice of sublimity, which ought to be built up in a solid and uniform structure.

XI

Closely associated with the part of our subject we have just treated of is that excellence of writing which is called amplification, when a writer or pleader, whose theme admits of many successive starting-points and pauses, brings on one impressive point after another in a continuous and ascending scale.[3] Now whether this is employed in the treatment of a commonplace, or in the way of exaggeration, whether to place arguments or facts in a strong light, or in the disposition of actions, or of passions — for amplification takes a hundred different shapes — in all cases the orator must be cautioned that none of these methods is complete without the aid of sublimity, — unless, indeed, it be our object to excite pity, or to depreciate an opponent's argument. In all other uses of amplification, if you subtract the element of sublimity you will take as it were the soul from the body. No sooner is the support of sublimity removed than the whole becomes lifeless, nerveless, and dull.

There is a difference, however, between the rules I am now giving and those just mentioned. Then I was speaking of the delineation and coördination of the principal circumstances. My next task, therefore, must be briefly to

* *De Cor.* 169.

define this difference, and with it the general distinction between amplification and sublimity. Our whole discourse will thus gain in clearness.

XII

I must first remark that I am not satisfied with the definition of amplification generally given by authorities on rhetoric. They explain it to be a form of language which invests the subject with a certain grandeur. Yes, but this definition may be applied indifferently to sublimity, pathos, and the use of figurative language, since all these invest the discourse with some sort of grandeur. The difference seems to me to lie in this, that sublimity gives elevation to a subject, while amplification gives extension as well. Thus the sublime is often conveyed in a single thought, but amplification can only subsist with a certain prolixity and diffusiveness. The most general definition of amplification would explain it to consist in the gathering together of all the constituent parts and topics of a subject, emphasizing the argument by repeated insistence, herein differing from proof, that whereas the object of proof is logical demonstration, . . .

Plato, like the sea, pours forth his riches in a copious and expansive flood. Hence the style of the orator, who is the greater master of our emotions, is often, as it were, red-hot and ablaze with passion, whereas Plato, whose strength lay in a sort of weighty and sober magnificence, though never frigid, does not rival the thunders of Demosthenes. And, if a Greek may be allowed to express an opinion on the subject of Latin literature, I think the same difference may be discerned in the grandeur of Cicero as compared with that of his Grecian rival. The sublimity of Demosthenes is generally sudden and abrupt: that of Cicero is equally diffused. Demosthenes is vehement, rapid, vigorous, terrible;

he burns and sweeps away all before him; and hence we may liken him to a whirlwind or a thunderbolt: Cicero is like a widespread conflagration, which rolls over and feeds on all around it, whose fire is extensive and burns long, breaking out successively in different places, and finding its fuel now here, now there. Such points, however, I resign to your more competent judgment.

To resume, then, the high-strung sublimity of Demosthenes is appropriate to all cases where it is desired to exaggerate, or to rouse some vehement emotion, and generally when we want to carry away our audience with us. We must employ the diffusive style, on the other hand, when we wish to overpower them with a flood of language. It is suitable, for example, to familiar topics, and to perorations in most cases, and to digressions, and to all descriptive and declamatory passages, and in dealing with history or natural science, and in numerous other cases.

XIII

To return, however, to Plato: how grand he can be with all that gentle and noiseless flow of eloquence you will be reminded by this characteristic passage, which you have read in his *Republic*: "They, therefore, who have no knowledge of wisdom and virtue, whose lives are passed in feasting and similar joys, are borne downwards, as is but natural, and in this region they wander all their lives; but they never lifted up their eyes nor were borne upwards to the true world above, nor ever tasted of pleasure abiding and unalloyed; but like beasts they ever look downwards, and their heads are bent to the ground, or rather to the table; they feed full their bellies and their lusts, and longing ever more and more for such things they kick and gore one another with horns and hoofs of iron, and slay·one another in their insatiable desires."*

We may learn from this author, if we would but observe his example, that there is yet another path besides those mentioned which leads to sublime heights. What path do I mean? The emulous imitation of the great poets and prose-writers of the past. On this mark, dear friend, let us keep our eyes ever steadfastly fixed. Many gather the divine impulse from another's spirit, just as we are told that the Pythian priestess, when she takes her seat on the tripod, where there is said to be a rent in the ground breathing upwards a heavenly emanation, straightway conceives from that source the godlike gift of prophecy, and utters her inspired oracles; so likewise from the mighty genius of the great writers of antiquity there is carried into the souls of their rivals, as from a fount of inspiration, an effluence which breathes upon them until, even though their natural temper be but cold, they share the sublime enthusiasm of others. Thus Homer's name is associated with a numerous band of illustrious disciples — not only Herodotus, but Stesichorus before him, and the great Archilochus, and above all Plato, who from the great fountain-head of Homer's genius drew into himself innumerable tributary streams. Perhaps it would have been necessary to illustrate this point, had not Ammonius and his school already classified and noted down the various examples. Now what I am speaking of is not plagiarism, but resembles the process of copying from fair forms or statues or works of skilled labor. Nor in my opinion would so many fair flowers of imagery have bloomed among the philosophical dogmas of Plato, nor would he have risen so often to the language and topics of poetry, had he not engaged heart and soul in a contest for precedence with

* *Rep.* ix. 586, A.

Homer, like a young champion entering the lists against a veteran. It may be that he showed too ambitious a spirit in venturing on such a duel; but nevertheless it was not without advantage to him: " for strife like this," as Hesiod says, " is good for men." *   And where shall we find a more glorious arena or a nobler crown than here, where even defeat at the hands of our predecessors is not ignoble?

XIV

Therefore it is good for us also, when we are laboring on some subject which demands a lofty and majestic style, to imagine to ourselves how Homer might have expressed this or that, or how Plato or Demosthenes would have clothed it with sublimity, or, in history, Thucydides. For by our fixing an eye of rivalry on those high examples they will become like beacons to guide us, and will perhaps lift up our souls to the fulness of the stature we conceive. And it would be still better should we try to realize this further thought, How would Homer, had he been here, or how would Demosthenes, have listened to what I have written, or how would they have been affected by it? For what higher incentive to exertion could a writer have than to imagine such judges or such an audience of his works, and to give an account of his writings with heroes like these to criticise and look on? Yet more inspiring would be the thought, With what feelings will future ages through all time read these my works? If this should awaken a fear in any writer that he will not be intelligible to his contemporaries it will necessarily follow that the conceptions of his mind will be crude, maimed, and abortive, and lacking that ripe perfection which alone can win the applause of ages to come.

* *Opp.* 29.

XV

The dignity, grandeur, and energy of a style largely depend on a proper employment of images, a term which I prefer to that usually given.* The term image in its most general acceptation includes every thought, howsoever presented, which issues in speech. But the term is now generally confined to those cases when he who is speaking, by reason of the rapt and excited state of his feelings, imagines himself to see what he is talking about, and produces a similar illusion in his hearers. Poets and orators both employ images, but with a very different object, as you are well aware. The poetical image is designed to astound; the oratorical image to give perspicuity. Both, however, seek to work on the emotions.

> " Mother, I pray thee, set not thou upon me
> Those maids with bloody face and serpent hair:
> See, see, they come, they're here, they spring upon me ! " †

And again —

> " Ah, ah, she'll slay me ! whither shall I fly ? " ‡

The poet when he wrote like this saw the Erinyes with his own eyes, and he almost compels his readers to see them too. Euripides found his chief delight in the labor of giving tragic expression to these two passions of madness and love, showing here a real mastery which I cannot think he exhibited elsewhere. Still, he is by no means diffident in venturing on other fields of the imagination. His genius was far from being of the highest order, but by taking pains he often raises himself to a tragic elevation. In his sublimer moments he generally reminds us of Homer's description of the lion —

---

* εἰδωλοποιίαι, "fictions of the imagination," Hickie.

† Eur. *Orest.* 255.   ‡ *Iph. Taur.* 291.

> " With tail he lashes both his flanks and sides,
> And spurs himself to battle." *

Take, for instance, that passage in which Helios, in handing
the reins to his son, says —

> " Drive on, but shun the burning Libyan tract;
> The hot dry air will let thine axle down:
> Toward the seven Pleiades keep thy steadfast way."

And then —

> " This said, his son undaunted snatched the reins,
> Then smote the winged coursers' sides: they bound
> Forth on the void and cavernous vault of air.
> His father mounts another steed, and rides
> With warning voice guiding his son.   ' Drive there!
> Turn, turn thy car this way.' " †

May we not say that the spirit of the poet mounts the chariot
with his hero, and accompanies the winged steeds in their
perilous flight?   Were it not so, — had not his imagination
soared side by side with them in that celestial passage, —
he would never have conceived so vivid an image.   Similar
is that passage in his " Cassandra," beginning

> " Ye Trojans, lovers of the steed." ‡

Æschylus is especially bold in forming images suited to his
heroic themes: as when he says of his " Seven against
Thebes " —

> " Seven mighty men, and valiant captains, slew
> Over an iron-bound shield a bull, then dipped
> Their fingers in the blood, and all invoked
> Ares, Enyo, and death-dealing Flight
> In witness of their oaths," §

and describes how they all mutually pledged themselves
without flinching to die.   Sometimes, however, his thoughts

---

* *Il.* xx. 170.   † Eur. *Phæt.*
‡ Perhaps from the lost " Alexander " (Jahn).   § *Sept. c. Th.* 42.

are unshapen, and as it were rough-hewn and rugged. Not observing this, Euripides, from too blind a rivalry, sometimes falls under the same censure. Æschylus with a strange violence of language represents the palace of Lycurgus as *possessed* at the appearance of Dionysus —

"The halls with rapture thrill, the roof's inspired." *

Here Euripides, in borrowing the image, softens its extravagance † —

"And all the mountain felt the god." ‡

Sophocles has also shown himself a great master of the imagination in the scene in which the dying Œdipus prepares himself for burial in the midst of a tempest, § and where he tells how Achilles appeared to the Greeks over his tomb just as they were putting out to sea on their departure from Troy. ‖ This last scene has also been delineated by Simonides with a vividness which leaves him inferior to none. But it would be an endless task to cite all possible examples.

To return, then, in poetry, as I observed, a certain mythical exaggeration is allowable, transcending altogether mere logical credence. But the chief beauties of an oratorical image are its energy and reality. Such digressions become offensive and monstrous when the language is cast in a poetical and fabulous mould, and runs into all sorts of impossibilities. Thus much may be learnt from the great orators of our own day, when they tell us in tragic tones that they see the Furies ¶ — good people, can't they understand that when Orestes cries out

---

* Aesch. *Lycurg.*

† Lit. "Giving it a different flavor," as Arist. *Poet.* ἡδυσμένῳ λόγῳ χωρὶς ἑκάστῳ τῶν εἰδῶν, vi. 2.

‡ *Bacch.* 726.   § *Oed. Col.* 1586.   ‖ In his lost "Polyxena."

¶ Comp. Petronius, *Satyricon*, ch. i. *passim.*

"Off, off, I say! I know thee who thou art,
One of the fiends that haunt me: I feel thine arms
About me cast, to drag me down to hell," *

these are the hallucinations of a madman?

Wherein, then, lies the force of an oratorical image? Doubtless in adding energy and passion in a hundred different ways to a speech; but especially in this, that when it is mingled with the practical, argumentative parts of an oration, it does not merely convince the hearer, but enthralls him. Such is the effect of those words of Demosthenes: † "Supposing, now, at this moment a cry of alarm were heard outside the assize courts, and the news came that the prison was broken open and the prisoners escaped, is there any man here who is such a trifler that he would not run to the rescue at the top of his speed? But suppose someone came forward with the information that they had been set at liberty by the defendant, what then? Why, he would be lynched on the spot!" Compare also the way in which Hyperides excused himself, when he was proceeded against for bringing in a bill to liberate the slaves after Chæronea. "This measure," he said, " was not drawn up by any orator, but by the battle of Chæronea." This striking image, being thrown in by the speaker in the midst of his proofs, enables him by one bold stroke to carry all mere logical objection before him. In all such cases our nature is drawn towards that which affects it most powerfully: hence an image lures us away from an argument: judgment is paralyzed, matters of fact disappear from view, eclipsed by the superior blaze. Nor is it surprising that we should be thus affected; for when two forces are thus placed in juxtaposition, the stronger must always absorb into itself the weaker.

On sublimity of thought, and the manner in which it arises

* *Orest.* 264.   † *c. Timocrat.* 208.

from native greatness of mind, from imitation, and from the employment of images, this brief outline must suffice.*

XVI

The subject which next claims our attention is that of figures of speech. I have already observed that figures, judiciously employed, play an important part in producing sublimity. It would be a tedious, or rather an endless task, to deal with every detail of this subject here; so in order to establish what I have laid down, I will just run over, without further preface, a few of those figures which are most effective in lending grandeur to language.

Demosthenes is defending his policy; his natural line of argument would have been: " You did not do wrong, men of Athens, to take upon yourselves the struggle for the liberties of Hellas. Of this you have home proofs. *They* did not wrong who fought at Marathon, at Salamis, and Platæa." Instead of this, in a sudden moment of supreme exaltation he bursts out like some inspired prophet with that famous appeal to the mighty dead: " Ye did not, could not have done wrong. I swear it by the men who faced the foe at Marathon ! " † He employs the figure of adjuration, to which I will here give the name of Apostrophe. And what does he gain by it? He exalts the Athenian ancestors to the rank of divinities, showing that we ought to invoke those who have fallen for their country as gods; he fills the hearts of his judges with the heroic pride of the old warriors of Hellas; forsaking the beaten path of argument he rises to the loftiest altitude of grandeur and passion, and commands assent by the startling novelty of his appeal; he applies the healing charm of eloquence, and thus " ministers to the mind diseased " of his countrymen, until lifted by his brave words

---

* He passes over chs. x. xi.   † *De Cor.* 208.

above their misfortunes they begin to feel that the disaster
of Chæronea is no less glorious than the victories of Marathon and Salamis. All this he effects by the use of one
figure, and so carries his hearers away with him. It is said
that the germ of this adjuration is found in Eupolis —

> "By mine own fight, by Marathon, I say,
> Who makes my heart to ache shall rue the day!" *

But there is nothing grand in the mere employment of an
oath. Its grandeur will depend on its being employed in the
right place and the right manner, on the right occasion, and
with the right motive. In Eupolis the oath is nothing beyond an oath; and the Athenians to whom it is addressed
are still prosperous, and in need of no consolation. Moreover, the poet does not, like Demosthenes, swear by the departed heroes as deities, so as to engender in his audience a
just conception of their valor, but diverges from the champions to the battle — a mere lifeless thing. But Demosthenes has so skilfully managed the oath that in addressing
his countrymen after the defeat of Chæronea he takes out of
their minds all sense of disaster; and at the same time, while
proving that no mistake has been made, he holds up an
example, confirms his arguments by an oath, and makes his
praise of the dead an incentive to the living. And to rebut
a possible objection which occurred to him — "Can you,
Demosthenes, whose policy ended in defeat, swear by a victory?" — the orator proceeds to measure his language,
choosing his very words so as to give no handle to opponents,
thus showing us that even in our most inspired moments
reason ought to hold the reins.† Let us mark his words:
"Those who *faced the foe* at Marathon; those who *fought*

---

* In his (lost) "Demi."

† Lit. "That even in the midst of the revels of Bacchus we ought to remain
sober."

in the sea-fights of Salamis and Artemisium; those who *stood in the ranks* at Platæa.'' Note that he nowhere says " those who *conquered*," artfully suppressing any word which might hint at the successful issue of those battles, which would have spoilt the parallel with Chæronea. And for the same reason he steals a march on his audience, adding immediately: "All of whom, Æschines, — not those who were successful only, — were buried by the state at the public expense.''

XVII

There is one truth which my studies have led me to observe, which perhaps it would be worth while to set down briefly here. It is this, that by a natural law the Sublime, besides receiving an acquisition of strength from figures, in its turn lends support in a remarkable manner to them. To explain: the use of figures has a peculiar tendency to rouse a suspicion of dishonesty, and to create an impression of treachery, scheming, and false reasoning; especially if the person addressed be a judge, who is master of the situation, and still more in the case of a despot, a king, a military potentate, or any of those who sit in high places.* If a man feels that this artful speaker is treating him like a silly boy and trying to throw dust in his eyes, he at once grows irritated, and thinking that such false reasoning implies a contempt of his understanding, he perhaps flies into a rage and will not hear another word; or even if he masters his resentment, still he is utterly indisposed to yield to the persuasive power of eloquence. Hence it follows that a figure is then most effectual when it appears in disguise. To allay, then, this distrust which attaches to the use of figures we must call in the powerful aid of sublimity and passion. For art, once associated with these great allies, will be overshadowed by

* Reading with Cobet, καὶ πάντας τοὺς ἐν ὑπεροχαῖς.

their grandeur and beauty, and pass beyond the reach of all suspicion. To prove this I need only refer to the passage already quoted: " I swear it by the men," etc. It is the very brilliancy of the orator's figure which blinds us to the fact that it *is* a figure. For as the fainter lustre of the stars is put out of sight by the all-encompassing rays of the sun, so when sublimity sheds its light all round the sophistries of rhetoric they become invisible. A similar illusion is produced by the painter's art. When light and shadow are represented in color, though they lie on the same surface side by side, it is the light which meets the eye first, and appears not only more conspicuous but also much nearer. In the same manner passion and grandeur of language, lying nearer to our souls by reason both of a certain natural affinity and of their radiance, always strike our mental eye before we become conscious of the figure, throwing its artificial character into the shade and hiding it as it were in a veil.

XVIII

The figures of question and interrogation also possess a specific quality which tends strongly to stir an audience and give energy to the speaker's words. "Or tell me, do you want to run about asking one another, is there any news? what greater news could you have than that a man of Macedon is making himself master of Hellas? Is Philip dead? Not he. However, he is ill. But what is that to you? Even if anything happens to him you will soon raise up another Philip." Or this passage: " Shall we sail against Macedon? And where, asks one, shall we effect a landing? The war itself will show us where Philip's weak places lie." * Now if this had been put baldly it would have lost greatly in force. As we see it, it is full of the quick alternation of question and

* *Phil.* i. 44.

answer. The orator replies to himself as though he were meeting another man's objections. And this figure not only raises the tone of his words but makes them more convincing. For an exhibition of feeling has then most effect on an audience when it appears to flow naturally from the occasion, not to have been labored by the art of the speaker; and this device of questioning and replying to himself reproduces the moment of passion. For as a sudden question addressed to an individual will·sometimes startle him into a reply which is an unguarded expression of his genuine sentiments, so the figure of question and interrogation blinds the judgment of an audience, and deceives them into a belief that what is really the result of labor in every detail has been struck out of the speaker by the inspiration of the moment.

There is one passage in Herodotus which is generally credited with extraordinary sublimity. . . .

XIX

. . . The removal of connecting particles gives a quick rush and " torrent rapture " to a passage, the writer appearing to be actually almost left behind by his own words. There is an example in Xenophon: " Clashing their shields together they pushed, they fought, they slew, they fell." * And the words of Eurylochus in the *Odyssey* —

> " We passed at thy command the woodland's shade;
> We found a stately hall built in a mountain glade." †

Words thus severed from one another without the intervention of stops give a lively impression of one who through distress of mind at once halts and hurries in his speech. And this is what Homer has expressed by using the figure *Asyndeton.*

* Xen. *Hel.* iv. 3. 19.   † *Od.* x. 251.

XX

But nothing is so conducive to energy as a combination of different figures, when two or three uniting their resources mutually contribute to the vigor, the cogency, and the beauty of a speech. So Demosthenes in his speech against Meidias repeats the same words and breaks up his sentences in one lively descriptive passage: " He who receives a blow is hurt in many ways which he could not even describe to another, by gesture, by look, by tone." Then, to vary the movement of his speech, and prevent it from standing still (for stillness produces rest, but passion requires a certain disorder of language, imitating the agitation and commotion of the soul), he at once dashes off in another direction, breaking up his words again, and repeating them in a different form, " by gesture, by look, by tone — when insult, when hatred, is added to violence, when he is struck with the fist, when he is struck as a slave ! " By such means the orator imitates the action of Meidias, dealing blow upon blow on the minds of his judges. Immediately after like a hurricane he makes a fresh attack: " When he is struck with the fist, when he is struck in the face; this is what moves, this is what maddens a man, unless he is inured to outrage; no one could describe all this so as to bring home to his hearers its bitterness." * •You see how he preserves, by continual variation, the intrinsic force of these repetitions and broken clauses, so that his order seems irregular, and conversely his irregularity acquires a certain measure of order.

XXI

Supposing we add the conjunctions, after the practice of Isocrates and his school: "Moreover, I must not omit to

* *Meid.* 72.

K

mention that he who strikes a blow may hurt in many ways, in the first place by gesture, in the second place by look, in the third and last place by his tone." If you compare the words thus set down in logical sequence with the expressions of the "Meidias," you will see that the rapidity and rugged abruptness of passion, when all is made regular by connecting links, will be smoothed away, and the whole point and fire of the passage will at once disappear. For as, if you were to bind two runners together, they will forthwith be deprived of all liberty of movement, even so passion rebels against the trammels of conjunctions and other particles, because they curb its free rush and destroy the impression of mechanical impulse.

XXII

The figure hyperbaton belongs to the same class. By hyperbaton we mean a transposition of words or thoughts from their usual order, bearing unmistakably the characteristic stamp of violent mental agitation. In real life we often see a man under the influence of rage, or fear, or indignation, or beside himself with jealousy, or with some other out of the interminable list of human passions, begin a sentence, and then swerve aside into some inconsequent parenthesis, and then again double back to his original statement, being borne with quick turns by his distress, as though by a shifting wind, now this way, now that, and playing a thousand capricious variations on his words, his thoughts, and the natural order of his discourse. Now the figure hyperbaton is the means which is employed by the best writers to imitate these signs of natural emotion. For art is then perfect when it seems to be nature, and nature, again, is most effective when pervaded by the unseen presence of art. An illustration will be found in the speech of Dionysius of

Phocæa in Herodotus: " A hair's breadth now decides our destiny, Ionians, whether we shall live as freemen or as slaves — ay, as runaway slaves. Now, therefore, if you choose to endure a little hardship, you will be able at the cost of some present exertion to overcome your enemies." * The regular sequence here would have been: " Ionians, now is the time for you to endure a little hardship; for a hair's breadth will now decide our destiny." But the Phocæan transposes the title " Ionians," rushing at once to the subject of alarm, as though in the terror of the moment he had forgotten the usual address to his audience. Moreover, he inverts the logical order of his thoughts, and instead of beginning with the necessity for exertion, which is the point he wishes to urge upon them, he first gives them the reason for that necessity in the words, " a hair's breadth now decides our destiny," so that his words seem unpremeditated, and forced upon him by the crisis.

Thucydides surpasses all other writers in the bold use of this figure, even breaking up sentences which are by their nature absolutely one and indivisible. But nowhere do we find it so unsparingly employed as in Demosthenes, who though not so daring in his manner of using it as the elder writer is very happy in giving to his speeches by frequent transpositions the lively air of unstudied debate. Moreover, he drags, as it were, his audience with him into the perils of a long inverted clause. He often begins to say something, then leaves the thought in suspense, meanwhile thrusting in between, in a position apparently foreign and unnatural, some extraneous matters, one upon another, and having thus made his hearers fear lest the whole discourse should break down, and forced them into eager sympathy with the danger of the speaker, when he is nearly at the end of a period

* vi. 11.

he adds just at the right moment, *i.e.* when it is least expected, the point which they have been waiting for so long.
And thus by the very boldness and hazard of his inversions
he produces a much more astounding effect. I forbear to
cite examples, as they are too numerous to require it.

XXIII

The juxtaposition of different cases, the enumeration of
particulars, and the use of contrast and climax, all, as you
know, add much vigor, and give beauty and great elevation
and life to a style. The diction also gains greatly in diversity
and movement by changes of case, time, person, number,
and gender.

With regard to change of number: not only is the style
improved by the use of those words which, though singular
in form, are found on inspection to be plural in meaning,
as in the lines —

"A countless host dispersed along the sand
With joyous cries the shoal of tunny hailed,"

but it is more worthy of observation that plurals for singulars sometimes fall with a more impressive dignity, rousing
the imagination by the mere sense of vast number. Such
is the effect of those words of Œdipus in Sophocles —

"Oh fatal, fatal ties!
Ye gave us birth, and we being born ye sowed
The self-same seed, and gave the world to view
Sons, brothers, sires, domestic murder foul,
Brides, mothers, wives. . . . Ay, ye laid bare
The blackest, deepest place where Shame can dwell." *

Here we have in either case but one person, first Œdipus,
then Jocasta; but the expansion of number into the plural
gives an impression of multiplied calamity. So in the following plurals —

* *O. R.* 1403.

"There came forth Hectors, and there came Sarpedons."

And in those words of Plato's (which we have already ad-
duced elsewhere), referring to the Athenians: " We have
no Pelopses or Cadmuses or Ægyptuses or Danauses, or any
others out of all the mob of Hellenized barbarians, dwelling
among us; no, this is the land of pure Greeks, with no mixture of foreign elements," * etc. Such an accumulation of
words in the plural number necessarily gives greater pomp
and sound to a subject. But we must only have recourse
to this device when the nature of our theme makes it allowable to amplify, to multiply, or to speak in the tones of
exaggeration or passion. To overlay every sentence with
ornament † is very pedantic.

XXIV

On the other hand, the contraction of plurals into singulars
sometimes creates an appearance of great dignity; as in that
phrase of Demosthenes: "Thereupon all Peloponnesus
was divided." ‡ There is another in Herodotus: " When
Phrynichus brought a drama on the stage entitled *The Taking
of Miletus*, the whole theatre fell a weeping " — instead of
" all the spectators." This knitting together of a number of
scattered particulars into one whole gives them an aspect of
corporate life. And the beauty of both uses lies, I think, in
their betokening emotion, by giving a sudden change of
complexion to the circumstances, — whether a word which
is strictly singular is unexpectedly changed into a plural, —
or whether a number of isolated units are combined by the
use of a single sonorous word under one head.

* *Menex.* 245, D.
† Lit. " To hang bells everywhere," a metaphor from the bells which were
attached to horses' trappings on festive occasions.
‡ *De Cor.* 18.

XXV

When past events are introduced as happening in present time the narrative form is changed into a dramatic action. Such is that description in Xenophon: " A man who has fallen and is being trampled under foot by Cyrus's horse strikes the belly of the animal with his scimitar; the horse starts aside and unseats Cyrus, and he falls." Similarly in many passages of Thucydides.

XXVI

Equally dramatic is the interchange of persons, often making a reader fancy himself to be moving in the midst of the perils described —

> " Unwearied, thou would'st deem, with toil unspent,
> They met in war; so furiously they fought " *

and that line in Aratus —

> " Beware that month to tempt the surging sea." †

In the same way Herodotus: "Passing from the city of Elephantine you will sail upwards until you reach a level plain. You cross this region, and there entering another ship you will sail on for two days, and so reach a great city, whose name is Meroe." ‡   Observe how he takes us, as it were, by the hand, and leads us in spirit through these places, making us no longer readers, but spectators.   Such a direct personal address always has the effect of placing the reader in the midst of the scene of action.   And by pointing your words to the individual reader, instead of to the reader generally, as in the line

> " Thou had'st not known for whom Tydides fought," §

and thus exciting him by an appeal to himself, you will rouse interest, and fix attention, and make him a partaker in the action of the book.

* *Il.* xv. 697.   † *Phæn.* 287.   ‡ ii. 29.   § *Il.* v. 85.

XXVII

Sometimes, again, a writer in the midst of a narrative ih the third person suddenly steps aside and makes a transition to the first. It is a kind of figure which strikes like a sudden outburst of passion. Thus Hector in the *Iliad*

> "With mighty voice called to the men of Troy
> To storm the ships, and leave the bloody spoils:
> If any I behold with willing foot
> Shunning the ships, and lingering on the plain,
> That hour I will contrive his death." *

The poet then takes upon himself the narrative part, as being his proper business; but this abrupt threat he attributes, without a word of warning, to the enraged Trojan chief. To have interposed any such words as " Hector said so and so " would have had a frigid effect. As the lines stand the writer is left behind by his own words, and the transition is effected while he is preparing for it. Accordingly the proper use of this figure is in dealing with some urgent crisis which will not allow the writer to linger, but compels him to make a rapid change from one person to another. So in Hecatæus: " Now Ceyx took this in dudgeon, and straightway bade the children of Heracles to depart. ' Behold, I can give you no help; lest, therefore, ye perish yourselves and bring hurt upon me also, get ye forth into some other land.' " There is a different use of the change of persons in the speech of Demosthenes against Aristogeiton, which places before us the quick turns of violent emotion. " Is there none to be found among you," he asks, " who even feels indignation at the outrageous conduct of a loathsome and shameless wretch who, — vilest of men, when you were debarred from freedom of speech, not by barriers or by

* *Il*. xv. 346.

doors, which might indeed be opened," * etc. Thus in the midst of a half-expressed thought he makes a quick change of front, and having almost in his anger torn one word into two persons, " who, vilest of men," etc., he then breaks off his address to Aristogeiton, and seems to leave him, nevertheless, by the passion of his utterance, rousing all the more the attention of the court. The same feature may be observed in a speech of Penelope's —

> " Why com'st thou, Medon, from the wooers proud?
> Com'st thou to bid the handmaids of my lord
> To cease their tasks, and make for them good cheer?
> Ill fare their wooing, and their gathering here!
> Would God that here this hour they all might take
> Their last, their latest meal!   Who day by day
> Make here your muster, to devour and waste
> The substance of my son: have ye not heard
> When children at your fathers' knee the deeds
> And prowess of your king? " †

XXVIII

None, I suppose, would dispute the fact that periphrasis tends much to sublimity. For, as in music the simple air is rendered more pleasing by the addition of harmony, so in language periphrasis often sounds in concord with a literal expression, adding much to the beauty of its tone, — provided always that it is not inflated and harsh, but agreeably blended. To confirm this one passage from Plato ⋅will suffice — the opening words of his Funeral Oration: " Indeed these men have now received from us their due, and that tribute paid they are now passing on their destined journey, with the State speeding them all and his own friends speeding each one of them on his way." ‡   Death, you see, he calls the " destined journey "; to receive the rites of

* *c. Aristog.* i. 27.   † *Od.* iv. 681.   ‡ *Menex.* 236, D.

burial is to be publicly " sped on your way " by the State. And these turns of language lend dignity in no common measure to the thought. He takes the words in their naked simplicity and handles them as a musician, investing them with melody, — harmonizing them, as it were, — by the use of periphrasis. So Xenophon: " Labor you regard as the guide to a pleasant life, and you have laid up in your souls the fairest and most soldier-like of all gifts: in praise is your delight, more than in anything else." * By saying, instead of " you are ready to labor," " you regard labor as the guide to a pleasant life," and by similarly expanding the rest of that passage, he gives to his eulogy a much wider and loftier range of sentiment. Let us add that inimitable phrase in Herodotus: " Those Scythians who pillaged the temple were smitten from heaven by a female malady."

XXIX

But this figure, more than any other, is very liable to abuse, and great restraint is required in employing it. It soon begins to carry an impression of feebleness, savors of vapid trifling, and arouses digust. Hence Plato, who is very bold and not always happy in his use of figures, is much ridiculed for saying in his *Laws* that " neither gold nor silver wealth must be allowed to establish itself in our State," † suggesting, it is said, that if he had forbidden property in oxen or sheep he would certainly have spoken of it as " bovine and ovine wealth."

Here we must quit this part of our subject, hoping, my dear friend Terentian, that your learned curiosity will be satisfied with this short excursion on the use of figures in their relation to the Sublime. All those which I have men-

* *Cyrop.* i. 5. 12.
† *De Legg.* vii. 801, B.

tioned help to render a style more energetic and impassioned; and passion contributes as largely to sublimity as the delineation of character to amusement.

XXX

But since the thoughts conveyed by words and the expression of those thoughts are for the most part interwoven with one another, we will now add some considerations which have hitherto been overlooked on the subject of expression. To say that the choice of appropriate and striking words has a marvellous power and an enthralling charm for the reader, that this is the main object of pursuit with all orators and writers, that it is this, and this alone, which causes the works of literature to exhibit the glowing perfections of the finest statues, their grandeur, their beauty, their mellowness, their dignity, their energy, their power, and all their other graces, and that it is this which endows the facts with a vocal soul; to say all this would, I fear, be, to the initiated, an impertinence. Indeed, we may say with strict truth that beautiful words are the very light of thought. I do not mean to say that imposing language is appropriate to every occasion. A trifling subject tricked out in grand and stately words would have the same effect as a huge tragic mask placed on the head of a little child. Only in poetry and . . .

XXXI

· . . . There is a genuine ring in that line of Anacreon's —

"The Thracian filly I no longer heed."

The same merit belongs to that original phrase in Theopompus; to me, at least, from the closeness of its analogy, it seems to have a peculiar expressiveness, though

Cæcilius censures it, without telling us why. "Philip," says
the historian, "showed a marvellous alacrity in *taking doses
of trouble.*" We see from this that the most homely language is sometimes far more vivid than the most ornamental,
being recognized at once as the language of common life, and
gaining immediate currency by its familiarity. In speaking,
then, of Philip as " taking doses of trouble," Theopompus has
laid hold on a phrase which describes with peculiar vividness
one who for the sake of advantage endured what was base and
sordid with patience and cheerfulness. The same may be
observed of two passages in Herodotus: "Cleomenes having
lost his wits, cut his own flesh into pieces with a short sword,
until by gradually *mincing* his whole body he destroyed
himself "; * and " Pythes continued fighting on his ship until
he was entirely *hacked to pieces.*" †   Such terms come home
at once to the vulgar reader, but their own vulgarity is re-
deemed by their expressiveness.

XXXII

Concerning the number of metaphors to be employed together Cæcilius seems to give his vote with those critics who
make a law that not more than two, or at the utmost three,
should be combined in the same place. The use, however,
must be determined by the occasion. Those outbursts of
passion which drive onwards like a winter torrent draw
with them as an indispensable accessory whole masses of
metaphor. It is thus in that passage of Demosthenes (who
here also is our safest guide) : " Those vile fawning wretches,
each one of whom has lopped from his country her fairest
members, who have toasted away their liberty, first to Philip,
now to Alexander, who measurè happiness by their belly and
their vilest appetites, who have overthrown the old landmarks

* vi. 75.   † vii. 181.

and standards of felicity among Greeks, — to be freemen, and to have no one for a master." * Here the number of the metaphors is obscured by the orator's indignation against the betrayers of his country. And to effect this Aristotle and Theophrastus recommend the softening of harsh metaphors by the use of some such phrase as " So to say," " As it were," " If I·may be permitted the expression," " If so bold a term is allowable." For thus to forestall criticism † mitigates, they assert, the boldness of the metaphors. And I will not deny that these have their use. Nevertheless I must repeat the remark which I made in the case of figures, ‡ and maintain that there are native antidotes to the number and boldness of metaphors, in well-timed displays of strong feeling, and in un-affected sublimity, because these have an innate power by the dash of their movement of sweeping along and carrying all else before them. Or should we not rather say that they absolutely demand as indispensable the use of daring metaphors, and will not allow the hearer to pause and criticise the number of them, because he shares the passion of the speaker?

In the treatment, again, of familiar topics and in descriptive passages nothing gives such distinctness as a close and continuous series of metaphor. It is by this means that Xenophon has so finely delineated the anatomy of the human frame.§ And there is a still more brilliant and life-like picture in Plato.‖ The human head he calls a *citadel;* the neck is an *isthmus* set to divide it from the chest; to support it beneath are the vertebræ, turning like *hinges;* pleasure he describes as a *bait* to tempt men to ill; the tongue is the *arbiter of tastes.* The heart is at once the *knot* of the veins and

---

* *De Cor.* 296.   † Reading ὑπoτίμησις.
‡ Ch. xvii.   § *Memorab.* i. 4, 5.
‖ *Timæus,* 69, D ; 74, A ; 65, C ; 72, G ; 74, B, D ; 80, E ; 77, G ; 78, E ; 85, E.

the *source* of the rapidly circulating blood, and is stationed in the *guard-room* of the body. The ramifying blood-vessels he calls *alleys*. " And casting about," he says, " for something to sustain the violent palpitation of the heart when it is alarmed by the approach of danger or agitated by passion, since at such times it is overheated, they (the gods) implanted in us the lungs, which are so fashioned that being soft and bloodless, and having cavities within, they act like a buffer, and when the heart boils with inward passion by yielding to its throbbing save it from injury." He compares the seat of the desires to the *women's quarters*, the seat of the passions to the *men's quarters*, in a house. The spleen, again, is the *napkin* of the internal organs, by whose excretions it is saturated from time to time, and swells to a great size with inward impurity. " After this," he continues, " they shrouded the whole with flesh, throwing it forward, like a cushion, as a barrier against injuries from without." The blood he terms the *pasture* of the flesh. "To assist the process of nutrition," he goes on, " they divided the body into ducts, cutting trenches like those in a garden, so that, the body being a system of narrow conduits, the current of the veins might flow as from a perennial fountain-head. And when the end is at hand," he says, " the soul is cast loose from her moorings like a ship, and free to wander whither she will." These, and a hundred similar fancies, follow one another in quick succession. But those which I have pointed out are sufficient to demonstrate how great is the natural power of figurative language, and how largely metaphors conduce to sublimity, and to illustrate the important part which they play in all impassioned and descriptive passages.

That the use of figurative language, as of all other beauties of style, has a constant tendency towards excess, is an obvious truth which I need not dwell upon. It is chiefly on this account that even Plato comes in for a large share of disparagement, because he is often carried away by a sort of frenzy of language into an intemperate use of violent metaphors and inflated allegory. " It is not easy to remark" (he says in one place) " that a city ought to be blended like a bowl, in which the mad wine boils when it is poured out, but being disciplined by another and a sober god in that fair society produces a good and temperate drink."* Really, it is said, to speak of water as a " sober god," and of the process of mixing as a " discipline," is to talk like a poet, and no very *sober* one either. It was such defects as these that the hostile critic † Cæcilius made his ground of attack, when he had the boldness in his essay "On the Beauties of Lysias" to pronounce that writer superior in every respect to Plato. Now Cæcilius was doubly unqualified for a judge: he loved Lysias better even than himself, and at the same time his hatred of Plato and all his works is greater even than his love for Lysias. Moreover, he is so blind a partisan that his very premises are open to dispute. He vaunts Lysias as a faultless and immaculate writer, while Plato is, according to him, full of blemishes. Now this is not the case: far from it.

XXXIII

But supposing now that we assume the existence of a really unblemished and irreproachable writer. Is it not worth while to raise the whole question whether in poetry and prose we should prefer sublimity accompanied by some faults, or a style which never rising above moderate excellence never stumbles and never requires correction? and again, whether the first place in literature is justly to be assigned to the more numerous, or the loftier excellences? For these are questions

* *Legg.* vi. 773, G.
† Reading ὁ μισῶν αὐτόν, by a conjecture of the translator.

proper to an inquiry on the Sublime, and urgently asking for settlement.

I know, then, that the largest intellects are far from being the most exact.[4] A mind always intent on correctness is apt to be dissipated in trifles; but in great affluence of thought, as in vast material wealth, there must needs be an occasional neglect of detail. And is it not inevitably so? Is it not by risking nothing, by never aiming high, that a writer of low or middling powers keeps generally clear of faults and secure of blame? whereas the loftier walks of literature are by their very loftiness perilous? I am well aware, again, that there is a law by which in all human productions the weak points catch the eye first, by which their faults remain indelibly stamped on the memory, while their beauties quickly fade away. Yet, though I have myself noted not a few faulty passages in Homer and in other authors of the highest rank, and though I am far from being partial to their failings, nevertheless I would call them not so much wilful blunders as oversights which were allowed to pass unregarded through that contempt of little things, that " brave disorder," which is natural to an exalted genius; and I still think that the greater excellences, though not everywhere equally sustained, ought always to be voted to the first place in literature, if for no other reason, for the mere grandeur of soul they evince. Let us take an instance: Apollonius in his *Argonautica* has given us a poem actually faultless; and in his pastoral poetry Theocritus is eminently happy, except when he occasionally attempts another style. And what then? Would you rather be a Homer or an Apollonius? Or take Eratosthenes and his *Erigone;* because that little work is without a flaw, is he therefore a greater poet than Archilochus, with all his disorderly profusion? greater than that impetuous, that god-gifted genius, which chafed against the restraints of law?

or in lyric poetry would you choose to be a Bacchylides or a Pindar? in tragedy a Sophocles or (save the mark!) an Io of Chios? Yet Io and Bacchylides never stumble, their style is always neat, always pretty; while Pindar and Sophocles sometimes move onwards with a wide blaze of splendor, but often drop out of view in sudden and disastrous eclipse. Nevertheless no one in his senses would deny that a single play of Sophocles, the *Œdipus*, is of higher value than all the dramas of Io put together.

XXXIV

If the number and not the loftiness of an author's merits is to be our standard of success, judged by this test we must admit that Hyperides is a far superior orator to Demosthenes. For in Hyperides there is a richer modulation, a greater variety of excellence. He is, we may say, in everything second-best, like the champion of the *pentathlon*, who, though in every contest he has to yield the prize to some other combatant, is superior to the unpractised in all five. Not only has he rivalled the success of Demosthenes in everything but his manner of composition, but, as though that were not enough, he has taken in all the excellences and graces of Lysias as well. He knows when it is proper to speak with simplicity, and does not, like Demosthenes, continue the same key throughout. His touches of character are racy and sparkling, and full of a delicate flavor. Then how admirable is his wit, how polished his raillery! How well-bred he is, how dexterous in the use of irony! His jests are pointed, but without any of the grossness and vulgarity of the old Attic comedy. He is skilled in making light of an opponent's argument, full of a well-aimed satire which amuses while it stings; and through all this there runs a pervading, may we not say, a matchless charm. He is most apt in moving compassion; his mythical digressions show a fluent ease, and he is perfect in bending his course and finding a way out of them without violence or effort. Thus when he tells the story of Leto he is really almost a poet; and his funeral oration shows a declamatory magnificence to which I hardly know a parallel. Demosthenes, on the other hand, has no touches of character, none of the versatility, fluency, or declamatory skill of Hyperides. He is, in fact, almost entirely destitute of all those excellences which I have just enumerated. When he makes violent efforts to be humorous and witty, the only laughter he arouses is against himself; and the nearer he tries to get to the winning grace of Hyperides, the farther he recedes from it. Had he, for instance, attempted such a task as the little speech in defence of Phryne or Athenagoras, he would only have added to the reputation of his rival. Nevertheless all the beauties of Hyperides, however numerous, cannot make him sublime. He never exhibits strong feeling, has little energy, rouses no emotion; certainly he never kindles terror in the breast of his readers. But Demosthenes followed a great master, * and drew his consummate excellences, his high-pitched eloquence, his living passion, his copiousness, his sagacity, his speed — that mastery and power which can never be approached — from the highest of sources. These mighty, these heaven-sent gifts (I dare not call them human), he made his own both one and all. Therefore, I say, by the noble qualities which he does possess he remains supreme above all rivals, and throws a cloud over his failings, silencing by his thunders and blinding by his lightnings the orators of all ages. Yes, it would be easier to meet the lightning-stroke with steady eye than to gaze unmoved when his impassioned eloquence is sending out flash after flash.

* *I.e.* Thucydides.

L

XXXV

But in the case of Plato and Lysias there is, as I said, a further difference. Not only is Lysias vastly inferior to Plato in the degree of his merits, but in their number as well; and at the same time he is as far ahead of Plato in the number of his faults as he is behind in that of his merits.

What truth, then, was it that was present to those mighty spirits of the past, who, making whatever is greatest in writing their aim, thought it beneath them to be exact in every detail? Among many others especially this, that it was not in nature's plan for us her chosen children to be creatures base and ignoble, — no, she brought us into life, and into the whole universe, as into some great field of contest, that we should be at once spectators and ambitious rivals of her mighty deeds, and from the first implanted in our souls an invincible yearning for all that is great, all that is diviner than ourselves. Therefore even the whole world is not wide enough for the soaring range of human thought, but man's mind often overleaps the very bounds of space.*   When we survey the whole circle of life, and see it abounding everywhere in what is elegant, grand, and beautiful, we learn at once what is the true end of man's being.   And this is why nature prompts us to admire, not the clearness and usefulness of a little stream, but the Nile, the Danube, the Rhine, and far beyond all the Ocean; not to turn our wandering eyes from the heavenly fires, though often darkened, to the little flame kindled by human hands, however pure and steady its light; not to think that tiny lamp more wondrous than the caverns of Ætna, from whose raging depths are hurled up stones and whole

---

* Comp. Lucretius on Epicurus: "Ergo vivida vis animi pervicit, et extra Processit longe flammantia mœnia mundi," etc.

masses of rock, and torrents sometimes come pouring from earth's centre of pure and living fire.

To sum the whole: whatever is useful or needful lies easily within man's reach; but he keeps his homage for what is astounding.

XXXVI

How much more do these principles apply to the Sublime in literature, where grandeur is never, as it sometimes is in nature, dissociated from utility and advantage. Therefore all those who have achieved it, however far from faultless, are still more than mortal. When a writer uses any other resource he shows himself to be a man; but the Sublime lifts him near to the great spirit of the Deity. He who makes no slips must be satisfied with negative approbation, but he who is sublime commands positive reverence. Why need I add that each one of those great writers often redeems all his errors by one grand and masterly stroke? But the strongest point of all is that, if you were to pick out all the blunders of Homer, Demosthenes, Plato, and all the greatest names in literature, and add them together, they would be found to bear a very small, or rather an infinitesimal proportion to the passages in which these supreme masters have attained absolute perfection. Therefore it is that all posterity, whose judgment envy herself cannot impeach, has brought and bestowed on them the crown of glory, has guarded their fame until this day against all attack, and is likely to preserve it

> "As long as lofty trees shall grow,
> And restless waters seaward flow."

It has been urged by one writer that we should not prefer the huge disproportioned Colossus to the Doryphorus of Polycleitus. But (to give one out of many possible answers) in art we admire exactness, in the works of nature magnificence;

and it is from nature that man derives the faculty of speech. Whereas, then, in statuary we look for close resemblance to humanity, in literature we require something which transcends humanity. Nevertheless (to reiterate the advice which we gave at the beginning of this essay), since that success which consists in avoidance of error is usually the gift of art, while high, though unequal excellence is the attribute of genius, it is proper on all occasions to call in art as an ally to nature. By the combined resources of these two we may hope to achieve perfection.

Such are the conclusions which were forced upon me concerning the points at issue; but every one may consult his own taste.

XXXVII

To return, however, from this long digression; closely allied to metaphors are comparisons and similes, differing only in this * * * *

XXXVIII

Such absurdities as, " Unless you carry your brains next to the ground in your heels." †   Hence it is necessary to know where to draw the line; for if ever it is overstepped the effect of the hyperbole is spoilt, being in such cases relaxed by over-straining, and producing the very opposite to the effect desired. Isocrates, for instance, from an ambitious desire of lending everything a strong rhetorical coloring, shows himself in quite a childish light. Having in his Panegyrical Oration set himself to prove that the Athenian state has surpassed that of Sparta in her services to Hellas, he starts off at the very outset with these words: " Such is the power of language that it can extenuate what is great, and lend greatness to what is little, give freshness to what is antiquated, and describe what

* The asterisks denote gaps in the original text.
† Pseud. Dem. de Halon. 45.

is recent so that it seems to be of the past." * Come, Isocrates (it might be asked), is it thus that you are going to tamper with the facts about Sparta and Athens? This flourish about the power of language is like a signal hung out to warn his audience not to believe him. We may repeat here what we said about figures, and say that the hyperbole is then most effective when it appears in disguise.† And this effect is produced when a writer, impelled by strong feeling, speaks in the accents of some tremendous crisis; as Thucydides does in describing the massacre in Sicily. "The Syracusans," he says, " went down after them, and slew those especially who were in the river, and the water was at once defiled, yet still they went on drinking it, though mingled with mud and gore, most of them even fighting for it." ‡ The drinking of mud and gore, and even the fighting for it, is made credible by the awful horror of the scene described. Similarly Herodotus on those who fell at Thermopylæ: " Here as they fought, those who still had them, with daggers, the rest with hands and teeth, the barbarians buried them under their javelins." § That they fought with the teeth against heavy-armed assailants, and that they were buried with javelins, are perhaps hard sayings, but not incredible, for the reasons already explained. We can see that these circumstances have not been dragged in to produce a hyperbole, but that the hyperbole has grown naturally out of the circumstances. For, as I am never tired of explaining, in actions and passions verging on frenzy there lies a kind of remission and palliation of any licence of language. Hence some comic extravagances, however improbable, gain credence by their humor, such as —

" He had a farm, a little farm, where space severely pinches;
'Twas smaller than the last despatch from Sparta by some inches."

* Paneg. 8.   † xvii.   ‡ Thuc. vii. 84.   § vii. 225.

For mirth is one of the passions, having its seat in pleasure. And hyperboles may be employed either to increase or to lessen — since exaggeration is common to both uses. Thus in extenuating an opponent's argument we try to make it seem smaller than it is.

XXXIX

We have still left, my dear sir, the fifth of those sources which we set down at the outset as contributing to sublimity, that which consists in the mere arrangement of words in a certain order. Having already published two books dealing fully with this subject — so far at least as our investigations had carried us — it will be sufficient for the purpose of our present inquiry to add that harmony is an instrument which has a natural power, not only to win and to delight, but also in a remarkable degree to exalt the soul and sway the heart of man. When we see that a flute kindles certain emotions in its hearers, rendering them almost beside themselves and full of an orgiastic frenzy, and that by starting some kind of rhythmical beat it compels him who listens to move in time and assimilate his gestures to the tune, even though he has no taste whatever for music; when we know that the sounds of a harp, which in themselves have no meaning, by the change of key, by the mutual relation of the notes, and their arrangement in symphony, often lay a wonderful spell on an audience — though these are mere shadows and spurious imitations of persuasion, not, as I have said, genuine manifestations of human nature:— can we doubt that composition (being a kind of harmony of that language which nature has taught us, and which reaches, not our ears only, but our very souls), when it raises changing forms of words, of thoughts, of actions, of beauty, of melody, all of which are engrained in and akin to ourselves, and when by the blending of its manifold tones it brings home to the minds of those who stand by the feelings present to the speaker, and ever disposes the hearer to sympathize with those feelings, adding word to word, until it has raised a majestic and harmonious structure: — can we wonder if all this enchants us, wherever we meet with it, and filling us with the sense of pomp and dignity and sublimity, and whatever else it embraces, gains a complete mastery over our minds? It would be mere infatuation to join issue on truths so universally acknowledged, and established by experience beyond dispute.*

Now to give an instance: that is doubtless a sublime thought, indeed wonderfully fine, which Demosthenes applies to his decree: τοῦτο τὸ ψήφισμα τὸν τότε τῇ πόλει περιστάντα κίνδυνον παρελθεῖν ἐποίησεν ὥσπερ νέφος, "This decree caused the danger which then hung round our city to pass away like a cloud." But the modulation is as perfect as the sentiment itself is weighty. It is uttered wholly in the dactylic measure, the noblest and most magnificent of all measures, and hence forming the chief constituent in the finest metre we know, the heroic. [And it is with great judgment that the words ὥσπερ νέφος are reserved till the end.†] Supposing we transpose them from their proper place and read, say τοῦτο τὸ ψήφισμα ὥσπερ νέφος ἐποίησε τὸν τότε κίνδυνον παρελθεῖν — nay, let us merely cut off one syllable, reading ἐποίησε παρελθεῖν ὡς νέφος — and you will understand how close is the unison between harmony and sublimity. In the passage before us the words ὥσπερ νέφος move first in a heavy measure, which is metrically equivalent to four short syllables: but on removing one syllable, and reading ὡς νέφος, the grandeur of movement is at once

---

* Reading ἀλλ' ἔοικε μανίᾳ, and putting a full stop at πίστις.

† There is a break here in the text; but the context indicates the sense of the words lost, which has accordingly been supplied.

crippled by the abridgment. So conversely if you lengthen into ὡσπερεὶ νέφος, the meaning is still the same, but it does not strike the ear in the same manner, because by lingering over the final syllables you at once dissipate and relax the abrupt grandeur of the passage.

XL

There is another method very efficient in exalting a style. As the different members of the body, none of which, if severed from its connection, has any intrinsic excellence, unite by their mutual combination to form a complete and perfect organism, so also the elements of a fine passage, by whose separation from one another its high quality is simultaneously dissipated and evaporates, when joined in one organic whole, and still further compacted by the bond of harmony, by the mere rounding of the period gain power of tone.[5]   In fact, a clause may be said to derive its sublimity from the joint contributions of a number of particulars.   And further (as we have shown at large elsewhere), many writers in prose and verse, though their natural powers were not high, were perhaps even low, and though the terms they employed were usually common and popular and conveying no impression of refinement, by the mere harmony of their composition have attained dignity and elevation, and avoided the appearance of meanness. Such among many others are Philistus, Aristophanes occasionally, Euripides almost always. Thus when Heracles says, after the murder of his children,

"I'm full of woes, I have no room for more," *

the words are quite common, but they are made sublime by being cast in a fine mould.   By changing their position you will see that the poetical quality of Euripides depends more on

* *H.F.* 1245.

his arrangement than on his thoughts. Compare his lines on Dirce dragged by the bull —

> "Whatever crossed his path,
> Caught in his victim's form, he seized, and dragging
> Oak, woman, rock, now here, now there, he flies." *

The circumstance is noble in itself, but it gains in vigor because the language is disposed so as not to hurry the movement, not running, as it were, on wheels, because there is a distinct stress on each word, and the time is delayed, advancing slowly to a pitch of stately sublimity.

XLI

Nothing so much degrades the tone of a style as an effeminate and hurried movement in the language, such as is produced by pyrrhics and trochees and dichorees falling in time together into a regular dance measure. Such abuse of rhythm is sure to savor of coxcombry and petty affectation, and grows tiresome in the highest degree by a monotonous sameness of tone. But its worst effect is that, as those who listen to a ballad have their attention distracted from its subject and can think of nothing but the tune, so an over-rhythmical passage does not affect the hearer by the meaning of its words, but merely by their cadence, so that sometimes, knowing where the pause must come, they beat time with the speaker, striking the expected close like dancers before the stop is reached. Equally undignified is the splitting up of a sentence into a number of little words and short syllables crowded too closely together and forced into cohesion, — hammered, as it were, successively together, — after the manner of mortice and tenon.†

* *Antiope* (Nauck, 222).
† I must refer to Weiske's Note, which I have followed, for the probable interpretation of this extraordinary passage.

XLII

Sublimity is further diminished by cramping the diction. Deformity instead of grandeur ensues from over-compression. Here I am not referring to a judicious compactness of phrase, but to a style which is dwarfed, and its force frittered away. To cut your words too short is to prune away their sense, but to be concise is to be direct. On the other hand, we know that a style becomes lifeless by over-extension, I mean by being relaxed to an unseasonable length.

XLIII

The use of mean words has also a strong tendency to degrade a lofty passage. Thus in that description of the storm in Herodotus the matter is admirable, but some of the words admitted are beneath the dignity of the subject; such, perhaps, as " the seas having *seethed*," because the ill-sounding phrase " having seethed " detracts much from its impressiveness: or when he says " the wind wore away," and " those who clung round the wreck met with an unwelcome end." * " Wore away " is ignoble and vulgar, and "unwelcome" inadequate to the extent of the disaster.

Similarly Theopompus, after giving a fine picture of the Persian king's descent against Egypt, has exposed the whole to censure by certain paltry expressions. "There was no city, no people of Asia, which did not send an embassy to the king; no product of the earth, no work of art, whether beautiful or precious, which was not among the gifts brought to him. Many and costly were the hangings and robes, some purple, some embroidered, some white; many the tents, of cloth of gold, furnished with all things useful; many the tapestries and couches of great price. Moreover, there was

* Hdt. vii. 188, 191, 13.

gold and silver plate richly wrought, goblets and bowls, some of which might be seen studded with gems, and others besides worked in relief with great skill and at vast expense. Besides these there were suits of armor in number past computation, partly Greek, partly foreign, endless trains of baggage animals and fat cattle for slaughter, many bushels of spices, many panniers and sacks and sheets of writing-paper; and all other necessaries in the same proportion. And there was salt meat of all kinds of beasts in immense quantity, heaped together to such a height as to show at a distance like mounds and hills thrown up one against another." He runs off from the grander parts of his subject to the meaner, and sinks where he ought to rise. Still worse, by his mixing up *panniers* and *spices* and *bags* with his wonderful recital of that vast and busy scene one would imagine that he was describing a kitchen. Let us suppose that in that show of magnificence someone had taken a set of wretched baskets and bags and placed them in the midst, among vessels of gold, jewelled bowls, silver plate, and tents and goblets of gold; how incongruous would have seemed the effect! Now just in the same way these petty words, introduced out of season, stand out like deformities and blots on the diction. These details might have been given in one or two broad strokes, as when he speaks of mounds being heaped together. So in dealing with the other preparations he might have told us of "wagons and camels and a long train of baggage animals loaded with all kinds of supplies for the luxury and enjoyment of the table," or have mentioned "piles of grain of every species, and of all the choicest delicacies required by the art of the cook or the taste of the epicure," or (if he must needs be so very precise) he might have spoken of "whatever dainties are supplied by those who lay or those who dress the banquet." In our sublimer efforts we should never stoop to what is sordid and despicable, unless very hard pressed by some urgent necessity. If we would write becomingly, our utterance should be worthy of our theme. We should take a lesson from nature, who when she planned the human frame did not set our grosser parts, or the ducts for purging the body, in our face, but as far as she could conceal them, " diverting," as Xenophon says, " those canals as far as possible from our senses," * and thus shunning in any part to mar the beauty of the whole creature.

However, it is not incumbent on us to specify and enumerate whatever diminishes a style. We have now pointed out the various means of giving it nobility and loftiness. It is clear, then, that whatever is contrary to these will generally degrade and deform it.

XLIV

There is still another point which remains to be cleared up, my dear Terentian, and on which I shall not hesitate to add some remarks, to gratify your inquiring spirit. It relates to a question which was recently put to me by a certain philosopher. "To me," he said, " in common, I may say, with many others, it is a matter of wonder that in the present age, which produces many highly skilled in the arts of popular persuasion, many of keen and active powers, many especially rich in every pleasing gift of language, the growth of highly exalted and wide-reaching genius has with a few rare exceptions almost entirely ceased. So universal is the dearth of eloquence which prevails throughout the world. Must we really," he asked, " give credit to that oft-repeated assertion that democracy is the kind nurse of genius, and that high literary excellence has flourished with her prime and faded with her decay? Liberty, it is said, is all-powerful to feed the aspirations of high intellects, to hold out hope, and keep alive

* *Mem.* i. 4. 6.

the flame of mutual rivalry and ambitious struggle for the highest place. Moreover, the prizes which are offered in every free state keep the spirits of her foremost orators whetted by perpetual exercise; * they are, as it were, ignited by friction, and naturally blaze forth freely because they are surrounded by freedom. But we of to-day," he continued, " seem to have learnt in our childhood the lessons of a benignant despotism, to have been cradled in her habits and customs from the time when our minds were still tender, and never to have tasted the fairest and most fruitful fountain of eloquence, I mean liberty. Hence we develop nothing but a fine genius for flattery. This is the reason why, though all other faculties are consistent with the servile condition, no slave ever became an orator; because in him there is a dumb spirit which will not be kept down: his soul is chained: he is like one who has learnt to be ever expecting a blow. For, as Homer says —

> " ' The day of slavery
> Takes half our manly worth away.' †

As, then (if what I have heard is credible), the cages in which those pygmies commonly called dwarfs are reared not only stop the growth of the imprisoned creature, but absolutely make him smaller by compressing every part of his body, so all despotism, however equitable, may be defined as a cage of the soul and a general prison."

My answer was as follows: "My dear friend, it is so easy, and so characteristic of human nature, always to find fault with the present.‡ Consider, now, whether the corruption of genius is to be attributed, not to a world-wide peace,§ but

---

* Comp. Pericles in Thuc. ii., ἆθλα γὰρ οἷς κεῖται ἀρετῆς μέγιστα τοῖς δὲ καὶ ἄνδρες ἄριστοι πολιτεύουσιν.

† *Od.* xvii. 322.

‡ Comp. Byron, "The good old times, — all times when old are good."

§ A euphemism for "a world-wide tyranny."

rather to the war within us which knows no limit, which engages all our desires, yes, and still further to the bad passions which lay siege to us to-day, and make utter havoc and spoil of our lives. Are we not enslaved, nay, are not our careers completely shipwrecked, by love of gain, that fever which rages unappeased in us all, and love of pleasure? — one the most debasing, the other the most ignoble of the mind's diseases. . When I consider it I can find no means by which we, who hold in such high honor, or, to speak more correctly, who idolize boundless riches, can close the door of our souls against those evil spirits which grow up with them. For Wealth unmeasured and unbridled is dogged by Extravagance: she sticks close to him, and treads in his footsteps: and as soon as he opens the gates of cities or of houses she enters with him and makes her abode with him. And after a time they build their nests (to use a wise man's words *) in that corner of life, and speedily set about breeding, and beget Boastfulness, and Vanity, and Wantonness, no baseborn children, but their very own. And if these also, the offspring of Wealth, be allowed to come to their prime, quickly they engender in the soul those pitiless tyrants, Violence, and Lawlessness, and Shamelessness. Whenever a man takes to worshipping what is mortal and irrational † in him, and neglects to cherish what is immortal, these are the inevitable results. He never looks up again; he has lost all care for good report; by slow degrees the ruin of his life goes on, until it is consummated all round; all that is great in his soul fades, withers away, and is despised.

" If a judge who passes sentence for a bribe can never more give a free and sound decision on a point of justice or honor (for to him who takes a bribe honor and justice must be measured by his own interests), how can we of to-day expect,

---

* Plato, *Rep.* ix. 573, E.   † Reading κάνόητα.

when the whole life of each one of us is controlled by bribery, while we lie in wait for other men's death and plan how to get a place in their wills, when we buy gain, from whatever source, each one of us, with our very souls in our slavish greed, how, I say, can we expect, in the midst of such a moral pestilence, that there is still left even one liberal and impartial critic, whose verdict will not be biassed by avarice in judging of those great works which live on through all time ? Alas ! I fear that for such men as we are it is better to serve than to be free. If our appetites were let loose altogether against our neighbors, they would be like wild beasts uncaged, and bring a deluge of calamity on the whole civilized world."

I ended by remarking generally that the genius of the present age is wasted by that indifference which with a few exceptions runs through the whole of life. If we ever shake off our apathy * and apply ourselves to work, it is always with a view to pleasure or applause, not for that solid advantage which is worthy to be striven for and held in honor.

We had better then leave this generation to its fate, and turn to what follows, which is the subject of the passions, to which we promised early in this treatise to devote a separate work.† They play an important part in literature generally, and especially in relation to the Sublime.

---

* Comp. Thuc. vi. 26. 2, for this sense of ἀναλαμβάνειν.　　† iii.

[1] Compare Buffon, below, p. 175.
[2] Compare Aristotle's *Rhetoric*, Book I, Chapter IX (Welldon's translation, p. 11).
[3] Compare the fault criticised by Socrates in the *Phædrus*, above, p. 31.
[4] Test this statement by examples in history.
[5] Observe a similar comparison in Plato, above, pp. 31–32.

V

JONATHAN SWIFT (1667-1745)

From A Letter to a Young Clergyman (1721)

[Save in the matter of punctuation, the text of this selection follows that of Swift's *Prose Works* in the standard (Bohn) edition by Temple Scott (London, Bell, 1898, Vol. 3, pp. 200-207). Swift's punctuation has been reduced in a measure to the current norm.

The selection amounts to about one third of: *A Letter to a Young Clergyman, Lately enter'd into Holy Orders.* By a Person of Quality. London, 1721. The " Letter " is dated " Dublin, *January the 9th*, 1719-1720." It contains the famous epigram: " Proper words in proper places make the true definition of a style " (see below, p. 161); this offers sufficient excuse for the inclusion of an excerpt in the present volume, even if the context were not pertinent reading for the student of composition. The epigram will be better understood in its context, although even thus the reader may be puzzled to say whether its author is here satirical or not. His irony is not always openly biting; at times it is wonderfully elusive, cloaking itself, when Swift desires, in the very simplicity and directness of his language. Covert or open, Swift is for English literature a commanding teacher through the medium of satire, an enduring power for good with those who have the imagination to interpret him aright. His advice in this selection is of wider range than merely for the clergymen of his or any subsequent day. Of course due allowance must be made for Swift's mental characteristics; he was by genius and habit an instinctive satirist, and he was a sharer in modes of thought peculiar to his age,—an age whose philosophers had long agreed that enthusiasm "should never prevail over reason." Such allowance made, his wholesome bitters may be taken to advantage, at least by all who desire to think and to write. For *his design in this paper is not so much to in-*

struct us in the business of a clergyman or a preacher, as to
warn us against some mistakes which are obvious to the
generality of mankind.

Swift's style is treated at some length in Minto's *Manual of*
English Prose Literature — a safe guide; in the present volume it is touched on by Coleridge (p. 206) and Mr. Harrison
(p. 446).]

I should likewise have been glad if you had applied yourself a little more to the study of the English language than
I fear you have done; the neglect whereof is one of the most
general defects among the scholars of this kingdom, who seem
not to have the least conception of a style, but run on in a
flat kind of phraseology, often mingled with barbarous terms
and expressions peculiar to the nation. Neither do I perceive that any person either finds or acknowledges his wants
upon this head, or in the least desires to have them supplied.
Proper words in proper places make the true definition of a
style. But this would require too ample a disquisition to be
now dwelt on; however, I shall venture to name one or two
faults which are easy to be remedied with a very small portion
of abilities.

The first is the frequent use of obscure terms, which by
the women are called hard words, and by the better sort of
vulgar, fine language; than which I do not know a more
universal, inexcusable, and unnecessary mistake among the
clergy of all distinctions, but especially the younger practitioners. I have been curious enough to take a list of several
hundred words in a sermon of a new beginner, which not one
of his hearers among a hundred could possibly understand;
neither can I easily call to mind any clergyman of my own
acquaintance who is wholly exempt from this error, although
many of them agree with me in the dislike of the thing. But
I am apt to put myself in the place of the vulgar, and think

M

many words difficult or obscure, which they will not allow to be so, because those words are obvious to scholars. I believe the method observed by the famous Lord Falkland [1] in some of his writings would not be an ill one for young divines. I was assured by an old person of quality who knew him well, that when he doubted whether a word was perfectly intelligible or no he used to consult one of his lady's chambermaids (not the waiting-woman, because it was possible she might be conversant in romances), and by her judgment was guided whether to receive or reject it. And if that great person thought such a caution necessary in treatises offered to the learned world, it will be sure at least as proper in sermons, where the meanest hearer is supposed to be concerned, and where very often a lady's chambermaid may be allowed to equal half the congregation both as to quality and under-standing. But I know not how it comes to pass that pro-fessors in most arts and sciences are generally the worst qualified to explain their meanings to those who are not of their tribe: a common farmer shall make you understand in three words that his foot is out of joint, or his collar-bone broken, wherein a surgeon, after a hundred terms of art, if you are not a scholar, shall leave you to seek. It is fre-quently the same case in law, physic, and even many of the meaner arts.

And upon this account it is that among hard words I number likewise those which are peculiar to divinity as it is a science, because I have observed several clergymen, other-wise little fond of obscure terms, yet in their sermons very liberal of those which they find in ecclesiastical writers, as if it were our duty to understand them; which I am sure it is not. And I defy the greatest divine to produce any law either of God or man which obliges me to comprehend the meaning of *omniscience, omnipresence, ubiquity, attribute, beatific vision*, with a thousand others so frequent in pulpits, any more than that of *eccentric, idiosyncracy, entity*, and the like. I believe I may venture to insist farther that many terms used in Holy Writ, particularly by St. Paul, might with more discretion be changed into plainer speech, except when they are introduced as part of a quotation.

I am the more earnest in this matter because it is a general complaint and the justest in the world. For a divine has nothing to say to the wisest congregation of any parish in this kingdom, which he may not express in a manner to be understood by the meanest among them. And this assertion must be true, or else God requires from us more than we are able to perform. However, not to contend whether a logician might possibly put a case that would serve for an exception, I will appeal to any man of letters whether at least nineteen in twenty of those perplexing words might not be changed into easy ones, such as naturally first occur to ordinary men, and probably did so at first to those very gentlemen who are so fond of the former.

We are often reproved by divines from the pulpits on account of our ignorance in things sacred, and perhaps with justice enough. However, it is not very reasonable for them to expect that common men should understand expressions which are never made use of in common life. No gentleman thinks it safe or prudent to send a servant with a message, without repeating it more than once, and endeavoring to put it into terms brought down to the capacity of the bearer; yet, after all this care, it is frequent for servants to mistake, and sometimes to occasion misunderstandings among friends; although the common domestics in some gentlemen's families have more opportunities of improving their minds than the ordinary sort of tradesmen.

It is usual for clergymen who are taxed with this learned

defect to quote Dr. Tillotson and other famous divines in their defence; without considering the difference between elaborate discourses upon important occasions, delivered to princes or parliaments, written with a view of being made public, and a plain sermon intended for the middle or lower size of people. Neither do they seem to remember the many alterations, additions, and expungings made by great authors in those treatises which they prepare for the public. Besides, that excellent prelate above-mentioned was known to preach after a much more popular manner in the city congregations; and if in those parts of his works he be any-where too obscure for the understandings of many who may be supposed to have been his hearers, it ought to be num-bered among his omissions.

The fear of being thought pedants hath been of pernicious consequence to young divines. This hath wholly taken many of them off from their severer studies in the university, which they have exchanged for plays, poems, and pamphlets, in order to qualify them for tea-tables and coffee-houses. This they usually call " polite conversation, — knowing the world, — and reading men instead of books." These accom-plishments when applied to the pulpit appear by a quaint, terse, florid style, rounded into periods and cadences, com-monly without either propriety or meaning. I have listened with my utmost attention for half an hour to an orator of this species without being able to understand, much less to carry away, one single sentence out of a whole sermon. Others, to show that their studies have not been confined to sciences or ancient authors, will talk in the style of a gaming ordinary and White Friars,[2] when I suppose the hearers can be little edified by the terms of *palming, shuffling, biting,*[3] *bamboozling*, and the like, if they have not been sometimes conversant among pickpockets and sharpers.

And truly, as they say a man is known by his company, so it should seem that a man's company may be known by his manner of expressing himself, either in public assemblies or private conversation.

It would be endless to run over the several defects of style among us; I shall therefore say nothing of the mean and paltry (which are usually attended by the fustian), much less of the slovenly or indecent. Two things I will just warn you against: the first is the frequency of flat, unnecessary epithets; and the other is the folly of using old, threadbare phrases, which will often make you go out of your way to find and apply them, are nauseous to rational hearers, and will seldom express your meaning as well as your own natural words.

Although, as I have already observed, our English tongue is too little cultivated in this kingdom, yet the faults are nine in ten owing to affectation and not to the want of understanding. When a man's thoughts are clear, the properest words will generally offer themselves first, and his own judgment will direct him in what order to place them, so as they may be best understood. Where men err against this method, it is usually on purpose, and to show their learning, their oratory, their politeness, or their knowledge of the world. In short, that simplicity without which no human performance can arrive to any great perfection is nowhere more eminently useful than in this.

I have been considering that part of oratory which relates to the moving of the passions; this, I observe, is in esteem and practice among some church divines as well as among all the preachers and hearers of the fanatic or enthusiastic strain. I will here deliver to you (perhaps with more freedom than prudence) my opinion upon the point.

The two great orators of Greece and Rome, Demosthenes

and Cicero, though each of them a leader (or as the Greeks call it, a demagogue) in a popular state, yet seem to differ in their practice upon this branch of their art: the former, who had to deal with a people of much more politeness, learning, and wit, laid the greatest weight of his oratory upon the strength of his arguments offered to their understanding and reason; whereas Tully considered the dispositions of a sincere, more ignorant, and less mercurial nation, by dwelling almost entirely on the pathetic part.

But the principal thing to be remembered is that the constant design of both these orators in all their speeches was to drive some one particular point, either the condemnation or acquittal of an accused person, a persuasive to war, the enforcing of a law, and the like; which was determined upon the spot, according as the orators on either side prevailed. And here it was often found of absolute necessity to inflame or cool the passions of the audience, especially at Rome, where Tully spoke, and with whose writings young divines (I mean those among them who read old authors) are more conversant than with those of Demosthenes, who by many degrees excelled the other at least as an orator.[4] But I do not see how this talent of moving the passions can be of any great use toward directing Christian men in the conduct of their lives, at least in these northern climates, where, I am confident, the strongest eloquence of that kind will leave few impressions upon any of our spirits deep enough to last till the next morning, or rather to the next meal.

But what hath chiefly put me out of conceit with this moving manner of preaching is the frequent disappointment it meets with. I know a gentleman who made it a rule in reading to skip over all sentences where he spied a note of admiration at the end. I believe those preachers who abound in *epiphonemas*,[5] if they look about them, would find one part of their congregation out of countenance and the other asleep, except perhaps an old female beggar or two in the aisles, who (if they be sincere) may probably groan at the sound.

Nor is it a wonder that this expedient should so often miscarry, which requires so much art and genius to arrive at any perfection in it, as any man will find, much sooner than learn, by consulting Cicero himself.[6]

I therefore entreat you to make use of this faculty (if you ever be so unfortunate as to think you have it) as seldom and with as much caution as you can, else I may probably have occasion to say of you as a great person said of another upon this very subject. A lady asked him coming out of church whether it were not a very moving discourse? " Yes," said he, " I was extremely sorry, for the man is my friend."

If in company you offer something for a jest and nobody second you in your own laughter nor seems to relish what you said, you may condemn their taste if you please and appeal to better judgments; but in the meantime, it must be agreed, you make a very indifferent figure. And it is at least equally ridiculous to be disappointed in endeavoring to make other folks grieve as to make them laugh.

A plain convincing reason may possibly operate upon the mind both of a learned and ignorant hearer as long as they live, and will edify a thousand times more than the art of wetting the handkerchiefs of a whole congregation, if you were sure to attain it.

If your arguments be strong, in God's name offer them in as moving a manner as the nature of the subject will properly admit, wherein reason and good advice will be your safest guides. But beware of letting the pathetic part swallow up the rational; for, I suppose, philosophers have long agreed that passion should never prevail over reason.

As I take it, the two principal branches of preaching are first to tell the people what is their duty, and then to convince them that it is so. The topics for both these, we know, are brought from Scripture and reason. Upon this first, I wish it were often practised to instruct the hearers in the limits, extent, and compass of every duty, which requires a good deal of skill and judgment; the other branch is, I think, not so difficult. But what I would offer them both is this: that it seems to be in the power of a reasonable clergyman, if he will be at the pains, to make the most ignorant man comprehend what is his duty, and to convince him by argument drawn to the level of his understanding that he ought to perform it.

But I must remember that my design in this paper was not so much to instruct you in your business either as a clergyman or a preacher as to warn you against some mistakes which are obvious to the generality of mankind as well as to me; and we who are hearers may be allowed to have some opportunities in the quality of being standers-by. Only perhaps I may now again transgress by desiring you to express the heads of your divisions in as few and clear words as you possibly can; otherwise I and many thousand others will never be able to retain them, nor consequently to carry away a syllable of the sermon.

---

[1] Lucius Cary, Viscount Falkland (1610?–1643), a royalist and a member of the Long Parliament, was killed at the first battle of Newbury. Dying prematurely, he was already known as a patron of letters and as himself a rare scholar and a writer of ability.

[2] At that time a retreat for sharpers.

[3] We still say "*bitten* by a swindler."

[4] and [6]. In these sentences, are the "proper words in proper places"?

[5] *Epiphonema:* "A striking reflection or an exclamatory sentence summing up a discourse, or a passage in a discourse" (*Standard Dictionary*); see also *Demetrius on Style*, ed. Roberts, p. 281.

VI

BUFFON (1707–1788)

"Discours sur le Style" (1753)

[Translated from *Œuvres Complètes de Buffon*, Paris, 1824, Vol. 1 (pp. cxlix–clxi).

It may be that the seeming inflation in Buffon's address is due to the usage of the Academy on such occasions; in the eighteenth century, grandiloquence was expected from the newly elected member. Nevertheless the author, as will be observed, merely announces that he will propound " some ideas on style." The address appears to have received the more ambitious title of *Discours sur le Style* from the Encyclopedist F. M. Grimm. It was delivered on August 25, 1753.

On Buffon and his *Discours*, see Petit de Julleville, *Histoire de la Langue et de la Littérature Française*, Vol. 6, pp. 240–249 (*V. — Buffon écrivain et théoricien du style*, by Félix Hémon); E. Géruzez, *Essais de Littérature Française*, Vol. 2, pp. 498–518 (*Buffon*); A. F. Villemain, *Tableau de la Littérature Française au XVIIIe Siècle*, Paris, 1868 (Vol. 2, pp. 200–217, *Vingt Deuxième Leçon, Buffon*, — esp. pp. 208–212); P. Flourens, *Travaux et Idées de Buffon*, Paris, 1870 (*Style de Buffon*, pp. 317–320). Buffon's *Discours* is in demand as a text in the secondary schools of France; probably the best of the school editions is that by René Nollet, Paris, Hachette, 1905.

Among the literary curiosities connected with Buffon's celebrated epigram, " the style is the man himself," is a story, *El Estilo es el Hombre*, by Antonio de Trueba (in *Coleccion de Autores Españoles*, Vol. 18, *Cuentos Campesinos*, Leipsic, Brockhaus). The story has been translated (*The Style is the Man*) by Professor T. F. Crane, in the *Cornell Review* (Vol. 6, pp. 68–79; 122–134).]

AN ADDRESS DELIVERED BEFORE THE FRENCH
ACADEMY

BY M. DE BUFFON

UPON THE DAY OF HIS RECEPTION

Gentlemen, in calling me to join your number you have
bestowed on me a great honor; yet glory is a good only in so
far as the recipient is worthy of it, and I am not convinced that
certain essays written without art, and devoid of other ornament than nature's own, are adequate title to make me dare
assume a place among the masters of art — among the eminent men [1] who here represent the literary splendor of France,
and whose names, celebrated to-day among the nations,
will resound on the lips of our remotest posterity. Gentlemen, in fixing your choice on me you have had other
motives: you have wished to give the illustrious body to which
I have for many years had the honor of belonging [2] a new
mark of respect. Though shared by others, my gratitude
is not the less lively. Yet how shall I fulfil the duty which it
lays on me to-day? I have nothing to offer you, Gentlemen,
but what is yours already: some ideas on Style, which I have
gathered from your works — which I have conceived in
reading and admiring you. Submitted to your intelligence,
they will not fail of proper recognition.

In all times there have been men with the ability to rule
their fellows by the power of speech. Yet only in enlightened
times have men written and spoken well. True eloquence
supposes the exercise of genius, and a cultivated mind. It is
far different from that natural facility in speaking which is
simply a talent, a gift accorded those whose passions are
strong, whose voices are flexible, whose imaginations are naturally quick. Such men perceive vividly, are affected vividly,

and display their emotions with force; and by an impression purely mechanical they transmit their own enthusiasm and feelings to others. It is body speaking to body; all movements and all gestures combine equally for service. What, indeed, is requisite in order to arouse and draw on the crowd? What do we need if we would agitate and persuade even the more intelligent? A vehement and affecting tone, expressive and frequent gestures, rapid and ringing words. But for the limited number of those whose heads are steady, whose taste is delicate, whose sense is refined, and who, like you, Gentlemen, set little value on cadence, gestures, and the empty sound of words, one must have substance, thoughts, arguments; and one must know how to present them and shade them and arrange them. It is not enough to strike the ear and hold the eye; one must work on the soul, and touch the sensibilities by addressing the mind.

Style is simply the order and movement one gives to one's thoughts. If these are connected closely, and rigorously compressed, the style will be firm, nervous, and concise. If they are allowed to follow one another loosely and merely at the lead of the diction, however choice this be, the style will be diffuse, nerveless, and languid.

However, before seeking the particular order in which actually to present his thoughts, the writer must first form another more general and more absolute order, where only primary aspects and fundamental ideas shall enter. It is in fixing their places in this prior plan that he sees his subject growing circumscribed, and comes to realize its true extent; and it is by keeping these first outlines continually before him that he is able to determine the proper intervals between the main ideas, and develops the accessory and intermediary ideas that shall serve to fill in. By sheer force of genius he will grasp the sum of these general and particular ideas in their true perspective; by a great delicacy of discernment he will distinguish thoughts that are fertile from such as are sterile; by a sagacity born of long experience in writing he will perceive in advance the ultimate result of all these mental operations. If a subject be at all vast or complex, very seldom can it be taken in at a glance, or penetrated in its entirety by a single and initial effort of genius; and seldom even after much reflection will all its relations be comprehended. Accordingly, one cannot give this matter too much attention; it is, indeed, the sole way to consolidate, develop, and elevate one's thoughts. The more substance and force they receive through meditation, the more easily will they afterward pass into concrete expression.

This plan, though not the resultant style, is nevertheless its basis, supporting it, directing it, regulating its movement, subjecting it to law. Without that basis the best of writers will wander; his pen running on unguided will form haphazard, irregular strokes and incongruous figures. However brilliant the colors he employs, whatever the beauties of detail he introduces, since the ensemble jars or else makes no adequate impression, the work will not really be a construction; hence, though admiring the brilliancy of the author, we may suspect him of lacking true genius.[3] Here is the reason why those who write as they speak, though they may speak excellently, write badly; that those who abandon themselves to the first flashes of their imagination assume a tone which they cannot sustain; that those who are in fear of losing their isolated and fugitive thoughts and who at separate times write in detached fragments, cannot unite these save by forced transitions; that, in a word, there are so many works made up by assemblage of pieces, and so few cast in a single mould.

Every subject, however, is a unit and, no matter how vast it be, can be comprised in a single treatise· hence, in-

terruptions, pauses, sections, and the like, should be employed
only when different subjects are under consideration, or
when, having to discuss great, thorny, and disparate questions,
genius finds its march broken by a multiplicity of obstacles
and is constrained by the force of circumstances.* Otherwise a great number of divisions, far from rendering a work
more solid, destroys its coherence. To the eye the book seems
clearer; but the author's design remains obscure. You cannot make an impression on your reader's mind, or even on his
feelings, but by continuity of the thread, by harmonious
interdependence of the ideas, by a successive development, a
sustained gradation, a uniform movement, which every interruption enfeebles or destroys.

Why is it that the works of nature are so perfect? Because each work is a whole, and because nature follows an
eternal plan from which she never departs. She prepares in
silence the germs of her productions. She sketches the original form of each living being in a single effort. This form
she develops and perfects by a continuous movement and in a
time prescribed. The result is wonderful; yet what should
strike us is the divine imprint that it bears. The human
spirit can *create* nothing, nor can it bring forth at all until
fertilized by experience and meditation; in its acquired
knowledge lie the germs of its productions. But if it imitates
nature in its procedure and labor; if it exalts itself by contemplation to the sublimest truths; if it unites these; if
it forms of them an entirety systematized by reflection: it
will build upon unshakable foundations monuments that cannot pass away.

It is for want of plan, for want of sufficient preliminary

---

* In what I said here I had in mind [Montesquieu's] *L'Esprit des Lois,*
in its substance an excellent work, and to be criticised solely on the score of
its too frequent sections.

reflection on his subject, that a man of intelligence finds himself embarrassed with uncertainty at what point to begin writing. Ideas come to him from many directions at a time; and since he has neither compared nor subordinated them, nothing determines him to prefer one set to another; hence he remains perplexed. When, however, he has made a plan, when he has collected and put in order all the essential thoughts on his subject, he recognizes without difficulty the instant when he ought to take up his pen; he is aware of the critical point when his mind is ready to bring forth; it is urgent with him to come to the birth; nay, he has now only pleasure in writing: his ideas follow one another easily, and the style is natural and smooth. A certain warmth born of that pleasure diffuses itself throughout, giving life to every phrase; there is a gradual increase of animation; the tone grows elevated; individual objects take on color; and a glow of feeling joins with the light of intellect to increase it and carry it on, making it spread from what one is saying to what one is about to say; and the style becomes interesting and luminous.

Nothing is more inimical to this warmth than the desire to be everywhere striking; nothing is more contrary to the light which should be at the centre of a work, and which should be diffused uniformly in any composition, than those sparks which are struck only at the cost of a violent collision between words, and which dazzle us for a moment or two, only to leave us in subsequent darkness.[4] These are thoughts that shine only by contrast, when but one aspect of an object is presented, while the remaining sides are put in shadow; and ordinarily the aspect chosen is a point or angle whereon the writer exercises his wit with the greater ease in proportion as he departs farther from the important sides on which good common sense is accustomed to view things.

Again, nothing is more opposed to true eloquence than the employment of superfine thoughts and the anxious search for such ideas as are slender, delicate, and without substance; ideas that, like leaves of beaten metal, acquire brilliancy only as they lose solidity. The more of this attenuated and shining wit there is in a composition, the less will there be of muscle, real illumination, warmth, and style; unless perchance this wit is the mainspring of the subject, and the writer has no other purpose than mere pleasantry. In that case the art of saying trifles will be found more difficult, perhaps, than that of saying things substantial.

Nothing is more opposed to the beauty of naturalness than the pains people take to express ordinary, every-day matters with an air of singularity or pretence; nor is there anything more degrading to the writer. Far from admiring him for this, we may pity him for having spent so much time in making new combinations of syllables, merely to say what everybody else has said already. This is the fault of minds that are cultivated but sterile; they have words in abundance but no ideas. Accordingly they juggle with diction, and fancy that they have put together ideas, because they have been arranging phrases, and that they have refined the language, when they have really corrupted it by warping the accepted forms. Such writers have no style; or, if you wish, they have only its shadow. A style ought to mean the engraving of thoughts; whereas they only know how to trace out words.[5]

To write well, then, an author must be in full possession of his subject: he must reflect on it enough to see clearly the order of his thoughts, and to put them in proper sequence — in a continuous chain, each of whose links represents a unified idea; and when he has taken up his pen, he must direct it successively from one main point to the next, not letting it stray therefrom, nor yet allowing it to dwell immoderately on any, nor, in fact, giving it other movement than that determined by the space to be traversed. Herein consists the rigor of style; and herein lies that which gives it unity and regulates its speed. It is this, too, and this alone, which suffices to render a style precise and simple, even and clear, lively and coherent. If to obedience to this principle — a principle dictated by genius — an author joins delicacy and taste, caution in the choice of phraseology, care in the matter of expressing things only in the most general terms,[6] his style will have positive nobility. If he has, further, a certain distrust of his first impulses, a contempt for what is superficially brilliant, and a steady aversion for what is equivocal and trifling, his style will be not simply grave, but even majestic. In fine, if he writes as he thinks, if he is himself convinced of what he wishes to prove, this good faith with himself, which is the foundation of propriety toward others and of sincerity in style, will make him accomplish his whole purpose; provided always that his inner conviction is not expressed with too violent enthusiasm, and that he shows throughout more candor than confidence and more light than heat.

Gentlemen, it is thus — as it seems to me when I read you — that you would speak to me for my instruction: my soul eagerly receiving such oracles of wisdom would fain take flight and mount on a level with you. How vain the effort ! Rules, I hear you add, can never take the place of genius. If that be lacking, they are useless. To write well — it is at once to think deeply, to feel vividly, and to express clearly; it is to have at once intelligence, sensibility, and taste. Style supposes the united exercise of all the intellectual faculties. Ideas and they alone are its foundation. Well-sounding words are a mere accessory, dependent simply upon the possession of an external sense. One needs only to possess something of an ear for avoiding awkwardness in sound, and to have trained and bettered it by reading the poets and orators, and one is mechanically led to imitate poetical cadence and the turns of oratory. Now imitation never created anything; hence this euphony of words forms neither the basis nor the tone of style. It is, in fact, often found in writings devoid of ideas.

The tone, which is simply an agreement of the style with the nature of the subject, should never be forced, but should arise naturally from the very essence of the material, depending to a large extent upon the generalization one has in mind. If the author rises to the most inclusive ideas, and if his subject itself is lofty, his tone will apparently rise to the same height; and if while sustaining the tone at that altitude his genius proves copious enough to surround each particular object with a brilliant light, if the author can unite beauty of color with vigor of design, if he can, in a word, represent each idea by a lively and well-defined image, and make of each sequence of ideas a picture that is harmonious and energetic, the tone will be not simply elevated but sublime. Here, Gentlemen, the application would avail more than the rule, and illustration be more instructive than precept; but since I am not permitted to cite the sublime passages that have so often transported me in reading your works, I am forced to limit myself simply to reflections. The well-written works are the only ones that will go down to posterity: the amount of knowledge in a book, the peculiarity of the facts, the novelty even of the discoveries, are not sure warrants of immortality. If the works that contain these are concerned with only minor objects; if they are written without taste, without nobility, without inspiration, they will perish; since the knowledge, facts, and discoveries, being easily detached, are passed on to others, and even gain intrinsically when appropriated by more gifted hands. These

N

things are external to the man; the style is the man himself.[7] Style, then, can be neither detached, nor transferred, nor altered by time: if it is elevated, noble, sublime, the author will be admired equally in all ages.   For it is truth alone that is permanent, that is even eternal.   Now a beautiful style is such in fact only by the infinite number of truths that it presents.   All the intellectual graces residing in it, all the interdependences of which it is composed, are truths not less useful, and for the human spirit possibly more precious, than those, whatsoever they be, that form the core of the subject.

The sublime is to be found only in lofty subjects.   Poetry, history, and philosophy all deal with the same material, and a most lofty material, namely, man and nature.   Philosophy describes and portrays nature; poetry paints and embellishes it; poetry paints men also, enlarges them, intensifies them, creates heroes and divinities.   History represents man only, and represents him as he is.   Accordingly, the tone of the historian will become sublime only when he draws a picture of the greatest men, when he exhibits the greatest actions, the greatest movements, and the greatest revolutions; under other circumstances it will suffice if he be always majestic and grave.   The tone of the philosopher might become sublime whenever he is to speak of the laws of nature, of creatures in general, of space, of matter, of time and motion, of the soul, of the human intellect, of the sentiments, and of the passions; elsewhere it will suffice if he be noble and elevated. But the tone of the orator and the poet, so soon as the subject is lofty, should be ever sublime, because they have the right to bring to the grandeur of their subject just as much color, as much movement, and as much illusion as they please; and because, having at all times to paint and enlarge the objects of their representation, they must at every point employ all the force and display all the extent of their genius.

[1] For example, Voltaire, Marivaux, Montesquieu, Maupertuis. Most of the others are now forgotten; that, however, is no sure ground for a belief that Buffon is here ironical.

[2] The Royal Academy of Sciences, to which Buffon had belonged since 1733.

[3] Géruzez supposes that Buffon is covertly thrusting at Voltaire. Compare below, p. 191, notes 24, 25.

[4] Here, according to Géruzez, Buffon refers to Fontenelle.

[5] Compare Wackernagel's etymology, above, p. 11.

[6] Compare Aristotle, above, p. 68, and Brunetière, below, p. 424.

[7] "Ces choses sont hors de l'homme, le style est l'homme même." Some of the earlier editions read: "Le style est *de* l'homme même." The expression did not occur in the original version which Buffon submitted to President de Ruffey. Its exact wording has been a matter of fruitless discussion in America. Buffon's thought is perfectly clear: whereas the subject-matter of a scientific treatise, say, is external to the man, and would exist whether the man existed or not, the style, or the order in which the man arranges his thoughts on the subject-matter, springs from the man himself; the style is so much of the man as exists in the ordering of his thoughts. See M. Nollet's edition of the *Discours*, p. 22, and the *Nation*, Jan. 25, 1906 ("Notes"). Compare Ben Jonson, *Timber*, ed. F. E. Schelling, p. 64.

VII

VOLTAIRE (1694–1778)

Style (1771–1774)

[Translated from Volume 4 of Voltaire's *Dictionnaire Philosophique —
Œuvres de Voltaire*, Paris, 1879, Vol. 20 (pp. 436 – 444).

Voltaire's " dictionary " article on *Style* is made up of
fragments originally published at widely different times,
Part I dating from 1771 and 1774, Part II having already
appeared in 1745. A criticism of Voltaire's habit of piecing
together his literary odds and ends may be drawn from Buffon (see above, pp. 172, 179). There is an enthusiastic appreciation of his style, applicable with slight abatement to this
article, in Mr. John Morley's excellent work on *Voltaire* (1882,
pp. 87–91). A briefer article entitled *Genre de Style* in Volume 3 of the *Dictionnaire Philosophique* insists on practically
the same ideas as the selection here translated, and contains
in some cases the same illustrations.]

PART FIRST

The style of Balzac's [1] letters would not have been bad
for a funeral oration; and we have various scraps of
physical science in the manner of the epic poem and the ode.
Everything is good in its place.

It is not that it does not require a great art, or rather a
very happy genius, to blend certain elements of a majestic
style in the treatment of subjects demanding simplicity, or to
introduce subtle touches of delicacy in a discourse full of
vehemence and power. Such graces, however, are not to be

taught. They presuppose much genius and taste. It would be hard to give lessons in either.

It is very strange that from the time the French first took to writing they did not produce a single book written in a good style until the year 1656, when the *Provincial Letters*[2] appeared. And why was it that no one wrote history in a fitting style prior to the *Venetian Conspiracy* by the Abbé de Saint-Réal?

How came it that Pellisson,[3] in his Memorial in behalf of Superintendent Fouquet, was the first to catch the true style of Ciceronian eloquence?

Nothing is rarer or more difficult than a style appropriate to the matter in hand.[4]

Never affect unusual turns and novel words in a religious treatise, as did the Abbé Houteville; do not declaim in a work on physics; avoid all trifling in mathematics; avoid bombast and forced figures in a legal plea. When a poor female drunkard, or *drunkardess*, dies of apoplexy, you observe, " She has joined the great majority." When they bury her, you aver that " Her mortal remains are consigned to the dust." If they ring for her funeral, you hear " a melancholy sound that is echoed to the skies." You fancy that you are imitating Cicero, when in fact you are aping Master Little-John.

I have often heard the question raised whether in our better tragedies the familiar style has not crept in too frequently, since it borders so closely on the style of simplicity and naturalness.

For example, in *Mithridates:* —

" My lord, you change countenance!"[5]

That is simple, even naïve. Placed where it is, this half verse has an effect that is terrible; it has a touch of the sublime. On the other hand, the same words when spoken by Berenice to Antiochus —

> " Prince, you are troubled and change countenance " [6]

are perfectly commonplace; here we have a transition rather than a situation.

Nothing could be more simple than the verse: —

> " Madam, I have letters from the army." [7]

It is the moment when Roxane pronounces these words that makes you tremble. This noble simplicity is very frequent in Racine, and constitutes one of his chief beauties.

Still, objection was raised to not a few verses that seemed merely familiar: —

> " That's enough; and what's Queen Berenice doing? "

> " I say, has any one seen the King of Commagene?
> Does he know that I am waiting? "

> " — I've run to the Queen's . . .
> He had gone out when I reached there." [8]

> " We know that she is charming; and such lovely hands
> Seem to ask of you the empire of the race." [9]

> " Like you, the more I think of it, the more I lose myself." [10]

> " What, my lord! The Sultan will see his face again? " [11]

> " And yet, to tell the truth,
> Your love must have long since foreseen it." [12]

> " Madam, once more, the choice is yours." [13]

> " Acomat, she wants to have me marry her.
> Well! " [14]

" I'm going to leave you.

        But I, I will not leave you." [15]

" In case I marry *her*, do you believe
Andromache will not at heart be jealous? " [16]

" You see it's settled; they are going to marry." [17]

" In order to do well, you should forestall him . . ." [18]

" Now wait.

        No — do you see? — it would be useless to deny
        it." [19]

People have found in Racine a large number of verses similarly prosaic and of a familiar tone that belongs only in comedy. These, however, are lost in the crowd of good verses; they are, so to speak, mere wires of baser metal that serve to unite the jewels.

The elegant style is indispensable, for without it beauty of sentiment is thrown away; whereas by itself it suffices to embellish the least noble and least tragic sentiments.

Would any one suppose it possible to bring on the stage, with an incestuous mother on the one hand and a parricidal father on the other, a young girl in the rôle of lover, who is to disdain the conquest of a gallant already successful with other mistresses and to stake her glory on triumphing over an austere man who has never loved anything? Yet observe what Aricia makes bold to say in the midst of the tragic theme of *Phædra*, putting it, however, in verses so fascinating that we have to pardon her for the sentiments of a stock comic coquette (Act II, Scene 1): —

> " Phèdre en vain s'honorait des soupirs de Thésée:
> Pour moi, je suis plus fière, et fuis la gloire aisée
> D'arracher un hommage à mille autres offert,
> Et d'entrer dans un cœur de toutes parts ouvert.

Mais de faire fléchir un courage inflexible,
De porter la douleur dans une âme insensible,
D'enchaîner un captif de ses fers étonné,
Contre un joug qui lui plaît vainement mutiné;
C'est là ce que je veux, c'est là ce qui m'irrite,
Hercule à désarmer coûtait moins qu'Hippolyte,
Et vaincu plus souvent, et plus tôt surmonté,
Préparait moins de gloire aux yeux qui l'ont dompté. " *

These verses are not tragic, but then not all verses need be; and if these are without effect on the stage, read in the closet they charm us merely by their elegance of style.

Nearly always the things a writer says are less striking than the way he puts them; for men in general have much the same ideas about the matters that form the stock in trade of all. It is the expression, the style, that makes all the difference. In the majority of our plays their tissue is made up of declarations of love, cases of jealousy, estrangements, reconciliations, and the like; this is true above all of Racine's, for his are built upon just such slender framework. Yet how few geniuses have been successful in reproducing these

---

* The stylistic qualities which Voltaire has in mind seem impossible of translation. Here is a somewhat literal version of Aricia's "sentiments": —

" Phædra's glory in Theseus's sighs was vain;
  As for me, I am prouder: I renounce the easy prize
  Of winning the homage a thousand others might have,
  And gaining a heart that is open on every side.
  But to force an inflexible spirit to bend,
  To strike a passionless soul with distress,
  To chain up a captive whose shackles astound him,
  One who vainly revolts at a yoke that he likes,
  There is my goal and the spur that incites me.
  To disarm Hercules cost less than it will to disarm Hippolytus;
  And vanquished more often and earlier defeated,
  Hercules brought less glory to the eyes that subdued him."

— Ed.

tints which every writer has tried to paint ! True style gives individuality to the commonest things, strength to the feeblest, dignity to the simplest.

Without style there is no possibility of a single good work in any form of eloquence or poetry.

The great vice in the style of almost all our modern philosophers and anti-philosophers is prolixity. A noteworthy example is the *System of Nature*. In this obscure book there are four times too many words; and it is in part on this account that it is so obscure.

At the beginning of the book [20] the author says that man is the product of nature, that he exists in nature, that he cannot escape from nature even in thought, etc.; that for a being formed by nature and circumscribed by it there exists nothing outside of the great entirety of which he is a part, and whose influences he is under; that consequently any beings that are supposed to be above nature or separate from it are necessarily pure chimeras.

He then adds : " It will never be possible for us to form real ideas of them." But how can any one form an idea, whether real or false, of a chimera, a thing that has no existence whatsoever? The words are futile and meaningless, having no other service than to round out an empty phrase. He continues: " . . . you can never form real ideas of the region these chimeras occupy, nor of the way they act." But how can chimeras occupy a position in space ? How can they have ways of acting ? What in the world would a non-existent chimera's waỳ of acting be ? The moment you have said *chimera*, you can go no further:

" For the satiate mind the superfluous runs to waste." [21]

" Let man learn the laws of nature; [22] let him submit to those laws from which nothing can release him; let him consent to remain ignorant of causes, since for him they are enshrouded by an impenetrable veil."

Here the latter clause is not at all in sequence with the preceding; on the contrary, the two clauses seem to contain an obvious contradiction. If man learns the laws of nature he will know what we generally understand as the causes of phenomena; hence these are by no means enshrouded by a veil to him impenetrable. It is a case of an author's betrayal through careless use of trite expressions.

"Let him endure without murmuring the decrees of a universal force that cannot retrace its steps or ever depart from the rules which its essence prescribes to it."

Now what in the world is a force that does not retrace its steps? The steps of a force! And not content with one false image, he straightway proffers you another, if you like it better, namely, a rule prescribed by an essence. Unfortunately, almost all the book is written in this obscure and diffuse style.

"All that human intelligence has gradually contrived in order to change or better its mode of existence is but a necessary consequence of the essence peculiar to man and of that of the beings which react on him. All our institutions, our reflections, our knowledge, have for their object simply the attainment of a happiness toward which our own nature unceasingly forces us to tend. All that we do or think, all that we are or shall be, is never anything but a result of what nature has made us."

I am not examining here the substance of this metaphysics; I do not inquire how our contrivances for changing our mode of existence, etc., are the necessary effects of an essence that undergoes no change. I confine myself to the style. *All that we shall be is never* (what a solecism!) *anything but a result of what nature has made us* (again what a solecism!).[23]

It ought to read: *will never be anything but a result of the laws of nature.* Only he has already said that four times in three pages.

It is extremely difficult to form distinct ideas of God and nature; it is perhaps just as difficult to acquire a good style.[24]

Here is a singular specimen of style, in a harangue that we heard in 1745 at Versailles.

Address to the King, delivered by M. Le Camus, First President of the Court of Imposts

SIRE:—

Your Majesty's conquests are so speedy that we must try to have a care for their acceptance by our descendants and to temper the surprise these wonders will cause, for fear that future heroes may dispense with emulating, and the nations with believing them.

But indeed, Sire, it is no longer possible that they will doubt, when they read in history how Your Majesty was seen upon the field of Mars and at the head of his troops, himself recording them upon a drum; for that is to have engraved them forever in the temple of memory.

Remotest ages will know that the English, that enemy proud and bold, that enemy jealous of your glory, have been forced to take roundabout advantage of your victory; that their allies have been witnesses of their shame; and that they have one and all rushed to the combat only to immortalize the triumph of the conqueror.

We dare not tell Your Majesty, in spite of his great love for his people, that there is but one more secret whereby to augment our joy — namely, to diminish his courage, and that Heaven would sell us its wonders too dear if it cost us your peril or that of the young hero who is our fondest hope.

*   *   *   *   *

Part Second

On the Corruption of Style [25]

Notwithstanding the models that we have of almost every kind, there is general complaint that our eloquence has become decadent. One of the great defects of the age, contributing most largely to this decadence, is the mixture of styles. We authors, as it seems to me, are not sufficiently given to imitating the painters, who never think of combining the attitudes of Callot with the faces of Raphael. Now and then in histories, otherwise well written, and in good dogmatic works, I observe a tendency to affect the most familiar tone of ordinary conversation. Somebody once upon a time said that we ought to write as we speak. The meaning of that law is that we should write naturally. In a letter we are accustomed to tolerate some irregularity, freedom of style, want of correctness, and venturesome pleasantries, because letters are usually written artlessly, without plan, and are in the nature of informal talk. But when we speak or write with consideration, we are bound to the proprieties. Now who, I ask, deserves more consideration than the public?

Is it permissible in works on mathematics to say that " a geometer who wants to save his soul will have to go up to heaven in a perpendicular line"; that " vanishing quantities tumble headforemost back to earth for having wished to rise too high"; that " a seed placed sprout downward sees through the trick and turns right side up"; that " were Saturn destroyed, its fifth satellite, not its first, would take its place, because kings always keep their heirs at a distance"; that " a vacuum exists only in a ruined man's purse"; that

"Hercules was a physicist" and that " a philosopher of such energy was irresistible"?

Really admirable books are infected with this blemish. Now the cause of so common a fault lies, I think, in the reproach that has been long, and justly, laid upon authors for their pedantry: " shunning an error they fall into a vice."[26] It has been urged so repeatedly upon our writers to copy the tone of good company that the most serious authors have grown jocose, and in order to be *good company* for their readers, have come to say things that are decidedly bad-mannered.

Some have tried to talk on science in the way Voiture talked to Mademoiselle Paulet on gallantry, never reflecting that Voiture himself failed to get the exact air of the little species of literature in which he is supposed to have excelled; — for he often takes insincerity for delicacy, and affectation for naturalness. The amusing is never good in the serious style, since it never bears on more than one side of any object, and that not the side to be considered: it turns in nearly every case on false analogies or on ambiguity; the result being that most professional wits have minds as untrustworthy as they are superficial.

In poetry, as it seems to me, it is quite as wrong to mix the styles as in prose. Now the Marotic style has for some time been exerting an injurious influence on our poetry, through its hodgepodge of vulgar and elevated, archaic and recent terms. Here, I fancy, is the reason why we catch the whistle of Rabelais mingling in some of our didactic poems with the notes of the Horatian flute.

> You must try to speak French; it sufficed for Boileau.
> Let his well-governed style and his justice of view
> Be your norms; and to ill-nurtured minds leave the part
> Of the teacher that imitates Rabelais's art.

I confess that I am shocked when I meet in a serious epistle such expressions as the following: —

> "Disjointed rimers with jangling brains,
> More bitter than aloes and colocynth juice,
> Your vices work mischief. Folk of such stripe —
> Ragpickers, Ostrogoths, rascals of God." [27]
>
> — To heap up words in such a reckless pile
> At once dishonors genius and style.

[1] Jean-Louis Guez de Balzac (1597–1654).

[2] By Pascal.

[3] Paul Pellisson-Fontanier. He had a place in Voltaire's *Temple du Goût*. For a similarly favorable opinion of his style see *Biographie Universelle*, Vol. 32, pp. 415–416.

[4] Compare Aristotle, above, p. 71.

[5] Racine, *Mithridate*, III, 5. Fourteen subsequent references are to the same author.

[6] *Bérénice*, I, 4.

[7] *Bajazet*, IV, 3.

[8] *Bérénice*, II, 1, l. 6; II, 1, ll. 1–3; II, 1, l. 5.

[9] *Ibid.*, II, 2.

[10] *Ibid.*, II, 5.

[11] *I.e.* the slave's face: *Bajazet*, I, 1.

[12] *Ibid.*, I, 4.

[13] *Ibid.*, II, 1.

[14] *Ibid.*, II, 3.

[15] *Ibid.*, II, 5.

[16] *Andromaque*, II, 5.

[17] *Bajazet*, III, 3.

[18] *Andromaque*, II, 1.

[19] *Bajazet*, III, 3.

[20] "Page 1" [Voltaire's note]. Voltaire refers to the atheistic work formerly supposed to be a posthumous publication of the Academician Mirabaud, now known to have been written by Holbach. In 1770 Goethe expressed a similar distaste for this work.

[21] *Omne supervacuum pleno de pectore manat:* Horace, *Art of Poetry*, l. 337.

[22] "Page 2" [Voltaire's note].

[23] Though it is hardly a matter of importance, we may observe that a better historical knowledge of the French language should have prevented Voltaire's second stricture on this sentence. His quibble cannot be adequately translated.

[24] This much of the article appeared in Part 8 of the *Questions sur l'encyclopédie*, 1771; the remainder was added in 1774.

[25] This fragment, originally part of a private letter, was first published in 1745. Notes 24 and 25 are given for the light they throw on Voltaire's method of composition.

[26] *In vitium ducit culpæ fuga:* Horace, *Art of Poetry*, l. 31.

[27] Voltaire quotes, very inexactly, from some lines by J. B. Rousseau (Bk. I, Epistle 3, to Clement Marot). Compare what he says above of the "Marotic" style.

VIII

GOETHE (1749–1832)

Simple Imitation of Nature; Manner; Style (1789)

[Translated from the Hempel edition of Goethe's *Werke*, 1877 (Vol. 24, ed. H. Düntzer, pp. 525–529); the Weimar edition (Vol. 47, 1896, pp. 77–83; p. 409) contains no variant readings of significance.]

The brief and sharp differentiation of *Einfache Nachahmung der Natur, Manier, Stil* was among the extracts which Goethe contributed to Wieland's *Merkur* in 1788-1789, on his return from Italy to Weimar. In his collected works (Hempel edition) it is printed as No. 4 in *Ueber Italien, Fragmente eines Tagebuchs* — a miscellany of observations on the fine arts, including notes on special topics in literature and music. " Fragment " 4, a compressed outline of Goethe's principles of artistic criticism at that time, with obvious reference to painting, might at first glance seem out of place in the present group of essays on style in literature. However, it is introduced purposely, partly on account of its author, but more for the valuable light that a sister art like painting ought, when properly considered, to throw upon the art of letters. Properly considered, the bearing of this selection on literature should not be hard to discover, if we transfer in a legitimate way the idea of an imitation of nature with which Goethe commences. Goethe temporarily limits his conception of nature to the inanimate world or to still life. His imaginary painter is to begin with an intense and continuous observation of separate objects at rest. There could be no better cue for the incipient writer, since there is no safer, perhaps no other, method of gaining that basis of faithfulness and accuracy in looking and ascertaining, which is indispensable for such lower procedures as simple description and explanation, not to speak of any higher forms of literature. " Homer," said Professor Palmer's friend — in *The Glory of the Imperfect,* — " looked long at his thumb"; this habit of patient and impartial study, thought the friend, was the secret of Homer's ever fresh and vigorous style.

Some such habit is the secret in the success of every artist, be he painter or writer. Other applications of Goethe's richly suggestive sentences must be left to the teacher's imagination; the student must do his own thinking: *this* point may be enforced profitably by the following quotation from a recent work on Velazquez by M. Auguste Bréal. It is copied from the *Nation* for June 1, 1905: —

" Velazquez is a perfect example of what dexterity and craftsmanship ought to be in a master, namely, the outcome of severe and protracted study. The painter who, later on, was able to indicate with a single touch — fleeting and decisive — a belt buckle, a sword hilt, the ribbon of a hoop, and the very life of a glance, began by meticulously elaborating portraits of pots and by patiently painting in every line of a model's grimace. Little by little, alone and by himself, he acquired and amassed the experience which is represented by a single trickle of paint in 'Las Meniñas.' Never has more audacious synthesis been produced by more careful analysis. This might furnish a subject of meditation for those young 'masters' who start by audacities which are all the easier for being unconscious. It is impossible to synthesize, it is impossible to epitomize (in painting) [or writing] what one has not studied. If one begins by the end, one is in danger of ending by the beginning ; and *if early works that are labored do not imply future mastery, early works that are masterly are the manifestation of an artist without personality.*" [The *Nation's* italics.]

The selection from *Ueber Italien* is aphoristic and sententious, not lacking in grace, yet unadorned, typical of Goethe's scientific vein in the treatment of fine art. References to Goethe's style are of course very frequent; G. H. Lewes's *Life and Works of Goethe*, 4th ed., 1890, p. 53 (Bk. II, Chap. II) may be cited.]

Since we shall have frequent use for these words from now on, it will not seem superfluous to point out exactly what we mean by them. For, though they have seen long literary

o

service, and though their meaning appears to be fixed through their employment in theoretical works, still every one uses them for the most part in some particular sense, and with more or less definite connotation according as he has a sharper or feebler conception of what they ought to express.

SIMPLE IMITATION OF NATURE

Suppose that an artist of requisite native talent, and one whose eye and hand had been trained to a certain extent on models, finally turning to objects in nature, began faithfully and industriously to imitate her forms and colors with utmost accuracy; suppose that he never consciously departed from her, and that he commenced and finished every one of his paintings in her immediate presence : such a person would always be an artist worthy of consideration, for he could not fail of an extraordinarily high grade of truth, and his work would necessarily be sure, powerful, and rich.

If we reflect on these conditions carefully, we readily see that a limited yet capable talent could in this way handle pleasing, if restricted, subjects.

Such subjects would have to be easily and always accessible —capable of being observed in comfort and copied in repose; the temper that is to engage in such work must be quiet, self-centred, and content with a moderate satisfaction.

This kind of imitation would accordingly be applied to so-called dead or inanimate objects by quiet, faithful men of limited endowment.   In its nature it does not preclude the attainment of a high perfection.

MANNER

Commonly, however, a man will find such procedure too painful or else insufficient.   He sees in many objects a certain harmony which he can put into a picture only by a sacrifice.

It irks him to make a mere letter for letter copy of the *a b c's* of nature ; he hits on a way of his own, invents for himself a language wherewith to express again after his own fashion what he has mentally conceived, and to give its own appropriate form to a subject that he has often repeated, — without having nature before him every time he repeats it, and without even recalling the original altogether vividly.

Thus there is engendered a language in which the soul of the speaker obtains direct expression and significance. And just as notions about morals take on a different form and arrangement in the mind of every one that does his own thinking, so will every artist of this description observe, conceive, and imitate the outer world differently; he will lay hold on its phenomena more circumspectly or more readily, and he will represent them again more firmly or more fleetingly.

We perceive that this kind of imitation may be applied most fitly in the case of objects where some large unity contains a great number of small subordinate details. The latter must be sacrificed, if a general expression of the large object is to be achieved; as, for example, in a landscape you would miss the mark badly, were you to lay punctilious stress upon the detail and not rather cleave to the conception of the whole.

STYLE

Granted now that through imitation of nature, through striving to provide itself with a general language, through accurate and penetrating study of objects, art at length reaches a point where with ever increasing nicety it learns to know the properties of things and the way they exist; until, with a sweeping view of images in their due order, it is competent to bring various characteristic forms together for unified imitation: then there arises *style,* the highest stage that art can reach, the stage where art may claim to rival the loftiest of human endeavors.[1]

Simple imitation has its basis in quiet existence and grateful proximity; *manner* is the seizing of a phenomenon with a facile and vigorous temper; *style* is founded upon the deepest principles of knowledge, upon the very nature of things, in so far as we can recognize this in visible and tangible forms.

*   *   *   *   *

The elaboration of what has been said would take up volumes, and as a matter of fact there are books in which a good deal about it may be found; however, the pure conception is to be studied only with reference to nature and the works of art. We may add one or two considerations, and shall have occasion hereafter to refer to these pages whenever the discussion turns on painting and sculpture.

It is not hard to see that the three kinds of artistic production here distinguished are intimately related one to another, and that one can insensibly shade into the next.

Simple imitation of objects easily comprehended (let us take for example fruits and flowers) can be carried to a high degree of excellence. Naturally, any one who is going to represent roses will quickly recognize and distinguish the most beautiful and the freshest, seeking them out among the thousands that summer offers him. Here, accordingly, the element of choice is already entering in, although the artist has supposedly formed no rigorous mental conception of the beauty of roses. His business is with tangible forms; the whole thing is a matter of various tone and superficial color. The downy peach, the delicately dusted plum, the smooth apple, the glistening cherry, the brilliant rose, the manifold pink, the variegated tulip — he can have them all before him in his studio, if he wishes, in their most perfect bloom and maturity; he can give them the most favorable light; his eye playing over the brilliant colors can accustom itself to their harmony; every year he can renew the same objects, and through quiet, imitative observation of existence pure and simple he can recognize and appropriate the characteristics of these objects without the effort of abstraction: and thus may arise the miraculous effects of a Huysum [2] or a Rachel Ruisch,[3] artists whose success almost oversteps the bounds of possibility. It is obvious that such an artist must become only the greater and surer if to his talent he adds a knowledge of botany, if he knows from the root up the influence of the different parts on the health and growth of the plant, their purposes and reciprocal activities; if he understands and ponders the successive development of leaves, flowers, fructification, fruit, and new germ. In that case he will show his taste not merely in his selection among phenomena; but he will also at once astonish and instruct us through the justice in his representation of particular qualities. In this sense you could say that he had formed a *style;* for you can readily see, on the other hand, how a master of this sort, by not going so deeply into detail, and by striving to give easy expression to the obvious and brilliant, would soon pass over into manner.

Simple imitation, consequently, labors, so to speak, in the outer court of style. The more honestly, carefully, purely, it goes to work; the more quiet its impression of what it beholds; the more patiently it copies, the more it acquires the habit of supplementary thought, that is, the more it learns to compare similarities, to distinguish dissimilarities, and to subordinate the particular object under the general concept: just in that measure it renders itself worthier to tread the threshold of the veritable sanctuary.

If now we consider manner we see that this can be in the highest sense, and according to the strictest value of the word, a *medium* between simple imitation and style. The closer this manner, after its lighter method, approaches true imitation; the more zealously, on the other hand, it seeks to grasp and comprehensibly to express what is characteristic in objects; the more firmly it unites both, by an unmixed, lively, vigorous individuality: the higher and more respectable will it prove. When an artist of this calibre ceases holding to nature and thinking on nature, he will gradually depart farther and farther from the foundation of art. His manner will grow more shallow and insignificant, the more it departs from simple imitation and from style.

We need not here repeat that we take the word manner in a good and respectful sense, and that consequently artists whose works to our thinking fall within the circle of manner have no ground of complaint against us. It is simply of importance for us to give the word style the highest position, so as to have on hand an expression with which to indicate the highest stage that art has reached and can reach. Indeed, merely to appreciate this stage is in itself a great felicity, and to converse about it with intelligent people, a noble satisfaction; such satisfaction we shall have many an opportunity to give ourselves in what follows.

[1] Among the loftiest of human endeavors would be the successful effort to order aright the life of an individual or of a family; or, still higher, the shaping of the life of a nation. However, the ordering of an individual life may itself be considered a work of art; *i.e.* an example of "the skilful and systematic arrangement or adaptation of means for the attainment of a desired end" *(Standard Dictionary)*. Compare Professor Albert S. Cook's address, *The Artistic Ordering of Life*, published by Crowell.

[2] Jan van Huysum (1682–1749), of Amsterdam, a Dutch painter of flowers and fruit.

[3] Rachel Ruisch (1664–1750), a painter of flowers, from The Hague.

IX

SAMUEL TAYLOR COLERIDGE (1772-1834)

On Style (1818)

[From Vol. 1 of Coleridge's *Literary Remains*, ed. H. N. Coleridge, 1836; cf. *The Complete Works of Samuel Taylor Coleridge*, New York, 1884, Vol. 4, pp. 337-343.

This corresponds to Lecture XIV, the last of the " various, rather than miscellaneous," series advertised by Coleridge for the winter and early spring of 1818. Of these lectures, says Dykes Campbell (*Athenæum*, March 16, 1889), " a deplorably scanty record is all that remains to us. A few preparatory notes of his own, a few jottings taken down from his lips by friends who attended the course — these, pieced out with some marginalia on the authors mentioned in the syllabus, were piously swept together by Mr. H. N. Coleridge, and printed . . . under the heading of 'Course of Lectures.' But the result was necessarily a mere ghost, not even a well-articulated skeleton, of what was probably the finest body of criticism ever produced by Coleridge." In the syllabus Lecture XIV was announced thus: —

"March 13. On the corruptions of the English language since the reign of Queen Anne in our style of writing prose. A few easy rules for the attainment of a manly, unaffected, and pure language, in our genuine mother tongue, whether for the purpose of writing, oratory, or conversation" (*Works*, 1884, Vol. 4, p. 232). How inadequately Coleridge's actual words and, above all, his illustrations are preserved in the *Literary Remains*, can be gathered by a comparison of this selection with a fragmentary report of the same lecture — entitled *Progressive Changes in English Prose-Writing* — published by an anonymous "Correspondent" in Leigh Hunt's *Tatler* for May 23, 1831, and reprinted by Dykes Campbell in the *Athenæum* for March 16, 1889 (1889, Vol. 1, pp. 345-346).

In the present selection a standard text has been supplied for the passage quoted by Coleridge from Chaucer.]

I have, I believe, formerly observed with regard to the character of the governments of the East, that their tendency was despotic, that is, towards unity; whilst that of the Greek governments, on the other hand, leaned to the manifold and the popular, the unity in them being purely ideal, namely of all as an identification of the whole. In the northern or Gothic nations the aim and purpose of the government were the preservation of the rights and interests of the individual in conjunction with those of the whole. The individual interest was sacred. In the character and tendency of the Greek and Gothic languages there is precisely the same relative difference. In Greek the sentences are long, and the structure architectural, so that each part or clause is insignificant when compared with the whole. The result is everything, the steps and processes nothing. But in the Gothic and, generally, in what we call the modern, languages, the structure is short, simple, and complete in each part, and the connection of the parts with the sum total of the discourse is maintained by the sequency of the logic, or the community of feelings excited between the writer and his readers. As an instance equally delightful and complete, of what may be called the Gothic structure as contradistinguished from that of the Greeks, let me cite a part of our famous Chaucer's character of a parish priest as he should be. Can it ever be quoted too often?

> " A good man was ther of religioun,
>   And was a POURE PERSOUN OF A TOUN;
>   But riche he was of hooly thoght and werk;
>   He was also a lernèd man, a clerk,
>   That Cristès Gospel trewèly wolde preche:
>   His parisshens devoutly wolde he teche.
>   Benygne he was, and wonder diligent,
>   And in adversitee ful pacient;
>   And swich he was y-prevèd oftè sithes.

Ful looth were hym to cursen for his tithes,
But rather wolde he yeven, out of doute,
Unto his pourė parisshens aboute,
Of his offrýng and eek of his substaunce:
He koude in litel thyng have suffisaunce.
Wyd was his parisshe, and houses fer asonder,
But he ne laftė nat for reyn ne thonder,
In siknesse nor in meschief to visíte
The ferreste in his parisshe, muche and lite,
Upon his feet, and in his hand a staf.
This noble ensample to his sheepe he yaf
That firste he wroghte and afterward he taughte.
Out of the gospel he tho wordės caughte,
And this figure he added eek therto,
That if gold rustė what shal iren doo?

*   *   *   *   *

He settė nat his benefice to hyre
And leet his sheepe encombred in the myre,
And ran to Londoun, unto Seïnt Poules,
To seken hym a chaunterie for soules;
Or with a bretherhed to been withholde,
But dwelte at hoom and keptė wel his folde,
So that the wolf ne made it nat myscarie, —
He was a shepherde, and noght a mercenarie:
And though he hooly were and vertuous,
He was to synful man nat despitous,
Ne of his speche daungerous ne digne,
But in his techyng déscreet and benygne,
To drawen folk to hevene by fairnesse,
By good ensample, this was his bisynesse:
But it were any persone obstinat,
What so he were, of heigh or lough estat,
Hym wolde he snybben sharply for the nonys.
A bettre preest I trowe that nowher noon ys;
He waited after no pompe and reverence,
Ne maked him a spicėd conscience,
But Cristės loore, and his Apostles twelve,
He taughte, but first he folwed it hym selve." [1]

Such change as really took place in the style of our literature after Chaucer's time is with difficulty perceptible, on account of the dearth of writers, during the civil wars of the fifteenth century. But the transition was not very great; and accordingly we find in Latimer and our other venerable authors about the time of Edward VI, as in Luther, the general characteristics of the earliest manner; — that is, every part popular, and the discourse addressed to all degrees of intellect; — the sentences short, the tone vehement, and the connection of the whole produced by honesty and singleness of purpose, intensity of passion, and pervading importance of the subject.

Another and a very different species of style is that which was derived from, and founded on, the admiration and cultivation of the classical writers, and which was more exclusively addressed to the learned class in society. I have previously mentioned Boccaccio as the original Italian introducer of this manner, and the great models of it in English are Hooker, Bacon, Milton, and Taylor, although it may be traced in many other authors of that age. In all these the language is dignified but plain, genuine English, although elevated and brightened by superiority of intellect in the writer. Individual words themselves are always used by them in their precise meaning, without either affectation or slipslop. The letters and state papers of Sir Francis Walsingham are remarkable for excellence in style of this description. In Jeremy Taylor the sentences are often extremely long, and yet are generally so perspicuous in consequence of their logical structure, that they require no perusal to be understood; and it is for the most part the same in Milton and Hooker.

Take the following sentence as a specimen of the sort of style to which I have been alluding: —

" Concerning Faith, the principal object whereof is that eternal verity which hath discovered the treasures of hidden wisdom in Christ; concerning Hope, the highest object whereof is that everlasting goodness which in Christ doth quicken the dead; concerning Charity, the final object whereof is that incomprehensible beauty which shineth in the countenance of Christ, the Son of the living God: concerning these virtues, the first of which beginning here with a weak apprehension of things not seen, endeth with the intuitive vision of God in the world to come; the second beginning here with a trembling expectation of things far removed, and as yet but only heard of, endeth with real and actual fruition of that which no tongue can express; the third beginning here with a weak inclination of heart towards him unto whom we are not able to approach, endeth with endless union, the mystery whereof is higher than the reach of the thoughts of men; concerning that Faith, Hope, and Charity, without which there can be no salvation, was there ever any mention made saving only in that Law which God himself hath from Heaven revealed? There is not in the world a syllable muttered with certain truth concerning any of these three, more than hath been supernaturally received from the mouth of the eternal God."

— *Eccles. Pol.* i. s. 11 [Bk. I, Ch. 11. 6].

The unity in these writers is produced by the unity of the subject, and the perpetual growth and evolution of the thoughts, one generating, and explaining, and justifying, the place of another ; not as it is in Seneca, where the thoughts, striking as they are, are merely strung together like beads, without any causation or progression.[2] The words are selected because they are the most appropriate, regard being had to the dignity of the total impression, and no merely big phrases are used where plain ones would have sufficed, even in the most learned of their works.

There is some truth in a remark, which I believe was made by Sir Joshua Reynolds, that the greatest man is he who forms the taste of a nation, and that the next greatest is he who corrupts it. The true classical style of Hooker and his fellows was easily open to corruption; and Sir Thomas Browne it was, who, though a writer of great genius, first effectually injured the literary taste of the nation by his introduction of learned words, merely because they were learned. It would be difficult to describe Browne adequately; exuberant in conception and conceit, dignified, hyperlatinistic, a quiet and sublime enthusiast; yet a fantast, a humorist, a brain with a twist; egotistic like Montaigne, yet with a feeling heart and an active curiosity, which, however, too often degenerates into a hunting after oddities. In his *Hydriotaphia*, and, indeed, almost all his works, the entireness of his mental action is very observable; he metamorphoses everything, be it what it may, into the subject under consideration. But Sir Thomas Browne with all his faults had a genuine idiom; and it is the existence of an individual idiom in each, that makes the principal writers before the Restoration the great patterns or integers of English style. In them the precise intended meaning of a word can never be mistaken; whereas in the latter writers, as especially in Pope, the use of words is for the most part purely arbitrary, so that the context will rarely show the true specific sense, but only that something of the sort is designed. A perusal of the authorities cited by Johnson in his dictionary under any leading word, will give you a lively sense of this declension in etymological truth of expression in the writers after the Restoration, or perhaps, strictly, after the middle of the reign of Charles II.

The general characteristic of the style of our literature down to the period which I have just mentioned, was gravity, and in Milton and some other writers of his day there are perceptible traces of the sternness of republicanism. Soon after the Restoration a material change took place, and the cause of royalism was graced, sometimes disgraced, by every shade of lightness of manner. A free and easy style was considered as a test of loyalty, or at all events, as a badge of the cavalier party; you may detect it occasionally even in Barrow, who is, however, in general remarkable for dignity and logical sequency of expression; but in L'Estrange, Collyer, and the writers of that class, this easy manner was carried out to the utmost extreme of slang and ribaldry. Yet still the works, even of these last authors, have considerable merit in one point of view; their language is level to the understandings of all men; it is an actual transcript of the colloquialism of the day, and is accordingly full of life and reality. Roger North's life of his brother, the Lord Keeper, is the most valuable specimen of this class of our literature; it is delightful, and much beyond any other of the writings of his contemporaries.

From the common opinion that the English style attained its greatest perfection in and about Queen Anne's reign I altogether dissent;[3] not only because it is in one species alone in which it can be pretended that the writers of that age excelled their predecessors; but also because the specimens themselves are not equal, upon sound principles of judgment, to much that had been produced before. The classical structure of Hooker — the impetuous, thought-agglomerating flood of Taylor — to these there is no pretence of a parallel; and for mere ease and grace, is Cowley inferior to Addison, being as he is so much more thoughtful and full of fancy? Cowley, with the omission of a quaintness here and there, is probably the best model of style for modern imitation in general. Taylor's periods have been frequently attempted by his admirers; you may, perhaps, just catch the turn of a simile or single image, but to write in the real manner of Jeremy Taylor would require as mighty a mind as his. Many parts of Algernon Sidney's treatises afford excellent exemplars of a good modern practical style; and Dryden in his prose works is a still better model, if you add a stricter and purer grammar. It is, indeed, worthy of remark that all our great poets have been good prose writers, as Chaucer, Spenser, Milton; and this probably arose from their just sense of metre. For a true poet will never confound verse and prose; whereas it is almost characteristic of indifferent prose writers that they should be constantly slipping into scraps of metre. Swift's style is, in its line, perfect; the manner is a complete expression of the matter, the terms appropriate, and the artifice concealed. It is simplicity in the true sense of the word.

After the Revolution, the spirit of the nation became much more commercial than it had been before; a learned body, or clerisy, as such, gradually disappeared, and literature in general began to be addressed to the common miscellaneous public. That public had become accustomed to, and required, a strong stimulus; and to meet the requisitions of the public taste, a style was produced which by combining triteness of thought with singularity and excess of manner of expression, was calculated at once to soothe ignorance and to flatter vanity. The thought was carefully kept down to the immediate apprehension of the commonest understanding, and the dress was as anxiously arranged for the purpose of making the thought appear something very profound. The essence of this style consisted in a mock antithesis, that is, an opposition of mere sounds, in a rage for personification, the abstract made animate, far-fetched metaphors, strange phrases, metrical scraps, in everything, in short, but genuine prose. Style is, of course, nothing else but the art of conveying the meaning appropriately and with perspicuity, whatever that meaning may be, and one criterion of style is that it shall not be translatable without injury to the meaning. Johnson's style has pleased many from the very fault of being perpetually translatable; he creates an impression of cleverness by never saying anything in a common way. The best specimen of this manner is in Junius, because his antithesis is less merely verbal than Johnson's. Gibbon's manner is the worst of all; it has every fault of which this peculiar style is capable. Tacitus is an example of it in Latin; in coming from Cicero you feel the *falsetto* immediately.

In order to form a good style, the primary rule and condition is, not to attempt to express ourselves in language before we thoroughly know our own meaning: — when a man perfectly understands himself, appropriate diction will generally be at his command either in writing or speaking. In such cases the thoughts and the words are associated. In the next place preciseness in the use of terms is required, and the test is whether you can translate the phrase adequately into simpler terms, regard being had to the feeling of the whole passage. Try this upon Shakespeare, or Milton, and see if you can substitute other simpler words in any given passage without a violation of the meaning or tone. The source of bad writing is the desire to be something more than a man of sense, — the straining to be thought a genius; and it is just the same in speech-making. If men would only say what they have to say in plain terms, how much more eloquent they would be ! Another rule is to avoid converting mere abstractions into persons. I believe you will very rarely find in any great writer before the Revolution the possessive case of an inanimate noun used in prose instead of the dependent case, as "the watch's hand," for "the hand of the watch." The possessive or Saxon genitive was confined to persons, or at least to animated subjects. And I cannot conclude this Lecture without insisting on the importance of accuracy of style as being near akin to veracity and truthful habits of mind; he who thinks loosely will write loosely, and, perhaps, there is some moral inconvenience in the common forms of our grammars which give our children so many obscure terms for material distinctions. Let me also exhort you to careful examination of what you read, if it be worth any perusal at all; such an examination will be a safeguard from fanaticism, the universal origin of which is in the contemplation of phenomena without investigation into their causes.[4]

[1] *Canterbury Tales, Prologue*, ll. 477–500; 507–528 (Chaucer, Globe Edition, 1898, p. 8).

[2] Compare Buffon, above, p. 174.

[3] Compare Mr. Harrison, below, pp. 445, 446.

[4] In his *History of Criticism* (see his Index), Professor Saintsbury expresses high appreciation of the following note by Coleridge on the "Wonderfulness of Prose":

"It has just struck my feelings that the Pherecydean origin of prose being granted, prose must have struck men with greater admiration than poetry. In the latter it was the language of passion and emotion: it [was] what they themselves spoke and heard in moments of exultation, indignation, &c. But to hear an evolving roll, or a succession of leaves, talk continually the language of deliberate reason in a form of continued preconception, of a *Z* already possessed when *A* was being uttered — this must have appeared godlike. I feel myself in the same state, when in the perusal of a sober, yet elevated and harmonious succession of sentences and periods, I abstract my mind from the particular passage and sympathize with the wonder of the common people, who say of an eloquent man: — 'He talks like a book.'"

— Coleridge, *Works*, ed. Shedd, Vol. 4, pp. 387–388.

X

THOMAS DE QUINCEY (1785-1859)

Style, Part IV (1841)

[De Quincey's essay on *Style*, in four successive papers, was first published in *Blackwood's Magazine* for July, September, and October, 1840, and February, 1841, was reprinted in Volume 11 of De Quincey's *Collective Writings*, and may be found in Volume 10 of the standard edition of his *Works* by Professor Masson, London, Black, 1897 (pp. 134-245). Together with the same author's essays on *Rhetoric* and *Language*, it has been edited by Professor F. N. Scott (Boston, Allyn & Bacon, 1893) in a fashion that leaves little to be desired. The student who wishes a critical apparatus must be referred to the excellent materials collected by Professor Scott, for, on account of the bulk and discursiveness of De Quincey's essay itself, an extended commentary, even on Part IV, is out of the question here.

In spite of its unrestrained digressions, this essay remains one of the notable modern contributions on the subject of literary style, full of brilliant suggestion, and, if not in itself either systematic or painfully exact, yet stimulating to further, scientific, research. It is stimulating in part through its incompleteness. For the long, heterogeneous preamble making up the first three papers in *Blackwood* seems to have been intended as preparatory to a discussion decidedly more extensive than the rather hastily concluded Part IV, in which De Quincey brings together his *results*.

Although the Opium-Eater is often at the mercy of his own habitual mannerisms, no English writer of a recent period has received more praise simply on the score of style. Out of a considerable literature touching on his style or dealing with it directly, may be noted: Minto, *Manual of English Prose Literature;* M. H. Turk, *Selections from De Quincey* (Ginn, Athenæum Press); J. M. Hart, *Joan of Arc, The English Mail-Coach*, etc. (Holt).]

P

" *Such being the state of preparation, what was the result?* "
These words concluded our last essay. There had been
two manifestations or bright epiphanies of the Grecian intellect, revelations in two separate forms: the first having
gathered about Pericles in the year 444 B.C., the second about
Alexander the Great in 333 B.C.; the first being a pure literature of creative power, the second in a great measure of
reflective power; the first fitted to call out the differences
of style, the second to observe, classify, and discuss them.
Under these circumstances of favorable preparation, what
had been the result? Where style exists in strong coloring
as a practice or art, we reasonably expect that style should
soon follow as a theory, as a science explaining that art,
tracing its varieties, and teaching its rules. To use ancient
distinctions, where the " *rhetorica utens* " has been cultivated
with eminent success (as in early Greece it had) it is but
natural to expect many consequent attempts at a " *rhetorica
docens.*" And especially it is natural to do so in a case where
the theorizing intellect had been powerfully awakened.
What, therefore, we ask again, had been in fact the result?

We must acknowledge that it had fallen far below the
reasonable standard of our expectations. Greece, it is
true, produced a long series of works on rhetoric, many of
which, though not easily met with,* survive to this day;
and one which stands first in order of time, viz. the great
work of Aristotle, is of such distinguished merit that some
eminent moderns have not scrupled to rank it as the very
foremost legacy in point of psychological knowledge which

---

* " *Not easily met with* " : — From Germany we have seen reprints of some
eight or nine; but once only, so far as our bibliography extends, were the
whole body published collectively. This was at the Aldine press in Venice
more than three centuries ago. Such an interval, and so solitary a publication, sufficiently explain the non-familiarity of modern scholars with this
section of Greek literature.

Pagan Literature has bequeathed to us. Without entering upon so large a comparison as that, we readily admit the commanding talent which this work displays. But it is under an equivocal use of the word " rhetoric " that the *Rhetoric* of Aristotle could ever have been classed with books treating of style. There is in fact a complex distinction to which the word Rhetoric is liable. 1st, it means the *rhetorica utens*, as when we praise the rhetoric of Seneca or Sir Thomas Browne, not meaning anything which they taught, but something which they practised, — not a doctrine which they delivered, but a machinery of composition which they employed. 2dly, it means the *rhetorica docens*, as when we praise the Rhetoric of Aristotle or Hermogenes, writers far enough from being rhetorical by their own style of writing,[1] but writers who professedly taught others to be rhetorical. 3dly, the *rhetorica utens* itself is subdivided into two meanings, so wide apart that they have very little bearing on each other: one being applied to the art of persuasion, the dexterous use of plausible topics for recommending any opinion whatever to the favor of an audience (this is the Grecian sense universally); the other being applied to the art of composition, the art of treating any subject ornamentally, gracefully, affectingly. There is another use of the word rhetoric distinct from all these, and hitherto, we believe, not consciously noticed; of which at some other time.

Now, this last subdivision of the word rhetoric, viz. " Rhetoric considered as a practising art, *rhetorica utens*," — which is the sense exclusively indicated by our modern use of the term, — is not at all concerned in the Rhetoric of Aristotle. It is rhetoric as a mode of moral suasion, as a technical system for obtaining a readiness in giving to the false a coloring of plausibility, to the doubtful a coloring of probability, or in giving to the true, when it happens to be ob-

scure, the benefit of a convincing exposition, — this it is
which Aristotle undertakes to teach, and not at all the art
of ornamental composition.   In fact, it is the whole body of
public *extempore* speakers whom he addresses, not the body
of deliberate writers in any section whatever.   And, therefore,
whilst conceding readily all the honor which is claimed for
that great man's Rhetoric, by this one distinction as to what
it was that he meant by Rhetoric, we evade at once all necessity for modifying our general proposition, — viz. that style
in our modern sense, as a theory of composition, as an art
of constructing sentences and weaving them into coherent
wholes, was not effectually cultivated amongst the Greeks.
It was not so well understood, nor so distinctly contemplated
in the light of a separate accomplishment, as afterwards
among the Romans.   And we repeat that this result from
circumstances *prima facie* so favorable to the very opposite
result is highly remarkable.   It is *so* remarkable that we shall
beg permission to linger a little upon those features in the
Greek Literature which most of all might seem to have war-
ranted our expecting from Greece the very consummation of
this delicate art.   For these same features, which would
separately have justified that expectation, may happen, when
taken in combination with others, to account for its disappointment.

There is, then, amongst the earliest phenomena of the
Greek Literature, and during its very inaugural period, one
which of itself and singly furnishes a presumption for expecting an exquisite investigation of style.   It lies in the fact
that two out of the three great tragic poets carried his own
characteristic quality of style to a morbid excess, — to such an
excess as should force itself, and in fact *did* force itself, into
popular notice.   Had these poets all alike exhibited that sustained and equable tenor of tragic style which we find in

Sophocles, it is not probable that the vulgar attention would have been fixed by its character. Where a standard of splendor is much raised, provided all parts are simultaneously raised on the same uniform scale, we know by repeated experience in many modes of display, whether in dress, in architecture, in the embellishment of rooms, &c., that this raising of the standard is not perceived with much vivacity, and that the feelings of the spectator are soon reconciled to alterations that are harmonized. It is always by some want of uniformity, some defect in following out the scale, that we become roused to conscious observation of the difference between this and our former standards. We exaggerate these differences in such a case as much as we undervalue them in a case where all is symmetrical. We might expect, therefore, beforehand, that the opposite characteristics as to style of Æschylus and Euripides would force themselves upon the notice of the Athenian populace; and, in fact, we learn from the Greek scholiasts on these poets that this effect did really follow. These scholiasts, indeed, belong to a later age. But we know by traditions which they have preserved, and we know from Aristotle himself, the immediate successor of the great tragic poets (indirectly we know also from the stormy ridicule of Aristophanes, who may be viewed as contemporary with those poets), that Æschylus was notorious to a proverb amongst the very mob for the stateliness, pomp, and towering character of his diction, whilst Euripides was equally notorious not merely for a diction in a lower key, more household, more natural, less elaborate, but also for cultivating such a diction by study and deliberate preference. Having such great models of contrasting style to begin with, having the attention converged upon these differences by the furious merriment of Aristophanes, less than a Grecian wit would have felt a challenge in all this to the investigation of style, as a great organ of difference between man and man, between poet and poet.

But there was a more enduring reason in the circumstances of Greece for entitling us to expect from her the perfect theory of style. It lay in those accidents of time and place which obliged Greece to spin most of her speculations, like a spider, out of her own bowels. Now, for such a kind of literature style is, generally speaking, paramount; for a literature less self-evolved style is more liable to neglect. Modern nations have labored under the very opposite disadvantage. The excess of external materials has sometimes oppressed their creative power, and sometimes their meditative power. The exuberance of *objective* knowledge — that knowledge which carries the mind to materials existing *out* of itself, such as natural philosophy, chemistry, physiology, astronomy, geology, where the mind of the student goes for little and the external object for much — has had the effect of weaning men from subjective speculation, where the mind is all in all and the alien object next to nothing, and in that degree has weaned them from the culture of style. Now, on the other hand, if you suppose a man in the situation of Baron Trenck at Spandau, or Spinoza in the situation of Robinson Crusoe at Juan Fernandez, or a contemplative monk of the thirteenth century in his cell, you will perceive that — unless he were a poor feeble-minded creature like Cowper's Bastille prisoner, thrown by utter want of energy upon counting the very nails of his dungeon in all permutations and combinations — rather than quit the external world, he must in his own defence, were it only as a relief from gnawing thoughts, cultivate some *subjective* science; that is, some branch of knowledge which, drawing everything from the mind itself, is independent of external resources. Such a science is found in the relations of man to God, — that is in theology; in the determinations

of space, — that is in geometry; in the relations of existence
or being universally to the human mind, — otherwise called
metaphysics or ontology; in the relations of the mind to itself,
— otherwise called logic. Hence it was that the scholastic
philosophy evolved itself, like a vast spider's loom, between
the years 1100 and 1400. Men shut up in solitude, with the
education oftentimes of scholars, with a life of leisure, but
with hardly any books, and no means of observation, were
absolutely forced, if they would avoid lunacy from energies
unoccupied with any object, to create an object out of those
very energies: they were driven by mere pressure of solitude,
and sometimes of eternal silence, into raising vast aërial
Jacob's ladders of vapory metaphysics, just as endless as
those meteorologic phenomena which technically bear that
name, just as sublime and aspiring in their tendency upwards,
and sometimes (but not always) just as unsubstantial. In
this present world of the practical and the ponderable, we so
little understand or value such abstractions, though once our
British schoolmen took the lead in these subtleties, that we
confound their very natures and names. Most people with us
mean by metaphysics what is properly called psychology.
Now, these two are so far from being the same thing that the
former could be pursued (and, to say the truth, was, in fact,
under Aristotle created) by the monk in his unfurnished cell,
where nothing ever entered but moonbeams. Whereas psychology is but in part a subjective science; in some proportion
it is also *objective*, depending on multiplied experience, or
on multiplied records of experience. Psychology, therefore,
could not have been cultivated extensively by the schoolmen,
and in fact would not have been cultivated at all but for the
precedent of Aristotle. He, who laid the foundation of their
metaphysics, which have nothing to do with man, had also
written a work on man, — viz. on the human soul, — besides

other smaller works on particular psychological phenomena (such as dreaming). Hence, through mere imitation, arose the short sketches of psychology amongst the schoolmen. Else *their* vocation lay to metaphysics, as a science which can dance upon moonbeams; and that vocation arose entirely out of their circumstances, — solitude, scholarship, and no books. Total extinction there was for them of all objective materials, and therefore, as a consequence inevitable, reliance on the solitary energies of their own minds. Like Christabel's chamber lamp, and the angels from which it was suspended, all was the invention of the unprompted artist, —

" All made out of the carver's brain."

Models he had none before him, for printed books were yet sleeping in futurity, and the gates of a grand asceticism were closed upon the world of life. We moderns, indeed, fancy that the necessities of the Romish Church—the mere instincts of self-protection in Popery — were what offered the bounty on this air-woven philosophy; and partly that is true; but it is most certain that all the bounties in this world would have failed to operate effectually, had they not met with those circumstances in the silent life of monasteries which favored the growth of such a self-spun metaphysical divinity. Monastic life predisposed the restlessness of human intellect to move in that direction. It was one of the few directions compatible with solitude and penury of books. It was the only one that opened an avenue at once to novelty and to freedom of thought. Now, then, precisely what the monastic life of the schoolmen was in relation to Philosophy, the Greece of Pericles had been in relation to Literature. What circumstances, what training, or predisposing influences existed for the monk in his cell, the same (or such as were tantamount) existed for the Grecian wit in the atmosphere of Athens.

Three great agencies were at work, and unconsciously moulding the efforts of the earliest schoolmen about the opening of
the Crusades, and of the latest some time after their close; —
three analogous agencies, the same in virtue, though varied
in circumstances, gave impulse and guidance to the men of
Greece, from Pericles, at the opening of Greek literature, to
Alexander of Macedon, who witnessed its second harvest.
And these agencies were: — 1*st*, Leisure in excess, with a
teeming intellect; the burden, under a new-born excitement,
of having nothing to do. 2*d*, Scarcity, without an absolute
famine, of books; enough to awake the dormant cravings,
but not enough to gratify them without personal participation in the labors of intellectual creation. 3*d*, A revolutionary
restlessness, produced by the recent establishment of a new
and growing public interest.

The two first of these agencies for stimulating intellects
already roused by agitating changes are sufficiently obvious;
though few perhaps are aware to what extent idleness prevailed in Pagan Greece, and even in Rome, under the system
of household slavery, and under the bigoted contempt of
commerce. But, waiving that point, and for the moment
waiving also the degree of scarcity which affected books at the
era of Pericles, we must say one word as to the two great
analogous public interests which had formed themselves
separately, and with a sense of revolutionary power, for the
Greeks on the one hand, and for the Schoolmen on the other.
As respected the Grecians, and especially the Athenians, this
excitement lay in the sentiment of nationality which had been
first powerfully organized by the Persian War. Previously
to that war the sentiment no doubt smouldered obscurely;
but the oriental invasion it was which kindled it into a torrent of flame. And it is interesting to remark that the very
same cause which fused and combined these scattered tribes

into the unity of Hellas, viz. their common interest in making head against an awful invader, was also the cause which most of all separated them into local parties by individual rivalship and by characteristic services. The arrogant Spartan, mad with a French-like self-glorification, boasted forever of his little Thermopylæ. Ten years earlier the far sublimer display of Athenian Marathon, to say nothing of after-services at Salamis or elsewhere, had placed Attica at the summit of the Greek family. No matter whether selfish jealousy would allow that preëminence to be recognized; doubtless it was felt. With this civic preëminence arose concurrently for Athens the development of an intellectual preëminence. On this we need say nothing. But even here, although the preëminence was too dazzling to have been at any time overlooked, yet, with some injustice in every age to Athens, her light has been recognized, but not what gave it value, — the contrasting darkness of all around her. This did not escape Paterculus, whose understanding is always vigilant. " We talk," says he, " of *Grecian* eloquence or *Grecian* poetry, when we should say *Attic;* for who has ever heard of Theban orators, of Lacedæmonian artists, or Corinthian poets ? " * Æschylus, the first great author of Athens (for Herodotus was not Athenian), personally fought in the Persian War. Consequently the two modes of glory for Athens were almost of simultaneous emergence. And

---

* People will here remind us that Aristotle was half a foreigner, being born at Stagira in Macedon. Ay, but amongst Athenian emigrants, and of an Athenian father! His mother, we think, was Thracian. The crossing of races almost uniformly terminates in producing splendor, at any rate energy, of intellect. If the roll of great men, or at least of energetic men, in Christendom were carefully examined, it would astonish us to observe how many have been the children of mixed marriages, — *i.e.* of alliances between two bloods as to nation, although the races might originally have been the same.

what we are now wishing to insist on is that precisely by and through this great unifying event, viz. the double inroad of Asia militant upon Greece, Greece first became generally and reciprocally known to Greece herself; that Greece was then first arranged and *cast*, as it were dramatically, according to her capacities, services, duties; that a general consciousness was then diffused of the prevailing relations in which each political family stood to the rest; and that in the leading states every intellectual citizen drew a most agitating excitement from the particular character of glory which had settled upon his own tribe, and the particular station which had devolved upon it amongst the champions of civilization.

That was the *positive* force acting upon Athens. Now, reverting to the monkish schoolmen, in order to complete the parallel, what was the corresponding force acting upon *them* ? Leisure and want of books were accidents common to both parties, — to the scholastic age and to the age of Pericles. These were the *negative* forces, concurring with others to sustain a movement once begun, but incapable of giving the original impulse. What was the active, the *affirmative*, force which effected for the scholastic monks that unity and sense of common purposes which had been effected for the Greeks by the sudden development of a Grecian interest opposed to a Persian, — of a civilized interest, under sudden peril, opposed to the barbarism of the universal planet ? What was there, for the race of monkish schoolmen laboring through three centuries, in the nature of a known palpable interest, which could balance so grand a principle of union and of effort as this acknowledged guardianship of civilization had suddenly unfolded, like a banner, for the Greeks during the infancy of Pericles ?* What *could* there be of corresponding grandeur?

---

* It is well to give unity to our grandest remembrances by connecting them, as many as can be, with the same centre. Pericles died in the year 429

Beforehand, this should have seemed impossible: but, in reality, a far grander mode of interest had arisen for the schoolmen: grander, because more indefinite; more indefinite, because spiritual. It was this:—The Western or Latin Church had slowly developed her earthly power. As an edifice of civil greatness throughout the western world, she stood erect and towering. In the eleventh century, beyond all others, she had settled her deep foundations. The work thus far was complete; but blank civil power, though indispensable, was the feeblest of her arms, and, taken separately, was too frail to last, besides that it was liable to revolutions. The authority by which chiefly she ruled, had ruled, and hoped to rule, was spiritual; and, with the growing institutions of the age, embodying so much of future resistance, it was essential that this spiritual influence should be founded on a subtle philosophy, difficult to learn, difficult to refute; as also that many dogmas already established, such as tradition by way of prop to infallibility, should receive a far ampler development. The Latin Church, we must remember, was not yet that Church of Papal Rome, in the maturity of its doctrines and its pretensions, which it afterwards became. And, when we consider how vast a benefactress this Church had been to early Christendom when moulding and settling her foundations, as also in what light she must have appeared to her own pious children in centuries where as yet only the first local breezes of opposition had begun to whisper amongst the Albigenses, &c., we are bound in all candor to see that a sublimer interest could not have existed for any series of philosophers than the profound persuasion that by marrying metaphysics to divinity, two sciences even separately

before Christ. Supposing his age to be fifty-six, he would then be born about 485 B.C., — that is, five years after the first Persian invasion under Darius, five years before the second under Xerxes.

so grand, and by the pursuit of labyrinthine truth, they were building up an edifice reaching to the heavens, — the great spiritual fortress of the Catholic Church.

Here let us retrace the course of our speculations, lest the reader should suppose us to be wandering.

First, for the sake of illustrating more vividly the influences which acted on the Greece of Pericles, we bring forward another case analogously circumstanced, as moulded by the same causes: — 1. The same condition of intellect under revolutionary excitement; 2. The same penury of books; 3. The same chilling gloom from the absence of female charities, — the consequent reaction of that oppressive *ennui* which Helvetius fancied, amongst all human agencies, to be the most potent stimulant for the intellect; 4. The same (though far different) enthusiasm and elevation of thought from disinterested participation in forwarding a great movement of the age: for the one side involving the glory of their own brilliant country and concurrent with civilization; for the other, coextensive with all spiritual truth and all spiritual power.

Next, we remark that men living permanently under such influences must, of mere necessity, resort to that order of intellectual pursuits which réquires little aid *ab extra,* — that order, in fact, which philosophically is called "subjective," as drawing much from our own proper selves, or little (if anything) from extraneous objects.

And then, thirdly, we remark that such pursuits are peculiarly favorable to the culture of style. In fact they force that culture. A man who has absolute facts to communicate from some branch of study external to himself, as physiology, suppose, or anatomy, or astronomy, is careless of style; or at least he may be so, because he is independent of style, for what he has to communicate neither readily admits, nor much needs, any graces in the mode of communication; the matter transcends and oppresses the manner. The matter tells without any manner at all. But he who has to treat a vague question, such as Cicero calls a *quæstio infinita*, where everything is to be finished out of his own peculiar feelings, or his own way of viewing things (in contradistinction to a *quæstio finita*, where determinate *data* from without already furnish the main materials), soon finds that the manner of treating it not only transcends the matter, but very often, and in a very great proportion, *is* the matter. In very many subjective exercises of the mind, — as, for instance, in that class of poetry which has been formally designated by this epithet (meditative poetry,[2] we mean, in opposition to the Homeric, which is intensely objective), the problem before the writer is to project his own inner mind; to bring out consciously what yet lurks by involution in many unanalyzed feelings; in short, to pass through a prism and radiate into distinct elements what previously had been even to himself but dim and confused ideas intermixed with each other. Now, in such cases, the skill with which detention or conscious arrest is given to the evanescent, external projection to what is internal, outline to what is fluxionary, and body to what is vague, — all this depends entirely on the command over language as the one sole means of embodying ideas; and in such cases the style, or, in the largest sense, *manner*, is confluent with the matter. But, at all events, even by those who are most impatient of any subtleties, or what they consider " metaphysical " distinctions, thus much must be conceded: viz. that those who rest upon external facts, tangible realities, and circumstantial details, — in short, generally upon the *objective*, whether in a case of narration or of argument, — must forever be less dependent upon style than those who have to draw upon their own understandings

and their own peculiar feelings for the furniture and matter of
their composition. A single illustration will make this plain.
It is an old remark, and, in fact, a subject of continual experience, that lawyers fail as public speakers in the House of
Commons. Even Erskine, the greatest of modern advocates,
was nobody as a senator; and the " fluent Murray," two
generations before him, had found his fluency give way under
that mode of trial. But why? How was it possible that a
man's fluency in one chamber of public business should thus
suddenly be defeated and confounded in another? The
reason is briefly expressed in Cicero's distinction between a
quæstio finita and a *quæstio infinita*. In the courts of law,
the orator was furnished with a brief, an abstract of facts,
downright statements upon oath, circumstances of presumption, and, in short, a whole volume of topics external to his
own mind. Sometimes, it is true, the advocate would
venture a little out to sea *proprio marte:* in a case of *crim.
con.*, for instance, he would attempt a little picture of domestic happiness drawn from his own funds. But he was
emboldened to do this from his certain knowledge that in the
facts of his brief he had always a hasty retreat in case of any
danger that he should founder. If the little picture prospered,
it was well: if not, if symptoms of weariness began to arise in
the audience, or of hesitation in himself, it was but to cut the
matter short, and return to the *terra firma* of his brief, when all
again was fluent motion. Besides that, each separate transition, and the distribution of the general subject, offered
themselves spontaneously in a law case; the logic was given
as well as the method. Very often the mere order of chro-
nology dictated the succession and arrangement of the topics.
Now, on the other hand, in a House of Commons oration,
although sometimes there may occur statements of fact and
operose calculations, still these are never more than a text,

at the very best, for the political discussion, but often no
more than a subsequent illustration or proof attached to
some one of its heads. The main staple of any long speech
must always be some general view of national policy; and,
in Cicero's language, such a view must always be *infinita;*
that is, not determined *ab extra*, but shaped and drawn from
the funds of one's own understanding. The facts are here
subordinate and ministerial; in the case before a jury the
facts are all in all. The forensic orator satisfies his duty if he
does but take the facts exactly as they stand in his brief, and
place them before his audience in that order, and even (if he
should choose it) in those words. The parliamentary orator
has no opening for facts at all, but as he himself may be able
to create such an opening by some previous expositions of
doctrine or opinion, of the probable or expedient. The one
is always creeping along shore; the other is always out at sea.
Accordingly, the degrees of anxiety which severally affect the
two cases are best brought to the test in this one question —
" *What shall I say next?* " — an anxiety besetting orators like
that which besets poor men in respect to their children's
daily bread. "This moment it is secured; but, alas for the
next!" Now, the judicial orator finds an instant relief: the
very points of the case are numbered; and, if he cannot find
more to say upon No. 7, he has only to pass on and call up
No. 8. Whereas the deliberative orator, in a senate or a
literary meeting, finds himself always in this situation, —
that, having reached with difficulty that topic which we have
supposed to be No. 7, one of three cases uniformly occurs:
either he does not perceive any No. 8 at all; or, secondly, he
sees a distracting choice of No. 8's — the ideas to which he
might next pass are many, but he does not see whither they
will lead him; or, thirdly, he sees a very fair and promising
No. 8, but cannot in any way discover off-hand how he is to

effect a transition to this new topic. He cannot, with the rapidity requisite, modulate out of the one key into the other. His anxiety increases, utter confusion masters him, and he breaks down.

We have made this digression by way of seeking, in a well-known case of public life, an illustration of the difference between a subjective and an objective exercise of the mind. It is the sudden translation from the one exercise to the other which, and which only, accounts for the failure of advocates when attempting senatorial efforts. Once used to depend on memorials or briefs of facts, or of evidence not self-derived, the advocate, like a child in leading-strings, loses that command over his own internal resources which otherwise he might have drawn from practice. In fact, the advocate, with his brief lying before him, is precisely in the condition of a parliamentary speaker who places a written speech or notes for a speech in his hat. This trick has sometimes been practised; and the consternation which would befall the orator in the case of such a hat-speech being suddenly blown away precisely realizes the situation of a *nisi prius* orator when first getting on his legs in the House of Commons. He has swum with bladders all his life: suddenly he must swim without them.

This case explains why it is that all subjective branches of study favor the cultivation of style. Whatsoever is entirely independent of the mind, and external to it, is generally equal to its own enunciation. Ponderable facts and external realities are intelligible in almost any language: they are self-explained and self-sustained. But, the more closely any exercise of mind is connected with what is internal and individual in the sensibilities,—that is, with what is philosophically termed *subjective*,—precisely in that degree, and the more subtly, does the style or the embodying of the thoughts cease to be a mere separable ornament, and in fact the more

Q

does the manner, as we expressed it before, become confluent with the matter. In saying this, we do but vary the form of what we once heard delivered on this subject by Mr. Wordsworth. His remark was by far the weightiest thing we ever heard on the subject of style; and it was this: that it is in the highest degree unphilosophic to call language or diction " the *dress* of thoughts." And what was it then that he would substitute? Why this: he would call it " the *incarnation* of thoughts." Never in one word was so profound a truth conveyed. Mr. Wordsworth was thinking, doubtless, of poetry like his own: viz. that which is eminently meditative. And the truth is apparent on consideration: for, if language were merely a dress, then you could separate the two; you could lay the thoughts on the left hand, the language on the right. But, generally speaking, you can no more deal thus with poetic thoughts than you can with soul and body. The union is too subtle, the intertexture too ineffable, — each coexisting not merely *with* the other, but each *in* and *through* the other. An image, for instance, a single word, often enters into a thought as a constituent part. In short, the two elements are not united as a body with a separable dress, but as a mysterious incarnation. And thus, in what proportion the thoughts are subjective, in that same proportion does the very essence become identical with the expression, and the style become confluent with the matter.

The Greeks, by want of books, philosophical instruments, and innumerable other aids to all objective researches, being thrown more exclusively than we upon their own unaided minds, cultivated logic, ethics, metaphysics, psychology, — all thoroughly subjective studies. The schoolmen, in the very same situation, cultivated precisely the same field of knowledge. The Greeks, indeed, added to their studies that of geometry; for the inscription over the gate of the Academy

("Let no one enter who is not instructed in geometry")
sufficiently argues that this science must have made some
progress in the days of Pericles, when it could thus be made a
general qualification for admission to a learned establishment
within thirty years after his death. But geometry is partly
an objective, partly a subjective, study. With this exception,
the Greeks and the Monastic Schoolmen trod the very same
path.

Consequently, in agreement with our principle, both ought
to have found themselves in circumstances favorable to the
cultivation of style. And it is certain that they did. As an
art, as a practice, it was felicitously pursued in both cases. It
is true that the harsh ascetic mode of treating philosophy by
the schoolmen generated a corresponding barrenness, aridity,
and repulsiveness, in the rigid forms of their technical language. But, however offensive to genial sensibilities, this
diction was a perfect thing in its kind; and, to do it justice,
we ought rather to compare it with the exquisite language of
algebra, — equally irreconcilable to all standards of æsthetic
beauty;[3] but yet, for the three qualities of elliptical rapidity
(that rapidity which constitutes very much of what is meant
by *elegance* in mathematics), of absolute precision, and of simplicity, this algebraic language is unrivalled amongst human
inventions. On the other hand, the Greeks, whose objects
did not confine them to these austere studies, carried out their
corresponding excellence in style upon a far wider, and indeed
a comprehensive, scale. Almost all modes of style were
exemplified amongst *them*. Thus we endeavor to show that
the subjective pursuits of the Greeks and the Schoolmen ought
to have favored a command of appropriate diction; and
afterwards that it did.

But, *fourthly*, we are entitled to expect that, wherever style
exists in great development as a practice, it will soon be

investigated with corresponding success as a theory. If fine music is produced spontaneously in short snatches by the musical sensibility of a people, it is a matter of certainty that the science of composition, that counterpoint, that thorough-bass, will soon be cultivated with a commensurate zeal. This is matter of such obvious inference that in any case where it fails we look for some extraordinary cause to account for it. Now, in Greece, with respect to style, the inference *did* fail. Style, as an art, was in a high state of culture; style, as a science, was nearly neglected. How is this to be accounted for? It arose naturally enough out of one great phenomenon in the condition of ancient times, and the relation which that bore to literature and to all human exertion of the intellect.

Did the reader ever happen to reflect on the great idea of *publication?* An idea we call it; because even in our own times, with all the mechanic aids of steam-presses, &c., this object is most imperfectly approached, and is destined, perhaps, forever to remain an unattainable ideal, — useful (like all ideals) in the way of regulating our aims, but also as a practicable object not reconcilable with the limitation of human power. For it is clear that, if books were multiplied by a thousandfold, and truths of all kinds were carried to the very fireside of every family, — nay, placed below the eyes of every individual, — still the purpose of any universal publication would be defeated and utterly confounded, were it only by the limited opportunities of readers. One condition of publication defeats another. Even so much as a general publication is a hopeless idea. Yet, on the other hand, publication in some degree, and by some mode, is a *sine qua non* condition for the generation of literature. Without a larger sympathy than that of his own personal circle, it is evident that no writer could have a motive for those exertions and previous preparations without which excellence is not attainable in any art whatsoever.

Now, in our own times, it is singular, and really philosophically curious, to remark the utter blindness of writers, readers, publishers, and all parties whatever interested in literature, as to the trivial fraction of publicity which settles upon each separate work. The very multiplication of books has continually defeated the object in growing progression. Readers have increased, the engines of publication have increased; but books, increasing in a still greater proportion, have left as the practical result an average quotient of publicity for each book, taken apart, continually decreasing. And, if the whole world were readers, probably the average publicity for each separate work would reach a *minimum;* such would be the concurrent increase of books. But even this view of the case keeps out of sight the most monstrous forms of this phenomenon. The inequality of the publication has the effect of keeping very many books absolutely without a reader. The majority of books are never opened; five hundred copies may be printed, or half as many more; of these it may happen that five are carelessly turned over. Popular journals, again, which carry a promiscuous miscellany of papers into the same number of hands, as a stage-coach must convey all its passengers at the same rate of speed, dupe the public with a notion that here at least all are read. Not at all. One or two are read from the interest attached to their subjects. Occasionally one is read a little from the ability with which it treats a subject not otherwise attractive. The rest have a better chance certainly than books, because they are at any rate placed under the eye and in the hand of readers. But this is no more than a variety of the same case. A hasty glance may be taken by one in a hundred at the less attractive papers; but reading is out of the question. Then, again, another delusion, by which all parties disguise the truth, is the absurd belief that, not being read at present, a book may, however, be revived hereafter. Believe it not! This is possible only with regard to books that demand to be studied, where the merit is slowly discovered. Every month, every day indeed, produces its own novelties, with the additional zest that they *are* novelties. Every future year, which will assuredly fail in finding time for its own books, — how should it find time for defunct books? No, no; every year buries its own literature. Since Waterloo there have been added upwards of fifty thousand books and pamphlets to the shelves of our *native* literature, taking no account of foreign importations. Of these fifty thousand possibly two hundred still survive; possibly twenty will survive for a couple of centuries; possibly five or six thousand may have been indifferently read; the rest not so much as opened. In this hasty sketch of a calulation we assume a single copy to represent a whole edition. But, in order to have the total sum of copies numerically neglected since Waterloo, it will be requisite to multiply forty-four thousand by five hundred at the least, but probably by a higher multiplier. At the very moment of writing this — by way of putting into a brighter light the inconceivable blunder as to publicity habitually committed by sensible men of the world — let us mention what we now see before us in a public journal. Speaking with disapprobation of a just but disparaging expression applied to the French war-mania by a London morning paper, the writer has described it as likely to irritate the people of France. O genius of arithmetic! The offending London journal has a circulation of four thousand copies daily; and it is assumed that thirty-three millions, of whom assuredly not twenty-five individuals will ever see the English paper as a visible object nor five ever read the passage in question, are to be mad-

dened by one word in a colossal paper laid this morning
on a table amongst fifty others, and to-morrow morning
pushed off that table by fifty others of more recent date.
How are such delusions possible? Simply from the previous
delusion, of ancient standing, connected with printed characters: what is printed seems to every man invested with
some fatal character of publicity such as cannot belong to
mere MS. ; whilst, in the meantime, out of every thousand
printed pages, one at the most, but at all events a very small
proportion indeed, is in any true sense more public when
printed than previously as a manuscript; and that one, even
that thousandth part, perishes as effectually in a few days to
each separate reader as the words perish in our daily conversation. Out of all that we talk, or hear others talk, through
the course of a year, how much remains on the memory at
the closing day of December? Quite as little, we may be
sure, survives from most people's reading. A book answers
its purpose by sustaining the intellectual faculties in motion
through the current act of reading, and a general deposition or
settling takes effect from the sum of what we read; even that,
however, chiefly according to the previous condition in which
the book finds us for understanding it, and referring them to
heads under some existing arrangement of our knowledge.
Publication is an idle term applied to what is not published;
and nothing is *published* which is not made known *publicly*
to the understanding as well as the eye; whereas, for the
enormous majority of what is printed, we cannot say so much
as that it is made known to the eyes.

For what reason have we insisted on this unpleasant view
of a phenomenon incident to the limitation of our faculties,
and apparently without remedy? Upon another occasion it
might have been useful to do so, were it only to impress upon
every writer the vast importance of compression. Simply to

retrench one word from each sentence, one superfluous epithet, for example, would probably increase the disposable time of the public by one-twelfth part; in other words, would add another month to the year, or raise any sum of volumes read from eleven to twelve hundred. A mechanic operation would effect *that* change; but, by cultivating a closer logic and more severe habits of thinking, perhaps two sentences out of each three might be pruned away, and the amount of possible publication might thus be increased in a threefold degree. A most serious duty, therefore, and a duty which is annually growing in solemnity, appears to be connected with the culture of an unwordy diction; much more, however, with the culture of clear thinking, — that being the main key to good writing, and consequently to fluent reading.

But all this, though not unconnected with our general theme, is wide of our immediate purpose. The course of our logic at this point runs in the following order. The Athenians, from causes assigned, ought to have consummated the whole science and theory of style. But they did *not.* Why? Simply from a remarkable deflection or bias given to their studies by a difficulty connected with *publication.* For some modes of literature the Greeks *had* a means of publication, for many they had *not.* That one difference, as we shall show, disturbed the just valuation of style.

Some mode of publication must have existed for Athens: that is evident. The mere *fact* of a literature proves it. For without public sympathy how can a literature arise? or public sympathy without a regular organ of publication? What poet would submit to the labors of his most difficult art, if he had no reasonable prospect of a large audience, and some-what of a permanent audience, to welcome and adopt his productions?

Now then, in the Athens of Pericles, what *was* the audience, how composed, and how insured, on which the literary composer might rely? By what channel, in short, did the Athenian writer calculate on a *publication?* This is a very interesting question, and, as regards much in the civilization of Greece, both for what it caused and what it prevented, is an important question. In the elder days, — in fact we may suppose through the five hundred years from the Trojan expedition to Pisistratus and Solon, — all *publication* was effected through two classes of men: the public reciters and the public singers. Thus, no doubt, it was that the Iliad and Odyssey were sent down to the hands of Pisistratus, who has the traditional reputation of having first arranged and revised these poems. These reciters or singers to the harp would probably rehearse one entire book of the Iliad at every splendid banquet. Every book would be kept in remembrance and currency by the peculiar local relations of particular states or particular families to ancestors connected with Troy. This mode of publication, however, had the disadvantage that it was among the arts ministerial to sensual enjoyment. And it is some argument for the extensive diffusion of such a practice in the early times of Greece that, both in the Greece of later times, and, by adoption from her, in the Rome of cultivated ages, we find the ἀκροαματα as commonly established by way of a dinner appurtenance — that is, exercises of display addressed to the ear, recitations of any kind with and without music — not at all less frequently than ὁραματα, or the corresponding display to the eye (dances or combats of gladiators). These were doubtless inheritances from the ancient usages of Greece, — modes of publication resorted to long before the Olympic Games by the mere necessitous cravings for sympathy, and kept up long after that institution, as in itself too brief and rare in its recurrence to satisfy the necessity.

Such was the earliest effort of publication, and in its feeble infancy; for this, besides its limitation in point of audience, was confined to narrative poetry. But, when the ideal of Greece was more and more exalted by nearer comparison with barbarous standards, after the sentiment of patriotism had coalesced with vindictive sentiments, and when towering cities began to reflect the grandeur of this land as in a visual mirror, these cravings for publicity became more restless and irrepressible. And at length, in the time of Pericles, concurrently with the external magnificence of the city, arose for Athens two modes of publication, each upon a scale of gigantic magnitude.

What were these? The *Theatre* and the *Agora* or *Forum:* publication by the Stage, and publication by the Hustings. These were the extraordinary modes of publication which arose for Athens: one by a sudden birth, like that of Minerva, in the very generation of Pericles; the other slowly maturing itself from the generation of Pisistratus, which preceded that of Pericles by a hundred years. This double publication, scenic and forensic, was virtually, and for all the loftier purposes of publication, the press of Athens. And, however imperfect a representative this may seem of a typographical publication, certain it is that in some important features the Athenian publication had separate advantages of its own. It was a far more effective and correct publication in the first place, enjoying every aid of powerful accompaniment from voice, gesture, scenery, music, and suffering in no instance from false reading or careless reading. Then, secondly, it was a far wider publication: each drama being read (or heard, which is a far better thing) by 25,000 or 30,000 persons, counterbalancing at least forty editions such as we on an average publish; each oration being delivered with just emphasis to perhaps 7000. But why, in this mention of a stage or hustings publication, as opposed to a publication by the printing-press, why was it, we are naturally admonished to ask, that the Greeks had no press? The ready answer will be, — because the art of printing had not been discovered. But that is an error, the detection of which we owe to the present Archbishop of Dublin. The art of printing *was* discovered. It had been discovered repeatedly. The art which multiplied the legends upon a coin or medal (a work which the ancients performed by many degrees better than we moderns, — for we make it a mechanic art, they a fine art) had in effect anticipated the art of printing.[4] It was an art, this typographic mystery, which awoke and went back to sleep many times over from mere defect of materials. Not the defect of typography as an art, but the defect of *paper* as a material for keeping this art in motion, — *there* lay the reason, as Dr. Whately most truly observes, why printed books had no existence amongst the Greeks of Pericles, or afterwards amongst the Romans of Cicero. And why was there no paper? The common reason applying to both countries was the want of linen rags, and that want arose from the universal habit of wearing woolen garments. In this respect Athens and Rome were on the same level. But for Athens the want was driven to a further extremity by the slenderness of her commerce with Egypt, whence only any substitute could have been drawn.

Even for Rome itself the scarcity of paper ran through many degrees. Horace, the poet, was amused with the town of Equotuticum for two reasons: as incapable of entering into hexameter verse from its prosodial quantity (*versu quod dicere non est*); and because it purchased water (*vænit vilissima rerum aqua*), — a circumstance in which it agrees with the well-known Clifton, above the hot wells of Bristol, where water is bought by the shilling's worth. But neither Horatian

Equotuticum nor Bristolian Clifton can ever have been as "hard up" for water as the Mecca caravan. And the differences were as great in respect to the want of paper between the Athens of Pericles or Alexander and the Rome of Augustus Cæsar. Athens had bad poets, whose names have come down to modern times; but Athens could no more have afforded to punish bad authors by sending their works to grocers —

> " in vicum vendentem pus et odores,
> Et piper, et quicquid *chartis amicitur ineptis* " —

than London, because gorged with the wealth of two Indies, can afford to pave her streets with silver. This practice of applying unsalable authors to the ignoble uses of retail dealers in petty articles must have existed in Rome for some time before it could have attracted the notice of Horace, and upon some considerable scale as a known public usage before it could have roused any echoes of public mirth as a satiric allusion, or have had any meaning and sting.

In that one revelation of Horace we see a proof how much paper had become more plentiful. It is true that so long as men dressed in woolen materials it was impossible to look for a *cheap* paper. Maga might have been printed at Rome very well for ten guineas a copy. Paper was dear, undoubtedly, but it could be had. On the other hand, how desperate must have been the bankruptcy at Athens in all materials for receiving the record of thoughts, when we find a polished people having no better tickets or cards for conveying their sentiments to the public than shells! Thence came the very name for civil banishment, viz. *ostracism*, because the votes were marked on an *ostracon*, or marine shell. Again, in another great city, viz. Syracuse, you see men reduced to *petalism*, or marking their votes by the petals of shrubs. Elsewhere, as indeed many centuries nearer to our own times in Constantinople, bull's hide was used for the same purpose.

Well might the poor Greeks adopt the desperate expedient of white plastered walls as the best memorandum-book for a man who had thoughts occurring to him in the night-time. Brass only, or marble, could offer any lasting memorial for thoughts; and upon what material the parts were written out for the actors on the Athenian stage, or how the elaborate revisals of the text could be carried on, is beyond our power of conjecture.

In this appalling state of embarrassment for the great poet or prose writer, what consequences would naturally arise? A king's favorite and friend like Aristotle might command the most costly materials. For instance, if you look back, from this day to 1800, into the advertising records or catalogues of great Parisian publishers, you will find more works of excessive luxury, costing from a thousand *francs* for each copy all the way up to as many *guineas*, in each separate period of fifteen years than in the whole forty among the wealthier and more enterprising publishers of Great Britain. What is the explanation? Can the very moderate incomes of the French gentry afford to patronize works which are beyond the purses of our British aristocracy, who, besides, are so much more of a reading class? Not so: the patronage for these Parisian works of luxury is not domestic, it is exotic: chiefly from emperors and kings; from great national libraries; from rich universities; from the grandees of Russia, Hungary, or Great Britain; and generally from those who, living in splendid castles or hotels, require corresponding furniture, and therefore corresponding books, because to such people books are necessarily furniture, —since, upon the principles of good taste, they must correspond with the splendor of all around them. And in the age of Alexander there were already purchasers enough among royal houses, or the imitators of such houses, to encourage costly copies of attractive works. Aristotle was a privileged man.

But in other less favored cases the strong yearnings for public sympathy were met by blank impossibilities. Much martyrdom, we feel assured, was then suffered by poets. Thousands, it is true, perish in our days, who have never had a solitary reader. But still the existence *in print* gives a delusive feeling that they *may* have been read. They are standing in the market all day, and somebody, unperceived by themselves, may have thrown an eye upon their wares. The thing is possible. But for the ancient writer there was a sheer physical impossibility that any man should sympathize with what he never could have seen, except under the two conditions we have mentioned.

These two cases there were of exemption from this dire physical resistance, — two conditions which made publication possible; and, under the horrible circumstances of sequestration for authors in general, need it be said that to benefit by either advantage was sought with such a zeal as, in effect, extinguished all other literature? If a man could be a poet for the stage, a *scriptor scenicus*, in that case he was published. If a man could be admitted as an orator, as a regular *demagogus*, upon the popular *bema* or hustings, in that case he was published. If his own thoughts were a torment to him, until they were reverberated from the hearts and flashing eyes and clamorous sympathy of a multitude, thus only an outlet was provided, a mouth was opened, for the volcano surging within his brain. The vast theatre was an organ of publication; the political forum was an organ of publication. And on this twofold arena a torch was applied to that inflammable gas which exhaled spontaneously from so excitable a mind as the mind of the Athenian.

Need we wonder, then, at the torrent-like determination with which Athenian literature, from the era 444 B.C. to the era 333 B.C., ran headlong into one or other channel, — the scenical poetry or the eloquence of the hustings? For an Athenian in search of popular applause or of sympathy there was no other avenue to either; unless, indeed, in the character of an artist, or of a leading soldier: but too often, in this latter class, it happened that mercenary foreigners had a preference. And thus it was that, during that period when the popular cast of government throughout Greece awakened patriotic emulation, scarcely anything is heard of in literature (allowing for the succession to philosophic chairs, which made it their pride to be private and exclusive) except dramatic poetry on the one hand, comic or tragic, and political oratory on the other.

As to this last avenue to the public ear, how it was abused, in what excess it became the nuisance and capital scourge of Athens, there needs only the testimony of all contemporary men who happened to stand aloof from that profession, or all subsequent men even of that very profession who were not blinded by some corresponding interest in some similar system of delusion. Euripides and Aristophanes, contemporary with the earliest practitioners of name and power on that stage of jugglers, are overrun with expressions of horror for these public pests. "You have every qualification," says Aristophanes to an aspirant, "that could be wished for a public orator: φωνη μιαρα — a voice like seven devils; κακος γεγονας — you are by nature a scamp; ἀγοραιος εἰ — you are up to snuff in the business of the forum." From Euripides might be gathered a small volume, relying merely upon so much of his works as yet survives, in illustration of the horror which possessed him for this gang of public misleaders: —

Τουτ' ἐσθ' ὁ θνητων εὐ πολεις οἰκουμενας
Δομους τ' ἀπολλυτ' — οἱ καλοι λιαν λογοι.

"This is what overthrows cities admirably organized, and the households of men, — your superfine harangues." Cicero, full four centuries later, looking back to this very period from Pericles to Alexander, friendly as he was by the *esprit de corps* to the order of orators, and professionally biassed to uphold the civil uses of eloquence, yet, as an honest man, cannot deny that it was this gift of oratory, hideously abused, which led to the overthrow of Athens and the ruin of Grecian liberty: " Illa vetus Græcia, quæ quondam opibus, imperio, gloria floruit, hoc uno malo concidit, — *libertate immoderata ac licentia concionum.*" Quintilian, standing on the very same ground of professional prejudice, all in favor of public orators, yet is forced into the same sorrowful confession. In one of the Declamations ascribed to him he says, "Civitatum status scimus ab oratoribus esse conversos " ; and in illustration he adds the example of Athens: " sive illam Atheniensium civitatem (quondam late principem) intueri placeat, accisas ejus vires animadvertemus *vitio concionantium.*" Root and branch, Athens was laid prostrate by her wicked Radical orators; for Radical, in the elliptic phrase of modern politics, they were almost to a man; and in this feature above all others (a feature often scornfully exposed by Euripides) those technically known as οἱ λεγοντες, the speaking men, and as οἱ δημαγωγοι,* the misleaders of the mob, offer a most suitable ancestry for the modern leaders

---

* With respect to the word "demagogues," as a technical designation for the political orators and partisans at Athens (otherwise called οἱ προσταται, those who headed any movement), it is singular that so accurate a Greek scholar as Henry Stephens should have supposed *linguas promptas ad plebem concitandum* (an expression of Livy's) *potius* των δημαγωγων *fuisse quam* των ῥητορων; as if the demagogues were a separate class from the popular orators. But, says Valckenaer, the relation is soon stated: not all the Athenian orators were demagogues, but all the demagogues were in fact, and technically were called, orators.

of Radicalism, — that with their base, fawning flatteries of the people they mixed up the venom of vipers against their opponents and against the aristocracy of the land.

Ὑπογλυκαίνειν ῥηματίοις μαγειρικοῖς —

" subtly to wheedle the people with honeyed words dressed to its palate ": this had been the ironical advice of the scoffing Aristophanes. That practice made the mob orator contemptible to manly tastes, rather than hateful. But the sacrifice of independence — the " pride which licks the dust" — is the readiest training for all uncharitableness and falsehood towards those who seem either rivals for the same base purposes, or open antagonists for nobler. And, accordingly, it is remarked by Euripides that these pestilent abusers of the popular confidence would bring a mischief upon Athens before they had finished, equally by their sycophancies to the mob and by their libels of foreign princes. Hundreds of years afterwards, a Greek writer, upon reviewing this most interesting period of one hundred and eleven years, from Pericles to Alexander, sums up and repeats the opinion of Euripides in this general representative portrait of Attic oratory, with respect, to which we wish to ask, Can any better delineation be given of a Chartist, or generically of a modern Jacobin?—Ὁ δημαγωγὸς κακοδιδασκαλεῖ τοὺς πολλούς, λέγων τὰ κεχαρισαμένα — "The mob-leader dupes the multitude with false doctrines, whilst delivering things soothing to their credulous vanity." This is one half of his office,—sycophancy to the immediate purseholders, and poison to the sources of truth; the other half is expressed with the same spirit of prophecy as regards the British future, καὶ διαβολαῖς αὐτοὺς ἐξαλλοτριοῖ πρὸς τοὺς ἀρίστους,— "and by lying calumnies he utterly alienates them in relation to their own native aristocracy."

Now this was a base pursuit, though somewhat relieved by

R

the closing example of Demosthenes, who, amidst much frailty, had a generous nature; and he showed it chiefly by his death, and in his lifetime, to use Milton's words, by uttering many times " odious truth," which, with noble courage, he compelled the mob to hear.   But one man could not redeem a national dishonor.   It *was* such, and such it was felt to be. Men, therefore, of elevated natures, and men of gentle pacific natures, equally revolted from a trade of lies, as regarded the audience, and of strife, as regarded the competitors.   There remained the one other pursuit of scenical poetry; and it hardly needs to be said what crowding there was amongst all the energetic minds of Athens into one or other of these pursuits: the one for the unworldly and idealizing, the other for the coarsely ambitious.   These, therefore, became the two *quasi* professions of Athens, and at the same time, in a sense more exclusive than can now be true of *our* professions, became the sole means of publication for truth of any class, and a publication by many degrees more certain, more extensive, and more immediate, than ours by the press.

The Athenian theatre published an edition of thirty thousand copies in one day, enabling, in effect, every male citizen capable of attending, from the age of twenty to sixty, together with many thousands of domiciled aliens, to read the drama, with the fullest understanding of its sense and poetic force that could be effected by natural powers of voice and action, combined with all possible auxiliaries of art, of music, of pantomimic dancing, and the whole carried home to the heart by visible and audible sympathy in excess.   This, but in a very inferior form as regarded the adjuncts of art, and the scale of the theatre, and the *mise en scène*, was precisely the advantage of Charles I for appreciating Shakespeare.

It was a standing reproach of the Puritans, adopted even by Milton, a leaden shaft feathered and made buoyant by *his* wit, that the King had adopted that stage poet as the companion of his closet retirements. So it would have been a pity if these malignant persecutors of the royal solitude should have been liars as well as fanatics. Doubtless, even when king, and in his afflictions, this storm-vexed man did read Shakespeare. But that was not the original way in which he acquired his acquaintance with the poet. A Prince of Wales, what between public claims and social claims, finds little time for reading after the period of childhood, — that is, at any period when he can comprehend a great poet. And it was as Prince of Wales that Charles prosecuted his studies of Shakespeare. He saw continually at Whitehall, personated by the best actors of the time, illustrated by the stage management, and assisted by the mechanic displays of Inigo Jones, all the principal dramas of Shakespeare actually performed. That was publication with an Athenian advantage. A thousand copies of a book may be brought into public libraries, and not one of them opened. But the three thousand copies of a play which Drury Lane used to publish in one night were in the most literal sense as well as in spirit read, — properly punctuated by the speakers, made intelligible by voice and action endowed with life and emphasis: in short, on each successive performance, a very large edition of a fine tragedy was published in the most impressive sense of publication, — not merely with accuracy, but with a mimic reality that forbade all forgetting, and was liable to no inattention.

Now, if Drury Lane published a drama for Shakespeare by three thousand copies in one night,[5] the Athenian theatre published ten times that amount for Sophocles. And this mode of publication in Athens, not coöperating (as in modern times) with other modes, but standing out in solitary conspicuous relief, gave an artificial bounty upon that one mode of poetic composition, as the hustings did upon one mode of prose composition. And those two modes, being thus cultivated to the utter exclusion of others which did not benefit by that bounty of publication, gave an unnatural bias to the national style, determined in effect upon too narrow a scale the operative ideal of composition, and finally made the dramatic artist and the mob orator the two sole intellectual professions for Athens. Hence came a great limitation of style in practice; and hence, secondly, for reasons connected with these two modes of composition, a general neglect of style as a didactic theory.

¹ Compare above, pp. 52-53.

² De Quincey has in mind the poetry of Wordsworth.

³ A statement to which mathematicians might demur.

⁴ A badly constructed sentence, meriting the censure of Schopenhauer (see below, p. 267).

⁵ As Masson points out, "*Drury Lane* was not the great theatrical centre of the metropolis till after the Restoration." "It was at the *Blackfriars* and the *Globe* . . . that Shakespeare's plays were first published in his own life-time."

XI

HENRY DAVID THOREAU (1817–1862)

[On Style] * (1849)

[From *A Week on the Concord and Merrimack Rivers*, Boston and New York (Houghton, Mifflin), 1893 (pp. 130–137).

A Week, etc., the earlier of the two works published by Thoreau himself, is, like his posthumous works, based upon his private journals and memoranda. His journal of a trip down the Concord and Merrimack (August 31–September 6, 1839) Thoreau elaborated at his hermitage by Walden Pond, whither he retired in 1845. He finished his manuscript presumably before March, 1847, and published the book at his own expense, in 1849. The selection offered here is from *Sunday* (September 1, 1839); being easily detached from its context, it makes by itself a definite and coherent excerpt.

It bears all the marks of conscientious literary workmanship. Thoreau's style, according to Lowell, " is compact," and his language has " an antique purity like wine grown colorless with age." " I thought," said Thoreau of his first book, " that it had little of the atmosphere of the house about it, but it might have been written wholly, as in fact it was to a great extent, out-of-doors." See also the impressions of William Ellery Channing in *Thoreau, The Poet-Naturalist* (ed. F. B. Sanborn, 1902), pp. 229–231, 234, 242.]

Enough has been said in these days of the charm of fluent writing. We hear it complained of some works of genius that they have fine thoughts, but are irregular and have no flow. But even the mountain peaks in the horizon are, to the eye of science, parts of one range. We should consider

---

* This selection is printed by permission of Messrs. Houghton, Mifflin, & Co., and by special arrangement with them as the authorized publishers of *Thoreau's Works*.

that the flow of thought is more like a tidal wave than a prone river, and is the result of a celestial influence, not of any declivity in its channel.   The river flows because it runs down hill, and flows the faster, the faster it descends.   The reader who expects to float downstream for the whole voyage may well complain of nauseating swells and choppings of the sea when his frail shore craft gets amidst the billows of the ocean stream, which flows as much to sun and moon as lesser streams to it.   But if we would appreciate the flow that is in these books, we must expect to feel it rise from the page like an exhalation, and wash away our critical brains like burr millstones, flowing to higher levels above and behind ourselves.   There is many a book which ripples on like a freshet, and flows as glibly as a mill-stream sucking under a causeway; and when their authors are in the full tide of their discourse, Pythagoras and Plato and Jamblichus halt beside them.   Their long, stringy, slimy sentences are of that con- sistency that they naturally flow and run together.   They read as if written for military men, for men of business, there is such a dispatch in them.   Compared with these, the grave thinkers and philosophers seem not to have got their swaddling- clothes off; they are slower than a Roman army in its march, the rear camping to-night where the van camped last night. The wise Jamblichus eddies and gleams like a watery slough.

> " How many thousands never heard the name
>   Of Sidney, or of Spenser, or their books?
>   And yet brave fellows, and presume of fame,
>   And seem to bear down all the world with looks." [1]

The ready writer seizes the pen and shouts " Forward ! Alamo and Fanning ! " and after rolls the tide of war.   The very walls and fences seem to travel.   But the most rapid trot is no flow after all; and thither, reader, you and I, at least, will not follow.

A perfectly healthy sentence, it is true, is extremely rare. For the most part we miss the hue and fragrance of the thought; as if we could be satisfied with the dews of the morning or evening without their colors, or the heavens without their azure. The most attractive sentences are, perhaps, not the wisest, but the surest and roundest. They are spoken firmly and conclusively, as if the speaker had a right to know what he says, and if not wise, they have at least been well learned. Sir Walter Raleigh might well be studied, if only for the excellence of his style, for he is remarkable in the midst of so many masters. There is a natural emphasis in his style, like a man's tread, and a breathing space between the sentences, which the best of modern writing does not furnish. His chapters are like English parks, or say rather like a Western forest, where the larger growth keeps down the underwood, and one may ride on horseback through the openings. All the distinguished writers of that period possess a greater vigor and naturalness than the more modern,[2] — for it is allowed to slander our own time, — and when we read a quotation from one of them in the midst of a modern author, we seem to have come suddenly upon a greener ground, a greater depth and strength of soil. It is as if a green bough were laid across the page, and we are refreshed as by the sight of fresh grass in midwinter or early spring. You have constantly the warrant of life and experience in what you read. The little that is said is eked out by implication of the much that was done. The sentences are verdurous and blooming as evergreen and flowers, because they are rooted in fact and experience, but our false and florid sentences have only the tints of flowers without their sap or roots. All men are really most attracted by the beauty of plain speech, and they even write in a florid style in imitation of this. They prefer to be misunderstood rather than to come short of its exuberance.   Hussein Effendi praised the epistolary style of Ibrahim Pasha to the French traveller Botta,[3] because of " the difficulty of understanding it; there was," he said, " but one person at Jidda who was capable of understanding and explaining the Pasha's correspondence." A man's whole life is taxed for the least thing well done.   It is its net result.   Every sentence is the result of a long probation.   Where shall we look for standard English but to the words of a standard man?   The word which is best said came nearest to not being spoken at all, for it is cousin to a deed which the speaker could have better done.   Nay, almost it must have taken the place of a deed by some urgent necessity, even by some misfortune, so that the truest writer will be some captive knight, after all.   And perhaps the fates had such a design, when, having stored Raleigh so richly with the substance of life and experience, they made him a fast prisoner, and compelled him to make his words his deeds, and transfer to his expression the emphasis and sincerity of his action.

Men have a respect for scholarship and learning greatly out of proportion to the use they commonly serve.   We are amused to read how Ben Jonson engaged that the dull masks with which the royal family and nobility were to be entertained should be " grounded upon antiquity and solid learning."   Can there be any greater reproach than an idle learning?   Learn to split wood, at least.   The necessity of labor and conversation with many men and things, to the scholar is rarely well remembered; steady labor with the hands, which engrosses the attention also, is unquestionably the best method of removing palaver and sentimentality out of one's style, both of speaking and writing.   If he has worked hard from morning till night, though he may have grieved that he could not be watching the train of his thoughts during that time, yet the few hasty lines which at evening

record his day's experience will be more musical and true
than his freest but idle fancy could have furnished. Surely
the writer is to address a world of laborers, and such therefore must be his own discipline. He will not idly dance at
his work who has wood to cut and cord before nightfall in
the short days of winter; but every stroke will be husbanded,
and ring soberly through the wood; and so will the strokes
of that scholar's pen, which at evening record the story of
the day, ring soberly, yet cheerily, on the ear of the reader,
long after the echoes of his axe have died away. The scholar
may be sure that he writes the tougher truth for the calluses
on his palms. They give firmness to the sentence. Indeed,
the mind never makes a great and successful effort, without
a corresponding energy of the body. We are often struck
by the force and precision of style to which hard-working
men, unpractised in writing, easily attain when required to
make the effort. As if plainness and vigor and sincerity, the
ornaments of style, were better learned on the farm and in
the workshop than in the schools. The sentences written by
such rude hands are nervous and tough, like hardened thongs,
the sinews of the deer, or the roots of the pine. As for the
graces of expression, a great thought is never found in a
mean dress; but though it proceed from the lips of the
Wolofs,[4] the nine Muses and the three Graces will have conspired to clothe it in fit phrase. Its education has always
been liberal, and its implied wit can endow a college. The
world, which the Greeks called Beauty, has been made such
by being gradually divested of every ornament which was not
fitted to endure. The Sibyl, " speaking with inspired mouth,
smileless, inornate, and unperfumed, pierces through centuries by the power of the god." The scholar might frequently emulate the propriety and emphasis of the farmer's
call to his team, and confess that if that were written it would

surpass his labored sentences. Whose are the truly *labored* sentences? From the weak and flimsy periods of the politician and literary man, we are glad to turn even to the description of work, the simple record of the month's labor in the farmer's almanac, to restore our tone and spirits. A sentence should read as if its author, had he held a plough instead of a pen, could have drawn a furrow deep and straight to the end. The scholar requires hard and serious labor to give an impetus to his thought. He will learn to grasp the pen firmly so, and wield it gracefully and effectively, as an axe or a sword. When we consider the weak and nerveless periods of some literary men, who perchance in feet and inches come up to the standard of their race, and are not deficient in girth also, we are amazed at the immense sacrifice of thews and sinews. What! these proportions, — these bones, — and this their work! Hands which could have felled an ox have hewed this fragile matter which would not have tasked a lady's fingers! Can this be a stalwart man's work, who has a marrow in his back and a tendon Achilles in his heel? They who set up the blocks of Stonehenge did somewhat, if they only laid out their strength for once, and stretched themselves.

[1] Samuel Daniel.

[2] Compare Coleridge, above, p. 205.

[3] Paolo Emilio Botta (1802–1870), of Italian extraction, an oriental traveller and Assyriologist.

[4] "Wolofs" — better "Yolof" (*i.e.* "Speakers"); a negro race of the western Sudan, whose language is "the medium of communication throughout Senegambia."   Thoreau may have been acquainted with De Roger's *Recherches philosophiques sur la langue oulofe*, Paris, 1829.

XII

ARTHUR SCHOPENHAUER (1788–1860)

On Style * (1851)

[From *The Art of Literature, A Series of Essays* by Arthur Schopenhauer, Selected and Translated, etc., by T. Bailey Saunders, M.A., London (Sonnenschein), 1904 (pp. 17–36).

Mr. Saunders's work, which first appeared in 1891, is a free arrangement of certain chapters in Schopenhauer's *Parerga* (1851), with a title " invented " by the translator. " The essays on *Authorship* and *Style* . . . are taken direct from the chapter headed *Ueber Schriftstellerei und Stil.*" Mr. Saunders's free handling of his original, entirely justified by his purpose, has made readable and unified English of German that is in the highest degree readable, but not always so compact. Schopenhauer's style is discussed with admiration, and with understanding also, in Kuno Fischer's *Geschichte der neueren Philosophie* (Vol. 8, 1893, *Schopenhauer*— especially pp. 491–495). More sweeping still is the praise given by Nietzsche (*Schopenhauer als Erzieher*, pp. 14–18 in Vol. 2 of *Unzeitgemässe Betrachtungen*, Leipzig, 1893).]

Style is the physiognomy of the mind, and a safer index to character than the face. To imitate another man's style is like wearing a mask, which, be it never so fine, is not long in arousing disgust and abhorrence, because it is lifeless; so that even the ugliest living face is better.[1] Hence those who write in Latin and copy the manner of ancient authors, may be said to speak through a mask; the reader, it is true, hears what they say, but he cannot observe their physiognomy too; he cannot see their *style*. With the Latin works of writers who think for themselves, the case is different, and their style

* With the permission of Messrs. Swan Sonnenschein & Co., Lim., London.

is visible; writers, I mean, who have not condescended to any sort of imitation, such as Scotus Erigena, Petrarch, Bacon, Descartes, Spinoza, and many others. And affectation in style is like making grimaces. Further, the language in which a man writes is the physiognomy of the nation to which he belongs; and here there are many hard and fast differences, beginning from the language of the Greeks, down to that of the Caribbean islanders.

To form a provisional estimate of the value of a writer's productions, it is not directly necessary to know the subject on which he has thought, or what it is that he has said about it; that would imply a perusal of all his works. It will be enough, in the main, to know *how* he has thought. This, which means the essential temper or general quality of his mind, may be precisely determined by his style. A man's style shows the *formal* nature of all his thoughts — the formal nature which can never change, be the subject or the character of his thoughts what it may: it is, as it were, the dough out of which all the contents of his mind are kneaded. When Eulenspiegel was asked how long it would take to walk to the next village, he gave the seemingly incongruous answer: *Walk.* He wanted to find out by the man's pace the distance he would cover in a given time. In the same way, when I have read a few pages of an author, I know fairly well how far he can bring me.

Every mediocre writer tries to mask his own natural style, because in his heart he knows the truth of what I am saying.[2] He is thus forced, at the outset, to give up any attempt at being frank or naïve — a privilege which is thereby reserved for superior minds, conscious of their own worth, and therefore sure of themselves. What I mean is that these everyday writers are absolutely unable to resolve upon writing just as they think; because they have a notion that, were they to do so, their work might possibly look very childish and simple. For all that, it would not be without its value. If they would only go honestly to work, and say, quite simply, the things they have really thought, and just as they have thought them, these writers would be readable and, within their own proper sphere, even instructive.

But instead of that, they try to make the reader believe that their thoughts have gone much further and deeper than is really the case. They say what they have to say in long sentences that wind about in a forced and unnatural way; they coin new words and write prolix periods which go round and round the thought and wrap it up in a sort of disguise. They tremble between the two separate aims of communicating what they want to say and of concealing it. Their object is to dress it up so that it may look learned or deep, in order to give people the impression that there is very much more in it than for the moment meets the eye. They either jot down their thoughts bit by bit, in short, ambiguous, and paradoxical sentences, which apparently mean much more than they say, — of this kind of writing Schelling's treatises on natural philosophy are a splendid instance; or else they hold forth with a deluge of words and the most intolerable diffusiveness, as though no end of fuss were necessary to make the reader understand the deep meaning of their sentences, whereas it is some quite simple if not actually trivial idea, — examples of which may be found in plenty in the popular works of Fichte, and the philosophical manuals of a hundred other miserable dunces not worth mentioning; or, again, they try to write in some particular style which they have been pleased to take up and think very grand, a style, for example, *par excellence* profound and scientific, where the reader is tormented to death by the narcotic effect of long-spun periods without a single idea in them, — such as are furnished in a special measure by those most impudent of all mortals, the Hegelians; * or it may be that it is an intellectual style they have striven after, where it seems as though their object were to go crazy altogether; and so on in many other cases. All these endeavors to put off the *nascetur ridiculus mus* — to avoid showing the funny little creature that is born after such mighty throes — often make it difficult to know what it is that they really mean. And then, too, they write down words, nay, even whole sentences, without attaching any meaning to them themselves, but in the hope that someone else will get sense out of them.

And what is at the bottom of all this? Nothing but the untiring effort to sell words for thoughts; a mode of merchandise that is always trying to make fresh openings for itself, and by means of odd expressions, turns of phrase, and combinations of every sort, whether new or used in a new sense, to produce the appearance of intellect in order to make up for the very painfully felt lack of it.

It is amusing to see how writers with this object in view will attempt first one mannerism and then another, as though they were putting on the mask of intellect! This mask may possibly deceive the inexperienced for a while, until it is seen to be a dead thing, with no life in it at all: it is then laughed at and exchanged for another. Such an author will at one moment write in a dithyrambic vein, as though he were tipsy; at another, nay, on the very next page, he will be pompous, severe, profoundly learned and prolix, stumbling on in the most cumbrous way, and chopping up everything very small; like the late Christian Wolf, only in a modern dress. Longest of all lasts the mask of unintelligibility; but this is only in Germany, whither it was introduced by Fichte,

* In their Hegel-gazette, commonly known as *Jahrbücher der wissenschaftlichen Litteratur.*

perfected by Schelling, and carried to its highest pitch in Hegel — always with the best results.

And yet nothing is easier than to write so that no one can understand; just as, contrarily, nothing is more difficult than to express deep things in such a way that everyone must necessarily grasp them. All the arts and tricks I have been mentioning are rendered superfluous if the author really has any brains; for that allows him to show himself as he is, and confirms to all time Horace's maxim that good sense is the source and origin of good style: —

Scribendi recte sapere est et principium et fons.[3]

But those authors I have named are like certain workers in metal, who try a hundred different compounds to take the place of gold — the only metal which can never have any substitute. Rather than do that, there is nothing against which a writer should be more upon his guard than the manifest endeavor to exhibit more intellect than he really has; because this makes the reader suspect that he possesses very little; since it is always the case that if a man affects anything, whatever it may be, it is just there that he is deficient.

That is why it is praise to an author to say that he is *naïve;* it means that he need not shrink from showing himself as he is. Generally speaking, to be naïve is to be attractive; while lack of naturalness is everywhere repulsive. As a matter of fact we find that every really great writer tries to express his thoughts as purely, clearly, definitely, and shortly as possible. Simplicity has always been held to be a mark of truth; it is also a mark of genius. Style receives its beauty from the thought it expresses; but with sham-thinkers the thoughts are supposed to be fine because of the style. Style is nothing but the mere silhouette of thought; and an obscure or bad style means a dull or confused brain.

The first rule, then, for a good style is that *the author should have something to say;* nay, this is in itself almost all that is necessary.   Ah, how much it means!   The neglect of this rule is a fundamental trait in the philosophical writing, and, in fact, in all the reflective literature, of my country, more especially since Fichte.   These writers all let it be seen that they want to appear as though they had something to say; whereas they have nothing to say.   Writing of this kind was brought in by the pseudo-philosophers at the Universities, and now it is current everywhere, even among the first literary notabilities of the age.   It is the mother of that strained and vague style, where there seem to be two or even more meanings in the sentence; also of that prolix and cumbrous manner of expression, called *le stile empesé;* again, of that mere waste of words which consists in pouring them out like a flood; finally, of that trick of concealing the direst poverty of thought under a farrago of never-ending chatter, which clacks away like a windmill and quite stupefies one — stuff which a man may read for hours together without getting hold of a single clearly expressed and definite idea.*   However, people are easy-going, and they have formed the habit of reading page upon page of all sorts of such verbiage, without having any particular idea of what the author really means.   They fancy it is all as it should be, and fail to discover that he is writing simply for writing's sake.

On the other hand, a good author, fertile in ideas, soon wins his reader's confidence that, when he writes, he has really and truly *something to say;* and this gives the intelligent reader patience to follow him with attention.   Such an author, just because he really has something to say, will never fail to

---

* Select examples of the art of writing in this style are to be found almost *passim* in the *Jahrbücher* published at Halle, afterwards called the *Deutschen Jahrbücher.*

express himself in the simplest and most straightforward manner; because his object is to awake the very same thought in the reader that he has in himself, and no other. So he will be able to affirm with Boileau that his thoughts are everywhere open to the light of day, and that his verse always says something, whether it says it well or ill: —

> *Ma pensée au grand jour partout s'offre et s'expose,*
> *Et mon vers, bien ou mal, dit toujours quelque chose;*

while of the writers previously described it may be asserted, in the words of the same poet, that they talk much and never say anything at all — *qui parlant beaucoup ne disent jamais rien.*

Another characteristic of such writers is that they always avoid a positive assertion wherever they can possibly do so, in order to leave a loophole for escape in case of need. Hence they never fail to choose the more *abstract* way of expressing themselves; whereas intelligent people use the more *concrete;* because the latter brings things more within the range of actual demonstration, which is the source of all evidence.[4]

There are many examples proving this preference for abstract expression; and a particularly ridiculous one is afforded by the use of the verb *to condition* in the sense of *to cause* or *to produce.* People say *to condition something* instead of *to cause it,* because being abstract and indefinite it says less; it affirms that A cannot happen without B, instead of that A is caused by B. A back door is always left open; and this suits people whose secret knowledge of their own incapacity inspires them with a perpetual terror of all positive assertion; while with other people it is merely the effect of that tendency by which everything that is stupid in literature or bad in life is immediately imitated — a fact proved in either case by the rapid way in which it spreads. The Englishman uses his

s

own judgment in what he writes as well as in what he does; but there is no nation of which this eulogy is less true than of the Germans. The consequence of this state of things is that the word *cause* has of late almost disappeared from the language of literature, and people talk only of *condition*. The fact is worth mentioning because it is so characteristically ridiculous.

The very fact that these commonplace authors are never more than half conscious when they write, would be enough to account for their dulness of mind and the tedious things they produce. I say they are only half conscious, because they really do not themselves understand the meaning of the words they use: they take words ready made and commit them to memory. Hence when they write, it is not so much words as whole phrases that they put together — *phrases banales*. This is the explanation of that palpable lack of clearly expressed thought in what they say. The fact is that they do not possess the die to give this stamp to their writing; clear thought of their own is just what they have not got. And what do we find in its place? — a vague, enigmatical intermixture of words, current phrases, hackneyed terms, and fashionable expressions. The result is that the foggy stuff they write is like a page printed with very old type.

On the other hand, an intelligent author really speaks to us when he writes, and that is why he is able to rouse our interest and commune with us. It is the intelligent author alone who puts individual words together with a full consciousness of their meaning, and chooses them with deliberate design. Consequently, his discourse stands to that of the writer described above, much as a picture that has been really painted to one that has been produced by the use of a stencil. In the one case, every word, every touch of the brush, has a special purpose; in the other, all is done mechanically.

The same distinction may be observed in music. For just as Lichtenberg says that Garrick's soul seemed to be in every muscle in his body, so it is the omnipresence of intellect that always and everywhere characterizes the work of genius.

I have alluded to the tediousness which marks the works of these writers; and in this connection it is to be observed, generally, that tediousness is of two kinds: objective and subjective. A work is objectively tedious when it contains the defect in question; that is to say, when its author has no perfectly clear thought or knowledge to communicate. For if a man has any clear thought or knowledge in him, his aim will be to communicate it, and he will direct his energies to this end; so that the ideas he furnishes are everywhere clearly expressed. The result is that he is neither diffuse, nor unmeaning, nor confused, and consequently not tedious. In such a case, even though the author is at bottom in error, the error is at any rate clearly worked out and well thought over, so that it is at least formally correct; and thus some value always attaches to the work. But for the same reason a work that is objectively tedious is at all times devoid of any value whatever.

The other kind of tediousness is only relative: a reader may find a work dull because he has no interest in the question treated of in it, and this means that his intellect is restricted. The best work may, therefore, be tedious subjectively, tedious, I mean, to this or that particular person; just as, contrarily, the worst work may be subjectively engrossing to this or that particular person who has an interest in the question treated of, or in the writer of the book.

It would generally serve writers in good stead if they would see that, whilst a man should, if possible, think like a great genius, he should talk the same language as everyone else. Authors should use common words to say uncommon things.

But they do just the opposite. We find them trying to wrap up trivial ideas in grand words, and to clothe their very ordinary thoughts in the most extraordinary phrases, the most far-fetched, unnatural, and out-of-the-way expressions. Their sentences perpetually stalk about on stilts. They take so much pleasure in bombast, and write in such a high-flown, bloated, affected, hyperbolical, and aerobatic[5] style that their prototype is Ancient Pistol, whom his friend Falstaff once impatiently told to say what he had to say *like a man of this world.**

There is no expression in any other language exactly answering to the French *stile empesé;* but the thing itself exists all the more often. When associated with affectation, it is in literature what assumption of dignity, grand airs, and primness are in society, and equally intolerable. Dulness of mind is fond of donning this dress; just as in ordinary life it is stupid people who like being demure and formal.

An author who writes in the prim style resembles a man who dresses himself up in order to avoid being confounded or put on the same level with the mob — a risk never run by the *gentleman,* even in his worst clothes. The plebeian may be known by a certain showiness of attire and a wish to have everything spick and span; and, in the same way, the commonplace person is betrayed by his style.

Nevertheless, an author follows a false aim if he tries to write exactly as he speaks. There is no style of writing but should have a certain trace of kinship with the *epigraphic* or *monumental* style, which is, indeed, the ancestor of all styles. For an author to write as he speaks is just as reprehensible as the opposite fault, to speak as he writes; for this gives a pedantic effect to what he says, and at the same time makes him hardly intelligible.

* *King Henry IV*, Part II, Act v, Sc. 3.

An obscure and vague manner of expression is always and everywhere a very bad sign. In ninety-nine cases out of a hundred it comes from vagueness of thought; and this again almost always means that there is something radically wrong and incongruous about the thought itself — in a word, that it is incorrect. When a right thought springs up in the mind, it strives after expression and is not long in reaching it; for clear thought easily finds words to fit it. If a man is capable of thinking anything at all, he is also always able to express it in clear, intelligible, and unambiguous terms. Those writers who construct difficult, obscure, involved, and equivocal sentences, most certainly do not know aright what it is that they want to say: they have only a dull consciousness of it, which is still in the stage of struggle to shape itself as thought. Often, indeed, their desire is to conceal from themselves and others that they really have nothing at all to say. They wish to appear to know what they do not know, to think what they do not think, to say what they do not say. If a man has some real communication to make, which will he choose — an indistinct or a clear way of expressing himself? Even Quintilian remarks that things which are said by a highly educated man are often easier to understand and much clearer; and that the less educated a man is, the more obscurely he will write — *plerumque accidit ut faciliora sint ad intelligendum et lucidiora multo quæ a doctissimo quoque dicuntur. . . . Erit ergo etiam obscurior quo quisque deterior.*[6]

An author should avoid enigmatical phrases: he should know whether he wants to say a thing or does not want to say it. It is this indecision of style that makes so many writers insipid. The only case that offers an exception to this rule arises when it is necessary to make a remark that is in some way improper.

As exaggeration generally produces an effect the opposite
of that aimed at; so words, it is true, serve to make thought
intelligible — but only up to a certain point. If words are
heaped up beyond it, the thought becomes more and more
obscure again. To find where the point lies is the problem
of style, and the business of the critical faculty; for a word
too much always defeats its purpose. This is what Voltaire
means when he says that *the adjective is the enemy of the
substantive.* But, as we have seen, many people try to conceal
their poverty of thought under a flood of verbiage.

Accordingly, let all redundancy be avoided, all stringing
together of remarks which have no meaning and are not
worth perusal. A writer must make a sparing use of the
reader's time, patience, and attention; so as to lead him to
believe that his author writes what is worth careful study, and
will reward the time spent upon it. It is always better to
omit something good than to add that which is not worth
saying at all. This is the right application of Hesiod's maxim,
πλέον ἥμισυ παντός * — the half is more than the whole.
Le secret pour être ennuyeux, c'est de tout dire. Therefore,
if possible, the quintessence only! mere leading thoughts!
nothing that the reader would think for himself. To use
many words to communicate few thoughts is everywhere the
unmistakable sign of mediocrity. To gather much thought
into few words stamps the man of genius.

Truth is most beautiful undraped; and the impression it
makes is deep in proportion as its expression has been simple.
This is so, partly because it then takes unobstructed possession
of the hearer's whole soul, and leaves him no by-thought to
distract him; partly, also, because he feels that here he is not
being corrupted or cheated by the arts of rhetoric, but that
all the effect of what is said comes from the thing itself. For

* *Works and Days,* 40.

instance, what declamation on the vanity of human existence could ever be more telling than the words of Job?—*Man that is born of a woman hath but a short time to live and is full of misery. He cometh up, and is cut down, like a flower; he fleeth as it were a shadow, and never continueth in one stay.*

For the same reason Goethe's naïve poetry is incomparably greater than Schiller's rhetoric. It is this, again, that makes many popular songs so affecting. As in architecture an excess of decoration is to be avoided, so in the art of literature a writer must guard against all rhetorical finery, all useless amplification, and all superfluity of expression in general; in a word, he must strive after *chastity* of style. Every word that can be spared is hurtful if it remains. The law of simplicity and naïvety holds good of all fine art; for it is quite possible to be at once simple and sublime.

True brevity of expression consists in everywhere saying only what is worth saying, and in avoiding tedious detail about things which everyone can supply for himself. This involves correct discrimination between what is necessary and what is superfluous. A writer should never be brief at the expense of being clear, to say nothing of being grammatical. It shows lamentable want of judgment to weaken the expression of a thought, or to stunt the meaning of a period for the sake of using a few words less. But this is the precise endeavor of that false brevity nowadays so much in vogue, which proceeds by leaving out useful words and even by sacrificing grammar and logic. It is not only that such writers spare a word by making a single verb or adjective do duty for several different periods, so that the reader, as it were, has to grope his way through them in the dark; they also practise, in many other respects, an unseemly economy of speech, in the effort to effect what they foolishly take to be brevity of expression and conciseness of style. By omitting something that might have thrown a light over the whole sentence, they turn it into a conundrum, which the reader tries to solve by going over it again and again.*

It is wealth and weight of thought, and nothing else, that gives brevity to style, and makes it concise and pregnant. If a writer's ideas are important, luminous, and generally worth communicating, they will necessarily furnish matter and substance enough to fill out the periods which give them expression, and make these in all their parts both grammatically and verbally complete; and so much will this be the case that no one will ever find them hollow, empty, or feeble. The diction will everywhere be brief and pregnant, and allow the thought to find intelligible and easy expression, and even unfold and move about with grace.

Therefore, instead of contracting his words and forms of speech, let a writer enlarge his thoughts. If a man has been thinned by illness and finds his clothes too big,. it is not by cutting them down, but by recovering his usual bodily condition, that he ought to make them fit him again.

Let me here mention an error of style very prevalent nowadays, and, in the degraded state of literature and the neglect of ancient languages, always on the increase; I mean *subjectivity*. A writer commits this error when he thinks it enough if he himself knows what he means and wants to say, and takes no thought for the reader, who is left to get at the bottom of it as best he can. This is as though the author were

* *Translator's Note.* In the original, Schopenhauer here enters upon a lengthy examination of certain common errors in the writing and speaking of German. His remarks are addressed to his own countrymen, and would lose all point, even if they were intelligible, in an English translation. But for those who practise their German by conversing or corresponding with Germans, let me recommend what he there says as a useful corrective to a slipshod style, such as can easily be contracted if it is assumed that the natives of a country always know their own language perfectly.

holding a monologue; whereas it ought to be a dialogue; and a dialogue, too, in which he must express himself all the more clearly inasmuch as he cannot hear the questions of his interlocutor.

Style should for this very reason never be subjective but *objective;* and it will not be objective unless the words are so set down that they directly force the reader to think precisely the same thing as the author thought when he wrote them. Nor will this result be obtained unless the author has always been careful to remember that thought so far follows the law of gravity that it travels from head to paper much more easily than from paper to head; so that he must assist the latter passage by every means in his power. If he does this, a writer's words will have a purely objective effect, like that of a finished picture in oils; whilst the subjective style is not much more certain in its working than spots on the wall, which look like figures only to one whose phantasy has been accidentally aroused by them; other people see nothing but spots and blurs. The difference in question applies to literary method as a whole; but it is often established also in particular instances. For example, in a recently published work I found the following sentence: *I have not written in order to increase the number of existing books.* This means just the opposite of what the writer wanted to say, and is nonsense as well.

He who writes carelessly confesses thereby at the very outset that he does not attach much importance to his own thoughts. For it is only where a man is convinced of the truth and importance of his thoughts, that he feels the enthusiasm necessary for an untiring and assiduous effort to find the clearest, finest, and strongest expression for them, — just as for sacred relics or priceless works of art there are provided silvern or golden receptacles. It was this feeling that led ancient authors, whose thoughts, expressed in their own words, have lived thousands of years, and therefore bear the honored title of *classics*, always to write with care. Plato, indeed, is said to have written the introduction to his *Republic* seven times over in different ways.*

As neglect of dress betrays want of respect for the company a man meets, so a hasty, careless, bad style shows an outrageous lack of regard for the reader, who then rightly punishes it by refusing to read the book.   It is especially amusing to see reviewers criticising the works of others in their own most careless style — the style of a hireling.   It is as though a judge were to come into court in dressing-gown and slippers! If I see a man badly and dirtily dressed, I feel some hesitation, at first, in entering into conversation with him : and when, on taking up a book, I am struck at once by the negligence of its style, I put it away.

Good writing should be governed by the rule that a man can think only one thing clearly at a time; and, therefore, that he should not be expected to think two or even more things in one and the same moment.   But this is what is done when a writer breaks up his principal sentence into little pieces, for the purpose of pushing into the gaps thus made two or three other thoughts by way of parenthesis; thereby unnecessarily and wantonly confusing the reader.   And here it is again my own countrymen who are chiefly in fault.   That German lends itself to this way of writing, makes the thing possible, but does not justify it.   No prose reads more easily or pleasantly than French, because, as a rule, it is free from the error in question.   The Frenchman strings his thoughts together, as far as he can, in the most logical and natural

---

* *Translator's Note.* It is a fact worth mentioning that the first twelve words of the *Republic* are placed in the exact order which would be natural in English.

order, and so lays them before his reader one after the other for convenient deliberation, so that every one of them may receive undivided attention. The German, on the other hand, weaves them together into a sentence which he twists and crosses, and crosses and twists again; because he wants to say six things all at once, instead of advancing them one by one. His aim should be to attract and hold the reader's attention; but, above and beyond neglect of this aim, he demands from the reader that he shall set the above-mentioned rule at defiance, and think three or four different thoughts at one and the same time; or since that is impossible, that his thoughts shall succeed each other as quickly as the vibrations of a cord. In this way an author lays the foundation of his *stile empesé*, which is then carried to perfection by the use of high-flown, pompous expressions to communicate the simplest things, and other artifices of the same kind.

In those long sentences rich in involved parentheses, like a box of boxes one within another, and padded out like roast geese stuffed with apples, it is really the *memory* that is chiefly taxed; while it is the understanding and the judgment which should be called into play, instead of having their activity thereby actually hindered and weakened.* This kind of sentence furnishes the reader with mere half-phrases, which he is then called upon to collect carefully and store up in his memory, as though they were the pieces of a torn letter, afterwards to be completed and made sense of by the other halves to which they respectively belong. He is expected to go on reading for a little without exercising any thought, nay, exerting only his memory, in the hope that, when he comes to the

---

* *Translator's Note.* This sentence in the original is obviously meant to illustrate the fault of which it speaks. It does so by the use of a construction very common in German, but happily unknown in English; where, however, the fault itself exists none the less, though in a different form.

end of the sentence, he may see its meaning and so receive something to think about; and he is thus given a great deal to learn by heart before obtaining anything to understand. This is manifestly wrong and an abuse of the reader's patience.

The ordinary writer has an unmistakable preference for this style, because it causes the reader to spend time and trouble in understanding that which he would have understood in a moment without it; and this makes it look as though the writer had more depth and intelligence than the reader. This is, indeed, one of those artifices referred to above, by means of which mediocre authors unconsciously, and as it were by instinct, strive to conceal their poverty of thought and give an appearance of the opposite. Their ingenuity in this respect is really astounding.

It is manifestly against all sound reason to put one thought obliquely on top of another, as though both together formed a wooden cross. But this is what is done where a writer interrupts what he has begun to say, for the purpose of inserting some quite alien matter; thus depositing with the reader a meaningless half-sentence, and bidding him keep it until the completion comes. It is much as though a man were to treat his guests by handing them an empty plate, in the hope of something appearing upon it. And commas used for a similar purpose belong to the same family as notes at the foot of the page and parentheses in the middle of the text; nay, all three differ only in degree. If Demosthenes and Cicero occasionally inserted words by way of parenthesis, they would have done better to have refrained.

But this style of writing becomes the height of absurdity when the parentheses are not even fitted into the frame of the sentence, but wedged in so as directly to shatter it. If, for instance, it is an impertinent thing to interrupt another person when he is speaking, it is no less impertinent to interrupt oneself. But all bad, careless, and hasty authors, who scribble with the bread actually before their eyes, use this style of writing six times on a page, and rejoice in it. It consists in — it is advisable to give rule and example together, wherever it is possible — breaking up one phrase in order to glue in another. Nor is it merely out of laziness that they write thus. They do it out of stupidity; they think there is a charming *légèreté* about it; that it gives life to what they say. No doubt there are a few rare cases where such a form of sentence may be pardonable.

Few write in the way in which an architect builds; who, before he sets to work, sketches out his plan, and thinks it over down to its smallest details. Nay, most people write only as though they were playing dominoes; and as in this game the pieces are arranged half by design, half by chance, so it is with the sequence and connection of their sentences. They only just have an idea of what the general shape of their work will be, and of the aim they set before themselves. Many are ignorant even of this, and write as the coral-insects build; period joins to period, and Lord knows what the author means.

Life nowadays goes at a gallop; and the way in which this affects literature is to make it extremely superficial and slovenly.

---

[1] Observe the strikingly similar diction used by Wackernagel, above, p. 10.

[2] Compare Wackernagel, above, pp. 15–16.

[3] Horace, *Art of Poetry*, l. 309.

[4] Compare Buffon, above, p. 176.

[5] Owing, very likely, to a printer's error, Mr. Saunders translates Schopenhauer's adjective *aerobatisch* "acrobatic." The German word is an inheritance from the Greek; cf. Aristophanes, *Clouds*, 225. The verb *aerobate* occurs in one or two English translations of the *Clouds;* the *New English Dictionary* does not record *aerobatic*.

[6] Compare Swift, above, p. 162.

XIII

HERBERT SPENCER (1820–1903)

The Philosophy of Style (1852)

[Spencer's essay on *The Philosophy of Style* appeared originally in the *Westminster Review* for October, 1852, as a review article upon Whately's *Elements of Rhetoric*, edited by J. W. Parker, Blair's *Lectures on Rhetoric and Belles Lettres*, Campbell's *Philosophy of Rhetoric,* and "Lord Kaimes' *Elements of Rhetoric.*" It was copied thence in the *Eclectic Magazine* for January, 1853 (Vol. 28, pp. 45–58). It has been republished separately as an annotated brochure (New York, Appleton, 1881, etc.), included in two collections of Spencer's essays (*Essays: Scientific, Political, and Speculative;* and *Essays: Moral, Political, and Æsthetic*), and "inserted in Boyd's edition of Lord Kames' *Elements of Criticism.*" It is contained also in Professor W. T. Brewster's collection, *Representative Essays on the Theory of Style* (1905). Finally, it has been edited by Professor F. N. Scott (Boston, Allyn & Bacon, second edition, 1905), "in the belief that *The Philosophy of Style* can be understood only in its proper connection with the Spencerian philosophy as a whole." In the latter edition Spencer's essay is accompanied by T. H. Wright's article on *Style*, which was a criticism of Spencer contributed to *Macmillan's Magazine* (Vol. 37, pp. 78 ff.), and copied by the *Popular Science Monthly* for January, 1878 (Vol. 12, pp. 340–349). To Professor Scott's useful bibliography should be added the titles of two subsequent publications: Spencer's *Autobiography,* New York (Appleton), 1904; and an estimate of Spencer by Professor Royce in the *International Quarterly* for June–September, 1904. Hiram M. Stanley's *Studies in the Evolutionary Psychology of Feeling*, London, 1895, criticises Spencer suggestively (Chap. XVIII, *The Psychology of Literary Style*).

Without adequate space, such as Professor Scott devotes to the matter, it is impossible to do more than hint at the necessary relation between Spencer's essay, with its salient doctrine of economy in literary expression, and the rest of the Spencerian social philosophy. This principle of economy is to be interpreted in the light of Spencer's fundamental conception of society as a unified and developing organism. The organism, being made up of individuals whose united activities constitute its manifold functions, demands at every instant the wisest expenditure of energy on the part of each individual, in the interests of the general welfare and progress — that is, of the more perfect functioning of the whole. Literature being a means of communication, therefore a social function, it follows that each separable portion of expressed thought, great or small — a dissertation, a paragraph, a phrase — is valuable according as it contributes with minimum waste of energy, not simply to the direct apprehension of what the writer wishes to say (since a given subject-matter, say a false philosophy, might be injurious to society as a whole), but to the progressive well-being and intelligence of the entire social complex.

If Spencer's essay inevitably loses when detached from the remainder of his work, it ought still to gain something when confronted with the opinions of others who have thought upon the same subject. " No general theory of expression," he says, " seems yet to have been enunciated; " a characteristically sweeping assertion, in which, however, he is striking chiefly at the rhetoricians of his own land. Of the ancients he knew less; and in the modern continental writers whom his slashing generalization would include, he was likewise not well-read. The worth of *The Philosophy of Style* must be settled to some extent by a comparison with both.]

PART I

Causes of Force in Language which depend upon Economy of the Mental Energies

I. The Principle of Economy applied to Words

Commenting on the seeming incongruity between his father's argumentative powers and his ignorance of formal logic, Tristram Shandy says: " It was a matter of just wonder with my worthy tutor, and two or three fellows of that learned society, that a man who knew not so much as the names of his tools, should be able to work after that fashion with them." Sterne's intended implication that a knowledge of the principles of reasoning neither makes, nor is essential to, a good reasoner, is doubtless true. Thus, too, is it with grammar. As Dr. Latham, condemning the usual school-drill in Lindley Murray, rightly remarks: "Gross vulgarity is a fault to be prevented; but the proper prevention is to be got from habit — not rules." Similarly, there can be little question that good composition is far less dependent upon acquaintance with its laws, than upon practice and natural aptitude. A clear head, a quick imagination, and a sensitive ear, will go far towards making all rhetorical precepts needless. He who daily hears and reads well-framed sentences, will naturally more or less tend to use similar ones. And where there exists any mental idiosyncrasy — where there is a deficient verbal memory, or an inadequate sense of logical dependence, or but little perception of order, or a lack of constructive ingenuity—no amount of instruction will remedy the defect. Nevertheless, *some* practical result may be expected from a familiarity with the principles of style. The endeavor to conform to laws may tell, though slowly. And if in no other way, yet, as facilitating revision, a knowledge of the thing to be achieved — a clear idea of what constitutes a beauty, and what a blemish — cannot fail to be of service.

No general theory of expression seems yet to have been enunciated. The maxims contained in works on composition and rhetoric, are presented in an unorganized form. Standing as isolated dogmas — as empirical generalizations, they are neither so clearly apprehended, nor so much respected, as they would be were they deduced from some simple first principle. We are told that " brevity is the soul of wit." We hear styles condemned as verbose or involved. Blair says that every needless part of a sentence " interrupts the description and clogs the image "; and again, that " long sentences fatigue the reader's attention." It is remarked by Lord Kaimes,[1] that "to give the utmost force to a period, it ought, if possible, to be closed with that word which makes the greatest figure." That parentheses should be avoided and that Saxon words should be used in preference to those of Latin origin, are established precepts. But, however influential the truths thus dogmatically embodied, they would be much more influential if reduced to something like scientific ordination. In this, as in other cases, conviction will be greatly strengthened when we understand the *why*. And we may be sure that a comprehension of the general principle from which the rules of composition result, will not only bring them home to us with greater force, but will discover to us other rules of like origin.

On seeking for some clue to the law underlying these current maxims, we may see shadowed forth in many of them, the importance of economizing the reader's or hearer's attention. To so present ideas that they may be apprehended with the least possible mental effort, is the desideratum towards which most of the rules above quoted point. When we condemn writing that is wordy, or confused, or intricate — when we praise this style as easy, and blame that as fatiguing, we consciously or unconsciously assume this desideratum as our standard of judgment. Regarding language as an apparatus of symbols for the conveyance of thought, we may say that, as in a mechanical apparatus, the more simple and the better arranged its parts, the greater will be the effect produced. In either case, whatever force is absorbed by the machine is

T

deducted from the result. A reader or listener has at each moment but a limited amount of mental power available. To recognize and interpret the symbols presented to him, requires part of this power; to arrange and combine the images suggested requires a further part; and only that part which remains can be used for realizing the thought conveyed. Hence, the more time and attention it takes to receive and understand each sentence, the less time and attention can be given to the contained idea; and the less vividly will that idea be conceived.

How truly language must be regarded as a hindrance to thought, though the necessary instrument of it, we shall clearly perceive on remembering the comparative force with which simple ideas are communicated by signs. To say, "Leave the room," is less expressive than to point to the door. Placing a finger on the lips is more forcible than whispering, "Do not speak." A beck of the hand is better than, "Come here." No phrase can convey the idea of surprise so vividly as opening the eyes and raising the eyebrows. A shrug of the shoulders would lose much by translation into words. Again, it may be remarked that when oral language is employed, the strongest effects are produced by interjections, which condense entire sentences into syllables. And in other cases, where custom allows us to express thoughts by single words, as in *Beware, Heigho, Fudge,* much force would be lost by expanding them into specific propositions. Hence, carrying out the metaphor that language is the vehicle of thought, there seems reason to think that in all cases the friction and inertia of the vehicle deduct from its efficiency; and that in composition, the chief, if not the sole thing to be done, is, to reduce this friction and inertia to the smallest possible amount. Let us then inquire whether economy of the recipient's attention is not the secret of effect, alike in the

right choice and collocation of words, in the best arrangement of clauses in a sentence, in the proper order of its
principal and subordinate propositions, in the judicious use
of simile, metaphor, and other figures of speech, and even in
the rhythmical sequence of syllables.

The greater forcibleness of Saxon English, or rather non-
Latin English, first claims our attention.[2] The several special
reasons assignable for this may all be reduced to the general
reason — economy. The most important of them is early
association. A child's vocabulary is almost wholly Saxon.
He says, *I have*, not *I possess* — *I wish*, not *I desire ;* he does
not *reflect*, he *thinks ;* he does not beg for *amusement*, but for
play; he calls things *nice* or *nasty*, not *pleasant* or *disagreeable.* The synonyms which he learns in after years, never
become so closely, so organically connected with the ideas
signified, as do these original words used in childhood; and
hence the association remains less strong. But in what does
a strong association between a word and an idea differ from
a weak one? Simply in the greater ease and rapidity of the
suggestive action. It can be in nothing else. Both of two
words, if they be strictly synonymous, eventually call up the
same image. The expression — It is *acid*, must in the end
give rise to the same thought as — It is *sour;* but because
the term *acid* was learnt later in life, and has not been so
often followed by the thought symbolized, it does not so readily
arouse that thought as the term *sour.* If we remember how
slowly and with what labor the appropriate ideas follow un-
familiar words in another language, and how increasing
familiarity with such words brings greater rapidity and ease
of comprehension; and if we consider that the same process
must have gone on with the words of our mother tongue from
childhood upwards, we shall clearly see that the earliest learnt
and oftenest used words, will, other things equal, call up

images with less loss of time and energy than their later learnt synonyms.

The further superiority possessed by Saxon English in its comparative brevity, obviously comes under the same generalization. If it be an advantage to express an idea in the smallest number of words, then will it be an advantage to express it in the smallest number of syllables. If circuitous phrases and needless expletives distract the attention and diminish the strength of the impression produced, then do surplus articulations do so. A certain effort, though commonly an inappreciable one, must be required to recognize every vowel and consonant. If, as all know, it is tiresome to listen to an indistinct speaker, or read a badly written manuscript; and if, as we cannot doubt, the fatigue is a cumulative result of the attention needed to catch successive syllables; it follows that attention is in such cases absorbed by each syllable. And if this be true when the syllables are difficult of recognition, it will also be true, though in a less degree, when the recognition of them is easy. Hence, the shortness of Saxon words becomes a reason for their greater force. One qualification, however, must not be overlooked. A word which in itself embodies the most important part of the idea to be conveyed, especially when that idea is an emotional one, may often with advantage be a polysyllabic word. Thus it seems more forcible to say, " It is *magnificent*," than " It is *grand*." The word *vast* is not so powerful a one as *stupendous*. Calling a thing *nasty* is not so effective as calling it *disgusting*.

There seem to be several causes for this exceptional superiority of certain long words. We may ascribe it partly to the fact that a voluminous, mouth-filling epithet is, by its very size, suggestive of largeness or strength; witness the immense pomposity of sesquipedalian verbiage: and when great power or intensity has to be suggested, this association of ideas aids the effect. A further cause may be that a word of several syllables admits of more emphatic articulation; and as emphatic articulation is a sign of emotion, the unusual impressiveness of the thing named is implied by it. Yet another cause is that a long word (of which the latter syllables are generally inferred as soon as the first are spoken) allows the hearer's consciousness a longer time to dwell upon the quality predicated; and where, as in the above cases, it is to this predicated quality that the entire attention is called, an advantage results from keeping it before the mind for an appreciable time. The reasons which we have given for preferring short words evidently do not hold here. So that to make our generalization quite correct we must say, that while in certain sentences expressing strong feeling, the word which more especially implies that feeling may often with advantage be a many-syllabled or Latin one; in the immense majority of cases, each word serving but as a step to the idea embodied by the whole sentence, should, if possible, be a one-syllabled or Saxon one.

Once more, that frequent cause of strength in Saxon and other primitive words — their imitative character, may be similarly resolved into the more general cause. Both those directly imitative, as *splash, bang, whiz, roar,* &c., and those analogically imitative, as *rough, smooth, keen, blunt, thin, hard, crag,* &c., have a greater or less likeness to the things symbolized; and by making on the senses impressions allied to the ideas to be called up, they save part of the effort needed to call up such ideas, and leave more attention for the ideas themselves.

The economy of the recipient's mental energy, into which are thus resolvable the several causes of the strength of Saxon English, may equally be traced in the superiority of specific over generic words. That concrete terms produce more vivid impressions than abstract ones, and should, when possible, be used instead, is a current maxim of composition. As Dr. Campbell says, "The more general the terms are, the picture is the fainter; the more special they are, 'tis the brighter." [3]   We should avoid such a sentence as:

In proportion as the manners, customs, and amusements of a nation are cruel and barbarous, the regulations of their penal code will be severe.

And in place of it we should write:

In proportion as men delight in battles, bull-fights, and combats of gladiators, will they punish by hanging, burning, and the rack.

This superiority of specific expressions is clearly due to a saving of the effort required to translate words into thoughts. As we do not think in generals but in particulars — as, whenever any class of things is referred to, we represent it to ourselves by calling to mind individual members of it; it follows that when an abstract word is used, the hearer or reader has to choose from his stock of images, one or more, by which he may figure to himself the genus mentioned.   In doing this, some delay must arise — some force be expended; and if, by employing a specific term, an appropriate image can be at once suggested, an economy is achieved, and a more vivid impression produced.

Turning now from the choice of words to their sequence, we shall find the same general principle hold good.   We have *a priori* reasons for believing that in every sentence there is some one order of words more effective than any other; and that this order is the one which presents the elements of the proposition in the succession in which they may be most readily put together.   As in a narrative, the events should be stated in such sequence that the mind may not have to go backwards and forwards in order to rightly connect them; as in a group of sentences, the arrangement should be such, that each of them may be understood as it comes, without waiting for subsequent ones; so in every sentence, the sequence of words should be that which suggests the constituents of the thought in the order most convenient for the building up that thought. Duly to enforce this truth, and to prepare the way for applications of it, we must briefly inquire into the mental act by which the meaning of a series of words is apprehended.

We cannot more simply do this than by considering the proper collocation of the substantive and adjective. Is it better to place the adjective before the substantive, or the substantive before the adjective? Ought we to say with the French — *un cheval noir;* or to say as we do — a black horse? Probably, most persons of culture would decide that one order is as good as the other. Alive to the bias produced by habit, they would ascribe to that the preference they feel for our own form of expression. They would expect those educated in the use of the opposite form to have an equal preference for that. And thus they would conclude that neither of these instinctive judgments is of any worth. There is, however, a philosophical ground for deciding in favor of the English custom. If " a horse black " be the arrangement, immediately on the utterance of the word " horse," there arises, or tends to arise, in the mind, a picture answering to that word; and as there has been nothing to indicate what *kind* of horse, any image of a horse suggests itself. Very likely, however, the image will be that of a brown horse, brown horses being the most familiar. The result is that when the word " black " is added, a check is given to the process of thought. Either the picture of a brown horse already present to the imagination has to be suppressed, and the picture of a black one summoned in its place; or else, if the picture of a brown horse be yet unformed, the tendency to form it has to be stopped. Whichever is the case, a certain amount of hindrance results. But if, on the other hand, " a black horse" be the expression used, no such mistake can be made. The word " black," indicating an abstract quality, arouses no definite idea. It simply prepares the mind for conceiving some object of that color; and the attention is kept suspended until that object is known. If, then, by the precedence of the adjective, the idea is conveyed without liability to error, whereas the precedence of the substantive is apt to produce a misconception, it follows that the one gives the mind less trouble than the other, and is therefore more forcible.

Possibly it will be objected that the adjective and substantive come so close together, that practically they may be considered as uttered at the same moment; and that on hearing the phrase " a horse black," there is not time to imagine a wrongly-colored horse before the word "black" follows to prevent it. It must be owned that it is not easy to decide by introspection whether this is so or not. But there are facts collaterally implying that it is not. Our ability to anticipate the words yet unspoken is one of them. If the ideas of the hearer kept considerably behind the expressions of the speaker, as the objection assumes, he could hardly foresee the end of a sentence by the time it was half delivered: yet this constantly happens. Were the supposition true, the mind, instead of anticipating, would be continually falling more and more in arrear. If the meanings of words are not realized as fast as the words are uttered, then the loss of time over each word must entail such an accumulation of delays as to leave a hearer entirely behind. But whether the force of these replies be or be not admitted, it will scarcely be denied that the right formation of a picture will be facilitated by presenting its elements in the order in which they are wanted;

even though the mind should do nothing until it has received them all.

What is here said respecting the succession of the adjective and substantive is obviously applicable, by change of terms, to the adverb and verb. And without further explanation, it will be manifest, that in the use of prepositions and other particles, most languages spontaneously conform with more or less completeness to this law.

On applying a like analysis to the larger divisions of a sentence, we find not only that the same principle holds good, but that the advantage of respecting it becomes marked. In the arrangement of predicate and subject, for example, we are at once shown that as the predicate determines the aspect under which the subject is to be conceived, it should be placed first; and the striking effect produced by so placing it becomes comprehensible. Take the often-quoted contrast between " Great is Diana of the Ephesians," and " Diana of the Ephesians is great." When the first arrangement is used, the utterance of the word " great " arouses those vague associations of an impressive nature with which it has been habitually connected; the imagination is prepared to clothe with high attributes whatever follows; and when the words " Diana of the Ephesians " are heard, all the appropriate imagery which can, on the instant, be summoned, is used in the formation of the picture: the mind being thus led directly, and without error, to the intended impression. When, on the contrary, the reverse order is followed, the idea " Diana of the Ephesians " is conceived with no special reference to greatness; and when the words " is great " are added, the conception has to be remodelled: whence arises a loss of mental energy, and a corresponding diminution of effect. The following verse from Coleridge's " Ancient Mariner," though somewhat irregular in structure, well illustrates the same truth:

> " *Alone, alone, all, all alone,*
> *Alone on a wide wide sea!*
> And never a saint took pity on
> My soul in agony."

Of course the principle equally applies when the predicate is a verb or a participle. And as effect is gained by placing first all words indicating the quality, conduct, or condition of the subject, it follows that the copula also should have precedence. It is true that the general habit of our language resists this arrangement of predicate, copula, and subject; but we may readily find instances of the additional force gained by conforming to it. Thus, in the line from " Julius Cæsar "—

> " Then *burst* his mighty heart,"

priority is given to a word embodying both predicate and copula. In a passage contained in "The Battle of Flodden Field," the like order is systematically employed with great effect:

> " The Border slogan rent the sky!
> *A home! a Gordon! was* the cry;
> *Loud were* the clanging blows:
> *Advanced, — forced back, — now low, now high,*
> The pennon sunk and rose;
> As *bends* the bark's mast in the gale
> When *rent are* rigging, shrouds, and sail,
> It wavered 'mid the foes."

Pursuing the principle yet further, it is obvious that for producing the greatest effect, not only should the main divisions of a sentence observe this sequence, but the subdivisions of these should be similarly arranged. In nearly all cases, the predicate is accompanied by some limit or qualification called its complement. Commonly, also, the circumstances of the subject, which form its complement, have to be specified.

And as these qualifications and circumstances must determine the mode in which the acts and things they belong to are conceived, precedence should be given to them. Lord Kaimes notices the fact that this order is preferable; though without giving the reason. He says: — " When a circumstance is placed at the beginning of the period, or near the beginning, the transition from it to the principal subject is agreeable: it is like ascending or going upward." A sentence arranged in illustration of this will be desirable. Here is one:

Whatever it may be in theory, it is clear that in practice the French idea of liberty is — the right of every man to be master of the rest.

In this case, were the first two clauses, up to the word " practice " inclusive, which qualify the subject, to be placed at the end instead of the beginning, much of the force would be lost; as thus:

The French idea of liberty is — the right of every man to be master of the rest; in practice at least, if not in theory.

Similarly, with respect to the conditions under which any fact is predicated. Observe in the following example the effect of putting them last:

How immense would be the stimulus to progress, were the honor now given to wealth and title given exclusively to high achievements and intrinsic worth !

And then observe the superior effect of putting them first:

Were the honor now given to wealth and title given exclusively to high achievements and intrinsic worth, how immense would be the stimulus to progress !

The effect of giving priority to the complement of the predicate, as well as the predicate itself, is finely displayed in the opening of " Hyperion ":

> " *Deep in the shady sadness of a vale*
> *Far sunken from the healthy breath of morn,*
> *Far from the fiery noon, and eve's one star,*
> *Sat* gray-haired Saturn, quiet as a stone."

Here it will be observed, not only that the predicate " sat "
precedes the subject " Saturn," and that the three lines in
italics, constituting the complement of the predicate, come
before it; but that in the structure of that complement also,
the same order is followed: each line being so arranged
that the qualifying words are placed before the words suggesting concrete images.

The right succession of the principal and subordinate propositions in a sentence manifestly depends on the same law.
Regard for economy of the recipient's attention, which, as
we find, determines the best order for the subject, copula,
predicate, and their complements, dictates that the subordinate
proposition shall precede the principal one, when the sentence
includes two. Containing, as the subordinate proposition
does, some qualifying or explanatory idea, its priority prevents misconception of the principal one; and therefore saves
the mental effort needed to correct such misconception. This
will be seen in the annexed example:

The secrecy once maintained in respect to the parliamentary
debates, is still thought needful in diplomacy; and in virtue
of this secret diplomacy, England may any day be unawares
betrayed by its ministers into a war costing a hundred thousand lives, and hundreds of millions of treasure: yet the
English pique themselves on being a self-governed people.

The two subordinate propositions, ending with the semi-
colon and colon respectively, almost wholly determine the
meaning of the principal proposition with which it concludes;
and the effect would be lost were they placed last instead of
first.

The general principle of right arrangement in sentences, which we have traced in its application to the leading divisions of them, equally determines the proper order of their minor divisions. In every sentence of any complexity the complement to the subject contains several clauses, and that to the predicate several others; and these may be arranged in greater or less conformity to the law of easy apprehension. Of course with these, as with the larger members, the succession should be from the less specific to the more specific — from the abstract to the concrete.

Now, however, we must notice a further condition to be fulfilled in the proper construction of a sentence; but still a condition dictated by the same general principle with the other: the condition, namely, that the words and expressions most nearly related in thought shall be brought the closest together. Evidently the single words, the minor clauses, and the leading divisions of every proposition, severally qualify each other. The longer the time that elapses between the mention of any qualifying member and the member qualified, the longer must the mind be exerted in carrying forward the qualifying member ready for use. And the more numerous the qualifications to be simultaneously remembered and rightly applied, the greater will be the mental power expended, and the smaller the effect produced. Hence, other things equal, force will be gained by so arranging the members of a sentence that these suspensions shall at any moment be the fewest in number; and shall also be of the shortest duration. The following is an instance of defective combination:

A modern newspaper-statement, though probably true, would be laughed at if quoted in a book as testimony; but the letter of a court gossip is thought good historical evidence, if written some centuries ago.

A rearrangement of this, in accordance with the principle indicated above, will be found to increase the effect. Thus:

Though probably true, a modern newspaper-statement quoted in a book as testimony, would be laughed at; but the letter of a court gossip, if written some centuries ago, is thought good historical evidence.

By making this change, some of the suspensions are avoided and others shortened; while there is less liability to produce premature conceptions. The passage quoted below from " Paradise Lost " affords a fine instance of a sentence well arranged; alike in the priority of the subordinate members, in the avoidance of long and numerous suspensions, and in the correspondence between the order of the clauses and the sequence of the phenomena described, which, by the way, is a further prerequisite to easy comprehension, and therefore to effect.

> " As when a prowling wolf,
> Whom hunger drives to seek new haunt for prey,
> Watching where shepherds pen their flocks at eve,
> In hurdled cotes amid the field secure,
> Leaps o'er the fence with ease into the fold;
> Or as a thief, bent to unhoard the cash
> Of some rich burgher, whose substantial doors,
> Cross-barred, and bolted fast, fear no assault,
> In at the window climbs, or o'er the tiles;
> So clomb this first grand thief into God's fold;
> So since into his church lewd hirelings climb." [4]

The habitual use of sentences in which all or most of the descriptive and limiting elements precede those described and limited, gives rise to what is called the inverted style: a title which is, however, by no means confined to this structure, but is often used where the order of the words is simply unusual. A more appropriate title would be the *direct*

style, as contrasted with the other, or *indirect style :* the peculiarity of the one being, that it conveys each thought into
the mind step by step with little liability to error; and of the
other, that it gets the right thought conceived by a series of
approximations.

The superiority of the direct over the indirect form of
sentence, implied by the several conclusions that have been
drawn, must not, however, be affirmed without reserva-
tion. Though, up to a certain point, it is well for the qualifying clauses of a period to precede those qualified; yet, as
carrying forward each qualifying clause costs some mental
effort, it follows that when the number of them and the time
they are carried become great, we reach a limit beyond which
more is lost than is gained. Other things equal, the arrangement should be such that no concrete image shall be suggested until the materials out of which it is to be made
have been presented. And yet, as lately pointed out, other
things equal, the fewer the materials to be held at once, and
the shorter the distance they have to be borne, the better.
Hence in some cases it becomes a question whether most
mental effort will be entailed by the many and long suspensions, or by the correction of successive misconceptions.

This question may sometimes be decided by considering
the capacity of the persons addressed. A greater grasp of
mind is required for the ready comprehension of thoughts
expressed in the direct manner, where the sentences are any-
wise intricate. To recollect a number of preliminaries stated
in elucidation of a coming idea, and to apply them all to
the formation of it when suggested, demands a good memory
and considerable power of concentration. To one possessing these, the direct method will mostly seem the best;
while to one deficient in them it will seem the worst. Just as it
may cost a strong man less effort to carry a hundred-weight

from place to place at once, than by a stone at a time; so, to an active mind it may be easier to bear along all the qualifications of an idea and at once rightly form it when named, than to first imperfectly conceive such idea and then carry back to it, one by one, the details and limitations afterwards mentioned. While conversely, as for a boy the only possible mode of transferring a hundred-weight is that of taking it in portions; so for a weak mind the only possible mode of forming a compound conception may be that of building it up by carrying separately its several parts.

That the indirect method — the method of conveying the meaning by a series of approximations—is best fitted for the uncultivated, may indeed be inferred from their habitual use of it. The form of expression adopted by the savage, as in — " Water, give me," is the simplest type of the approximate arrangement. In pleonasms, which are comparatively prevalent among the uneducated, the same essential structure is seen; as, for instance, in—"The men, they were there." Again, the old possessive case — "The king, his crown," conforms to the like order of thought. Moreover, the fact that the indirect mode is called the natural one, implies that it is the one spontaneously employed by the common people: that is — the one easiest for undisciplined minds.

There are many cases, however, in which neither the direct nor the indirect structure is the best; but where an intermediate structure is preferable to both. When the number of circumstances and qualifications to be included in the sentence is great, the most judicious course is neither to enumerate them all before introducing the idea to which they belong, nor to put this idea first and let it be remodelled to agree with the particulars afterwards mentioned; but to do a little of each. Take a case. It is desirable to avoid so extremely indirect an arrangement as the following:

" We came to our journey's end, at last, with no small difficulty, after much fatigue, through deep roads, and bad
weather."

Yet to transform this into an entirely direct sentence would
not produce a satisfactory effect; as witness:

At last, with no small difficulty, after much fatigue, through
deep roads, and bad weather, we came to our journey's
end.

Dr. Whately, from whom we quote the first of these two
arrangements, proposes this construction:

" At last, after much fatigue, through deep roads and bad
weather, we came, with no small difficulty, to our journey's
end."

Here it will be observed that by introducing the words " we
came " a little earlier in the sentence, the labor of carrying
forward so many particulars is diminished, and the subsequent qualification "with no small difficulty " entails an
addition to the thought that is very easily made. But a
further improvement may be produced by introducing the
words " we came " still earlier; especially if at the same
time the qualifications be rearranged in conformity with the
principle already explained, that the more abstract elements
of the thought should come before the more concrete. Observe the better effect obtained by making these two changes:

At last, with no small difficulty, and after much fatigue,
we came, through deep roads and bad weather, to our journey's end.

This reads with comparative smoothness; that is, with less
hindrance from suspensions and reconstructions of thought —
with less mental effort.

U

Before dismissing this branch of our subject, it should be further remarked, that even when addressing the most vigorous intellects, the direct style is unfit for communicating ideas of a complex or abstract character. So long as the mind has not much to do, it may be well able to grasp all the preparatory clauses of a sentence, and to use them effectively; but if some subtlety in the argument absorb the attention — if every faculty be strained in endeavoring to catch the speaker's or writer's drift, it may happen that the mind, unable to carry on both processes at once, will break down, and allow the elements of the thought to lapse into confusion.

II. The Effect of Figurative Language Explained

Turning now to consider figures of speech, we may equally discern the same general law of effect. Underlying all the rules given for the choice and right use of them, we shall find the same fundamental requirement — economy of attention. It is indeed chiefly because they so well subserve this requirement, that figures of speech are employed. To bring the mind more easily to the desired conception, is in many cases solely, and in all cases mainly, their object.

Let us begin with the figure called Synecdoche. The advantage sometimes gained by putting a part for the whole, is due to the more convenient, or more accurate, presentation of the idea. If, instead of saying " a fleet of ten ships," we say " a fleet of ten *sail*," the picture of a group of vessels at sea is more readily suggested; and is so because the sails constitute the most conspicuous parts of vessels so circumstanced: whereas the word *ships* would very likely remind us of vessels in dock. Again, to say, "All *hands* to the pumps," is better than to say, "All *men* to the pumps "; as it suggests the men in the special attitude intended, and so saves effort. Bringing "*gray hairs* with sorrow to the grave," is another expression, the effect of which has the same cause.

The occasional increase of force produced by Metonymy may be similarly accounted for. "The low morality of *the bar*," is a phrase both more brief and significant than the literal one it stands for. A belief in the ultimate supremacy of intelligence over brute force, is conveyed in a more concrete, and therefore more realizable form, if we substitute *the pen* and *the sword* for the two abstract terms. To say, " Beware of drinking! " is less effective than to say, " Beware of *the bottle!* " and is so, clearly because it calls up a less specific image.

The Simile is in many cases used chiefly with a view to ornament; but whenever it increases the *force* of a passage, it does so by being an economy. Here is an instance:

The illusion that great men and great events came oftener in early times than now, is partly due to historical perspective. As in a range of equidistant columns, the furthest off look the closest; so, the conspicuous objects of the past seem more thickly clustered the more remote they are.

To construct by a process of literal explanation the thought thus conveyed, would take many sentences, and the first elements of the picture would become faint while the imagination was busy in adding the others. But by the help of a comparison all effort is saved; the picture is instantly realized, and its full effect produced.

Of the position of the Simile,* it needs only to remark,

---

* Properly the term "simile" is applicable only to the entire figure, inclusive of the two things compared and the comparison drawn between them. But as there exists no name for the illustrative member of the figure, there seems no alternative but to employ "simile" to express this also. This context will in each case show in which sense the word is used.

that what has been said respecting the order of the adjective and substantive, predicate and subject, principal and subordinate propositions, &c., is applicable here. As whatever qualifies should precede whatever is qualified, force will generally be gained by placing the simile before the object to which it is applied. That this arrangement is the best, may be seen in the following passage from the " Lady of the Lake " :

> " As wreath of snow, on mountain-breast,
> Slides from the rock that gave it rest,
> Poor Ellen glided from her stay,
> And at the Monarch's feet she lay."

Inverting these couplets will be found to diminish the effect considerably. There are cases, however, even where the simile is a simple one, in which it may with advantage be placed last; as in these lines from Alexander Smith's " Life Drama " :

> " I see the future stretch
> All dark and barren as a rainy sea."

The reason for this seems to be, that so abstract an idea as that attaching to the word " future," does not present itself to the mind in any definite form, and hence the subsequent arrival at the simile entails no reconstruction of the thought.

Such, however, are not the only cases in which this order is the most forcible. As the advantage of putting the simile before the object depends on its being carried forward in the mind to assist in forming an image of the object, it must happen that if, from length or complexity, it cannot be so carried forward, the advantage is not gained. The annexed sonnet, by Coleridge, is defective from this cause:

> " As when a child on some long winter's night
> Affrighted clinging to its grandam's knees
> With eager wond'ring and perturb'd delight
> Listens strange tales of fearful dark decrees

Mutter'd to wretch by necromantic spell;
    Or of those hags, who at the witching time
    Of murky midnight ride the air sublime,
And mingle foul embrace with fiends of hell:

Cold horror drinks its blood! Anon the tear
    More gentle starts, to hear the beldame tell
    Of pretty babes, that loved each other dear,
Murder'd by cruel uncle's mandate fell:

Even such the shivering joys thy tones impart,
Even so thou, Siddons! meltest my sad heart!"

Here, from the lapse of time and accumulation of circumstances, the first part of the comparison is forgotten before its application is reached, and requires rereading. Had the main idea been first mentioned, less effort would have been required to retain it, and to modify the conception of it into harmony with the comparison, than to remember the comparison, and refer back to its successive features for help in forming the final image.

The superiority of the Metaphor to the Simile is ascribed by Dr. Whately to the fact that " all men are more gratified at catching the resemblance for themselves, than in having it pointed out to them." But after what has been said, the great economy it achieves will seem the more probable cause. Lear's exclamation —

" Ingratitude! thou marble-hearted fiend,"

would lose part of its effect were it changed into —

" Ingratitude! thou fiend with heart like marble";

and the loss would result partly from the position of the simile and partly from the extra number of words required. When the comparison is an involved one, the greater force of the metaphor, consequent on its greater brevity, becomes much more conspicuous. If, drawing an analogy between mental and physical phenomena, we say,

As, in passing through the crystal, beams of white light are decomposed into the colors of the rainbow; so, in traversing the soul of the poet, the colorless rays of truth are transformed into brightly-tinted poetry,

it is clear that in receiving the double set of words expressing the two halves of the comparison, and in carrying the one half to the other, considerable attention is absorbed. Most of this is saved, however, by putting the comparison in a metaphorical form, thus:

The white light of truth, in traversing the many-sided transparent soul of the poet, is refracted into iris-hued poetry.

How much is conveyed in a few words by the help of the Metaphor, and how vivid the effect consequently produced, may be abundantly exemplified. From " A Life Drama " may be quoted the phrase,

" I speared him with a jest,"

as a fine instance among the many which that poem contains. A passage in the " Prometheus Unbound," of Shelley, displays the power of the Metaphor to great advantage:

> " Methought among the lawns together
> We wandered, underneath the young gray dawn,
> And multitudes of dense white fleecy clouds
> Were wandering in thick flocks along the mountains
> *Shepherded* by the slow, unwilling wind."

This last expression is remarkable for the distinctness with which it realizes the features of the scene: bringing the mind, as it were, by a bound to the desired conception.

But a limit is put to the advantageous use of the Metaphor, by the condition that it must be sufficiently simple to be understood from a hint. Evidently, if there be any obscurity in the meaning or application of it, no economy of attention will be gained; but rather the reverse. Hence, when the comparison is complex, it is usual to have recourse to the Simile. There is, however, a species of figure, some-times classed under Allegory, but which might, perhaps, be better called Compound Metaphor, that enables us to retain the brevity of the metaphorical form even where the analogy is intricate. This is done by indicating the application of the figure at the outset, and then leaving the mind to continue the parallel. Emerson has employed it with great effect in the first of his " Lectures on the Times ":

"The main interest which any aspects of the Times can have for us, is the great spirit which gazes through them, the light which they can shed on the wonderful questions, What are we, and Whither we tend ? We do not wish to be deceived. Here we drift, like white sail across the wild ocean, now bright on the wave, now darkling in the trough of the sea; but from what port did we sail ? Who knows ? Or to what port are we bound ? Who knows ? There is no one to tell us but such poor weather-tossed mariners as ourselves, whom we speak as we pass, or who have hoisted some signal, or floated to us some letter in a bottle from far. But what know they more than we ? They also found themselves on this wondrous sea. No; from the older sailors nothing. Over all their speaking-trumpets the gray sea and the loud winds answer, Not in us; not in Time."

The division of the Simile from the Metaphor is by no means a definite one. Between the one extreme in which the two elements of the comparison are detailed at full length and the analogy pointed out, and the other extreme in which the comparison is implied instead of stated, come intermediate forms, in which the comparison is partly stated and partly implied. For instance:

"Astonished at the performances of the English plough, the Hindoos paint it, set it up, and worship it; thus turning a tool into an idol: linguists do the same with language."

There is an evident advantage in leaving the reader or hearer to complete the figure. And generally these intermediate forms are good in proportion as they do this; provided the mode of completing it be obvious.

Passing over much that may be said of like purport upon Hyberbole, Personification, Apostrophe, &c., let us close our remarks upon construction by a typical example. The general principle which has been enunciated is, that other things equal, the force of all verbal forms and arrangements is great, in proportion as the time and mental effort they demand from the recipient is small. The corollaries from this general principle have been severally illustrated; and it has been shown that the relative goodness of any two modes of expressing an idea, may be determined by observing which requires the shortest process of thought for its comprehension. But though conformity in particular points has been exemplified, no cases of complete conformity have yet been quoted. It is indeed difficult to find them; for the English idiom does not commonly permit the order which theory dictates. A few, however, occur in Ossian. Here is one:

" As autumn's dark storms pour from two echoing hills, so towards each other approached the heroes. As two dark streams from high rocks meet and mix, and roar on the plain: loud, rough, and dark in battle meet Lochlin and Inisfail. . . . As the troubled noise of the ocean when roll the waves on high; as the last peal of the thunder of heaven; such is noise of the battle."

Except in the position of the verb in the first two similes, the theoretically best arrangement is fully carried out in each of these sentences. The simile comes before the qualified image, the adjectives before the substantives, the predicate and copula before the subject, and their respective complements before them. That the passage is open to the charge of being bombastic proves nothing; or rather, proves our case. For what is bombast but a force of expression too great for the magnitude of the ideas embodied? All that may rightly be inferred is, that only in very rare cases, and then only to produce a climax, should *all* the conditions of effective expression be fulfilled.

III. Arrangement of Minor Images in Building up a Thought

Passing on to a more complex application of the doctrine with which we set out, it must now be remarked, that not only in the structure of sentences, and the use of figures of speech, may economy of the recipient's mental energy be assigned as the cause of force; but that in the choice and arrangement of the minor images, out of which some large thought is to be built up, we may trace the same condition to effect. To select from the sentiment, scene, or event described those typical elements which carry many others along with them; and so, by saying a few things but suggesting many, to abridge the description; is the secret of producing a vivid impression. An extract from Tennyson's "Mariana" will well illustrate this:

> "All day within the dreamy house,
> The doors upon their hinges creak'd,
> The blue fly sung in the pane; the mouse
> Behind the mouldering wainscot shriek'd,
> Or from the crevice peer'd about."

The several circumstances here specified bring with them many appropriate associations. Our attention is rarely drawn by the buzzing of a fly in the window, save when everything is still. While the inmates are moving about the house, mice usually keep silence; and it is only when extreme quietness reigns that they peep from their retreats. Hence each of the facts mentioned, presupposing numerous others, calls up these with more or less distinctness; and revives the feeling of dull solitude with which they are connected in our experience. Were all these facts detailed instead of suggested, the attention would be so frittered away that little impression of dreariness would be produced. Similarly in other cases. Whatever the nature of the thought to be conveyed, this skilful selection of a few particulars which imply the rest, is the key to success. In the choice of component ideas, as in the choice of expressions, the aim must be to convey the greatest quantity of thoughts with the smallest quantity of words.

The same principle may in some cases be advantageously carried yet further, by indirectly suggesting some entirely distinct thought in addition to the one expressed. Thus, if we say,

The head of a good classic is as full of ancient myths, as that of a servant-girl of ghost stories;

it is manifest that besides the fact asserted, there is an implied opinion respecting the small value of classical knowledge: and as this implied opinion is recognized much sooner than it can be put into words, there is gain in omitting it. In other cases, again, great effect is produced by an overt omission; provided the nature of the idea left out is obvious. A good instance of this occurs in "Heroes and Hero-worship." After describing the way in which Burns was sacrificed to the idle curiosity of Lion-hunters — people who came not out of sympathy, but merely to *see* him — people who sought a little amusement, and who got their amusement while "the Hero's life went for it!" Carlyle suggests a parallel thus:

" Richter says, in the Island of Sumatra there is a kind of
' Light-chafers,' large Fire-flies, which people stick upon spits,
and illuminate the ways with at night. Persons of condition
can thus travel with a pleasant radiance, which they much
admire. Great honor to the Fire-flies! But — ! — "

IV. The Superiority of Poetry to Prose Explained

Before inquiring whether the law of effect, thus far traced,
explains the superiority of poetry to prose, it will be needful to
notice some supplementary causes of force in expression, that
have not yet been mentioned. These are not, properly speaking, additional causes; but rather secondary ones, originating
from those already specified — reflex results of them. In
the first place, then, we may remark that mental excitement
spontaneously prompts the use of those forms of speech which
have been pointed out as the most effective. " Out with
him!" " Away with him!" are the natural utterances
of angry citizens at a disturbed meeting. A voyager, describing a terrible storm he had witnessed, would rise to some such
climax as — "Crack went the ropes and down came the
mast." Astonishment may be heard expressed in the phrase
— " Never was there such a sight!" All of which sentences
are, it will be observed, constructed after the direct type.
Again, everyone knows that excited persons are given to
figures of speech. The vituperation of the vulgar abounds
with them: often, indeed, consists of little else. " Beast,"
" brute," " gallows rogue," " cut-throat villain," these, and
other like metaphors and metaphorical epithets, at once call
to mind a street quarrel. Further, it may be noticed that
extreme brevity is another characteristic of passionate language. The sentences are generally incomplete; the particles
are omitted; and frequently important words are left to be
gathered from the context. Great admiration does not vent

itself in a precise proposition, as — " It is beautiful "; but in the simple exclamation, — " Beautiful ! " He who, when reading a lawyer's letter, should say, " Vile rascal ! " would be thought angry; while, " He is a vile rascal ! " would imply comparative coolness. Thus we see that alike in the order of the words, in the frequent use of figures, and in extreme conciseness, the natural utterances of excitement conform to the theoretical conditions of forcible expression.

Hence, then, the higher forms of speech acquire a secondary strength from association. Having, in actual life, habitually heard them in connection with vivid mental impressions, and having been accustomed to meet with them in the most powerful writing, they come to have in themselves a species of force. The emotions that have from time to time been produced by the strong thoughts wrapped up in these forms, are partially aroused by the forms themselves. They create a certain degree of animation; they induce a preparatory sympathy ; and when the striking ideas looked for are reached, they are the more vividly realized.

The continuous use of these modes of expression that are alike forcible in themselves and forcible from their associations, produces the peculiarly impressive species of composition which we call poetry. Poetry, we shall find, habitually adopts those symbols of thought, and those methods of using them, which instinct and analysis agree in choosing as most effective ; and becomes poetry by virtue of doing this. On turning back to the various specimens that have been quoted, it will be seen that the direct or inverted form of sentence predominates in them; and that to a degree quite inadmissible in prose. And not only in the frequency, but in what is termed the violence of the inversions, will this distinction be remarked. In the abundant use of figures, again, we may recognize the same truth. Metaphors, similes, hyperboles, and personifications, are the poet's colors, which he has liberty to employ almost without limit. We characterize as "poetical" the prose which uses these appliances of language with any frequency, and condemn it as "over florid" or "affected" long before they occur with the profusion allowed in verse. Further, let it be remarked that in brevity — the other requisite of forcible expression which theory points out, and emotion spontaneously fulfils — poetical phraseology similarly differs from ordinary phraseology. Imperfect periods are frequent; elisions are perpetual; and many of the minor words, which would be deemed essential in prose, are dispensed with.

Thus poetry, regarded as a vehicle of thought, is especially impressive partly because it obeys all the laws of effective speech, and partly because in so doing it imitates the natural utterances of excitement. While the matter embodied is idealized emotion, the vehicle is the idealized language of emotion. As the musical composer catches the cadences in which our feelings of joy and sympathy, grief and despair, vent themselves, and out of these germs evolves melodies suggesting higher phases of these feelings; so, the poet develops from the typical expressions in which men utter passion and sentiment, those choice forms of verbal combination in which concentrated passion and sentiment may be fitly presented.

There is one peculiarity of poetry conducing much to its effect — the peculiarity which is indeed usually thought its characteristic one — still remaining to be considered: we mean its rhythmical structure. This, improbable though it seems, will be found to come under the same generalization with the others. Like each of them, it is an idealization of the natural language of strong emotion, which is known to be more or less metrical if the emotion be not too violent;

and like each of them it is an economy of the reader's or hearer's attention. In the peculiar tone and manner we adopt in uttering versified language, may be discerned its relationship to the feelings; and the pleasure which its measured movement gives us, is ascribable to the comparative ease with which words metrically arranged can be recognized.

This last position will scarcely be at once admitted; but a little explanation will show its reasonableness. For if, as we have seen, there is an expenditure of mental energy in the mere act of listening to verbal articulations, or in that silent repetition of them which goes on in reading — if the perceptive faculties must be in active exercise to identify every syllable — then, any mode of so combining words as to present a regular recurrence of certain traits which the mind can anticipate, will diminish that strain upon the attention required by the total irregularity of prose. Just as the body, in receiving a series of varying concussions, must keep the muscles ready to meet the most violent of them, as not knowing when such may come; so, the mind in receiving unarranged articulations, must keep its perceptives active enough to recognize the least easily caught sounds. And as, if the concussions recur in a definite order, the body may husband its forces by adjusting the resistance needful for each concussion; so, if the syllables be rhythmically arranged, the mind may economize its energies by anticipating the attention required for each syllable.

Far-fetched though this idea will perhaps be thought, a little introspection will countenance it. That we *do* take advantage of metrical language to adjust our perceptive faculties to the force of the expected articulations, is clear from the fact that we are balked by halting versification. Much as at the bottom of a flight of stairs, a step more or less than we counted upon gives us a shock; so, too, does a misplaced accent or a supernumerary syllable. In the one case, we *know* that there is. an erroneous preadjustment; and we can scarcely doubt that there is one in the other. But if we habitually preadjust our perceptions to the measured movement of verse, the physical analogy above given renders it probable that by so doing we economize attention; and hence that metrical language is more effective than prose, because it enables us to do this.[5]

Were there space, it might be worth while to inquire whether the pleasure we take in rhyme, and also that which we take in euphony, are not partly ascribable to the same general cause.

Part II

Causes of Force in Language which depend upon Economy of the Mental Sensibilities

A few paragraphs only can be devoted to a second division of our subject that here presents itself. To pursue in detail the laws of effect, as applying to the larger features of composition, would carry us beyond our limits. But we may briefly indicate a further aspect of the general principle hitherto traced out, and hint a few cf its wider applications.

Thus far, then, we have considered only those causes of force in language which depend upon economy of the mental *energies:* we have now to glance at those which depend upon economy of the mental *sensibilities*. Questionable though this division may be as a psychological one, it will yet serve roughly to indicate the remaining field of investigation. It will suggest that besides considering the extent to which any faculty or group of faculties is tasked in receiving a form of words and realizing its contained idea, we have to consider the state in which this faculty or group of faculties is left; and how the reception of subsequent sentences and images will be influenced by that state. Without going at length into so wide a topic as the exercise of faculties and its reactive effects, it will be sufficient here to call to mind that every faculty (when in a state of normal activity) is most capable at the outset; and that the change in its condition, which ends in what we term exhaustion, begins simultaneously with its exercise. This generalization, with which we are all familiar in our bodily experiences, and which our daily language recognizes as true of the mind as a whole, is equally true of each mental power, from the simplest of the senses to the most complex of the sentiments. If we hold a flower to the nose for long, we become insensible to its scent. We say of a very brilliant flash of lightning that it blinds us; which means that our eyes have for a time lost their ability to appreciate light. After eating a quantity of honey, we are apt to think our tea is without sugar. The phrase " a deafening roar," implies that men find a very loud sound temporarily incapacitates them for hearing faint ones. To a hand which has for some time carried a heavy body, small bodies afterwards lifted seem to have lost their weight. Now, the truth at once recognized in these, its extreme manifestations, may be traced throughout. It may be shown that alike in the reflective faculties, in the imagination, in the perceptions of the beautiful, the ludicrous, the sublime, in the sentiments, the instincts, in all the mental powers, however we may classify them — action exhausts; and that in proportion as the action is violent, the subsequent prostration is great.

Equally, throughout the whole nature, may be traced the law that exercised faculties are ever tending to resume their original state. Not only after continued rest, do they

regain their full power — not only do brief cessations partially reinvigorate them; but even while they are in action,
the resulting exhaustion is ever being neutralized. The
two processes of waste and repair go on together. Hence
with faculties habitually exercised — as the senses of all
persons, or the muscles of any one who is strong — it happens that, during moderate activity, the repair is so nearly
equal to the waste, that the diminution of power is scarcely
appreciable; and it is only when the activity has been long
continued, or has been very violent, that the repair becomes
so far in arrear of the waste as to produce a perceptible prostration. In all cases, however, when, by the action of a
faculty, waste has been incurred, *some* lapse of time must
take place before full efficiency can be reacquired; and this
time must be long in proportion as the waste has been
great.

Keeping in mind these general truths, we shall be in
a condition to understand certain causes of effect in composition now to be considered. Every perception received, and
every conception realized, entailing some amount of waste —
or, as Liebig would say, some change of matter in the brain;
and the efficiency of the faculties subject to this waste being
thereby temporarily, though often but momentarily, diminished; the resulting partial inability must affect the acts of
perception and conception that immediately succeed. And
hence we may expect that the vividness with which images
are realized will, in many cases, depend on the order of
their presentation: even when one order is as convenient to
the understanding as the other.

There are sundry facts which alike illustrate this, and
are explained by it. Climax is one of them. The marked
effect obtained by placing last the most striking of any series
of images, and the weakness — often the ludicrous weakness

x

— produced by reversing this arrangement, depends on the general law indicated. As immediately after looking at the sun we cannot perceive the light of a fire, while by looking at the fire first and the sun afterwards we can perceive both; so, after receiving a brilliant, or weighty, or terrible thought, we cannot appreciate a less brilliant, less weighty, or less terrible one, while, by reversing the order, we can appreciate each. In Antithesis, again, we may recognize the same general truth. The opposition of two thoughts that are the reverse of each other in some prominent trait, insures an impressive effect; and does this by giving a momentary relaxation to the faculties addressed. If, after a series of images of an ordinary character, appealing in a moderate degree to the sentiment of reverence, or approbation, or beauty, the mind has presented to it a very insignificant, a very unworthy, or a very ugly image; the faculty of reverence, or approbation, or beauty, as the case may be, having for the time nothing to do, tends to resume its full power; and will immediately afterwards appreciate a vast, admirable, or beautiful image better than it would otherwise do. Conversely, where the idea of absurdity due to extreme insignificance is to be produced, it may be greatly intensified by placing it after something highly impressive: especially if the form of phrase implies that something still more impressive is coming. A good illustration of the effect gained by thus presenting a petty idea to a consciousness that has not yet recovered from the shock of an exciting one, occurs in a sketch by Balzac. His hero writes to a mistress who has cooled towards him, the following letter:

"MADAME, — Votre conduite m'étonne autant qu'elle m'afflige. Non contente de me déchirer le cœur par vos dédains, vous avez l'indélicatesse de me retenir une brosse à dents, que mes moyens ne me permettent pas de remplacer, mes propriétés étant grevées d'hypothèques.

" Adieu, trop belle et trop ingrate amie! Puissions-nous nous revoir dans un monde meilleur!

" CHARLES EDOUARD."

Thus we see that the phenomena of Climax, Antithesis, and Anticlimax, alike result from this general principle. Improbable as these momentary variations in susceptibility may seem, we cannot doubt their occurrence when we contemplate the analogous variations in the susceptibility of the senses. Referring once more to phenomena of vision, everyone knows that a patch of black on a white ground looks blacker, and a patch of white on a black ground looks whiter, than elsewhere. As the blackness and the whiteness must really be the same, the only assignable cause for this is a difference in their actions upon us, dependent upon the different states of our faculties. It is simply a visual antithesis.

But this extension of the general principle of economy — this further condition to effective composition, that the sensitiveness of the faculties must be continuously husbanded — includes much more than has been yet hinted. It implies not only that certain arrangements and certain juxtapositions of connected ideas are best; but that some modes of dividing and presenting a subject will be more striking than others; and that, too, irrespective of its logical cohesion. It shows why we must progress from the less interesting to the more interesting; and why not only the composition as a whole, but each of its successive portions, should tend towards a climax. At the same time, it forbids long continuity of the same kind of thought, or repeated production of like effects. It warns us against the error committed both by Pope in his poems and by Bacon in his essays — the error, namely, of constantly employing forcible forms of expression: and it points out that as the easiest posture by and by becomes fatiguing, and is with pleasure exchanged for one less easy, so, the most perfectly constructed sentences will soon weary, and relief will be given by using those of an inferior kind.

Further, we may infer from it not only that we should avoid generally combining our words in one manner, however good, or working out our figures and illustrations in one way, however telling ; but that we should avoid anything like uniform adherence, . even to the wider conditions of effect. We should not make every section of our subject progress in interest; we should not always rise to a climax. As we saw that, in single sentences, it is but rarely allowable to fulfil all the conditions to strength; so, in the larger sections of a composition we must not often conform entirely to the law indicated. We must subordinate the component effect to the total effect.

In deciding how practically to carry out the principles of artistic composition, we may derive help by bearing in mind a fact already pointed out — the fitness of certain verbal arrangements for certain kinds of thought. That constant variety in the mode of presenting ideas which the theory demands, will in a great degree result from a skilful adaptation of the form to the matter. We saw how the direct or inverted sentence is spontaneously used by excited people; and how their language is also characterized by figures of speech and by extreme brevity. Hence these may with advantage predominate in emotional passages; and may increase as the emotion rises. On the other hand, for complex ideas, the indirect sentence seems the best vehicle. In conversation, the excitement produced by the near approach to a desired conclusion, will often show itself in a series of short, sharp sentences; while, in impressing a view already enunciated, we generally make our periods voluminous by piling thought upon thought. These natural modes of procedure may serve as guides in writing. Keen observation and skilful analysis would, in like manner, detect further peculiarities of expression produced by other attitudes of mind; and by paying due attention to all such traits, a writer possessed of sufficient versatility might make some approach to a completely organized work.

This species of composition which the law of effect points out as the perfect one, is the one which high genius tends naturally to produce. As we found that the kinds of sentence which are theoretically best, are those generally employed by superior minds, and by inferior minds when excitement has raised them; so, we shall find that the ideal form for a poem, essay, or fiction, is that which the ideal writer would evolve spontaneously. One in whom the powers of expression fully responded to the state of feeling, would unconsciously use that variety in the mode of presenting his thoughts, which Art demands. This constant employment of one species of phraseology, which all have now to strive against, implies an undeveloped faculty of language. To have a specific style is to be poor in speech. If we remember that, in the far past, men had only nouns and verbs to convey their ideas with,[6] and that from then to now the growth has been towards a greater number of implements of thought, and consequently towards a greater complexity and variety in their combinations; we may infer that we are now, in our use of sentences, much what the primitive man was in his use of words; and that a continuance of the process that has hitherto gone on, must produce increasing heterogeneity in our modes of expression. As now, in a fine nature, the play of the features, the tones of the voice and its cadences, vary in harmony with every thought uttered; so, in one possessed of a fully developed power of speech, the mould in which each combination of words is cast will similarly vary with, and be appropriate to, the sentiment.

That a perfectly endowed man must unconsciously write in all styles, we may infer from considering how styles originate. Why is Johnson pompous, Goldsmith simple? Why is one author abrupt, another rhythmical, another concise? Evidently in each case the habitual mode of utterance must depend upon the habitual balance of the nature. The predominant feelings have by use trained the intellect to represent them. But while long, though unconscious, discipline has made it do this efficiently, it remains, from lack of practice, incapable of doing the same for the less active feelings; and when these are excited, the usual verbal forms undergo but slight modifications. Let the powers of speech be fully developed, however — let the ability of the intellect to utter the emotions be complete; and this fixity of style will disappear. The perfect writer will express himself as Junius, when in the Junius frame of mind; when he feels as Lamb felt, will use a like familiar speech; and will fall into the ruggedness of Carlyle when in a Carlylean mood. Now he will be rhythmical and now irregular; here his language will be plain and there ornate; sometimes his sentences will be balanced and at other times unsymmetrical; for a while there will be considerable sameness, and then again great variety. His mode of expression naturally responding to his state of feeling, there will flow from his pen a composition changing to the same degree that the aspects of his subject change. He will thus without effort conform to what we have seen to be the laws of effect. And while his work presents to the reader that variety needful to prevent continuous exertion of the same faculties, it will also answer to the description of all highly organized products, both of man and of nature: it will be, not a series of like parts simply placed in juxtaposition, but one whole made up of unlike parts that are mutually dependent.

[1] Henry Home, Lord Kames (1696–1782); observe the preferable spelling.

[2] On this head consult Jespersen's *Growth and Structure of the English Language* — a fascinating work; see also Greenough and Kittredge, *Words and their Ways in English Speech* (1901), Chap. III, *Learned Words and Popular Words* (pp. 19–28).

[3] Compare Buffon, above, p. 176.

[4] *Paradise Lost*, Book IV, ll. 183–193.

[5] Compare Aristotle, above, pp. 73–74.

[6] This is necessarily a matter of conjecture.

XIV

GEORGE HENRY LEWES (1817–1878)

The Principles of Success in Literature, Chapters V, VI
(1865)

[These two chapters constitute the last third of the serial treatise contributed by Lewes to the *Fortnightly Review* in the capacity of its first editor. The treatise was commenced in the initial number, May 15, 1865, as an indication of the literary standards which the new periodical was to represent. Chapters II and III appeared in the numbers for July 1 and July 15, respectively, of that year. Chapters IV, V, and VI followed on August 1, September 15, and November 1. The separate articles were collected in 1885 by Professor Albert S. Cook in a pamphlet that is now out of print. Professor F. N. Scott rendered the treatise accessible again in convenient form by his painstaking edition of 1891 (Boston, Allyn & Bacon, second edition, 1892), in which many typographical and other slips of the *Fortnightly* are corrected. To the accuracy of Professor Scott's second edition the text of the two chapters here presented is greatly indebted, aiming to improve thereon only in one or two minor points, such as uniformity in spelling the name *De Quincey*.

The latter three chapters of Lewes's *Principles of Success* are concerned with the outer and secondary requisites of expression rather than the inner and primary requisites of native endowment in the writer; that is, so far as manner can be treated separately from matter, they have to do with questions of style rather than questions of substance and conception. This is notably true of the last two chapters, of which the fifth, on *The Principle of Beauty*, is preliminary to the sixth, on *The Laws of Style*. Taken together, these two sections form a unit of inspiring doctrine that finds its place naturally in a collection like the present. All six chapters are, indeed, salutary reading for the undeveloped writer.

The first editor of the *Fortnightly* pronounced his name *Lewis*. In Professor Scott's edition, noted above, there is a good sketch of Lewes's life, supplemented by numerous critical references.]

Chapter V

The Principle of Beauty

It is not enough that a man have clearness of Vision, and reliance on Sincerity; he must also have the art of Expression, or he will remain obscure. Many have had

> " The visionary eye, the faculty to see
> The thing that hath been as the thing which is,"

but either from native defect, or the mistaken bias of education, have been frustrated in the attempt to give their visions beautiful or intelligible shape. The art which could give them shape is doubtless intimately dependent on clearness of eye and sincerity of purpose, but it is also something over and above these, and comes from an organic aptitude not less special, when possessed with fulness, than the aptitude for music or drawing. Any instructed person can write, as any one can learn to draw; but to write well, to express ideas with felicity and force, is not an accomplishment but a talent. The power of seizing unapparent relations of things is not always conjoined with the power of selecting the fittest verbal symbols by which they can be made apparent to others: the one is the power of the thinker, the other the power of the writer.

" Style," says De Quincey, " has two separate functions — first, to brighten the *intelligibility* of a subject which is obscure to the understanding; secondly, to regenerate the normal *power* and impressiveness of a subject which has become dormant to the sensibilities. . . . Decaying lineaments are to be retraced, and faded coloring to be refreshed." [1] To effect these purposes we require a rich verbal memory from which to select the symbols best fitted to call up images in the reader's mind, and we also require the delicate selective instinct to guide us in the choice and arrangement of those symbols, so that the rhythm and cadence may agreeably attune the mind, rendering it receptive to the impressions meant to be communicated. A copious verbal memory, like a copious memory of facts, is only one source of power, and without the high controlling faculty of the artist may lead to diffusive indecision. Just as one man, gifted with keen insight, will from a small stock of facts extricate unapparent relations to which others, rich in knowledge, have been blind; so will a writer, gifted with a fine instinct, select from a narrow range of phrases symbols of beauty and of power utterly beyond the reach of commonplace minds. It is often considered, both by writers and readers, that fine language makes fine writers; yet no one supposes that fine colors make a fine painter. The *copia verborum* is often a weakness and a snare. As Arthur Helps says, men use several epithets in the hope that one of them may fit. But the artist knows which epithet does fit, uses that, and rejects the rest. The characteristic weakness of bad writers is inaccuracy: their symbols do not adequately express their ideas. Pause but for a moment over their sentences, and you perceive that they are using language at random, the choice being guided rather by some indistinct association of phrases, or some broken echoes of familiar sounds, than by any selection of words to represent ideas. I read the other day of the truck system being " rampant" in a certain district; and every day we may meet with similar echoes of familiar words which betray the flaccid condition of the writer's mind drooping under the labor of expression.

Except in the rare cases of great dynamic thinkers whose thoughts are as turning-points in the history of our race, it is by Style that writers gain distinction, by Style they secure their immortality.[2] In a lower sphere many are remarked as writers although they may lay no claim to distinction as thinkers, if they have the faculty of felicitously expressing the ideas of others; and many who are really remarkable as thinkers gain but slight recognition from the public, simply because in them the faculty of expression is feeble. In proportion as the work passes from the sphere of passionless intelligence to that of impassioned intelligence, from the region of demonstration to the region of emotion, the art of Style becomes more complex, its necessity more imperious. But even in Philosophy and Science the art is both subtle and necessary; the choice and arrangement of the fitting symbols, though less difficult than in Art, is quite indispensable to success. If the distinction which I formerly drew between the Scientific and the Artistic tendencies be accepted, it will disclose a corresponding difference in the Style which suits a ratiocinative exposition fixing attention on abstract relations, and an emotive exposition fixing attention on objects as related to the feelings. We do not expect the scientific writer to stir our emotions, otherwise than by the secondary influences which arise from our awe and delight at the unveiling of new truths In his own researches he should extricate himself from the perturbing influences of emotion, and consequently he should protect us from such suggestions in his exposition. Feeling too often smites intellect with blindness, and intellect too often paralyzes the free play of emotion, not to call for a decisive separation of the two. But this separation is no ground for the disregard of Style in works of pure demonstration — as we shall see by and by.

The Principle of Beauty is only another name for Style, which is an art, incommunicable as are all other arts, but like them subordinated to laws founded on psychological conditions. The laws constitute the Philosophy of Criticism; and I shall have to ask the reader's indulgence if for the first time I attempt to expound them scientifically in the chapter to which the present is only an introduction. A knowledge of these laws, even presuming them to be accurately expounded, will no more give a writer the power of felicitous expression than a knowledge of the laws of color, perspective, and proportion will enable a critic to paint a picture. But all good writing must conform to these laws; all bad writing will be found to violate them. And the utility of the knowledge will be that of a constant monitor, warning the artist of the errors into which he has slipped, or into which he may slip if unwarned.

How is it that while every one acknowledges the importance of Style, and numerous critics from Quintilian and Longinus down to Quarterly Reviewers have written upon it, very little has been done towards a satisfactory establishment of principles? Is it not partly because the critics have seldom held the true purpose of Style steadily before their eyes, and still seldomer justified their canons by deducing them from psychological conditions? To my apprehension they seem to have mistaken the real sources of influence, and have fastened attention upon some accidental or collateral details, instead of tracing the direct connection between effects and causes. Misled by the splendor of some great renown they have concluded that to write like Cicero or to paint like Titian must be the pathway to success; which is true in one sense, and profoundly false as they understand it. One pestilent contagious error issued from this misconception, namely, that all maxims confirmed by the practice of the great artists must be maxims for the art; although a close examination might reveal that the practice of these artists may have been the result of their peculiar individualities or of the state of culture at their epoch.   A true Philosophy of Criticism would exhibit in how far such maxims were universal, as founded on laws of human nature, and in how far adaptations to particular individualities.   A great talent will discover new methods.   A great success ought to put us on the track of new principles.   But the fundamental laws of Style, resting on the truths of human nature, may be illustrated, they cannot be guaranteed by any individual success.   Moreover, the strong individuality of the artist will create special modifications of the laws to suit himself, making that excellent or endurable which in other hands would be intolerable.   If the purpose of Literature be the sincere expression of the individual's own ideas and feelings it is obvious that the cant about the " best models " tends to pervert and obstruct that expression.   Unless a man thinks and feels precisely after the manner of Cicero and Titian it is manifestly wrong for him to express himself in their way.   He may study in them the principles of effect, and try to surprise some of their secrets, but he should resolutely shun all imitation of them.   They ought to be illustrations not authorities, studies not models.

The fallacy about models is seen at once if we ask this simple question : Will the practice of a great writer justify a solecism in grammar or a confusion in logic?   No.   Then why should it justify any other detail not to be reconciled with universal truth ?   If we are forced to invoke the arbitration of reason in the one case, we must do so in the other.   Unless we set aside the individual practice whenever it is irreconcilable with general principles, we shall be unable to discriminate in a successful work those merits which *secured* from those demerits which *accompanied* success.   Now this is precisely the condition in which Criticism has always been.   It has been formal instead of being psychological: it has drawn its maxims from the works of successful artists, instead of ascertaining the psychological principles involved in the effects of those works. When the perplexed dramatist called down curses on the man who invented fifth acts, he never thought of escaping from his tribulation by writing a play in four acts; the formal canon which made five acts indispensable to a tragedy was drawn from the practice of great dramatists, but there was no demonstration of any psychological demand on the part of the audience for precisely five acts.*

Although no instructed mind will for a moment doubt the immense advantage of the stimulus and culture derived from a reverent familiarity with the works of our great predecessors and contemporaries, there is a pernicious error which has been fostered by many instructed minds, rising out of their reverence for greatness and their forgetfulness of the ends of Literature. This error is the notion of " models," and of fixed canons drawn from the practice of great artists. It substitutes Imitation for Invention; reproduction of old types instead of the creation of new. There is more bad than good work produced in consequence of the assiduous following of models. And we shall seldom be very wide of the mark if in our estimation of youthful productions we place more reliance on their departures from what has been already done, than on their resemblances to the best artists. An energetic crudity, even a riotous absurdity, has more promise in it than a clever and elegant mediocrity, because it shows that the young man is speaking out of his own heart, and struggling

---

* English critics are much less pedantic in adherence to "rules" than the French, yet when, many years ago, there appeared a tragedy in three acts, and without a death, these innovations were considered inadmissible; and if the success of the work had been such as to elicit critical discussion, the necessity of five acts and a death would doubtless have been generally insisted on.

to express himself in his own way rather than in the way he finds in other men's books. The early works of original writers are usually very bad; then succeeds a short interval of imitation in which the influence of some favorite author is distinctly traceable; but this does not last long: the native independence of the mind reasserts itself, and although perhaps academic and critical demands are somewhat disregarded, so that the original writer on account of his very originality receives but slight recognition from the authorities, nevertheless if there is any real power in the voice it soon makes itself felt in the world. There is one word of counsel I would give to young authors, which is that they should be humbly obedient to the truth proclaimed by their own souls, and haughtily indifferent to the remonstrances of critics founded solely on any departure from the truths expressed by others. It by no means follows that because a work is unlike works that have gone before it, therefore it is excellent or even tolerable; it may be original in error or in ugliness; but one thing is certain, that in proportion to its close fidelity to the matter and manner of existing works will be its intrinsic worthlessness. And one of the severest assaults on the fortitude of an unacknowledged writer comes from the knowledge that his critics, with rare exceptions, will judge his work in reference to preëxisting models, and not in reference to the ends of Literature and the laws of human nature. He knows that he will be compared with artists whom he ought not to resemble if his work have truth and originality; and finds himself teased with disparaging remarks which are really compliments in their objections. He can comfort himself by his trust in truth and the sincerity of his own work. He may also draw strength from the reflection that the public and posterity may cordially appreciate the work in which constituted authorities see nothing but failure. The history of Literature abounds in examples of critics being entirely at fault; — missing the old familiar landmarks, these guides at once set up a shout of warning that the path has been missed.

Very noticeable is the fact that of the thousands who have devoted years to the study of the classics, especially to the " niceties of phrase ". and " chastity of composition," so much prized in these classics, very few have learned to write with felicity, and not many with accuracy. Native incompetence has doubtless largely influenced this result in men who are insensible to the nicer shades of distinction in terms, and want the subtle sense of congruity; but the false plan of studying " models " without clearly understanding the psychological conditions which the effects involve, without seeing why great writing is effective and where it is merely individual expression, has injured even vigorous minds and paralyzed the weak. From a similar mistake hundreds have deceived themselves in trying to catch the trick of phrase peculiar to some distinguished contemporary. In vain do they imitate the Latinisms and antitheses of Johnson, the epigrammatic sentences of Macaulay, the colloquial ease of Thackeray, the cumulative pomp of Milton, the diffusive play of De Quincey: a few friendly or ignorant reviewers may applaud it as " brilliant writing," but the public remains unmoved. It is imitation, and as such it is lifeless.

We see at once the mistake directly we understand that a genuine style is the living body of thought, not a costume that can be put on and off; it is the expression of the writer's mind; it is not less the incarnation of his thoughts in verbal symbols than a picture is the painter's incarnation of his thoughts in symbols of form and color.[3] A man may, if it please him, dress his thoughts in the tawdry splendor of a masquerade. But this is no more Literature than the masquerade is Life.

No Style can be good that is not sincere. It must be the expression of its author's mind. There are, of course, certain elements of composition which must be mastered as a dancer learns his steps, but the style of the writer, like the grace of the dancer, is only made effective by such mastery; it springs from a deeper source. Initiation into the rules of construction will save us from some gross errors of composition, but it will not make a style. Still less will imitation of another's manner make one. In our day there are many who imitate Macaulay's short sentences, iterations, antitheses, geographical and historical illustrations, and eighteenth-century diction, but who accepts them as Macaulays?[4] They cannot seize the secret of his charm, because that charm lies in the felicity of his talent, not in the structure of his sentences; in the fulness of his knowledge, not in the character of his illustrations. Other men aim at ease and vigor by discarding Latinisms, and admitting colloquialisms; but vigor and ease are not to be had on recipe. No study of models, no attention to rules, will give the easy turn, the graceful phrase, the simple word, the fervid movement, or the large clearness; a picturesque talent will express itself in concrete images; a genial nature will smile in pleasant turns and innuendoes; a rapid, unhesitating, imperious mind will deliver its quick incisive phrases; a full, deliberating mind will overflow in ample paragraphs laden with the weight of parentheses and qualifying suggestions. The style which is good in one case would be vicious in another. The broken rhythm which increases the energy of one style would ruin the *largo* of another. Both are excellencies where both are natural.

We are always disagreeably impressed by an obvious imitation of the manner of another, because we feel it to be an insincerity, and also because it withdraws our attention from the thing said, to the way of saying it. And here lies the

Y

great lesson writers have to learn — namely, that they should think of the immediate purpose of their writing, which is to convey truths and emotions, in symbols and images, intelligible and suggestive. The racket-player keeps his eye on the ball he is to strike, not on the racket with which he strikes. If the writer sees vividly, and will say honestly what he sees, and how he sees it, he may want something of the grace and felicity of other men, but he will have all the strength and felicity with which nature has endowed him. More than that he cannot attain, and he will fall very short of it in snatching at the grace which is another's. Do what he will, he cannot escape from the infirmities of his own mind: the affectation, arrogance, ostentation, hesitation, native in the man will taint his style, no matter how closely he may copy the manner of another. For evil and for good, *le style est de l'homme même.*[5]

The French critics, who are singularly servile to all established reputations, and whose unreasoning idolatry of their own classics is one of the reasons why their Literature is not richer, are fond of declaring with magisterial emphasis that the rules of good taste and the canons of style were fixed once and forever by their great writers in the seventeenth century. The true ambition of every modern is said to be by careful study of these models to approach (though with no hope of equalling) their chastity and elegance. That a writer of the nineteenth century should express himself in the manner which was admirable in the seventeenth is an absurdity which needs only to be stated. It is not worth refuting. But it never presents itself thus to the French. In their minds it is a lingering remnant of that older superstition which believed the Ancients to have discovered all wisdom, so that if we could only surprise the secret of Aristotle's thoughts and clearly comprehend the drift of Plato's theories (which unhappily was not clear) we should compass all knowledge. How long this superstition lasted cannot accurately be settled; perhaps it is not quite extinct even yet; but we know how little the most earnest students succeeded in surprising the secrets of the universe by reading Greek treatises, and how much by studying the universe itself. Advancing Science daily discredits the superstition; yet the advance of Criticism has not yet wholly discredited the parallel superstition in Art. The earliest thinkers are no longer considered the wisest, but the earliest artists are still proclaimed the finest. Even those who do not believe in this superiority are, for the most part, overawed by tradition and dare not openly question the supremacy of works which in their private convictions hold a very subordinate rank. And this reserve is encouraged by the intemperate scorn of those who question the supremacy without having the knowledge or the sympathy which could fairly appreciate the earlier artists. Attacks on the classics by men ignorant of the classical languages tend to perpetuate the superstition.

But be the merit of the classics, ancient and modern, what it may, no writer can become a classic by imitating them. The principle of Sincerity here ministers to the principle of Beauty by forbidding imitation and enforcing rivalry. Write what you can, and if you have the grace of felicitous expression or the power of energetic expression your style will be admirable and admired. At any rate see that it be your own, and not another's; on no other terms will the world listen to it. You cannot be eloquent by borrowing from the opulence of another; you cannot be humorous by mimicking the whims of another; what was a pleasant smile dimpling his features becomes a grimace on yours.

It will not be supposed that I would have the great writers disregarded, as if nothing were to be learned from them; but the study of great writers should be the study of general principles as illustrated or revealed in these writers; and if properly pursued it will of itself lead to a condemnation of the notion of models.   What we may learn from them is a nice discrimination of the symbols which intelligibly express the shades of meaning and kindle emotion.   The writer wishes to give his thoughts a literary form.   This is for others, not for himself; consequently he must, before all things, desire to be intelligible, and to be so he must adapt his expressions to the mental condition of his audience.   If he employs arbitrary symbols, such as old words in new and unexpected senses, he may be clear as daylight to himself, but to others, dark as fog. And the difficulty of original writing lies in this, that what is new and individual must find expression in old symbols.   This difficulty can only be mastered by a peculiar talent, strengthened and rendered nimble by practice, and the commerce with original minds.   Great writers should be our companions if we would learn to write greatly; but no familiarity with their manner will supply the place of native endowment. Writers are born, no less than poets, and like poets, they learn to make their native gifts effective.   Practice, aiding their vigilant sensibility, teaches them, perhaps unconsciously, certain methods of effective presentation, how one arrangement of words carries with it more power than another, how familiar and concrete expressions are demanded in one place, and in another place abstract expressions unclogged with disturbing suggestions.   Every author thus silently amasses a store of empirical rules, furnished by his own practice, and confirmed by the practice of others.   A true Philosophy of Criticism would reduce these empirical rules to science by ranging them under psychological laws, thus demonstrating the validity of the rules, not in virtue of their having been employed by Cicero or Addison, by Burke or Sydney Smith, but in virtue of their conformity with the constancies of human nature.

The importance of Style is generally unsuspected by philosophers and men of science, who are quite aware of its advantage in all departments of *belles lettres;* and if you allude in their presence to the deplorably defective presentation of the ideas in some work distinguished for its learning, its profundity, or its novelty, it is probable that you will be despised as a frivolous setter up of manner over matter, a light-minded *dilettante,* unfitted for the simple austerities of science. But this is itself a light-minded contempt; a deeper insight would change the tone, and help to remove the disgraceful slovenliness and feebleness of composition which deface the majority of grave works, except those written by Frenchmen, who have been taught that composition is an art and that no writer may neglect it. In England and Germany, men who will spare no labor in research, grudge all labor in style; a morning is cheerfully devoted to verifying a quotation, by one who will not spare ten minutes to reconstruct a clumsy sentence; a reference is sought with ardor, an appropriate expression in lieu of the inexact phrase which first suggests itself does not seem worth seeking. What are we to say to a man who spends a quarter's income on a diamond pin which he sticks in a greasy cravat? a man who calls public attention on him, and appears in a slovenly undress? Am I to bestow applause on some insignificant parade of erudition, and withhold blame from the stupidities of style which surround it?

Had there been a clear understanding of Style as the living body of thought, and not its " dress," which might be more or less ornamental, the error I am noticing would not have spread so widely. But, naturally, when men regarded the grace of style as mere grace of manner, and not as the delicate precision giving form and relief to matter — as mere ornament, stuck on to arrest incurious eyes, and not as effective expression — their sense of the deeper value of matter made them despise such aid. A clearer conception would have rectified this error. The matter is confluent with the manner; and only *through* the style can thought reach the reader's mind. If the manner is involved, awkward, abrupt, obscure, the reader will either be oppressed with a confused sense of cumbrous material which awaits an artist to give it shape, or he will have the labor thrown upon him of extricating the material and reshaping it in his own mind.

How entirely men misconceive the relation of style to thought may be seen in the replies they make when their writing is objected to, or in the ludicrous attempts of clumsy playfulness and tawdry eloquence when they wish to be regarded as writers.

" Le style le moins noble a pourtant sa noblesse," [6]

and the principle of Sincerity, not less than the suggestions of taste, will preserve the integrity of each style. A philosopher, an investigator, an historian, or a moralist, so far from being required to present the graces of a wit, an essayist, a pamphleteer, or a novelist, would be warned off such ground by the necessity of expressing himself sincerely. Pascal, Biot, Buffon, or Laplace are examples of the clearness and beauty with which ideas may be presented wearing all the graces of fine literature, and losing none of the severity of science. Bacon, also, having an opulent and active intellect, spontaneously expressed himself in forms of various excellence. But what a pitiable contrast is presented by Kant ! It is true that Kant having a much narrower range of sensibility could have no such ample resource of expression, and he was wise in not attempting to rival the splendor of the *Novum Organum;* but he was not simply unwise, he was extremely culpable in sending forth his thoughts as so much raw material which the public was invited to put into shape as it could. Had he been aware that much of his bad writing was imperfect thinking, and always imperfect adaptation of means to ends, he might have been induced to recast it into more logical and more intelligible sentences, which would have stimulated the reader's mind as much as they now oppress it. Nor had Kant the excuse of a subject too abstruse for clear presentation. The examples of Descartes, Spinoza, Hobbes, and Hume are enough to show how such subjects can be mastered, and the very implication of writing a book is that the writer has mastered his material and can give it intelligible form.

A grave treatise, dealing with a narrow range of subjects or moving amid severe abstractions, demands a gravity and severity of style which is dissimilar to that demanded by subjects of a wider scope or more impassioned impulse; but abstract philosophy has its appropriate elegance no less than mathematics. I do not mean that each subject should necessarily be confined to one special mode of treatment, in the sense which was understood when people spoke of the " dignity of history," and so forth. The style must express the writer's mind; and as variously constituted minds will treat one and the same subject, there will be varieties in their styles. If a severe thinker be also a man of wit, like Bacon, Hobbes, Pascal, or Galileo, the wit will flash its sudden illuminations on the argument; but if he be not a man of wit, and condescends to jest under the impression that by jesting he is giving an airy grace to his argument, we resent it as an impertinence.

I have throughout used Style in the narrower sense of expression rather than in the wider sense of " treatment " which is sometimes affixed to it. The mode of treating a subject is also no doubt the writer's or the artist's way of expressing what is in his mind, but this is Style in the more general sense, and does not admit of being reduced to laws apart from those of Vision and Sincerity. A man necessarily sees a subject in a particular light — ideal or grotesque, familiar or fanciful, tragic or humorous. He may wander into fairy-land, or move amid representative abstractions; he may follow his wayward fancy in its grotesque combinations, or he may settle down amid the homeliest details of daily life. But having chosen he must be true to his choice. He is not allowed to represent fairy-land as if it resembled Walworth, nor to paint Walworth in the colors of Venice. The truth of consistency must be preserved in his treatment, truth in art meaning of course only truth within the limits of the art; thus the painter may produce the utmost relief he can by means of light and shade, but is peremptorily forbidden to use actual solidities on a plane surface. He must represent gold by color, not by sticking gold on his figures.* Our applause is greatly determined by our sense of difficulty overcome, and to stick gold on a picture is an avoidance of the difficulty of painting it.

Truth of presentation has an inexplicable charm for us, and throws a halo round even ignoble objects. A policeman idly standing at the corner of the street, or a sow lazily sleeping against the sun, are not in nature objects to excite a thrill of delight, but a painter may, by the cunning of his art, represent them so as to delight every spectator. The same objects represented by an inferior painter will move only a languid interest; by a still more inferior painter they may be

---

* This was done with *naïveté* by the early painters, and is really very effective in the pictures of Gentile da Fabriano — that Paul Veronese of the fifteenth century — as the reader will confess if he has seen the "Adoration of the Magi," in the Florence Academy; but it could not be tolerated now.

represented so as to please none but the most uncultivated eye. Each spectator is charmed in proportion to his recognition of a triumph over difficulty which is measured by the degree of verisimilitude. The degrees are many. In the lowest the pictured object is so remote from the reality that we simply recognize what the artist meant to represent. In like manner we recognize in poor novels and dramas what the authors mean to be characters, rather than what our experience of life suggests as characteristic.

Not only do we apportion our applause according to the degree of verisimilitude attained, but also according to the difficulty each involves. It is a higher difficulty, and implies a nobler art, to represent the movement and complexity of life and emotion than to catch the fixed lineaments of outward aspect. To paint a policeman idly lounging at the street corner with such verisimilitude that we are pleased with the representation, admiring the solidity of the figure, the texture of the clothes, and the human aspect of the features, is so difficult that we loudly applaud the skill which enables an artist to imitate what in itself is uninteresting; and if the imitation be carried to a certain degree of verisimilitude the picture may be of immense value. But no excellence of representation can make this high art. To carry it into the region of high art, another and far greater difficulty must be overcome; the man must be represented under the strain of great emotion, and we must recognize an equal truthfulness in the subtle indications of great mental agitation, the fleeting characters of which are far less easy to observe and to reproduce, than the stationary characters of form and costume. We may often observe how the novelist or dramatist has tolerable success so long as his personages are quiet, or moved only by the vulgar motives of ordinary life, and how fatally uninteresting, because unreal, these very personages become as soon as they are exhibited under the stress of emotion: their language ceases at once to be truthful, and becomes stagey; their conduct is no longer recognizable as that of human beings such as we have known. Here we note a defect of treatment, a mingling of styles, arising partly from defect of vision, and partly from an imperfect sincerity; and success in art will always be found dependent on integrity of style. The Dutch painters, so admirable in their own style, would become pitiable on quitting it for a higher.[7]

But I need not entér at any length upon this subject of treatment. Obviously a work must have charm or it cannot succeed; and the charm will depend on very complex conditions in the artist's mind. What treatment is in Art, composition is in Philosophy. The general conception of the point of view, and the skilful distribution of the masses, so as to secure the due preparation, development, and culmination, without wasteful prodigality or confusing want of symmetry, constitute Composition, which is to the structure of a treatise what Style — in the narrower sense — is to the structure of sentences. How far Style is reducible to law will be examined in the next chapter.

Chapter VI

The Laws of Style

From what was said in the preceding chapter, the reader will understand that our present inquiry is only into the laws which regulate the mechanism of Style. In such an analysis all that constitutes the individuality, the life, the charm of a great writer, must escape. But we may dissect Style, as we dissect an organism, and lay bare the fundamental laws by which each is regulated. And this analogy may indicate the utility of our attempt; the grace and luminousness of a happy talent will no more be acquired by a knowledge of these laws, than the force and elasticity of a healthy organism will be given by a knowledge of anatomy; but the mistakes in Style, and the diseases of the organism, may be often avoided, and sometimes remedied, by such knowledge.

On a subject like this, which has for many years engaged the researches of many minds, I shall not be expected to bring forward discoveries; indeed, novelty would not unjustly be suspected of fallacy. The only claim my exposition can have on the reader's attention is that of being an attempt to systematize what has been hitherto either empirical observation, or the establishment of critical rules on a false basis. I know but of one exception to this sweeping censure, and that is the essay on the *Philosophy of Style*, by Mr. Herbert Spencer, where for the first time, I believe, the right method was pursued of seeking in psychological conditions for the true laws of expression.

The aims of Literature being instruction and delight, Style must in varying degrees appeal to our intellect and our sensibilities: sometimes reaching the intellect through the presentation of simple ideas, and at others through the agitating influence of emotions; sometimes awakening the sensibilities through the reflexes of ideas, and sometimes through a direct appeal. A truth may be nakedly expressed so as to stir the intellect alone; or it may be expressed in terms which, without disturbing its clearness, may appeal to our sensibility by their harmony or energy. It is not possible to distinguish the combined influences of clearness, movement, and harmony, so as to assign to each its relative effect; and if in the ensuing pages one law is isolated from another, this must be understood as an artifice inevitable in such investigations.

There are five laws under which all the conditions of Style may be grouped: 1. The Law of Economy. 2. The Law

of Simplicity.   3. The Law of Sequence.   4. The Law of
Climax.   5. The Law of Variety.

It would be easy to reduce these five to three, and range all
considerations under Economy, Climax, and Variety; or we
might amplify the divisions; but there are reasons of convenience as well as symmetry which give a preference to the
five.   I had arranged them thus for convenience some years
ago, and I now find they express the equivalence of the two
great factors of Style — Intelligence and Sensibility.   Two
out of the five, Economy and Simplicity, more specially derive
their significance from intellectual needs; another two,
Climax and Variety, from emotional needs; and between
these is the Law of Sequence, which is intermediate in its
nature, and may be claimed with equal justice by both.   The
laws of force and the laws of pleasure can only be provisionally
isolated in our inquiry; in style they are blended.   The following brief estimate of each considers it as an isolated principle
undetermined by any other.

I. The Law of Economy

Our inquiry is scientific, not empirical; it therefore seeks
the psychological basis for every law, endeavoring to ascertain what condition of a reader's receptivity determines the
law.   Fortunately for us, in the case of the first and most
important law the psychological basis is extremely simple,
and may be easily appreciated by a reference to its analogue
in Mechanics.[8]

What is the first object of a machine?   Effective work —
vis viva.   Every means by which friction can be reduced, and
the force thus economized be rendered available, necessarily
solicits the constructor's care.   He seeks as far as possible
to liberate the motion which is absorbed in the working of

the machine, and to use it as *vis viva.* He knows that every superfluous detail, every retarding influence, is at the cost of so much power, and is a mechanical defect, though it may perhaps be an æsthetic beauty or a practical convenience. He may retain it because of the beauty, because of the convenience, but he knows the price of effective power at which it is obtained.

And thus it stands with Style. The first object of a writer is effective expression, the power of communicating distinct thoughts and emotional suggestions. He has to overcome the friction of ignorance and preoccupation. He has to arrest a wandering attention, and to clear away the misconceptions which cling around verbal symbols. Words are not like iron and wood, coal and water, invariable in their properties, calculable in their effects. They are mutable in their powers, deriving force and subtle variations of force from very trifling changes of position; coloring and colored by the words which precede and succeed; significant or insignificant from the powers of rhythm and cadence. It is the writer's art so to arrange words that they shall suffer the least possible retardation from the inevitable friction of the reader's mind. The analogy of a machine is perfect. In both cases the object is to secure the maximum of disposable force, by diminishing the amount absorbed in the working. Obviously, if a reader is engaged in extricating the meaning from a sentence which ought to have reflected its meaning as in a mirror, the mental energy thus employed is abstracted from the amount of force which he has to bestow on the subject; he has mentally to form anew the sentence which has been clumsily formed by the writer; he wastes, on interpretation of the symbols, force which might have been concentrated on meditation of the propositions. This waste is inappreciable in writing of ordinary excellence, and on subjects not severely tasking to the attention; but if inappreciable, it is always waste; and in bad writing, especially on topics of philosophy and science, the waste is important. And it is this which greatly narrows the circle for serious works. Interest in the subjects treated of may not be wanting; but the abundant energy is wanting which to the fatigue of consecutive thinking will add the labor of deciphering the language. Many of us are but too familiar with the fatigue of reconstructing unwieldy sentences in which the clauses are not logically dependent, nor the terms free from equivoque; we know what it is to have to hunt for the meaning hidden in a maze of words; and we can understand the yawning indifference which must soon settle upon every reader of such writing, unless he has some strong external impulse or abundant energy.

Economy dictates that the meaning should be presented in a form which claims the least possible attention to itself as form, unless when that form is part of the writer's object, and when the simple thought is less important than the manner of presenting it. And even when the manner is playful or impassioned, the law of Economy still presides, and insists on the rejection of whatever is superfluous. Only a delicate susceptibility can discriminate a superfluity in passages of humor or rhetoric; but elsewhere a very ordinary understanding can recognize the clauses and the epithets which are out of place, and in excess, retarding or confusing the direct appreciation of the thought. If we have written a clumsy or confused sentence, we shall often find that the removal of an awkward inversion liberates the idea, or that the modification of a cadence increases the effect. This is sometimes strikingly seen at the rehearsal of a play: a passage which has fallen flat upon the ear is suddenly brightened into effectiveness by the removal of a superfluous phrase, which, by its retarding influence, had thwarted the declamatory crescendo.

Young writers may learn something of the secrets of Economy by careful revision of their own compositions, and by careful dissection of passages selected both from good and bad writers. They have simply to strike out every word, every clause, and every sentence, the removal of which will not carry away any of the constituent elements of the thought. Having done this, let them compare the revised with the unrevised passages, and see where the excision has improved, and where it has injured, the effect. For Economy, although a primal law, is not the only law of Style. It is subject to various limitations from the pressure of other laws; and thus the removal of a trifling superfluity will not be justified by a wise economy if that loss entails a dissonance, or prevents a climax, or robs the expression of its ease and variety. Economy is rejection of whatever is superfluous; it is not Miserliness. A liberal expenditure is often the best economy, and is always so when dictated by a generous impulse, not by a prodigal carelessness or ostentatious vanity. That man would greatly err who tried to make his style effective by stripping it of all redundancy and ornament, presenting it naked before the indifferent public. Perhaps the very redundancy which he lops away might have aided the reader to see the thought more clearly, because it would have kept the thought a little longer before his mind, and thus prevented him from hurrying on to the next while this one was still imperfectly conceived.

As a general rule, redundancy is injurious; and the reason of the rule will enable us to discriminate when redundancy is injurious and when beneficial. It is injurious when it hampers the rapid movement of the reader's mind, diverting his attention to some collateral detail. But it is beneficial when its retarding influence is such as only to detain the mind longer on the thought, and thus to secure the fuller effect of the thought. For rapid reading is often imperfect reading. The mind is satisfied with a glimpse of that which it ought to have steadily contemplated; and any artifice by which the thought can be kept long enough before the mind, may indeed be a redundancy as regards the meaning, but is an economy of power. Thus we see that the phrase or the clause which we might be tempted to lop away because it threw no light upon the proposition, would be retained by a skilful writer because it added power. You may know the character of a redundancy by this one test: does it divert the attention, or simply retard it? The former is always a loss of power; the latter is sometimes a gain of power. The art of the writer consists in rejecting all redundancies that do not conduce to clearness. The shortest sentences are not necessarily the clearest. Concision gives energy, but it also adds restraint. The labor of expanding a terse sentence to its full meaning is often greater than the labor of picking out the meaning from a diffuse and loitering passage. Tacitus is more tiresome than Cicero.

There are occasions when the simplest and fewest words surpass in effect all the wealth of rhetorical amplification. An example may be seen in the passage which has been a favorite illustration from the days of Longinus [9] to our own. " God said: Let there be light! and there was light." This is a conception of power so calm and simple that it needs only to be presented in the fewest and the plainest words, and would be confused or weakened by any suggestion of accessories. Let us amplify the expression in the redundant style of miscalled eloquent writers: " God, in the magnificent fulness of creative energy, exclaimed: Let there be light! and lo! the agitating fiat immediately went forth, and thus

in one indivisible moment the whole universe was illumined."
We have here a sentence which I am certain many a writer
would, in secret, prefer to the masterly plainness of Genesis.
It is not a sentence which would have captivated critics.

Although this sentence from Genesis is sublime in its
simplicity, we are not to conclude that simple sentences are
uniformly the best, or that a style composed of propositions
briefly expressed would obey a wise Economy. The reader's
pleasure must not be forgotten; and he cannot be pleased
by a style which always leaps and never flows. A harsh,
abrupt, and dislocated manner irritates and perplexes him
by its sudden jerks. It is easier to write short sentences than
to read them. An easy, fluent, and harmonious phrase steals
unobtrusively upon the mind, and allows the thought to expand quietly like an opening flower.[10] But the very suasive-
ness of harmonious writing needs to be varied lest it become
a drowsy monotony; and the sharp, short sentences which
are intolerable when abundant, when used sparingly act like
a trumpet-call to the drooping attention.

II. The Law of Simplicity

The first obligation of Economy is that of using the fewest
words to secure the fullest effect. It rejects whatever is
superfluous; but the question of superfluity must, as I
showed just now, be determined in each individual case by
various conditions too complex and numerous to be reduced
within a formula. The same may be said of Simplicity, which
is indeed so intimately allied with Economy that I have only
given it a separate station for purposes of convenience. The
psychological basis is the same for both. The desire for
Simplicity is impatience at superfluity, and the impatience
arises from a sense of hindrance.

z

The first obligation of Simplicity is that of using the simplest means to secure the fullest effect. But although the mind instinctively rejects all needless complexity, we shall greatly err if we fail to recognize the fact, that what the mind recoils from is not the complexity, but the needlessness. When two men are set to the work of one, there is a waste of means; when two phrases are used to express one meaning twice, there is a waste of power; when incidents are multiplied and illustrations crowded without increase of illumination, there is prodigality which only the vulgar can mistake for opulence. Simplicity is a relative term. If in sketching the head of a man the artist wishes only to convey the general characteristics of that head, the fewest touches show the greatest power, selecting as they do only those details which carry with them characteristic significance. The means are simple, as the effect is simple. But if, besides the general characteristics, he wishes to convey the modelling of the forms, the play of light and shade, the textures, and the very complex effect of a human head, he must use more complex means. The simplicity which was adequate in the one case becomes totally inadequate in the other.

Obvious as this is, it has not been sufficiently present to the mind of critics who have called for plain, familiar, and concrete diction, as if that alone could claim to be simple; who have demanded a style unadorned by the artifices of involution, cadence, imagery, and epigram, as if Simplicity were incompatible with these; and have praised meagreness, mistaking it for Simplicity. Saxon words are words which in their homeliness have deep-seated power, and in some places they are the simplest because the most powerful words we can employ; but their very homeliness excludes them from certain places where their very power of suggestion is a disturbance of the general effect. The selective instinct of

the artist tells him when his language should be homely, and
when it should be more elevated; and it is precisely in the
imperceptible blending of the plain with the ornate that a
great writer is distinguished. He uses the simplest phrases
without triviality, and the grandest without a suggestion of
grandiloquence.

Simplicity of Style will therefore be understood as meaning
absence of needless superfluity:

"Without o'erflowing full." [11]

Its plainness is never meagreness, but unity. Obedient to
the primary impulse of *adequate* expression, the style of a
complex subject should be complex; of a technical subject,
technical; of an abstract subject, abstract; of a familiar subject, familiar; of a pictorial subject, picturesque. The structure of the "Antigone" is simple; but so also is the structure
of "Othello," though it contains many more elements; the
simplicity of both lies in their fulness without superfluity.

Whatever is outside the purpose, or the feeling, of a scene,
a speech, a sentence, or a phrase, whatever may be omitted
without sacrifice of effect, is a sin against this law. I do not
say that the incident, description, or dialogue, which may be
omitted without injury to the unity of the work, is necessarily
a sin against art; still less that, even when acknowledged as
a sin, it may not sometimes be condoned by its success. The
law of Simplicity is not the only law of art; and, moreover,
audiences are, unhappily, so little accustomed to judge works
as wholes, and so ready to seize upon any detail which pleases
them, no matter how incongruously the detail may be placed,*
that a felicitous fault will captivate applause, let critics shake
reproving heads as they may. Nevertheless the law of Sim-

---

* "Was hilft's, wenn ihr ein Ganzes dargebracht?
Das Publikum wird es euch doch zerpflücken." — GOETHE.

plicity remains unshaken, and ought only to give way to the pressure of the law of Variety.

The drama offers a good opportunity for studying the operation of this law, because the limitations of time compel the dramatist to attend closely to what is and what is not needful for his purpose. A drama must compress into two or three hours material which may be diffused through three volumes of a novel, because spectators are more impatient than readers, and more unequivocally resent by their signs of weariness any disregard of economy, which in the novel may be skipped. The dramatist, having little time in which to evolve his story, feels that every scene which does not forward the progress of the action or intensify the interest in the characters is an artistic defect; though in itself it may be charmingly written, and may excite applause, it is away from his immediate purpose. And what is true of purpose-less scenes and characters which divert the current of progress, is equally true, in a minor degree, of speeches and sentences which arrest the culminating interest by calling attention away to other objects. It is an error which arises from a deficient earnestness on the writer's part, or from a too pliant facility. The *dramatis personæ* wander in their dialogue, not swayed by the fluctuations of feeling, but by the author's desire to show his wit and wisdom, or else by his want of power to control the vagrant suggestions of his fancy. The desire for display and the inability to control are weaknesses that lead to almost every transgression of Simplicity; but sometimes the transgressions are made in more or less con-scious obedience to the law of Variety, although the highest reach of art is to secure variety by an opulent simplicity.

The novelist is not under the same limitations of time, nor has he to contend against the same mental impatience on the part of his public. He may therefore linger where the dramatist must hurry; he may digress, and gain fresh impetus from the digression, where the dramatist would seriously endanger the effect of his scene by retarding its evolution. The novelist with a prudent prodigality may employ descriptions, dialogues, and episodes, which would be fatal in a drama. Characters may be introduced and dismissed without having any important connection with the plot; it is enough if they serve the purpose of the chapter in which they appear. Although as a matter of fine art no character should have a place in a novel unless it form an integral element of the story, and no episode should be introduced unless it reflect some strong light on the characters or incidents, this is a critical demand which only fine artists think of satisfying, and only delicate tastes appreciate. For the mass of readers it is enough if they are amused; and indeed all readers, no matter how critical their taste, would rather be pleased by a transgression of the law than wearied by prescription. Delight condones offence. The only question for the writer is, whether the offence is so trivial as to be submerged in the delight. And he will do well to remember that the greater flexibility belonging to the novel by no means removes the novel from the laws which rule the drama. The parts of a novel should have organic relations. Push the license to excess, and stitch together a volume of unrelated chapters, — a patchwork of descriptions, dialogues, and incidents, — no one will call that a novel; and the less the work has of this unorganized character the greater will be its value, not only in the eyes of critics, but in its effect on the emotions of the reader.

Simplicity of structure means organic unity, whether the organism be simple or complex; and hence in all times the emphasis which critics have laid upon Simplicity, though they have not unfrequently confounded it with narrowness of range.

In like manner, as we said just now, when treating of diction they have overlooked the fact that the simplest must be that which best expresses the thought.   Simplicity of diction is integrity of speech; that which admits of least equivocation, that which by the clearest verbal symbols most readily calls up in the reader's mind the images and feelings which the writer wishes to call up.   Such diction may be concrete or abstract, familiar or technical; its simplicity is determined by the nature of the thought.   We shall often be simpler in using abstract and technical terms than in using concrete and familiar terms which by their very concreteness and familiarity call up images and feelings foreign to our immediate purpose. If we desire the attention to fall upon some general idea we only blur its outlines by using words that call up particulars. Thus, although it may be needful to give some definite direction to the reader's thoughts by the suggestion of a particular fact, we must be careful not to arrest his attention on the fact itself, still less to divert it by calling up vivid images of facts unrelated to our present purpose.   For example, I wish to fix in the reader's mind a conception of a lonely meditative man walking on the seashore, and I fall into the vicious style of our day which is lauded as word-painting, and write something like this: —

"The fishermen mending their storm-beaten boats upon the shore would lay down the hammer to gaze after him as he passed abstractedly before their huts, his hair streaming in the salt breeze, his feet crushing the scattered seaweed, his eyes dreamily fixed upon the purple heights of the precipitous crags."

Now it is obvious that the details here assembled are mostly foreign to my purpose, which has nothing whatever to do with fishermen, storms, boats, seaweeds, or purple crags; and by calling up images of these I only divert the attention from

my thought.   Whereas, if it had been my purpose to picture
the scene itself, or the man's delight in it, then the enumeration of details would give color and distinctness to the picture.

The art of a great writer is seen in the perfect fitness of his
expressions.   He knows how to blend vividness with vagueness, knows where images are needed, and where by their
vivacity they would be obstacles to the rapid appreciation of
his thought.   The value of concrete illustration artfully used
may be seen illustrated in a passage from Macaulay's invective
against Frederick the Great: " On the head of Frederick is all
the blood which was shed in a war which raged during many
years and in every quarter of the globe, the blood of the
column at Fontenoy, the blood of the mountaineers who were
slaughtered at Culloden.   The evils produced by his wicked-
ness were felt in lands where the name of Prussia was unknown; and in order that he might rob a neighbor whom he
had promised to defend, black men fought on the coast of
Coromandel, and red men scalped each other by the Great
Lakes of North America."   Disregarding the justice or injustice of the thought, note the singular force and beauty of
this passage, delightful alike to ear and mind; and observe
how its very elaborateness has the effect of the finest simplicity,
because the successive pictures are constituents of the general
thought, and by their vividness render the conclusion more
impressive.   Let us suppose him to have written with the
vague generality of expression much patronized by dignified
historians, and told us that " Frederick was the cause of great
European conflicts extending over long periods; and in consequence of his political aggression hideous crimes were per-
petrated in the most distant parts of the globe."   This absence
of concrete images would not have been simplicity, inasmuch
as the labor of converting the general expressions into definite
meanings would thus have been thrown upon the reader.

Pictorial illustration has its dangers, as we daily see in the clumsy imitators of Macaulay, who have not the fine instinct of style, but obey the vulgar instinct of display, and imagine they can produce a brilliant effect by the use of strong lights, whereas they distract the attention with images alien to the general impression, just as crude colorists vex the eye with importunate splendors. Nay, even good writers sometimes sacrifice the large effect of a diffusive light to the small effect of a brilliant point. This is a defect of taste frequently noticeable in two very good writers, De Quincey and Ruskin, whose command of expression is so varied that it tempts them into *fioritura* as flexibility of voice tempts singers to sin against simplicity. At the close of an eloquent passage De Quincey writes: —

"Gravitation, again, that works without holiday forever, and searches every corner of the universe, what intellect can follow it to its fountains? And yet, shyer than gravitation, less to be counted than the fluxions of sun-dials, stealthier than the growth of a forest, are the footsteps of Christianity amongst the political workings of man."

The association of holidays and shyness with an idea so abstract as that of gravitation, the use of the learned word fluxions to express the movements of the shadows on a dial, and the discordant suggestion of stealthiness applied to vegetable growth and Christianity, are so many offences against simplicity. Let the passage be contrasted with one in which wealth of imagery is in accordance with the thought it expresses: —

"In the edifices of Man there should be found reverent worship and following, not only of the spirit which rounds the pillars of the forest, and arches the vault of the avenue — which gives veining to the leaf and polish to the shell, and grace to every pulse that agitates animal organization — but of that also which reproves the pillars of the earth, and builds up her barren precipices into the coldness of the clouds, and lifts her shadowy cones of mountain purple into the pale arch of the sky; for these, and other glories more than these, refuse not to connect themselves, in his thoughts, with the work of his own hand; the gray cliff loses not its nobleness when it reminds us of some Cyclopean waste of mural stone; the pinnacles of the rocky promontory arrange themselves, undegraded, into fantastic semblances of fortress towers, and even the awful cone of the far-off mountain has a melancholy mixed with that of its own solitude, which is cast from the images of nameless tumuli on white sea-shores, and of the heaps of reedy clay, into which chambered cities melt in their mortality." *

I shall notice but two points in this singularly beautiful passage. The one is the exquisite instinct of Sequence in several of the phrases, not only as to harmony, but as to the evolution of the meaning, especially in " builds up her barren precipices into the coldness of the clouds, and lifts her shadowy cones of mountain purple into the pale arch of the sky." The other is the injurious effect of three words in the sentence, " for these, and other glories more than these, *refuse not to* connect themselves in his thoughts." Strike out the words printed in italics, and you not only improve the harmony, but free the sentence from a disturbing use of what Ruskin has named the " pathetic fallacy." There are times in which Nature may be assumed as in sympathy with our moods; and at such times the pathetic fallacy is a source of subtle effect. But in the passage just quoted the introduction seems to me a mistake: the simplicity of the thought is disturbed by this hint of an active participation of Nature in man's feelings; it is preserved in its integrity by the omission of that hint.

* Ruskin.

These illustrations will suffice to show how the law we are considering will command and forbid the use of concrete expressions and vivid imagery according to the purpose of the writer. A fine taste guided by Sincerity will determine that use. Nothing more than a general rule can be laid down. Eloquence, as I said before, cannot spring from the simple desire to be eloquent; the desire usually leads to grandiloquence. But Sincerity will save us. We have but to remember Montesquieu's advice: " Il faut prendre garde aux grandes phrases dans les humbles sujets; elles produisent l'effet d'une masque à barbe blanche sur la joue d'un enfant."

Here another warning may be placed. In our anxiety lest we err on the side of grandiloquence we may perhaps fall into the opposite error of tameness. Sincerity will save us here also. Let us but express the thought and feeling actually in our minds, then our very grandiloquence (if that is our weakness) will have a certain movement and vivacity not without effect, and our tameness (if we are tame) will have a gentleness not without its charm.

Finally, let us banish from our critical superstitions the notion that chastity of composition, or simplicity of Style, is in any respect allied to timidity. There are two kinds of timidity, or rather it has two different origins, both of which cripple the free movement of thought. The one is the timidity of fastidiousness, the other of placid stupidity: the one shrinks from originality lest it should be regarded as impertinent; the other lest, being new, it should be wrong. We detect the one in the sensitive discreetness of the style. We detect the other in the complacency of its platitudes and the stereotyped commonness of its metaphors. The writer who is afraid of originality feels himself in deep water when he launches into a commonplace. For him who is timid because weak, there is no advice, except suggesting the propriety of silence. For him who is timid because fastidious, there is this advice: get rid of the superstition about chastity, and recognize the truth that a style may be simple, even if it move amid abstractions, or employ few Saxon words, or abound in concrete images and novel turns of expression.

III. The Law of Sequence

Much that might be included under this head would equally well find its place under that of Economy or that of Climax. Indeed it is obvious that to secure perfect Economy there must be that sequence of the words which will present the least obstacle to the unfolding of the thought, and that Climax is only attainable through a properly graduated sequence. But there is another element we have to take into account, and that is the rhythmical effect of Style. Mr. Herbert Spencer in his Essay very clearly states the law of Sequence, but I infer that he would include it entirely under the law of Economy; at any rate he treats of it solely in reference to intelligibility, and not at all in its scarcely less important relation to harmony. " We have *à priori* reasons," he says, " for believing that in every sentence there is some one order of words more effective than any other; and that this order is the one which presents the elements of the proposition in the succession in which they may be most readily put together. As in a narrative, the events should be stated in such sequence that the mind may not have to go backwards and forwards in order to rightly connect them; as in a group of sentences, the arrangement should be such, that each of them may be understood as it comes, without waiting for subsequent ones; so in every sentence, the sequence of words should be that which suggests the constituents of the thought in the order most convenient for the building up that thought." [12]

But Style appeals to the emotions as well as to the intellect, and the arrangement of words and sentences which will be the most economical may not be the most musical, and the most musical may not be the most pleasurably effective. For Climax and Variety it may be necessary to sacrifice something of rapid intelligibility: hence involutions, antitheses, and suspensions, which disturb the most orderly arrangement, may yet, in virtue of their own subtle influences, be counted as improvements on that arrangement.

Tested by the Intellect and the Feelings, the law of Sequence is seen to be a curious compound of the two. If we isolate these elements for the purposes of exposition, we shall find that the principle of the first is much simpler and more easy of obedience than the principle of the second. It may be thus stated: —

The constituent elements of the conception expressed in the sentence and the paragraph should be arranged in strict correspondence with an inductive or a deductive progression.

All exposition, like all research, is either inductive or deductive. It groups particulars so as to lead up to a general conception which embraces them all, but which could not be fully understood until they had been estimated; or else it starts from some general conception, already familiar to the mind, and as it moves along, casts its light upon numerous particulars, which are thus shown to be related to it, but which without that light would have been overlooked.

If the reader will meditate on that brief statement of the principle, he will, I think, find it explain many doubtful points. Let me merely notice one, namely, the dispute as to whether the direct or the indirect style should be preferred. Some writers insist, and others practise the precept without in-

sistence, that the proposition should be stated first, and all
its qualifications as well as its evidences be made to follow;
others maintain that the proposition should be made to grow
up step by step with all its evidences and qualifications in
their due order, and the conclusion disclose itself as crowning the whole. Are not both methods right under different
circumstances? If my object is to convince you of a general
truth, or to impress you with a feeling, which you are not
already prepared to accept, it is obvious that the most effective
method is the inductive, which leads your mind upon a culminating wave of evidence or emotion to the very point I aim
at. But the deductive method is best when I wish to direct
the light of familiar truths and roused emotions, upon new
particulars, or upon details in unsuspected relation to those
truths; and when I wish the attention to be absorbed by
these particulars which are of interest in themselves, not upon
the general truths which are of no present interest except
in as far as they light up these details. A growing thought
requires the inductive exposition, an applied thought the
deductive.

This principle, which is of very wide application, is subject
to two important qualifications — one pressed on it by the
necessities of Climax and Variety, the other by the feebleness
of memory, which cannot keep a long hold of details unless
their significance is apprehended; so that a paragraph of
suspended meaning should never be long, and when the
necessities of the case bring together numerous particulars in
evidence of the conclusion, they should be so arranged as to
have culminating force: one clause leading up to another,
and throwing its impetus into it, instead of being linked on
to another, and dragging the mind down with its weight.

It is surprising how few men understand that Style is a
Fine Art; and how few of those who are fastidious in their

diction give much care to the arrangement of their sentences, paragraphs, and chapters — in a word, to Composition. The painter distributes his masses with a view to general effect; so does the musician: writers seldom do so. Nor do they usually arrange the members of their sentences in that sequence which shall secure for each its proper emphasis and its determining influence on the others — influence reflected back and influence projected forward. As an example of the charm that lies in unostentatious antiphony, consider this passage from Ruskin: — " Originality in expression does not depend on invention of new words; nor originality in poetry on invention of new measures; nor in painting on invention of new colors or new modes of using them. The chords of music, the harmonies of color, the general principles of the arrangement of sculptural masses, have been determined long ago, and in all probability cannot be added to any more than they can be altered." Men write like this by instinct; and I by no means wish to suggest that writing like this can be produced by rule. What I suggest is, that in this, as in every other Fine Art, instinct does mostly find itself in accordance with rule; and a knowledge of rules helps to direct the blind gropings of feeling, and to correct the occasional mistakes of instinct. If, after working his way through a long and involved sentence in which the meaning is rough-hewn, the writer were to try its effect upon ear and intellect, he might see its defects and reshape it into beauty and clearness. But in general men shirk this labor, partly because it is irksome, and partly because they have no distinct conception of the rules which would make the labor light.

The law of Sequence, we have seen, rests upon the two requisites of Clearness and Harmony. Men with a delicate sense of rhythm will instinctively distribute their phrases in an order that falls agreeably on the ear, without monotony, and without an echo of other voices; and men with a keen sense of logical relation will instinctively arrange their sentences in an order that best unfolds the meaning. The French are great masters of the law of Sequence, and, did space permit, I could cite many excellent examples. One brief passage from Royer-Collard must suffice: " Les faits que l'observation laisse épars et muets la causalité les rassemble, les enchaîne, leur prête un langage. Chaque fait révèle celui qui a précédé, prophétise celui qui va suivre."

The ear is only a guide to the harmony of a period, and often tempts us into the feebleness of expletives or approximative expressions for the sake of a cadence. Yet, on the other hand, if we disregard the subtle influences of harmonious arrangement, our thoughts lose much of the force which would otherwise result from their logical subordination. The easy evolution of thought in a melodious period, quietly taking up on its way a variety of incidental details, yet never lingering long enough over them to divert the attention or to suspend the continuous crescendo of interest, but by subtle influences of proportion allowing each clause of the sentence its separate significance, is the product of a natural gift, as rare as the gift of music, or of poetry.[13] But until men come to understand that Style is an art, and an amazingly difficult art, they will continue with careless presumption to tumble out their sentences as they would lilt stones from a cart, trusting very much to accident or gravitation for the shapeliness of the result. I will write a passage which may serve as an example of what I mean, although the defect is purposely kept within very ordinary limits: —

"To construct a sentence with many loosely and not obviously dependent clauses, each clause containing an important meaning or a concrete image the vivacity of which, like a boulder in a shallow stream, disturbs the equable current of thought, — and in such a case the more beautiful the image the greater the obstacle, so that the laws of Simplicity and Economy are violated by it, — while each clause really requires for its interpretation a proposition that is however kept suspended till the close, — is a defect."

The weariness produced by such writing as this is very great, and yet the recasting of the passage is easy. Thus: —

" It is a defect when a sentence is constructed with many loosely and not obviously dependent clauses, each of which requires for its interpretation a proposition that is kept suspended till the close; and this defect is exaggerated when each clause contains an important meaning, or a concrete image which, like a boulder in a shallow stream, disturbs the equable current of thought: the more beautiful the image, the greater its violation of the laws of Simplicity and Economy."

In this second form the sentence has no long suspension of the main idea, no diversions of the current. The proposition is stated and illustrated directly, and the mind of the reader follows that of the writer. How injurious it is to keep the key in your pocket until all the locks in succession have been displayed may be seen in such a sentence as this: —

" Phantoms of lost power, sudden intuitions, and shadowy restorations of forgotten feelings, sometimes dim and perplexing, sometimes by bright but furtive glimpses, sometimes by a full and steady revelation, overcharged with light — throw us back in a moment upon scenes and remembrances that we have left full thirty years behind us."

Had De Quincey liberated our minds from suspense by first presenting the thought which first arose in his own mind, — namely, that we are thrown back upon scenes and remembrances by phantoms of lost power, &c. — the beauty of his language in its pregnant suggestiveness would have been felt at once. Instead of that, he makes us accompany him in darkness, and when the light appears we have to travel backward over the ground again to see what we have passed. The passage continues: —

" In solitude, and chiefly in the solitudes of nature, and, above all, amongst the great and *enduring* features of nature, such as mountains, and quiet dells, and the lawny recesses of forests, and the silent shores of lakes, features with which (as being themselves less liable to change) our feelings have a more abiding association — under these circumstances it is, that such evanescent hauntings of our past and forgotten selves are most apt to startle and to waylay us."

The beauty of this passage seems to me marred by the awkward yet necessary interruption, " under these circumstances it is," which would have been avoided by opening the sentence with " Such evanescent hauntings of our forgotten selves are most apt to startle us in solitudes," &c. Compare the effect of directness in the following: —

"This was one, and the most common, shape of extinguished power from which Coleridge fled to the great city. But sometimes the same decay came back upon his heart in the more poignant shape of intimations and vanishing glimpses, recovered for one moment from the paradise of youth, and from fields of joy and power, over which for him, too certainly, he felt that the cloud of night was settling forever." [14]

Obedience to the law of Sequence gives strength by giving clearness and beauty of rhythm; it economizes force and creates music. A very trifling disregard of it will mar an effect. See an example both of obedience and trifling disobedience in the following passage from Ruskin: —

" People speak in this working age, when they speak from their hearts, as if houses and lands, and food and raiment were alone useful, and as if Sight, Thought, and Admiration were all profitless, so that men insolently call themselves Utilitarians, who would turn, if they had their way, themselves and their race into vegetables; men who think, as far as such can be said to think, that the meat is more than the life and the raiment than the body, who look to the earth as a stable and to its fruit as fodder; vine-dressers and husbandmen, who love the corn they grind, and the grapes they crush, better than the gardens of the angels upon the slopes of Eden."

It is instructive to contrast the dislocated sentence, "who would turn, if they had their way, themselves and their race," with the sentence which succeeds it, "men who think, as far as such can be said to think, that the meat," &c. In the latter the parenthetic interruption is a source of power : it dams the current to increase its force; in the former the inversion is a loss of power: it is a dissonance to the ear and a diversion of the thought.

As illustrations of Sequence in composition, two passages may be quoted from Macaulay which display the power of pictorial suggestions when, instead of diverting attention from the main purpose, they are arranged with progressive and culminating effect.

" Such or nearly such was the change which passed on the Mogul empire during the forty years which followed the death of Aurungzebe. A succession of nominal sovereigns, sunk in indolence and debauchery, sauntered away life in secluded palaces, chewing bhang, fondling concubines, and listening to buffoons. A succession of ferocious invaders descended through the western passes, to prey on the defenceless wealth of Hindustan. A Persian conqueror crossed the Indus, marched through the gates of Delhi, and bore away in triumph those treasures of which the magnificence had astounded Roe and Bernier, the Peacock Throne, on which the

richest jewels of Golconda had been disposed by the most
skilful hands of Europe, and the inestimable Mountain of
Light, which, after many strange vicissitudes, lately shone in
the bracelet of Runjeet-Singh, and is now destined to adorn the
hideous idol of Orissa. The Afghan soon followed to complete the work of devastation which the Persian had begun.
The warlike tribes of Rajpootana threw off the Mussulman
yoke. A band of mercenary soldiers occupied Rohilcund.
The Seiks ruled on the Indus. The Jauts spread dismay along
the Jumnah. The high lands which border on the western
seacoast of India poured forth a yet more formidable race, a
race which was long the terror of every native power, and
which, after many desperate and doubtful struggles, yielded
only to the fortune and genius of England. It was under the
reign of Aurungzebe that this wild clan of plunderers first
descended from their mountains; and soon after his death,
every corner of his wide empire learned to tremble at the
mighty name of the Mahrattas. Many fertile viceroyalties
were entirely subdued by them. Their dominions stretched
across the peninsula from sea to sea. Mahratta captains
reigned at Poonah, at Gualior, in Guzerat, in Berar, and in
Tanjore."

Such prose as this affects us like poetry. The pictures and
suggestions might possibly have been gathered together by
any other historian; but the artful succession, the perfect
sequence, could only have been found by a fine writer. I pass
over a few paragraphs, and pause at this second example of a
sentence simple in structure, though complex in its elements,
fed but not overfed with material, and almost perfect in its
cadence and logical connection. "Scarcely any man, however sagacious, would have thought it possible that a trading
company, separated from India by fifteen thousand miles of
sea, and possessing in India only a few acres for purposes of

commerce, would, in less than a hundred years, spread its empire from Cape Comorin to the eternal snow of the Himalayas; would compel Mahratta and Mahommedan to forget their mutual feuds in common subjection; would tame down even thòse wild races which had resisted the most powerful of the Moguls; and having united under its laws a hundred millions of subjects, would carry its victorious arms far to the east of the Burrampooter, and far to the west of the Hydaspes, dictate terms of peace at the gates of Ava, and seat its vassal on the throne of Candahar."

Let us see the same principle exhibited in a passage at once pictorial and argumentative. " We know more certainly every day," says Ruskin, " that whatever appears to us harmful in the universe has some beneficent or necessary operation; that the storm which destroys a harvest brightens the sunbeams for harvests yet unsown, and that the volcano which buries a city preserves a thousand from destruction. But the evil is not for the time less fearful because we have learned it to be necessary; and we easily understand the timidity or the tenderness of the spirit which would withdraw itself from the presence of destruction, and create in its imagination a world of which the peace should be unbroken, in which the sky should not darken nor the sea rage, in which the leaf should not change nor the blossom wither. That man is greater, however, who contemplates with an equal mind the alternation of terror and of beauty; who, not rejoicing less beneath the sunny sky, can bear also to watch the bars of twilight narrowing on the horizon; and, not less sensible to the blessing of the peace of nature, can rejoice in the magnificence of the ordinances by which that peace is protected and secured. But separated from both by an immeasurable distance would be the man who delighted in convulsion and disease for their own sake; who found his daily food in the disorder of nature mingled with the suffering of humanity; and watched joyfully at the right hand of the Angel whose appointed work is to destroy as well as to accuse, while the corners of the House of Feasting were struck by the wind from the wilderness."

I will now cite a passage from Burke, which will seem tame after the pictorial animation of the passages from Macaulay and Ruskin; but which, because it is simply an exposition of opinions addressed to the understanding, will excellently illustrate the principle I am enforcing. He is treating of the dethronement of kings. " As it was not made for common abuses, so it is not to be agitated by common minds. The speculative line of demarcation, where obedience ought to end, and resistance must begin, is faint, obscure, and not easily definable. It is not a single act, or a single event, which determines it. Governments must be abused and deranged indeed, before it can be thought of; and the prospect of the future must be as bad as the experience of the past. When things are in that lamentable condition, the nature of the disease is to indicate the remedy to those whom nature has qualified to administer in extremities this critical, ambiguous, bitter potion to a distempered state. Times and occasions, and provocations, will teach their own lessons. The wise will determine from the gravity of the case; the irritable from sensibility to oppression; the high-minded from disdain and indignation at abusive power in unworthy hands; the brave and bold from the love of honorable danger in a generous cause: but, with or without right, a revolution will be the very last resource of the thinking and the good." [15]

As a final example I will cite a passage from M. Taine: —
" De là encore cette insolence contre les inférieurs, et ce mépris versé d'étage en étage depuis le premier jusqu'au dernier. Lorsque dans une société la loi consacre les conditions inégales,

personne n'est exempt d'insulte; le grand seigneur, outragé par le roi, outrage le noble qui outrage le peuple; la nature humaine est humilié à tous les étages, et la société n'est plus qu'un commerce d'affronts."

The law of Sequence by no means prescribes that we should invariably state the proposition before its qualifications — the thought before its illustrations; it merely prescribes that we should arrange our phrases in the order of logical dependence and rhythmical cadence, the order best suited for clearness and for harmony. The nature of the thought will determine the one, our sense of euphony the other.

IV. The Law of Climax

We need not pause long over this; it is generally understood. The condition of our sensibilities is such that to produce their effect stimulants must be progressive in intensity and varied in kind. On this condition rest the laws of Climax and Variety. The phrase or image which in one position will have a mild power of occupying the thoughts, or stimulating the emotions, loses this power if made to succeed one of like kind but more agitating influence, and will gain an accession of power if it be artfully placed on the wave of a climax. We laugh at

> " Then came Dalhousie, that great God of War,
>   Lieutenant-Colonel to the Earl of Mar,"

because of the relaxation which follows the sudden tension of the mind; but if we remove the idea of the colonelcy from this position of anti-climax, the same couplet becomes energetic rather than ludicrous: —

> " Lieutenant-Colonel to the Earl of Mar,
>   Then came Dalhousie, that great God of War."

I have selected this strongly marked case, instead of several feeble passages which might be chosen from the first book at hand, wherein carelessness allows the sentences to close with the least important phrases, and the style droops under frequent anti-climax. Let me now cite a passage from Macaulay which vividly illustrates the effect of Climax: —

" Never, perhaps, was the change which the progress of civilization has produced in the art of war more strikingly illustrated than on that day. Ajax beating down the Trojan leader with a rock which two ordinary men could scarcely lift, Horatius defending the bridge against an army, Richard the Lion-hearted spurring along the whole Saracen line without finding an enemy to withstand his assault, Robert Bruce crushing with one blow the helmet and head of Sir Henry Bohun in sight of the whole array of England and Scotland, such are the heroes of a dark age. [Here is an example of suspended meaning, where the suspense intensifies the effect, because each particular is vividly apprehended in itself; and all culminate in the conclusion; they do not complicate the thought, or puzzle us, they only heighten expectation.] In such an age bodily vigor is the most indispensable qualification of a warrior. At Landen two poor sickly beings, who, in a rude state of society, would have been regarded as too puny to bear any part in combats, were the souls of two great armies. In some heathen countries they would have been exposed while infants. In Christendom they would, six hundred years earlier, have been sent to some quiet cloister. But their lot had fallen on a time when men had discovered that the strength of the muscles is far inferior in value to the strength of the mind. It is probable that, among the hundred and twenty thousand soldiers who were marshalled round Neerwinden under all the standards of Western Europe, the two feeblest in body were the hunchbacked dwarf who urged forward the fiery onset of France, and the asthmatic skeleton who covered the slow retreat of England."

The effect of Climax is very marked in the drama. Every speech, every scene, every act, should have its progressive sequence. Nothing can be more injudicious than a trivial phrase following an energetic phrase, a feeble thought succeeding a burst of passion, or even a passionate thought succeeding one more passionate. Yet this error is frequently committed.

In the drama all laws of Style are more imperious than in fiction or prose of any kind, because the art is more intense. But Climax is demanded in every species of composition, for it springs from a psychological necessity. It is pressed upon, however, by the law of Variety in a way to make it far from safe to be too rigidly followed. It easily degenerates into monotony.

V. The Law of Variety

Someone, after detailing an elaborate recipe for a salad, wound up the enumeration of ingredients and quantities with the advice to " open the window and throw it all away." This advice might be applied to the foregoing enumeration of the laws of Style, unless these were supplemented by the important law of Variety. A style which rigidly interpreted the precepts of economy, simplicity, sequence, and climax, which rejected all superfluous words and redundant ornaments, adopted the easiest and most logical arrangement, and closed every sentence and every paragraph with a climax, might be a very perfect bit of mosaic, but would want the glow and movement of a living mind. Monotony would settle on it like a paralyzing frost. A series of sentences in which every phrase was a distinct thought, would no more serve as pabulum for the mind, than portable soup freed from all the fibrous tissues of meat and vegetable would serve as food for the body. Animals perish from hunger in the presence of pure albumen; and minds would lapse into idiocy in the presence of unadulterated thought. But without invoking extreme cases, let us simply remember the psychological fact that it is as easy for sentences to be too compact as for food to be too concentrated; and that many a happy negligence, which to microscopic criticism may appear defective, will be the means of giving clearness and grace to a style. Of course the indolent indulgence in this laxity robs style of all grace and power. But monotony in the structure of sentences, monotony of cadence, monotony of climax, monotony anywhere, necessarily defeats the very aim and end of style; it calls attention to the manner; it blunts the sensibilities; it renders excellences odious.

" Beauty deprived of its proper foils and adjuncts ceases to be enjoyed as beauty, just as light deprived of all shadow ceases to be enjoyed as light. A white canvas cannot produce an effect of sunshine; the painter must darken it in some places before he can make it look luminous in others; nor can an uninterrupted succession of beauty produce the true effect of beauty; it must be foiled by inferiority before its own power can be developed. Nature has for the most part mingled her inferior and noble elements as she mingles sunshine with shade, giving due use and influence to both, and the painter who chooses to remove the shadow, perishes in the burning desert he has created. The truly high and beautiful art of Angelico is continually refreshed and strengthened by his frank portraiture of the most ordinary features of his brother monks and of the recorded peculiarities of ungainly sanctity; but the modern German and Raphaelesque schools lose all honor and nobleness in barber-like admiration of handsome faces, and have, in fact, no real faith except in straight noses, and curled hair. Paul Veronese opposes the dwarf to the soldier, and the negress to the queen; Shakespeare places Caliban beside Miranda, and Autolycus beside Perdita; but the vulgar idealist withdraws his beauty to the safety of the saloon, and his innocence to the seclusion of the cloister; he pretends that he does this in delicacy of choice and purity of sentiment, while in truth he has neither courage to front the monster, nor wit enough to furnish the knave." *

And how is Variety to be secured? The plan is simple, but like many other simple plans, is not without difficulty. It is for the writer to obey the great cardinal principle of Sincerity, and be brave enough to express himself in his own way, following the moods of his own mind, rather than endeavoring to catch the accents of another, or to adapt himself to some standard of taste. No man really thinks and feels monotonously. If he is monotonous in his manner of setting forth his thoughts and feelings, that is either because he has not learned the art of writing, or because he is more or less consciously imitating the manner of others. The subtle play of thought will give movement and life to his style if he do not clog it with critical superstitions. I do not say that it will give him grace and power; I do not say that relying on perfect sincerity will make him a fine writer, because sincerity will not give talent; but I say that sincerity will give him all the power that is possible to him, and will secure him the inestimable excellence of Variety.

* Ruskin.

[1] From De Quincey's essay on *Language* (*Works*, ed. Masson, Vol. 10, pp. 260, 261).

[2] Professor Scott points out a parallel in Buffon; see above, p. 177.

[3] Compare Wackernagel, above, p. 10, and De Quincey, above, p. 226.

[4] Compare Wackernagel, above, p. 16.

[5] Compare above, p. 179.

[6] Boileau, *L'Art Poétique*, Canto I, l. 80.

[7] Compare Goethe, above, p. 197.

[8] Compare Spencer, above, p. 273.

[9] See above, p. 110.

[10] Compare the translator's note on p. 267, and Schopenhauer's sentence on p. 269, commencing with the words, "It consists in . . . ."

[11] Denham: *Cooper's Hill*, l. 192.

[12] See above, p. 278.

[13] Compare Note 10.

[14] De Quincey on *Coleridge* (De Quincey's *Works*, ed. Masson, Vol. 2, pp. 204, 205).

[15] Burke's *Works* (Bohn Ed.), Vol. 2, p. 304.

XV

ROBERT LOUIS STEVENSON (1850–1894)

On Some Technical Elements of Style in Literature* (1885)

[From *The Works of Robert Louis Stevenson*, New York (Scribner's), 1898 (Vol. 22, pp. 243–265).

This paper was first printed in the *Contemporary Review* for April, 1885 (Vol. 47, pp. 548–561), under the rather sweeping title, *On Style in Literature: Its Technical Elements;* a heading subsequently modified so as to seem less inclusive. "*Some* Technical Elements of Style" more appropriately describes the purport of Stevenson's essay, for, as a matter of fact, the author's views, though original, are not too broad; his attention is fixed upon the minuter tissues of expression rather than such larger, structural elements as still fall within the province of a theory of style. The wisest theory will disregard neither. Without question, Stevenson's views are original, first, in that he speaks from a successful experience in his craft — he has practised what he preaches; second, in that he puts novel emphasis upon matters usually neglected or held incapable of being taught (cf. Mr. Harrison's query, — " Whence comes the music of language? " — below, p. 439) ; third, in that he betrays no influence from the classical authorities on rhetoric, since, unfortunately, he appears never to have read them (cf. his *Life* by Graham Balfour, Vol. 2, p. 14). We can scarcely suppose that a wholesome contact with the broad and sane writings of the ancients would have diminished the spontaneity of his unusual insight.

It is proper to observe that Stevenson hardly considered this paper — " the work of five days in bed " — as his final pronouncement upon the subject of literary technique, although he set a high value on it. " I have written," he says in a contemporary letter to W. E. Henley, " a long and peculiarly solemn paper on the technical elements of style.

It is path-breaking and epoch-making; but I do not think the public will be readily convoked to its perusal " (*Letters*, Vol. 1, p. 408). Elsewhere he mentions it in a similar strain of irony, yet perhaps with less real confidence: " It is a sort of start upon my treatise on The Art of Literature: a small arid book that shall some day appear" (*Letters*, Vol. 1, p. 420). Since Stevenson's death his various papers on literary technique have been published in a single volume, entitled *Essays in the Art of Writing* (London, Chatto & Windus). It cannot be said, however, that he ever worked out a comprehensive theory.

Stevenson's practice as a stylist has had the fortune of a methodical treatment in German: *Characteristische Eigenschaften von R. L. Stevenson's Stil* von Wm. P. Chalmers, *Marburger Studien zur englischen Philologie*, Heft 4 (1903); a praiseworthy effort, valuable for its analysis and examples; it should, however, have been put into English. Incidental observations on Stevenson's style are made, by a most competent judge, in the *Nation* for January 9, 1896 (Vol. 62, p. 37).

In the following text the paragraphing of the *Contemporary* has in several instances been restored.]

There is nothing more disenchanting to man than to be shown the springs and mechanism of any art. All our arts and occupations lie wholly on the surface; it is on the surface that we perceive their beauty, fitness, and significance; and to pry below is to be appalled by their emptiness and shocked by the coarseness of the strings and pulleys. In a similar way, psychology itself, when pushed to any nicety, discovers an abhorrent baldness, but rather from the fault of our analysis than from any poverty native to the mind. And perhaps in æsthetics the reason is the same: those disclosures which seem fatal to the dignity of art, seem so perhaps only in the proportion of our ignorance; and those conscious and unconscious artifices which it seems unworthy of the serious artist to employ, were yet, if we had the power to trace them to their springs, indications of a delicacy of the sense finer than we conceive, and hints of ancient harmonies in nature. This ignorance at least is largely irremediable. We shall never learn the affinities of beauty, for they lie too deep in nature and too far back in the mysterious history of man. The amateur, in consequence, will always grudgingly receive details of method, which can be stated but can never wholly be explained; nay, on the principle laid down in Hudibras, that

> " still the less they understand,
> The more they admire the sleight-of-hand,"

many are conscious at each new disclosure of a diminution in the ardor of their pleasure. I must therefore warn that well-known character, the general reader, that I am here embarked upon a most distasteful business: taking down the picture from the wall and looking on the back; and like the inquiring child, pulling the musical cart to pieces.

1. *Choice of Words.* — The art of literature stands apart from among its sisters, because the material in which the literary artist works is the dialect of life; hence, on the one hand, a strange freshness and immediacy of address to the public mind, which is ready prepared to understand it; but hence, on the other, a singular limitation. The sister arts enjoy the use of a plastic and ductile material, like the modeller's clay; literature alone is condemned to work in mosaic with finite and quite rigid words. You have seen these blocks, dear to the nursery: this one a pillar, that a pediment, a third a window or a vase. It is with blocks of just such arbitrary size and figure that the literary architect is condemned to design the palace of his art. Nor is this all; for since these blocks, or words, are the acknowledged currency of our daily affairs, there are here possible none of those suppressions by which other arts obtain relief, continu-

ify, and vigor: no hieroglyphic touch, no smoothed impasto, no inscrutable shadow, as in painting; no blank wall, as in architecture; but every word, phrase, sentence, and paragraph must move in a logical progression, and convey a definite conventional import.

Now the first merit which attracts in the pages of a good writer, or the talk of a brilliant conversationalist, is the apt choice and contrast of the words employed. It is, indeed, a strange art to take these blocks, rudely conceived for the purpose of the market or the bar, and by tact of application touch them to the finest meanings and distinctions, restore to them their primal energy, wittily shift them to another issue, or make of them a drum to rouse the passions. But though this form of merit is without doubt the most sensible and seizing, it is far from being equally present in all writers. The effect of words in Shakespeare, their singular justice, significance, and poetic charm, is different, indeed, from the effect of words in Addison or Fielding. Or, to take an example nearer home, the words in Carlyle seem electrified into an energy of lineament, like the faces of men furiously moved; whilst the words in Macaulay, apt enough to convey his meaning, harmonious enough in sound, yet glide from the memory like undistinguished elements in a general effect. But the first class of writers have no monopoly of literary merit. There is a sense in which Addison is superior to Carlyle; a sense in which Cicero is better than Tacitus, in which Voltaire excels Montaigne: it certainly lies not in the choice of words; it lies not in the interest or value of the matter; it lies not in force of intellect, of poetry, or of humor. The three first are but infants to the three second; and yet each, in a particular point of literary art, excels his superior in the whole. What is that point?

2. *The Web.* — Literature, although it stands apart by

reason of the great destiny and general use of its medium in the affairs of men, is yet an art like other arts. Of these we may distinguish two great classes: those arts, like sculpture, painting, acting, which are representative, or, as used to be said very clumsily, imitative; and those, like architecture, music, and the dance, which are self-sufficient, and merely presentative.[1] Each class, in right of this distinction, obeys principles apart; yet both may claim a common ground of existence, and it may be said with sufficient justice that the motive and end of any art whatever is to make a pattern; a pattern, it may be, of colors, of sounds, of changing attitudes, geometrical figures, or imitative lines; but still a pattern. That is the plane on which these sisters meet; it is by this that they are arts; and if it be well they should at times forget their childish origin, addressing their intelligence to virile tasks, and performing unconsciously that necessary function of their life, to make a pattern, it is still imperative that the pattern shall be made.

Music and literature, the two temporal arts, contrive their pattern of sounds in time; or, in other words, of sounds and pauses. Communication may be made in broken words, the business of life be carried on with substantives alone; but that is not what we call literature; and the true business of the literary artist is to plait or weave his meaning, involving it around itself; so that each sentence, by successive phrases, shall first come into a kind of knot, and then, after a moment of suspended meaning, solve and clear itself. In every properly constructed sentence there should be observed this knot or hitch; so that (however delicately) we are led to foresee, to expect, and then to welcome the successive phrases. The pleasure may be heightened by an element of surprise, as, very grossly, in the common figure of the antithesis, or, with much greater subtlety, where an antithesis is first suggested and then deftly evaded. Each phrase, besides, is to be comely in itself; and between the implication and the evolution of the sentence there should be a satisfying equipoise of sound; for nothing more often disappoints the ear than a sentence solemnly and sonorously prepared, and hastily and weakly finished. Nor should the balance be too striking and exact, for the one rule is to be infinitely various; to interest, to disappoint, to surprise, and yet still to gratify; to be ever changing, as it were, the stitch, and yet still to give the effect of an ingenious neatness.

The conjuror juggles with two oranges, and our pleasure in beholding him springs from this, that neither is for an instant overlooked or sacrificed. So with the writer. His pattern, which is to please the supersensual ear, is yet addressed, throughout and first of all, to the demands of logic. Whatever be the obscurities, whatever the intricacies of the argument, the neatness of the fabric must not suffer, or the artist has been proved unequal to his design. And, on the other hand, no form of words must be selected, no knot must be ied among the phrases, unless knot and word be precisely what is wanted to forward and illuminate the argument; for to fail in this is to swindle in the game. The genius of prose rejects the *cheville* no less emphatically than the laws of verse; and the *cheville*, I should perhaps explain to some of my readers, is any meaningless or very watered phrase employed to strike a balance in the sound. Pattern and argument live in each other; and it is by the brevity, clearness, charm, or emphasis of the second, that we judge the strength and fitness of the first.

Style is synthetic; and the artist, seeking, so to speak, a peg to plait about, takes up at once two or more elements or two or more views of the subject in hand; combines, implicates, and contrasts them; and while, in one sense, he was merely

2 B

seeking an occasion for the necessary knot, he will be found, in the other, to have greatly enriched the meaning, or to have transacted the work of two sentences in the space of one. In the change from the successive shallow statements of the old chronicler to the dense and luminous flow of highly synthetic narrative, there is implied a vast amount of both philosophy and wit. The philosophy we clearly see, recognizing in the synthetic writer a far more deep and stimulating view of life, and a far keener sense of the generation and affinity of events. The wit we might imagine to be lost; but it is not so, for it is just that wit, these perpetual nice contrivances, these difficulties overcome, this double purpose attained, these two oranges kept simultaneously dancing in the air, that, consciously or not, afford the reader his delight. Nay, and this wit, so little recognized, is the necessary organ of that philosophy which we so much admire. That style is therefore the most perfect, not, as fools say, which is the most natural, for the most natural is the disjointed babble of the chronicler; but which attains the highest degree of elegant and pregnant implication unobtrusively; or if obtrusively, then with the greatest gain to sense and vigor. Even the derangement of the phrases from their (so-called) natural order is luminous for the mind; and it is by the means of such designed reversal that the elements of a judgment may be most pertinently marshalled, or the stages of a complicated action most perspicuously bound into one.

The web, then, or the pattern: a web at once sensuous and logical, an elegant and pregnant texture: that is style, that is the foundation of the art of literature. Books indeed continue to be read, for the interest of the fact or fable, in which this quality is poorly represented, but still it will be there. And, on the other hand, how many do we continue to peruse and reperuse with pleasure whose only merit is the elegance of texture ? I am tempted to mention Cicero; and since Mr. Anthony Trollope is dead, I will. It is a poor diet for the mind, a very colorless and toothless " criticism of life "; but we enjoy the pleasure of a most intricate and dexterous pattern, every stitch a model at once of elegance and of good sense; and the two oranges, even if one of them be rotten, kept dancing with inimitable grace.

Up to this moment I have had my eye mainly upon prose; for though in verse also the implication of the logical texture is a crowning beauty, yet in verse it may be dispensed with. You would think that here was a death-blow to all I have been saying; and far from that, it is but a new illustration of the principle involved. For if the versifier is not bound to weave a pattern of his own, it is because another pattern has been formally imposed upon him by the laws of verse. For that is the essence of a prosody. Verse may be rhythmical; it may be merely alliterative; it may, like the French, depend wholly on the (quasi) regular recurrence of the rhyme; or, like the Hebrew, it may consist in the strangely fanciful device of repeating the same idea.[2] It does not matter on what principle the law is based, so it be a law. It may be pure convention; it may have no inherent beauty; all that we have a right to ask of any prosody is, that it shall lay down a pattern for the writer, and that what it lays down shall be neither too easy nor too hard. Hence it comes that it is much easier for men of equal facility to write fairly pleasing verse than reasonably interesting prose; for in prose the pattern itself has to be invented, and the difficulties first created before they can be solved. Hence, again, there follows the peculiar greatness of the true versifier: such as Shakespeare, Milton, and Victor Hugo, whom I place beside them as versifier merely, not as poet. These not only knit and knot the logical texture of the style with all the dexterity and strength of prose;

they not only fill up the pattern of the verse with infinite variety and sober wit; but they give us, besides, a rare and special pleasure, by the art, comparable to that of counter-point, with which they follow at the same time, and now contrast, and now combine, the double pattern of the texture and the verse. Here the sounding line concludes; a little further on, the well-knit sentence; and yet a little further, and both will reach their solution on the same ringing syllable. The best that can be offered by the best writer of prose is to show us the development of the idea and the stylistic pattern proceed hand in hand, sometimes by an obvious and triumphant effort, sometimes with a great air of ease and nature. The writer of verse, by virtue of conquering another difficulty, delights us with a new series of triumphs. He follows three purposes where his rival followed only two; and the change is of precisely the same nature as that from melody to harmony. Or if you prefer to return to the juggler, behold him now, to the vastly increased enthusiasm of the spectators, juggling with three oranges instead of two. Thus it is: added difficulty, added beauty; and the pattern, with every fresh element, becoming more interesting in itself.

Yet it must not be thought that verse is simply an addition; something is lost as well as something gained; and there remains plainly traceable, in comparing the best prose with the best verse, a certain broad distinction of method in the web. Tight as the versifier may draw the knot of logic, yet for the ear he still leaves the tissue of the sentence floating somewhat loose. In prose, the sentence turns upon a pivot, nicely balanced, and fits into itself with an obtrusive neatness like a puzzle. The ear remarks and is singly gratified by this return and balance; while in verse it is all diverted to the measure. To find comparable passages is hard; for either the versifier is hugely the superior of the rival, or, if he be not, and still persist in his more delicate enterprise, he falls to be as widely his inferior. But let us select them from the pages of the same writer, one who was ambidexter; let us take, for instance, Rumour's Prologue to the Second Part of *Henry IV*, a fine flourish of eloquence in Shakespeare's second manner, and set it side by side with Falstaff's praise of sherris, act iv, scene 1; or let us compare the beautiful prose spoken throughout by Rosalind and Orlando, compare, for example, the first speech of all, Orlando's speech to Adam, with what passage it shall please you to select — the Seven Ages from the same play, or even such a stave of nobility as Othello's farewell to war; and still you will be able to perceive, if you have an ear for that class of music, a certain superior degree of organization in the prose; a compacter fitting of the parts; a balance in the swing and the return as of a throbbing pendulum. We must not, in things temporal, take from those who have little, the little that they have; the merits of prose are inferior, but they are not the same; it is a little kingdom, but an independent.

3. *Rhythm of the Phrase.* — Some way back, I used a word which still awaits an application. Each phrase, I said, was to be comely; but what is a comely phrase? In all ideal and material points, literature, being a representative art, must look for analogies to painting and the like; but in what is technical and executive, being a temporal art, it must seek for them in music. Each phrase of each sentence, like an air or a recitative in music, should be so artfully compounded out of long and short, out of accented and unaccented, as to gratify the sensual ear. And of this the ear is the sole judge. It is impossible to lay down laws. Even in our accentual and rhythmic language no analysis can find the secret of the beauty of a verse; how much less, then, of those phrases, such as prose is built of, which obey no law but to be lawless

and yet to please?[3] The little that we know of verse (and for my part I owe it all to my friend Professor Fleeming Jenkin) is, however, particularly interesting in the present connection. We have been accustomed to describe the heroic line as five iambic feet, and to be filled with pain and confusion whenever, as by the conscientious schoolboy, we have heard our own description put in practice.

"All nìght | the dreàd | less àn | gel ùn | pursùed,"*

goes the schoolboy; but though we close our ears, we cling to our definition, in spite of its proved and naked insufficiency. Mr. Jenkin was not so easily pleased, and readily discovered that the heroic line consists of four groups, or, if you prefer the phrase, contains four pauses:

"All night | the dreadless | angel | unpursued."

Four groups, each practically uttered as one word: the first, in this case, an iamb; the second, an amphibrachys; the third, a trochee; and the fourth an amphimacer; and yet our schoolboy, with no other liberty but that of inflicting pain, had triumphantly scanned it as five iambs. Perceive, now, this fresh richness of intricacy in the web; this fourth orange, hitherto unremarked, but still kept flying with the others. What had seemed to be one thing it now appears is two; and, like some puzzle in arithmetic, the verse is made at the same time to read in fives and to read in fours.

But again, four is not necessary. We do not, indeed, find verses in six groups, because there is not room for six in the ten syllables; and we do not find verses of two, because one of the main distinctions of verse from prose resides in the comparative shortness of the group; but it is even common to find verses of three. Five is the one forbidden number; because five is the number of the feet; and if five were chosen,

* Milton.

the two patterns would coincide, and that opposition which is the life of verse would instantly be lost. We have here a clue to the effect of polysyllables, above all in Latin, where they are so common and make so brave an architecture in the verse; for the polysyllable is a group of Nature's making. If but some Roman would return from Hades (Martial, for choice), and tell me by what conduct of the voice these thundering verses should be uttered — " *Aut Lacedæmonium Tarentum,*" for a case in point — I feel as if I should enter at last into the full enjoyment of the best of human verses.

But, again, the five feet are all iambic, or supposed to be; by the mere count of syllables the four groups cannot be all iambic; as a question of elegance, I doubt if any one of them requires to be so; and I am certain that for choice no two of them should scan the same. The singular beauty of the verse analyzed above is due, so far as analysis can carry us, part, indeed, to the clever repetition of L, D, and N, but part to this variety of scansion in the groups. The groups which, like the bar in music, break up the verse for utterance, fall uniambically; and in declaiming a so-called iambic verse, it may so happen that we never utter one iambic foot. And yet to this neglect of the original beat there is a limit.

"Athens, the eye of Greece, mother of arts,"*

is, with all its eccentricities, a good heroic line; for though it scarcely can be said to indicate the beat of the iamb, it certainly suggests no other measure to the ear. But begin

"Mother Athens, eye of Greece,"

or merely "Mother Athens," and the game is up, for the trochaic beat has been suggested. The eccentric scansion of the groups is an adornment; but as soon as the original beat has been forgotten, they cease implicitly to be eccentric.

* Milton.

Variety is what is sought; but if we destroy the original mould, one of the terms of this variety is lost, and we fall back on sameness. Thus, both as to the arithmetical measure of the verse, and the degree of regularity in scansion, we see the laws of prosody to have one common purpose: to keep alive the opposition of two schemes simultaneously followed; to keep them notably apart, though still coincident; and to balance them with such judicial nicety before the reader, that neither shall be unperceived and neither signally prevail.

The rule of rhythm in prose is not so intricate. Here, too, we write in groups, or phrases, as I prefer to call them, for· the prose phrase is greatly longer and is much more nonchalantly uttered than the group in verse; so that not only is there a greater interval of continuous sound between the pauses, but, for that very reason, word is linked more readily to word by a more summary enunciation. Still, the phrase is the strict analogue of the group, and successive phrases, like successive groups, must differ openly in length and rhythm. The rule of scansion in verse is to suggest no measure but the one in hand; in prose, to suggest no measure at all. Prose must be rhythmical, and it may be as much so as you will; but it must not be metrical. It may be anything, but it must not be verse. A single heroic line may very well pass and not disturb the somewhat larger stride of the prose style; but one following another will produce an instant impression of poverty, flatness, and disenchantment. The same lines delivered with the measured utterance of verse, would perhaps seem rich in variety. By the more summary enunciation proper to prose, as to a more distant vision, these niceties of difference are lost. A whole verse is uttered as one phrase; and the ear is soon wearied by a succession of groups identical in length. The prose writer, in fact, since he is allowed to be so much less harmonious, is condemned to a perpetually fresh variety of movement on a larger scale, and must never disappoint the ear by the trot of an accepted metre. And this obligation is the third orange with which he has to juggle, the third quality which the prose writer must work into his pattern of words. It may be thought perhaps that this is a quality of ease rather than a fresh difficulty; but such is the inherently rhythmical strain of the English language, that the bad writer — and must I take for example that admired friend of my boyhood, Captain Reid? — the inexperienced writer, as Dickens in his earlier attempts to be impressive, and the jaded writer, as any one may see for himself, all tend to fall at once into the production of bad blank verse. And here it may be pertinently asked, Why bad? And I suppose it might be enough to answer that no man ever made good verse by accident, and that no verse can ever sound otherwise than trivial when uttered with the delivery of prose. But we can go beyond such answers. The weak side of verse is the regularity of the beat, which in itself is decidedly less impressive than the movement of the nobler prose; and it is just into this weak side, and this alone, that our careless writer falls. A peculiar density and mass, consequent on the nearness of the pauses, is one of the chief good qualities of verse; but this our accidental versifier, still following after the swift gait and large gestures of prose, does not so much as aspire to imitate. Lastly, since he remains unconscious that he is making verse at all, it can never occur to him to extract those effects of counterpoint and opposition which I have referred to as the final grace and justification of verse, and, I may add, of blank verse in particular.

4. *Contents of the Phrase.* — Here is a great deal of talk about rhythm — and naturally; for in our canorous language rhythm is always at the door. But it must not be forgotten that in some languages this element is almost, if not quite, extinct,

and that in our own it is probably decaying. The even speech of many educated Americans sounds the note of danger. I should see it go with something as bitter as despair, but I should not be desperate.   As in verse, no element, not even rhythm, is necessary; so, in prose also, other sorts of beauty will arise and take the place and play the part of those that we outlive. The beauty of the expected beat in verse, the beauty in prose of its larger and more lawless melody, patent as they are to English hearing, are already silent in the ears of our next neighbors; for in France the oratorical accent and the pattern of the web have almost or altogether succeeded to their places; and the French prose writer would be astounded at the labors of his brother across the Channel, and how a good quarter of his toil, above all *invita Minerva*, is to avoid writing verse.   So wonderfully far apart have races wandered in spirit, and so hard it is to understand the literature next door!

Yet French prose is distinctly better than English; and French verse, above all while Hugo lives, it will not do to place upon one side.   What is more to our purpose, a phrase or a verse in French is easily distinguishable as comely or un- comely. There is then another element of comeliness hither- to overlooked in this analysis: the contents of the phrase. Each phrase in literature is built of sounds, as each phrase in music consists of notes. One sound suggests, echoes, de- mands, and harmonizes with another; and the art of rightly using these concordances is the final art in literature.   It used to be a piece of good advice to all young writers to avoid alliteration; and the advice was sound, in so far as it pre- vented daubing. None the less for that, was it abominable nonsense, and the mere raving of those blindest of the blind who will not see. The beauty of the contents of a phrase, or of a sentence, depends implicitly upon alliteration and upon assonance. The vowel demands to be repeated; the consonant demands to be repeated; and both cry aloud to be perpetually varied. You may follow the adventures of a letter through any passage that has particularly pleased you; find it, perhaps, denied awhile, to tantalize the ear; find it fired again at you in a whole broadside; or find it pass into congenerous sounds, one liquid or labial melting away into another. And you will find another and much stranger circumstance. Literature is written by and for two senses: a sort of internal ear, quick to perceive " unheard melodies "; and the eye, which directs the pen and deciphers the printed phrase. Well, even as there are rhymes for the eye, so you will find that there are assonances and alliterations; that where an author is running the open A, deceived by the eye and our strange English spelling, he will often show a tenderness for the flat A; and that where he is running a particular consonant, he will not improbably rejoice to write it down even when it is mute or bears a different value.

Here, then, we have a fresh pattern — a pattern, to speak grossly, of letters — which makes the fourth preoccupation of the prose writer, and the fifth of the versifier. At times it is very delicate and hard to perceive, and then perhaps most excellent and winning (I say perhaps); but at times again the elements of this literal melody stand more boldly forward and usurp the ear. It becomes, therefore, somewhat a matter of conscience to select examples; and as I cannot very well ask the reader to help me, I shall do the next best by giving him the reason or the history of each selection. The two first, one in prose, one in verse, I chose without previous analysis, simply as engaging passages that had long reëchoed in my ear.

" I cannot praise a fugitive and cloistered virtue, unexercised and unbreathed, that never sallies out and sees her adversary, but slinks out of the race where that immortal garland is to be run for, not without dust and heat." * Down to " virtue," the current s and r are both announced and repeated unobtrusively, and by way of a grace-note that almost inseparable group PVF is given entire.† The next phrase is a period of repose, almost ugly in itself, both s and r still audible, and B given as the last fulfilment of PVF. In the next four phrases, from " that never " down to " run for," the mask is thrown off, and, but for a slight repetition of the F and V, the whole matter turns, almost too obtrusively, on s and R; first s coming to the front, and then R. In the concluding phrase all these favorite letters, and even the flat A, a timid preference for which is just perceptible, are discarded at a blow and in a bundle; and to make the break more obvious, every word ends with a dental, and all but one with T, for which we have been cautiously prepared since the beginning. The singular dignity of the first clause, and this hammer-stroke of the last, go far to make the charm of this exquisite sentence. But it is fair to own that s and R are used a little coarsely.

" In Xanadu did Kubla Khan	(kǎndl)
A stately pleasure-dome decree,	(kdlsr)
Where Alph, the sacred river, ran,	(kǎndlsr)
Through caverns measureless to man	(kǎnlsr)
Down to a sunless sea." ‡	(ndls)

Here I have put the analysis of the main group alongside the lines; and the more it is looked at, the more interesting it will seem. But there are further niceties. In lines two and four,

* Milton.

† As PVF will continue to haunt us through our English examples, take, by way of comparison, this Latin verse, of which it forms a chief adornment, and do not hold me answerable for the all too Roman freedom of the sense: "Hanc volo, quæ facilis, quæ palliolata vagatur."

‡ Coleridge.

the current s is most delicately varied with z. In line three, the current flat A is twice varied with the open A, already suggested in line two, and both times (" where " and " sacred ") in conjunction with the current R. In the same line F and V (a harmony in themselves, even when shorn of their comrade P) are admirably contrasted. And in line four there is a marked subsidiary M, which again was announced in line two. I stop from weariness, for more might yet be said.

My next example was recently quoted from Shakespeare as an example of the poet's color sense. Now, I do not think literature has anything to do with color, or poets any way the better of such a sense; and I instantly attacked this passage, since " purple " was the word that had so pleased the writer of the article, to see if there might not be some literary reason for its use. It will be seen that I succeeded amply; and I am bound to sav I think the passage exceptional in Shakespeare — exceptional, indeed, in literature; but it was not I who chose it.

> " The BARge she sat iN, like a BURNished throNe
> BURNt oN the water: the POOP was BEateN gold,
> PURPle the sails and so PUR*FUMèd that
> The wiNds were love-sick with them." †

It may be asked why I have put the F of "perfumèd" in capitals; and I reply, because this change from P to F is the completion of that from B to P, already so adroitly carried out. Indeed, the whole passage is a monument of curious ingenuity; and it seems scarce worth while to indicate the subsidiary s, L, and w. In the same article, a second passage from Shakespeare was quoted, once again as an example of his color sense:

> " A mole cinque-spotted like the crimson drops
> I' the bottom of a cowslip." ‡

* per † *Antony and Cleopatra.* ‡ *Cymbeline.*

It is very curious, very artificial, and not worth while to analyze at length: I leave it to the reader.   But before I turn my back on Shakespeare, I should like to quote a passage, for my own pleasure, and for a very model of every technical art:

"But, in the wind and tempest of her frown,	w. p. v. f. (st) (ow)*
Distinction, with a loud and powerful fan,	w. p. f. (st) (ow) l
Puffing at all, winnows the light away;	w. p. f. l
And what hath mass or matter, by itself	w. f. l. m. Ă
Lies rich in virtue and unmingled." †	v. l. m

From these delicate and choice writers I turned with some curiosity to a player of the big drum — Macaulay.   I had in hand the two-volume edition, and I opened at the beginning of the second volume.   Here was what I read:

"The violence of revolutions is generally proportioned to the degree of the maladministration which has produced them. It is therefore not strange that the government of Scotland, having been during many years greatly more corrupt than the government of England, should have fallen with a far heavier ruin.   The movement against the last king of the house of Stuart was in England conservative, in Scotland destructive.   The English complained not of the law, but of the violation of the law."

This was plain-sailing enough; it was our old friend PVF, floated by the liquids in a body; but as I read on, and turned the page, and still found PVF with his attendant liquids, I confess my mind misgave me utterly.   This could be no trick of Macaulay's; it must be the nature of the English tongue. In a kind of despair, I turned half-way through the volume; and coming upon his lordship dealing with General Cannon, and fresh from Claverhouse and Killiecrankie, here, with elucidative spelling, was my reward:

"Meanwhile the disorders of Kannon's ĸamp went on inĸreasing. He ĸalled a ĸouncil of war to ĸonsider what ĸourse it would be ad-

* The v is in "of."   † *Troilus and Cressida.*

visable to таке. But as soon as the кouncil had met, a preliminary кuestion was raised. The army was almost eкскlusively a Highland army. The recent viкtory had been won eкскlusively by Highland warriors. Great chie*f*s who had brought siкs or se*v*en hundred *f*ighting men into the *f*ield did not think it *f*air that they should be out*v*oted by gentlemen *f*rom Ireland, and *f*rom the Low Kountries, who bore indeed King James's кommission, and were кalled кolonels and кaptains, but who were кolonels without regiments and кaptains without кompanies."

A moment of fv in all this world of к's! It was not the English language, then, that was an instrument of one string, but Macaulay that was an incomparable dauber.

It was probably from this barbaric love of repeating the same sound, rather than from any design of clearness, that he acquired his irritating habit of repeating words; I say the one rather than the other, because such a trick of the ear is deeper-seated and more original in man than any logical consideration.[4] Few writers, indeed, are probably conscious of the length to which they push this melody of letters. One, writing very diligently, and only concerned about the meaning of his words and the rhythm of his phrases, was struck into amazement by the eager triumph with which he cancelled one expression to substitute another. Neither changed the sense; both being monosyllables, neither could affect the scansion; and it was only by looking back on what he had already written that the mystery was solved: the second word contained an open a, and for nearly half a page he had been riding that vowel to the death.

In practice, I should add, the ear is not always so exacting; and ordinary writers, in ordinary moments, content themselves with avoiding what is harsh, and here and there, upon a rare occasion, buttressing a phrase, or linking two together, with a patch of assonance or a momentary jingle of alliteration. To understand how constant is this preoccupation of good writers, even where its results are least obtrusive, it is only necessary to turn to the bad. There, indeed, you will find cacophony supreme, the rattle of incongruous consonants only relieved by the jaw-breaking hiatus, and whole phrases not to be articulated by the powers of man.

Conclusion. — We may now briefly enumerate the elements of style. We have, peculiar to the prose writer, the task of keeping his phrases large, rhythmical, and pleasing to the ear, without ever allowing them to fall into the strictly metrical: peculiar to the versifier, the task of combining and contrasting his double, treble, and quadruple pattern, feet and groups, logic and metre — harmonious in diversity: common to both, the task of artfully combining the prime elements of language into phrases that shall be musical in the mouth; the task of weaving their argument into a texture of committed phrases and of rounded periods — but this particularly binding in the case of prose: and, again common to both, the task of choosing apt, explicit, and communicative words. We begin to see now what an intricate affair is any perfect passage; how many faculties, whether of taste or pure reason, must be held upon the stretch to make it; and why, when it is made, it should afford us so complete a pleasure. From the arrangement of according letters, which is altogether arabesque and sensual,[5] up to the architecture of the elegant and pregnant sentence, which is a vigorous act of the pure intellect, there is scarce a faculty in man but has been exercised. We need not wonder, then, if perfect sentences are rare, and perfect pages rarer.

[1] In the *Contemporary* Stevenson at this point appends the following note:
The division of the arts may best be shown in a tabular form, thus:

	In time.	In space.	In time and space.
Presentative . . .	Music	Painting	Dance
Representative . .	Literature	Sculpture, &c. Architecture	Acting

[2] A traditional belief, half erroneous, for which Stevenson should not be held responsible. Recent scholars are pretty much agreed upon the existence of a metrical form in Old Testament poetry; see the *Athenæum*, July 29, 1905 (p. 140); *Nation*, Aug. 3, 1905 (p. 107); *Jewish Encyclopedia*, under *Meter* and *Poetry*. Compare also Sidney, *Defense of Poesy*, ed. Albert S. Cook, p. 6.

[3] But see F. N. Scott, *The Scansion of Prose Rhythm*, *Publications of the Modern Language Association of America*, Vol. 20, pp. 707–728; and compare E. Sievers, *Ueber Sprachmelodisches in der deutschen Dichtung*, *Annalen der Naturphilosophie*, Vol. 1, pp. 76–94.

[4] Compare Wackernagel, above, p. 6.

[5] "Sensual" : Stevenson evidently intended this word, though not in its ordinary meaning; we should expect *sensuous*.

XVI

WALTER PATER (1839-1894)

Style (1888)

[From *Appreciations, With an Essay on Style*, New York (Macmillan), 1905 (pp. 1-36).

Pater first published his essay as a separate article, in the *Fortnightly Review* for December 1, 1888 (Old Series, Vol. 50, pp. 728-743), whence it was copied by *Living Age* for January, 1889 (Vol. 180, pp. 3-13). In the latter year, after a characteristic revision of the wording, the author issued it again as an introduction to his " Appreciations " of Wordsworth, Coleridge, Lamb, etc. These appreciations, however, are general literary estimates; they are not in any ordinary sense studies in style.

On its appearance in that volume, the introductory essay, though it has since won an abiding station in the literature of criticism, was not everywhere received with immediate favor. For example, Mr. William Watson, reviewing the volume for the London *Academy* (Dec. 21, 1889), delivered himself without enthusiasm: —

" The opening paper, on ' Style ' — in reality concerning itself rather with diction, or with artifices of prose composition, than with that abstract effect, that air and carriage, which the word 'style' has almost insensibly come to stand for — is perhaps for this reason a little disappointing."

Other contemporary criticisms may be consulted in the *Athenæum* for December 14, 1889 (1889, Vol. 2, pp. 813-814), and the *Nation* for December 26, 1889 (Vol. 49, p. 524). For good reasons, a safer and less disappointed valuation than Mr. Watson's has been offered later by Professors Gayley and Scott, who characterize the essay thus (*Literary Criticism*, 1899, p. 225): —

" Structural unity pervading all the elements of composition, from the largest to the smallest, is the requirement upon which the author most strenuously insists."

Pater's strenuous insistence on stylistic unity is illustrated in his own practice, where his success was bought at the expense of slow and unremitting toil. The personal significance of his remarks on Flaubert's "tardy and painful" labor in composition is obvious. (Compare M. Faguet's spirited account of *Flaubert Ecrivain:* E. Faguet, *Flaubert,* Chap. X.) For a partial insight into Pater's way of working, study the first two sentences of the article in the *Fortnightly*, and then the same two sentences, as revised, in the essay below. In the *Fortnightly* they run: —

" Since all progress of mind consists for the most part in differentiation, in the severance of an obscure complex into its parts or phases, it is surely the stupidest of losses to wear off the edge of achieved distinctions, and confuse things which right reason has put asunder — poetry and prose, for instance; or, to speak more exactly, the characteristic laws and excellences of prose and verse composition. On the other hand, those who have dwelt most emphatically on the distinction between prose and verse, prose and poetry, may sometimes have been tempted to limit the proper functions of prose too narrowly; which again is at least false economy, as being, in effect, the renunciation of a certain means or faculty, in a world where after all we must needs make the most of things."]

Since all progress of mind consists for the most part in differentiation, in the resolution of an obscure and complex object into its component aspects, it is surely the stupidest of losses to confuse things which right reason has put asunder, to lose the sense of achieved distinctions, the distinction between poetry and prose, for instance, or, to speak more exactly, between the laws and characteristic excellences of verse and prose composition. On the other hand, those who have dwelt most emphatically on the distinction between prose and verse, prose and poetry, may sometimes have been tempted to limit the proper functions of prose too narrowly; and this again is at least false economy, as being, in effect, the renunciation of a certain means or faculty, in a world where after all we must needs make the most of things. Critical efforts to limit art *à priori*, by anticipations regarding the natural incapacity of the material with which this or that artist works, as the sculptor with solid form, or the prose-writer with the ordinary language of men, are always liable to be discredited by the facts of artistic production; and while prose is actually found to be a colored thing with Bacon, picturesque with Livy and Carlyle, musical with Cicero and Newman, mystical and intimate with Plato and Michelet and Sir Thomas Browne, exalted or florid, it may be, with Milton and Taylor, it will be useless to protest that it can be nothing at all, except something very tamely and narrowly confined to mainly practical ends — a kind of " good round-hand "; as useless as the protest that poetry might not touch prosaic subjects as with Wordsworth, or an abtruse matter as with Browning, or treat contemporary life nobly as with Tennyson. In subordination to one essential beauty in all good literary style, in all literature as a fine art, as there are many beauties of poetry so the beauties of prose are many, and it is the business of criticism to estimate them as such; as it is good in the criticism of verse to look for those hard, logical, and quasi-prosaic excellences which that too has, or needs. To find in the poem, amid the flowers, the allusions, the mixed perspectives, of *Lycidas*, for instance, the thought, the logical structure: — how wholesome! how delightful! as to identify in prose what we call the poetry, the imaginative power, not treating it as out of place and a kind of vagrant intruder, but by way of an estimate of its rights, that is, of its achieved powers, there.

Dryden, with the characteristic instinct of his age, loved to emphasize the distinction between poetry and prose, the protest against their confusion with each other coming with somewhat diminished effect from one whose poetry was so prosaic. In truth, his sense of prosaic excellence affected his verse rather than his prose, which is not only fervid, richly figured, poetic, as we say, but vitiated, all unconsciously, by many a scanning line. Setting up correctness, that humble merit of prose, as the central literary excellence, he is really a less correct writer than he may seem, still with an imperfect mastery of the relative pronoun. It might have been foreseen that, in the rotations of mind, the province of poetry in prose would find its assertor; and, a century after Dryden, amid very different intellectual needs, and with the need therefore of great modifications in literary form, the range of the poetic force in literature was effectively enlarged by Wordsworth. The true distinction between prose and poetry he regarded as the almost technical or accidental one of the absence or presence of metrical beauty, or, say! metrical restraint; [1] and for him the opposition came to be between verse and prose of course; but, as the essential dichotomy in this matter, between imaginative and unimaginative writing, parallel to De Quincey's distinction [2] between " the literature of power and the literature of knowledge," in the former of which the composer gives us not fact, but his peculiar sense of fact, whether past or present.

Dismissing then, under sanction of Wordsworth, that harsher opposition of poetry to prose, as savoring in fact of the arbitrary psychology of the last century, and with it the prejudice that there can be but one only beauty of prose style, I propose here to point out certain qualities of all literature as a fine art, which, if they apply to the literature of fact, apply still more to the literature of the imaginative sense of fact, while they apply indifferently to verse and prose, so far as either is really imaginative — certain conditions of true art in both alike, which conditions may also contain in them the secret of the proper discrimination and guardianship of the peculiar excellences of either.

The line between fact and something quite different from external fact is, indeed, hard to draw. In Pascal, for instance, in the persuasive writers generally, how difficult to define the point where, from time to time, argument which, if it is to be worth anything at all, must consist of facts or groups of facts, becomes a pleading—a theorem no longer, but essentially an appeal to the reader to catch the writer's spirit, to think with him, if one can or will — an expression no longer of fact but of his sense of it, his peculiar intuition of a world, prospective, or discerned below the faulty conditions of the present, in either case changed somewhat from the actual world. In science, on the other hand, in history so far as it conforms to scientific rule, we have a literary domain where the imagination may be thought to be always an intruder. And as, in all science, the functions of literature reduce themselves eventually to the transcribing of fact, so all the excellences of literary form in regard to science are reducible to various kinds of painstaking; this good quality being involved in all " skilled work " whatever, in the drafting of an act of parliament, as in sewing. Yet here again, the writer's sense of fact, in history especially, and in all those complex subjects which do but lie on the borders of science, will still take the place of fact, in various degrees. Your historian, for instance, with absolutely truthful intention, amid the multitude of facts presented to him must needs select, and in selecting assert something of his own humor, something that comes not of the world without but of a vision within. So Gibbon moulds his unwieldy material to a preconceived view. Livy, Tacitus, Michelet, moving full of poignant sensibility amid the records of the past, each, after his own sense, modifies — who can tell where and to what degree?—and becomes something else than a transcriber; each, as he thus modifies, passing into the domain of art proper. For just in proportion as the writer's aim, consciously or unconsciously, comes to be the transcribing, not of the world, not of mere fact, but of his sense of it, he becomes an artist, his work *fine* art; and good art (as I hope ultimately to show) in proportion to the truth of his presentment of that sense; as in those humbler or plainer functions of literature also, truth — truth to bare fact, there — is the essence of such artistic quality as they may have. Truth! there can be no merit, no craft at all, without that. And further, all beauty is in the long run only *fineness* of truth, or what we call expression, the finer accommodation of speech to that vision within.

—The transcript of his sense of fact rather than the fact, as being preferable, pleasanter, more beautiful to the writer himself. In literature, as in every other product of human skill, in the moulding of a bell or a platter for instance, wherever this sense asserts itself, wherever the producer so modifies his work as, over and above its primary use or intention, to make it pleasing (to himself, of course, in the first instance) there, " fine " as opposed to merely serviceable art, exists. Literary art, that is, like all art which is in any way imitative or reproductive of fact — form, or color, or incident — is the representation of such fact as connected with soul, of a specific personality, in its preferences, its volition and power.

Such is the matter of imaginative or artistic literature — this transcript, not of mere fact, but of fact in its infinite variety, as modified by human preference in all its infinitely varied forms. It will be good literary art not because it is brilliant or sober, or rich, or impulsive, or severe, but just in proportion as its representation of that sense, that soul-fact, is true, verse being only one department of such literature, and imaginative prose, it may be thought, being the special art of the modern world. That imaginative prose should be the special and opportune art of the modern world results from two important facts about the latter: first, the chaotic variety and complexity of its interests, making the intellectual issue, the really master currents of the present time incalculable — a condition of mind little susceptible of the restraint proper to verse form, so that the most characteristic verse of the nineteenth century has been lawless verse; and secondly, an all-pervading naturalism, a curiosity about everything whatever as it really is, involving a certain humility of attitude, cognate to what must, after all, be the less ambitious form of literature. And prose thus asserting itself as the special and privileged artistic faculty of the present day, will be, however critics may try to narrow its scope, as varied in its excellence as humanity itself reflecting on the facts of its latest experience — an instrument of many stops, meditative, observant, descriptive, eloquent, analytic, plaintive, fervid. Its beauties will be not exclusively " pedestrian ": it will exert, in due measure, all the varied charms of poetry, down to the rhythm which, as in Cicero, or Michelet, or Newman, at their best, gives its musical value to every syllable.*

The literary artist is of necessity a scholar, and in what he proposes to do will have in mind, first of all, the scholar and the scholarly conscience — the male conscience in this matter, as we must think it, under a system of education which still to so large an extent limits real scholarship to men. In his

---

* Mr. Saintsbury, in his *Specimens of English Prose, from Malory to Macaulay*, has succeeded in tracing, through successive English prose-writers, the tradition of that severer beauty in them, of which this admirable scholar of our literature is known to be a lover. *English Prose, from Mandeville to Thackeray*, more recently "chosen and edited" by a younger scholar, Mr. Arthur Galton, of New College, Oxford, a lover of our literature at once enthusiastic and discreet, aims at a more various illustration of the eloquent powers of English prose, and is a delightful companion.

self-criticism, he supposes always that sort of reader who will go (full of eyes) warily, considerately, though without consideration for him, over the ground which the female conscience traverses so lightly, so amiably. For the material in which he works is no more a creation of his own than the sculptor's marble. Product of a myriad various minds and contending tongues, compact of obscure and minute association, a language has its own abundant and often recondite laws, in the habitual and summary recognition of which scholarship consists. A writer, full of a matter he is before all things anxious to express, may think of those laws, the limitations of vocabulary, structure, and the like, as a restriction, but if a real artist, will find in them an opportunity. His punctilious observance of the proprieties of his medium will diffuse through all he writes a general air of sensibility, of refined usage. *Exclusiones debitæ naturæ*—the exclusions, or rejections, which nature demands — we know how large a part these play, according to Bacon, in the science of nature. In a somewhat changed sense, we might say that the art of the scholar is summed up in the observance of those rejections demanded by the nature of his medium, the material he must use. Alive to the value of an atmosphere in which every term finds its utmost degree of expression, and with all the jealousy of a lover of words, he will resist a constant tendency òn the part of the majority of those who use them to efface the distinctions of language, the facility of writers often reënforcing in this respect the work of the vulgar. He will feel the obligation not of the laws only, but of those affinities, avoidances, those mere preferences, of his language, which through the associations of literary history have become a part of its nature, prescribing the rejection of many a neology, many a license, many a gipsy phrase which might present itself as actually expressive. His appeal, again, is to the scholar, who has great experience in literature and will show no favor to short-cuts, or hackneyed illustration, or an affectation of learning designed for the unlearned. Hence a contention, a sense of self-restraint and renunciation, having for the susceptible reader the effect of a challenge for minute consideration; the attention of the writer, in every minutest detail, being a pledge that it is worth the reader's while to be attentive too, that the writer is dealing scrupulously with his instrument, and therefore, indirectly, with the reader himself also, that he has the science of the instrument he plays on, perhaps, after all, with a freedom which in such case will be the freedom of a master.

For meanwhile, braced only by those restraints, he is really vindicating his liberty in the making of a vocabulary, an entire system of composition, for himself, his own true manner; and when we speak of the manner of a true master we mean what is essential in his art. Pedantry being only the scholarship of *le cuistre* (we have no English equivalent) he is no pedant, and does but show his intelligence of the rules of language in his freedoms with it, addition or expansion, which like the spontaneities of manner in a well-bred person will still further illustrate good taste. — The right vocabulary! Translators have not invariably seen how all-important that is in the work of translation, driving for the most part at idiom or construction; whereas, if the original be first-rate, one's first care should be with its elementary particles, Plato, for instance, being often reproducible by an exact following, with no variation in structure, of word after word, as the pencil follows a drawing under tracing-paper, so only each word or syllable be not of false color, to change my illustration a little.

Well! that is because any writer worth translating at all has winnowed and searched through his vocabulary, is conscious of the words he would select in systematic reading of a dictionary, and still more of the words he would reject were the dictionary other than Johnson's; and doing this with his peculiar sense of the world ever in view, in search of an instrument for the adequate expression of that, he begets a vocabulary faithful to the coloring of his own spirit, and in the strictest sense original. That living authority which language needs lies, in truth, in its scholars, who, recognizing always that every language possesses a genius, a very fastidious genius, of its own, expand at once and purify its very elements, which must needs change along with the changing thoughts of living people. Ninety years ago, for instance, great mental force, certainly, was needed by Wordsworth, to break through the consecrated poetic associations of a century, and speak the language that was his, that was to become in a measure the language of the next generation. But he did it with the tact of a scholar also. English, for a quarter of a century past, has been assimilating the phraseology of pictorial art; for half a century, the phraseology of the great German metaphysical movement of eighty years ago; in part also the language of mystical theology: and none but pedants will regret a great consequent increase of its resources. For many years to come its enterprise may well lie in the naturalization of the vocabulary of science, so only it be under the eye of a sensitive scholarship — in a liberal naturalization of the ideas of science too, for after all the chief stimulus of good style is to possess a full, rich, complex matter to grapple with The literary artist, therefore, will be well aware of physical science; science also attaining, in its turn, its true literary ideal.   And then, as the scholar is nothing without the historic sense, he will be apt to restore not really obsolete or really worn-out words, but the finer edge of words still in use: *ascertain, communicate, discover* — words like these it has been part of our " business " to misuse. And still, as language was made for man, he will be no authority for correctnesses which, limiting freedom of utterance, were yet but accidents in their origin; as if one vowed not to say " *its*," which ought to have been in Shakespeare; "*his* " and " *hers*," for inanimate objects, being but a barbarous and really inexpressive survival. Yet we have known many things like this. Racy Saxon monosyllables, close to us as touch and sight, he will intermix readily with those long, savorsome, Latin words, rich in " second intention." In this late day certainly, no critical process can be conducted reasonably without eclecticism. Of such eclecticism we have a justifying example in one of the first poets of our time. How illustrative of monosyllabic effect, of sonorous Latin, of the phraseology of science, of metaphysic, of colloquialism even, are the writings of Tennyson; yet with what a fine, fastidious scholarship throughout!

A scholar writing for the scholarly, he will of course leave something to the willing intelligence of his reader. "To go preach to the first passer-by," says Montaigne, " to become tutor to the ignorance of the first I meet, is a thing I abhor; " a thing, in fact, naturally distressing to the scholar, who will therefore ever be shy of offering uncomplimentary assistance to the reader's wit. To really strenuous minds there is a pleasurable [3] stimulus in the challenge for a continuous effort on their part, to be rewarded by securer and more intimate grasp of the author's sense. Self-restraint, a skilful economy of means, *ascêsis*, that too has a beauty of its own; and for the reader supposed there will be an æsthetic satisfaction in that frugal closeness of style which makes the most of a word, in the exaction from every sentence of a precise relief, in the just spacing out of word to thought, in the logically filled space connected always with the delightful sense of difficulty overcome.

Different classes of persons, at different times, make, of course, very various demands upon literature. Still, scholars, I suppose, and not only scholars, but all disinterested lovers of books, will always look to it, as to all other fine art, for a refuge, a sort of cloistral refuge, from a certain vulgarity in the actual world. A perfect poem like *Lycidas*, a perfect fiction like *Esmond*,[4] the perfect handling of a theory like Newman's *Idea of a University*, has for them something of the uses of a religious " retreat." Here, then, with a view to the central need of a select few, those " men of a finer thread " who have formed and maintain the literary ideal, everything, every component element, will have undergone exact trial, and, above all, there will be no uncharacteristic or tarnished or vulgar decoration, permissible ornament being for the most part structural, or necessary. As the painter in his picture, so the artist in his book, aims at the production by honorable artifice of a peculiar atmosphere. " The artist," says Schiller, " may be known rather by what he *omits* "; and in literature, too, the true artist may be best recognized by his tact of omission. For to the grave reader words too are grave; and the ornamental word, the figure, the accessory form or color or reference, is rarely content to die to thought precisely at the right moment, but will inevitably linger awhile, stirring a long " brain-wave " behind it of perhaps quite alien associations.

Just there, it may be, is the detrimental tendency of the sort of scholarly attentiveness of mind I am recommending. But the true artist allows for it. He will remember that, as the very word ornament indicates what is in itself non-essential, so the " one beauty " of all literary style is of its very essence, and independent, in prose and verse alike, of all removable decoration; that it may exist in its fullest lustre, as in Flaubert's *Madame Bovary*, for instance, or in Sten-

dhal's *Le Rouge et Le Noir*, in a composition utterly unadorned, with hardly a single suggestion of visibly beautiful
things.   Parallel, allusion, the allusive way generally, the
flowers in the garden: — he knows the narcotic force of these
upon the negligent intelligence to which any *diversion*, literally,
is welcome, any vagrant intruder, because one can go wandering away with it from the immediate subject.   Jealous,
if he have a really quickening motive within, of all that does
not hold directly to that, of the facile, the otiose, he will never
depart from the strictly pedestrian process, unless he gains
a ponderable something thereby.   Even assured of its congruity, he will still question its serviceableness.   Is it worth
while, can we afford, to attend to just that, to just that figure
or literary reference, just then? — Surplusage! he will dread
that, as the runner on his muscles.   For in truth all art does
but consist in the removal of surplusage, from the last finish
of the gem-engraver blowing away the last particle of invisible
dust, back to the earliest divination of the finished work to be,
lying somewhere, according to Michelangelo's fancy, in the
rough-hewn block of stone.

And what applies to figure or flower must be understood of
all other accidental or removable ornaments of writing whatever; and not of specific ornament only, but of all that latent
color and imagery which language as such carries in it.   A
lover of words for their own sake, to whom nothing about them
is unimportant, a minute and constant observer of their
physiognomy, he will be on the alert not only for obviously
mixed metaphors of course, but for the metaphor that is
mixed in all our speech, though a rapid use may involve no
cognition of it.   Currently recognizing the incident, the color,
the physical elements or particles in words like *absorb, consider, extract*, to take the first that occur, he will avail himself
of them, as further adding to the resources of expression.

The elementary particles of language will be realized as color and light and shade through his scholarly living in the full sense of them. Still opposing the constant degradation of language by those who use it carelessly, he will not treat colored glass as if it were clear; and while half the world is using figure unconsciously, will be fully aware not only of all that latent figurative texture in speech, but of the vague, lazy, half-formed personification — a rhetoric, depressing, and worse than nothing, because it has no really rhetorical motive — which plays so large a part there, and, as in the case of more ostentatious ornament, scrupulously exact of it, from syllable to syllable, its precise value.

So far I have been speaking of certain conditions of the literary art arising out of the medium or material in or upon which it works, the essential qualities of language and its aptitudes for contingent ornamentation, matters which define scholarship as science and good taste respectively. They are both subservient to a more intimate quality of good style: more intimate, as coming nearer to the artist himself. The otiose, the facile, surplusage: why are these abhorrent to the true literary artist, except because, in literary as in all other art, structure is all-important, felt, or painfully missed, every-where? — that architectural conception of work, which foresees the end in the beginning and never loses sight of it, and in every part is conscious of all the rest, till the last sentence does but, with undiminished vigor, unfold and justify the first — a condition of literary art, which, in contradistinction to another quality of the artist himself, to be spoken of later, I shall call the necessity of *mind* in style.

An acute philosophical writer, the late Dean Mansel (a writer whose works illustrate the literary beauty there may be in closeness, and with obvious repression or economy of a fine rhetorical gift) wrote a book, of fascinating precision in a very obscure subject, to show that all the technical laws of logic are but means of securing, in each and all of its apprehensions, the unity, the strict identity with itself, of the apprehending mind. All the laws of good writing aim at a similar unity or identity of the mind in all the processes by which the word is associated to its import. The term is right, and has its essential beauty, when it becomes, in a manner, what it signifies, as with the names of simple sensations. To give the phrase, the sentence, the structural member, the entire composition, song, or essay, a similar unity with its subject and with itself : — style is in the right way when it tends towards that. All depends upon the original unity, the vital wholeness and identity, of the initiatory apprehension or view. So much is true of all art, which therefore requires always its logic, its comprehensive reason — insight, foresight, retrospect, in simultaneous action — true, most of all, of the literary art, as being of all the arts most closely cognate to the abstract intelligence. Such logical coherency may be evidenced not merely in the lines of composition as a whole, but in the choice of a single word, while it by no means interferes with, but may even prescribe, much variety, in the building of the sentence for instance, or in the manner, argumentative, descriptive, discursive, of this or that part or member of the entire design. The blithe, crisp sentence, decisive as a child's expression of its needs, may alternate with the long-contending, victoriously intricate sentence; the sentence born with the integrity of a single word, relieving the sort of sentence in which, if you look closely, you can see much contrivance, much adjustment, to bring a highly qualified matter into compass at one view. For the literary architecture, if it is to be rich and expressive, involves not only foresight of the end in the beginning, but also development or growth of design, in the process of execution, with many irregularities, surprises, and afterthoughts; the contingent as well as the necessary being subsumed under the unity of the whole. As truly, to the lack of such architectural design, of a single, almost visual, image, vigorously informing an entire, perhaps very intricate, composition, which shall be austere, ornate, argumentative, fanciful, yet true from first to last to that vision within, may be attributed those weaknesses of conscious or unconscious repetition of word, phrase, motive, or member of the whole matter, indicating, as Flaubert was aware, an original structure in thought not organically complete. With such foresight, the actual conclusion will most often get itself written out of hand, before, in the more obvious sense, the work is finished. With some strong and leading sense of the world, the tight hold of which secures true *composition* and not mere loose accretion, the literary artist, I suppose, goes on considerately, setting joint to joint, sustained by yet restraining the productive ardor, retracing the negligences of his first sketch, repeating his steps only that he may give the reader a sense of secure and restful progress, readjusting mere assonances even, that they may soothe the reader, or at least not interrupt him on his way; and then, somewhere before the end comes, is burdened, inspired, with his conclusion, and betimes delivered of it, leaving off, not in weariness and because he finds *himself* at an end, but in all the freshness of volition. His work now structurally complete, with all the accumulating effect of secondary shades of meaning, he finishes the whole up to the just proportion of that antepenultimate conclusion, and all becomes expressive. The house he has built is rather a body he has informed. And so it happens, to its greater credit, that the better interest even of a narrative to be recounted, a story to be told, will often be in its second reading. And though there are instances of great writers who have been no artists,

2 D

an unconscious tact sometimes directing work in which we may detect, very pleasurably, many of the effects of conscious art, yet one of the greatest pleasures of really good prose literature is in the critical tracing out of that conscious artistic structure, and the pervading sense of it as we read. Yet of poetic literature too; for, in truth, the kind of constructive intelligence here supposed is one of the forms of the imagination.

That is the special function of mind, in style. Mind and soul: — hard to ascertain philosophically, the distinction is real enough practically, for they often interfere, are sometimes in conflict, with each other. Blake, in the last century, is an instance of preponderating soul, embarrassed, at a loss, in an era of preponderating mind. As a quality of style, at all events, soul is a fact, in certain writers — the way they have of absorbing language, of attracting it into the peculiar spirit they are of, with a subtlety which makes the actual result seem like some inexplicable inspiration. By mind, the literary artist reaches us, through static and objective indications of design in his work, legible to all. By soul, he reaches us, somewhat capriciously perhaps, one and not another, through vagrant sympathy and a kind of immediate contact. Mind we cannot choose but approve where we recognize it; soul may repel us, not because we misunderstand it. The way in which theological interests sometimes avail themselves of language is perhaps the best illustration of the force I mean to indicate generally in literature, by the word *soul*. Ardent religious persuasion may exist, may make its way, without finding any equivalent heat in language: or, again, it may enkindle words to various degrees, and when it really takes hold of them doubles its force. Religious history presents many remarkable instances in which, through no mere phrase-worship, an unconscious literary tact has, for the sensitive, laid open a privileged pathway from one to another. "The altar-fire," people say, "has touched those lips!" The Vulgate, the English Bible, the English Prayer-Book, the writings of Swedenborg, the Tracts for the Times:—there, we have instances of widely different and largely diffused phases of religious feeling in operation as soul in style. But something of the same kind acts with similar power in certain writers of quite other than theological literature, on behalf of some wholly personal and peculiar sense of theirs. Most easily illustrated by theological literature, this quality lends to profane writers a kind of religious influence. At their best, these writers become, as we say sometimes, " prophets "; such character depending on the effect not merely of their matter, but of their matter as allied to, in " electric affinity " with, peculiar form, and working in all cases by an immediate sympathetic contact, on which account it is that it may be called soul, as opposed to mind, in style. And this too is a faculty of choosing and rejecting what is congruous or otherwise, with a drift towards unity — unity of atmosphere here, as there of design — soul securing color (or perfume, might we say?) as mind secures form, the latter being essentially finite, the former vague or infinite, as the influence of a living person is practically infinite. There are some to whom nothing has any real interest, or real meaning, except as operative in a given person; and it is they who best appreciate the quality of soul in literary art. They seem to know a *person*, in a book, and make way by intuition: yet, although they thus enjoy the completeness of a personal information, it is still a characteristic of soul, in this sense of the word, that it does but suggest what can never be uttered, not as being different from, or more obscure than, what actually gets said, but as containing that plenary substance of which there is only one phase or facet in what is there expressed.

If all high things have their martyrs, Gustave Flaubert

might perhaps rank as the martyr of literary style. In his printed correspondence, a curious series of letters, written in his twenty-fifth year, records what seems to have been his one other passion — a series of letters which, with its fine casuistries, its firmly repressed anguish, its tone of harmonious gray, and the sense of disillusion in which the whole matter ends, might have been, a few slight changes supposed, one of his own fictions. Writing to Madame X. certainly he does display, by " taking thought " mainly, by constant and delicate pondering, as in his love for literature, a heart really moved, but still more, and as the pledge of that emotion, a loyalty to his work. Madame X., too, is a literary artist, and the best gifts he can send her are precepts of perfection in art, counsels for the effectual pursuit of that better love. In his love-letters it is the pains and pleasures of art he insists on, its solaces: he communicates secrets, reproves, encourages, with a view to that. Whether the lady was dissatisfied with such divided or indirect service, the reader is not enabled to see; but sees that, on Flaubert's part at least, a living person could be no rival of what was, from first to last, his leading passion, a somewhat solitary and exclusive one.

"I must scold you," he writes, "for one thing, which shocks, scandalizes me, the small concern, namely, you show for art just now. As regards glory be it so: there, I approve. But for art! — the one thing in life that is good and real — can you compare with it an earthly love? — prefer the adoration of a relative beauty to the *cultus* of the true beauty? Well! I tell you the truth. That is the one thing good in me: the one thing I have, to me estimable. For yourself, you blend with the beautiful a heap of alien things, the useful, the agreeable, what not? —

"The only way not to be unhappy is to shut yourself up in art, and count everything else as nothing. Pride takes the place of all beside when it is established on a large basis. Work! God wills it. That, it seems to me, is clear. —

"I am reading over again the *Æneid*, certain verses of which I repeat to myself to satiety. There are phrases there which stay in one's head, by which I find myself beset, as with those musical airs which are forever returning, and cause you pain, you love them so much. I observe that I no longer laugh much, and am no longer depressed. I am ripe. You talk of my serenity, and envy me. It may well surprise you. Sick, irritated, the prey a thousand times a day of cruel pain, I continue my labor like a true working-man, who, with sleeves turned up, in the sweat of his brow, beats away at his anvil, never troubling himself whether it rains or blows, for hail or thunder. I was not like that formerly. The change has taken place naturally, though my will has counted for something in the matter. —

"Those who write in good style are sometimes accused of a neglect of ideas, and of the moral end, as if the end of the physician were something else than healing, of the painter than painting — as if the end of art were not, before all else, the beautiful."

What, then, did Flaubert understand by beauty, in the art he pursued with so much fervor, with so much self-command? Let us hear a sympathetic commentator: —

"Possessed of an absolute belief that there exists but one way of expressing one thing, one word to call it by, one adjective to qualify, one verb to animate it, he gave himself to superhuman labor for the discovery, in every phrase, of that word, that verb, that epithet. In this way, he believed in some mysterious harmony of expression, and when a true word seemed to him to lack euphony still went on seeking another, with invincible patience, certain that he had not yet got hold of the *unique* word. . . . A thousand preoccupations would beset him at the same moment, always with this desperate certitude fixed in his spirit: Among all the expressions in the world, all forms and turns of expression, there is but *one* — one form, one mode — to express what I want to say."

The one word for the one thing, the one thought, amid the multitude of words, terms, that might just do: the problem of style was there! — the unique word, phrase, sentence, paragraph, essay, or song, absolutely proper to the single mental presentation or vision within. In that perfect justice, over

and above the many contingent and removable beauties with
which beautiful style may charm us, but which it can exist
without, independent of them yet dexterously availing itself
of them, omnipresent in good work, in function at every
point, from single epithets to the rhythm of a whole book,
lay the specific, indispensable, very intellectual, beauty of
literature, the possibility of which constitutes it a fine
art.

One seems to detect the influence of a philosophic idea there,
the idea of a natural economy, of some preëxistent adaptation,
between a relative, somewhere in the world of thought, and its
correlative, somewhere in the world of language — both alike,
rather, somewhere in the mind of the artist, desiderative,
expectant, inventive — meeting each other with the readiness
of " soul and body reunited," in Blake's rapturous design;
and, in fact, Flaubert was fond of giving his theory philosophical expression. —

" There are no beautiful thoughts," he would say, " without beautiful
forms, and conversely. As it is impossible to extract from a physical
body the qualities which really constitute it — color, extension, and the
like — without reducing it to a hollow abstraction, in a word, without
destroying it; just so it is impossible to detach the form from the idea,
for the idea only exists by virtue of the form."

All the recognized flowers, the removable ornaments of
literature (including harmony and ease in reading aloud, very
carefully considered by him) counted certainly; for these too
are part of the actual value of what one says. But still, after
all, with Flaubert, the search, the unwearied research, was
not for the smooth, or winsome, or forcible word, as such, as
with false Ciceronians, but quite simply and honestly, for the
word's adjustment to its meaning. The first condition of this
must be, of course, to know yourself, to have ascertained your
own sense exactly. Then, if we suppose an artist, he says

to the reader, — I want you to see precisely what I see. Into
the mind sensitive to " form," a flood of random sounds,
colors, incidents, is ever penetrating from the world without,
to become, by sympathetic selection, a part of its very structure, and, in turn, the visible vesture and expression of that
other world it sees so steadily within, nay, already with a
partial conformity thereto, to be refined, enlarged, corrected,
at a hundred points; and it is just there, just at those doubtful
points that the function of style, as tact or taste, intervenes.
The unique term will come more quickly to one than another,
at one time than another, according also to the kind of matter
in question. Quickness and slowness, ease and closeness
alike, have nothing to do with the artistic character of the
true word found at last. As there is a charm of ease, so there
is also a special charm in the signs of discovery, of effort and
contention towards a due end, as so often with Flaubert himself — in the style which has been pliant, as only obstinate,
durable metal can be, to the inherent perplexities and re-
cusancy of a certain difficult thought.

If Flaubert had not told us, perhaps we should never have
guessed how tardy and painful his own procedure really was,
and after reading his confession may think that his almost
endless hesitation had much to do with diseased nerves.
Often, perhaps, the felicity supposed will be the product of
a happier, a more exuberant nature than Flaubert's. Aggra-
vated, certainly, by a morbid physical condition, that anxiety
in " seeking the phrase," which gathered all the other small
ennuis of a really quiet existence into a kind of battle, was
connected with his lifelong contention against facile poetry,
facile art — art, facile and flimsy; and what constitutes the
true artist is not the slowness or quickness of the process, but
the absolute success of the result. As with those laborers in
the parable, the prize is independent of the mere length of

the actual day's work. "You talk," he writes, odd, trying lover, to Madame X. —

"You talk of the exclusiveness of my literary tastes. That might have enabled you to divine what kind of a person I am in the matter of love. I grow so hard to please as a literary artist, that I am driven to despair. I shall end by not writing another line."

"Happy," he cries, in a moment of discouragement at that patient labor, which for him, certainly, was the condition of a great success —

"Happy those who have no doubts of themselves! who lengthen out, as the pen runs on, all that flows forth from their brains. As for me, I hesitate, I disappoint myself, turn round upon myself in despite: my taste is augmented in proportion as my natural vigor decreases, and I afflict my soul over some dubious word out of all proportion to the pleasure I get from a whole page of good writing. One would have to live two centuries to attain a true idea of any matter whatever. What Buffon said is a big blasphemy: genius is not long-continued patience. Still, there is some truth in the statement, and more than people think, especially as regards our own day. Art! art! art! bitter deception! phantom that glows with light, only to lead one on to destruction."

Again —

"I am growing so peevish about my writing. I am like a man whose ear is true but who plays falsely on the violin: his fingers refuse to reproduce precisely those sounds of which he has the inward sense. Then the tears come rolling down from the poor scraper's eyes and the bow falls from his hand."

Coming slowly or quickly, when it comes, as it came with so much labor of mind, but also with so much lustre, to Gustave Flaubert, this discovery of the word will be, like all artistic success and felicity, incapable of strict analysis: effect of an intuitive condition of mind, it must be recognized by like intuition on the part of the reader, and a sort of immediate sense. In every one of those masterly sentences of

Flaubert there was, below all mere contrivance, shaping, and afterthought, by some happy instantaneous concourse of the various faculties of the mind with each other, the exact apprehension of what was *needed* to carry the meaning. And that it fits with absolute justice will be a judgment of immediate sense in the appreciative reader. We all feel this in what may be called inspired translation. Well! all language involves translation from inward to outward. In literature, as in all forms of art, there are the absolute and the merely relative or accessory beauties; and precisely in that exact proportion of the term to its purpose is the absolute beauty of style, prose or verse. All the good qualities, the beauties, of verse also, are such, only as precise expression.

In the highest as in the lowliest literature, then, the one indispensable beauty is, after all, truth: — truth to bare fact in the latter, as to some personal sense of fact, diverted somewhat from men's ordinary sense of it, in the former; truth there as accuracy, truth here as expression, that finest and most intimate form of truth, the *vraie vérité*. And what an eclectic principle this really is! employing for its one sole purpose — that absolute accordance of expression to idea — all other literary beauties and excellences whatever: how many kinds of style it covers, explains, justifies, and at the same time safeguards! Scott's facility, Flaubert's deeply pondered evocation of " the phrase," are equally good art. Say what you have to say, what you have a will to say, in the simplest, the most direct and exact manner possible, with no surplusage: — there, is the justification of the sentence so fortunately born, " entire, smooth, and round," that it needs no punctuation, and also (that is the point!) of the most elaborate period, if it be right in its elaboration. Here is the office of ornament: here also the purpose of restraint in ornament. As the exponent of truth, that austerity (the beauty, the function, of which in literature Flaubert understood so well) becomes not the correctness or purism of the mere scholar, but a security against the otiose, a jealous exclusion of what does not really tell towards the pursuit of relief, of life and vigor in the portraiture of one's sense. License again, the making free with rule, if it be indeed, as people fancy, a habit of genius, flinging aside or transforming all that opposes the liberty of beautiful production, will be but faith to one's own meaning. The seeming baldness of *Le Rouge et Le Noir* is nothing in itself; the wild ornament of *Les Misérables* is nothing in itself; and the restraint of Flaubert, amid a real natural opulence, only redoubled beauty — the phrase so large and so precise at the same time, hard as bronze, in service to the more perfect adaptation of words to their matter. Afterthoughts, retouchings, finish, will be of profit only so far as they too really serve to bring out the original, initiative, generative, sense in them.

In this way, according to the well-known saying, "The style is the man," [5] complex or simple, in his individuality, his plenary sense of what he really has to say, his sense of the world; all cautions regarding style arising out of so many natural scruples as to the medium through which alone he can expose that inward sense of things, the purity of this medium, its laws or tricks of refraction: nothing is to be left there which might give conveyance to any matter save that. Style in all its varieties, reserved or opulent, terse, abundant, musical, stimulant, academic, so long as each is really characteristic or expressive, finds thus its justification, the sumptuous good taste of Cicero being as truly the man himself, and not another, justified, yet insured inalienably to him, thereby, as would have been his portrait by Raffaelle, in full consular splendor, on his ivory chair.

A relegation, you may say perhaps — a relegation of style

to the subjectivity, the mere caprice, of the individual, which must soon transform it into mannerism. Not so! since there is, under the conditions supposed, for those elements of the man, for every lineament of the vision within, the one word, the one acceptable word, recognizable by the sensitive, by others " who have intelligence " in the matter, as absolutely as ever anything can be in the evanescent and delicate region of human language. The style, the manner, would be the man, not in his unreasoned and really uncharacteristic caprices, involuntary or affected, but in absolutely sincere apprehension of what is most real to him. But let us hear our French guide again. —

" Styles," says Flaubert's commentator, " *Styles,* as so many peculiar moulds, each of which bears the mark of a particular writer, who is to pour into it the whole content of his ideas, were no part of his theory. What he believed in was *Style:* that is to say, a certain absolute and unique manner of expressing a thing, in all its intensity and color. For him the *form* was the work itself. As in living creatures, the blood, nourishing the body, determines its very contour and external aspect, just so, to his mind, the *matter,* the basis, in a work of art, imposed, necessarily, the unique, the just expression, the measure, the rhythm — the *form* in all its characteristics."

If the style be the man, in all the color and intensity of a veritable apprehension, it will be in a real sense " impersonal."

I said, thinking of books like Victor Hugo's *Les Misérables,* that prose literature was the characteristic art of the nineteenth century, as others, thinking of its triumphs since the youth of Bach, have assigned that place to music. Music and prose literature are, in one sense, the opposite terms of art; the art of literature presenting to the imagination, through the intelligence, a range of interests, as free and various as those which music presents to it through sense. And certainly the tendency of what has been here said is to bring literature too under those conditions, by conformity to which music takes rank as the typically perfect art. If music be the ideal of all art whatever, precisely because in music it is impossible to distinguish the form from the substance or matter, the subject from the expression, then, literature, by finding its specific excellence in the absolute correspondence of the term to its import, will be but fulfilling the condition of all artistic quality in things everywhere, of all good art.

Good art, but not necessarily great art; the distinction between great art and good art depending immediately, as regards literature at all events, not on its form, but on the matter. Thackeray's *Esmond*, surely, is greater art than *Vanity Fair*, by the greater dignity of its interests. It is on the quality of the matter it informs or controls, its compass, its variety, its alliance to great ends, or the depth of the note of revolt, or the largeness of hope in it, that the greatness of literary art depends, as *The Divine Comedy, Paradise Lost, Les Misérables, The English Bible*, are great art. Given the conditions I have tried to explain as constituting good art; — then, if it be devoted further to the increase of men's happiness, to the redemption of the oppressed, or the enlargement of our sympathies with each other, or to such presentment of new or old truth about ourselves and our relation to the world as may ennoble and fortify us in our sojourn here, or immediately, as with Dante, to the glory of God, it will be also great art; if, over and above those qualities I summed up as mind and soul — that color and mystic perfume, and that reasonable structure, it has something of the soul of humanity in it, and finds its logical, its architectural place, in the great structure of human life.

---

[1] So also Leigh Hunt (*What is Poetry?* Professor Albert S. Cook's edition, Ginn, 1893, p. 38): "Verse is the final proof to the poet that his mastery over his art is complete."

[2] The distinction passes generally for De Quincey's; but, as he himself pointed out, De Quincey took it originally from Wordsworth; see his *Works*, ed. Masson, Vol. 10, p. 48, foot-note, and Wordsworth, *Prelude*, Book V, 1. 425.

[3] " Pleasurable ": a " barbarous " word, though sanctioned by the usage not merely of Pater, but of Wordsworth, Coleridge, Carlyle, and others.

"*Esmond*": in the *Fortnightly* stands "*Transformation*"; *i.e.* Hawthorne's *Marble Faun*. The substitution of Thackeray's novel is probably in the interests of " structural unity " in the smaller elements of composition; see Pater's reference to *Esmond* at the end of the essay (p. 412). Minor textual variants may also be traced in the essay between the first and subsequent imprints of *Appreciations*.

[5] Buffon; see above, p. 178.

XVII

FERDINAND BRUNETIÈRE (1849–1906)

The French Mastery of Style * (1897)

[Brunetière's article, translated from the author's manuscript by Mr. Irving Babbitt, appeared in the *Atlantic Monthly* for October, 1897 (Vol. 80, pp. 442–451). It has not been republished elsewhere.

As the French critic whose opinion carried, latterly, most weight in America, Brunetière should obtain a welcome rehearing upon a matter where his studies made him so competent to judge. With no injustice to his knowledge of other periods in French literature, it may be said that he was exceptionally well versed in the authors of the seventeenth century, above all in the theologians, whose controversial writings show the commencement of modern French style in prose. This familiarity, for example with Bossuet, seems to have reacted upon Brunetière's own habit of expression. His style tolerates a sentence on the whole longer and more involved than is customary in France to-day; other, less obtrusive reminiscences of an elder mode may be felt in him rather than explained.

Since his death, Dec. 9, 1906, notices of Brunetière have appeared in the *Revue des Deux Mondes* (Dec. 15, 1906, following p. 120), the *Nation* (Dec. 15, 1906, Apr. 4, 1907), and the *Atlantic Monthly* (April, 1907).

There is an important article on *Style* by the same author in *La Grande Encyclopédie* (Vol. 30, pp. 558–562).]

"The natural bent, the need, the mania, to influence others is the most salient trait of French character. . . . Every people has its mission; this is the mission of the French. The most trifling idea they launch upon Europe is a battering-ram driven forward by thirty million men. Ever hunger-

---

* With the permission of Messrs. Houghton, Mifflin and Company, publishers of the *Atlantic Monthly*.

ing for success and influence, the French would seem to live only to gratify this craving; and inasmuch as a nation cannot have been given a mission without the means of fulfilling it, the French have been given this means in their language, by which they rule much more effectually than by their arms, though their arms have shaken the world." This praise, possibly the highest the French language has ever received, cannot be said to emanate from one who was an entire foreigner: he was a native of Savoy, and everybody knows what affection, frequently chiding and captious, the Savoyards, from Vaugelas to François Buloz, have shown toward the French language. On the other hand, it can hardly be called the utterance of a Frenchman, coming as it does from Joseph de Maistre, ambassador from his Majesty the King of Sardinia to his Majesty the Tsar of all the Russias: and that is why I venture to quote it. There are things that modesty forbids us to say ourselves, but which we have the right to appropriate when others have said them, especially when their way of saying them makes us feel that there is a little jealousy mingled with the genuineness of their admiration. This same Joseph de Maistre writes furthermore: " I recollect having read formerly a letter of the famous architect Christopher Wren, in which he discusses the right dimensions for a church. He fixes upon them solely with reference to the carrying power of the human voice, and he sets the limits beyond which the voice for any English ear becomes inaudible; ' but,' he says on this point, ' a French orator would make himself heard farther away, his pronunciation being firmer and more distinct.' " And finally, de Maistre adds by way of comment on this quotation: " What Wren has said of oral speech appears to me still truer of that far more penetrating speech heard in books. The speech of Frenchmen is always audible farther away." Let us take his word for it.

What, then, is the reason of this fact? It is a question which has seemed to me worth discussing, now that all the great American universities are organizing their " departments of Romance languages " on a more liberal scale than they have done hitherto. If, speaking from the other side of the Atlantic, I could give them good reasons for persevering in this path, I should possibly be rendering them a service. For, these reasons being purely literary, the American universities would doubtless then grant to " literature " proper an attention that several of them seem up to the present to have reserved entirely for " philology." We, for our part, should gain through coming into closer relations with these universities, and thereby with what is best in the American democracy. It is hard to see who in Europe or America could take exception to this exchange of kindly offices, at least if it be true that the French language and literature possess the distinctive features which I shall attempt to show.

Let us put aside at the start all thought of any superiority in French as a natural organism over other languages, especially over the other Romance languages. If our language has its native points of excellence, other languages have theirs: Italian, for instance, is sweeter, and Spanish more sonorous. Sonorousness and sweetness are neither of them points of excellence which we can afford to despise in a language; and because they are to a certain extent " physical," they are none the less real or unusual. A fine voice, too, is only a fine voice; and yet how much does it not contribute to the success of a great orator. It may even be said almost literally of Demosthenes and Cicero that they are the " greatest voices " that have been heard among men. It must be confessed that the physical properties of the French language are not at all out of the common; and the truth is that, before turning them to account, most of our great writers in prose and verse have had a preliminary struggle to surmount them.

We must not be led, either, into thinking that we have had greater writers than the English or the Germans. This would be mere impertinence. If we could be tempted into believing it, all the labor of criticism for more than a hundred years would have been thrown away. Victor Hugo is a great poet, but Goethe and Shakespeare are great poets also. Genius has no national preferences.

But what may be truthfully said is that in France, from the very start, and especially during the last four hundred years, everybody has conspired to make of the French language that instrument of international exchange and universal communication which it has become. Noble ladies, from Marguerite de Valois, author of the Heptameron, to the Marquise de Rambouillet; ministers of state, like the Cardinal de Richelieu; princes and kings, Francis I, Charles IX (the protector and rival of Ronsard), Louis XIV, have formed, as it were, part of a conspiracy which had as its definite object to gain for French universal acceptance in place of the classics. The French Academy was founded with no other purpose; its charter attests the fact, as also its membership, which, happily, has never been entirely confined to men of letters. Our writers, in order to conform to this design, have usually consented to give up a part of their originality. It has not been enough for them to understand themselves, or to be understood by their countrymen and within the limits of their frontiers. They believed long before Rivarol said it — in an Essay on the Universal Diffusion of the French Language, a subject for the best treatment of which the Berlin Academy had offered a prize in 1781 — that " what is not clear is not French." To achieve this transparent and radiant clearness, to make some approach, at least, to this

2 E

universal diffusion, so that in Germany and England, in Italy and America, the knowledge of the French language is a sign of culture, a mark of education, — to arrive at these results, I do not deny that they have been forced to make some sacrifices. These, however, I shall choose to ignore for the present, and I propose simply to discuss here two or three of the principal means that these conspirators of a somewhat unusual kind have taken to compass their end.

I

In the first place, for three or four hundred years back, French writers, and we the public in common with them, have treated our language as a work of art. Let us have a clear understanding of the meaning of this word " art." The Greeks in antiquity, the Italians of the Renaissance, gave an artistic stamp or character to the commonest utensils, — to an earthen jar or a tin plate, an amphora, a ewer. It is a stamp of a similar kind that our writers from the time of Ronsard have tried to give the French language. They have thought that every language, apart from the services it renders in the ordinary usage and every-day intercourse of life, is capable of receiving an artistic form, and this form they have desired to bestow upon our own language. Read with reference to this point the manifesto of the Pléiade, The Defense and Ennoblement of the French Language by Joachim du Bellay, which bears the date of 1549, and you will see that such is throughout not merely its general spirit, but its special and particular object. Since then not only have French prose writers and poets had the same ambition, but all their readers, even princes themselves, have encouraged it, have made it almost a question of state; and the consequence is that no literary revolution or transformation has taken place in France which did not begin by being, knowingly and deliberately, a transformation or a modification of the language. This is what Malherbe, after Ronsard and in opposition to him, desired to do: namely, to give to the French language a precision and a clearness of outline, a musical cadence, a harmony of phrase, and finally a fullness of sense and sound, which seemed to him to be still lacking in the work of Ronsard; and along with Malherbe, by other means, but in a parallel direction, this was likewise the aim of the *précieuses*. The same is true of Boileau, as well as of Molière. It was through language, since it was by the means of style and the criticism of style, as is seen in works like the Satires and the Précieuses Ridicules, that they brought the art of their time back to the imitation of nature. Even in our own days, what was romanticism, what were realism and naturalism, at the start? The answer is always the same: they were theories of style before being doctrines of art; ways of writing before being ways of feeling or thinking; a reform of the language and an emancipation of the vocabulary, the striving after a greater flexibility of syntax, before it was known what use would be made of these conquests.

There is, then, in French, in the method of handling the language, a continuous artistic tradition. By very different and sometimes even opposing means, our writers have desired to please, in the best sense of the word, — to please themselves first of all, to please the public, to please foreigners; to make of their language a universal language, analogous in a fashion to the language of music, to that of sounds or colors; and as the crowning triumph to make of a page of Bossuet or Racine, for instance, a monument of art, for qualities of the same order as a statue of Michael Angelo or a painting of Raphael.

From our great writers, and the cultivated and intelligent readers who are their natural judges, this concern for art has

spread to the whole race, if indeed it were not truer to say
that it was a matter of instinct. Who is not familiar with
the phrase, " Duas res . . . gens Gallica industriosissime
persequitur : rem militarem et argute loqui "?   " Argute
loqui," — this is to be artistic in one's speech, and this everybody has been and tries to be among us; and nowhere, surely,
possibly not even in Greece, in the Athenian cafés, would you
come across more " elegant talkers " (*beaux parleurs*) than
in France: they are to be met with in the villages; they are
to be found in the workshops.   Some of them, I am well
aware, are insufferable withal, as for example the druggist
Homais in Madame Bovary, and again the illustrious Gau-
dissart in the Comédie Humaine of Honoré de Balzac.   But
what medal is without its reverse?   If we have so many
" elegant talkers," it is because, in our whole system of public
education, and even in our primary schools, this concern for
art prevails.   The fact is worthy of remark.   What our little
children learn in the schools under the name of orthography
— the word itself, when connected with its etymology, expresses the idea clearly enough — is to see in their language
a work of art, since it is to recognize and enjoy what is well
written.   It is not possible, indeed, to fix in the memory the
outer form of a word, its appearance, its physiognomy, so as
not to confuse it with any other word, without its exact meaning being also stamped in the mind.

In this respect, the oddities, or, as we sometimes call them,
the "Chinese puzzles " (*chinoiseries*) of orthography help to
preserve shades of thought.   The same may be said of the
peculiarities of syntax.   You will not teach children that
Goliath was a tall man (*un homme grand*), and David a great
man (*un grand homme*), without teaching them at the same
time a number of ideas that are epitomized in these two ways
of placing the adjective.   You will not explain to little

Walloons or to little Picards that a *bonnet blanc* is a white. cap, and that a *blanc bonnet* is a woman, in their patois, without their deriving some profit even from this pastime or playing on words. Need I speak of the rules of our participles, — those participles which, as the vaudeville says, are always getting one into a muddle,* so much apparent fancifulness and caprice there is in their agreements; and is it necessary for me to show that the most delicate analysis of the relations of ideas is implied in these very rules? The whole question here is not whether our farmers or our workingmen have need of all this knowledge, whether it would not be more profitable for them to learn other things, and whether they might not give less time to picking up the peculiarities of orthography or the *exceptions* of French grammar. I am not passing judgment; I am simply taking cognizance of the facts, and trying to arrive at an explanation. Whatever qualities, then, are to be peculiarly admired in French, we may say without hesitation, are due less to the language itself, to its original nature, than to the intensive cultivation which it has always received at every step of our educational system, and which, for my part, I hope it may long continue to receive.

Not that this cultivation may not have and has not had its dangers, like those to which "euphuism," "Marinism," and "Gongorism" have, in their time, exposed English, Italian, and Spanish. So much importance must not be attached to form as to lead to the sacrifice of substance; more than one writer in French could be named who has fallen into this mistake, — for it is a mistake. They are the writers to whom we have given the name of *précieux*. However, before condemning them in a lump on the authority of

---

* Ces *participes* avec lesquels, comme dit le vaudeville, on ne sait jamais quel *parti prendre.*

Molière, it is well to remember that we find in their number men like Fontenelle, Marivaux, Massillon, and Montesquieu. But it remains true that to treat a language as a work of art is to run the risk of seeing in it, sooner or later, only itself. Its words take on a mystical value, independent and entirely apart, as it were, from the ideas they are meant to convey. " Examine," said Baudelaire, " this word," — any ordinary word. " Is it not of a glowing vermilion, and is the heavenly azure as blue as that word? Look: has not this word the gentle lustre of the morning stars, and that one the livid paleness of the moon? " And Flaubert has written: " I recollect that my heart throbbed violently . . . from looking at a wall of the Acropolis, a perfectly bare wall! . . . The question occurs to me, then, Cannot a book, *quite apart from what it says*, produce the same effect? Is there not an intrinsic virtue in the choiceness of the materials, in the nicety with which they are put together, in the polish of the surfaces, in the harmony of the total effect? " They both failed to remember one thing, — which is that words express ideas before having a " color " or " virtue " peculiar to themselves, and that they are precise and luminous only with the clearness or the precision of these ideas. But Flaubert and Baudelaire are consistent with the principles of their school, and they show us what a man comes to when he no longer sees in language anything more than a work of art. Like them, he values words for themselves, for their appearance, for the sound they render, for various reasons which have nothing to do with the art of thinking. He detects genius in the turn of a phrase. Style becomes something intrinsic and mysterious, existing in and for itself. Virtuosity, which is only the indifference to the content of forms, gets possession of art, makes a plaything of it, perverts it or corrupts it; and through the sheer desire " to write well," one finally comes, as George Sand pointed out to Flaubert, to write only for a dozen initiates; even they do not always understand one, and besides, they never admire one for the reasons one would prefer.

II

In what way may we avoid this danger? Is it possible to point out several ways, or is there perhaps only one? In any case, we can easily define and characterize the one our great writers have taken, although not always of their own accord. They have understood, or have been made to understand, that language, though a work of art, still continues to be above all a medium for the communication of thoughts and feelings, — what may be called their instrument of exchange, their current coin; and that consequently perfect art cannot be conceived or sought for apart from those attributes which are the attributes of thought itself.

In French, as in English or German, and I presume also in Chinese, both prose writers and poets have always tended to make of their art an image or expression of themselves. It is for this very reason that they are writers, — because the things that had been said did not satisfy them, or because they wished to say them in another way, or else to say things that had not been said. Only in France, the court, " society," criticism, have reminded them that if they wrote, it was in order to be understood. From Ronsard to Victor Hugo, they have had imposed upon them, as a rule, the twofold condition to remain themselves, and at the same time to talk the language of everybody. The interest which they had inspired in a whole people for the things of literature turned in some sort against them. Having themselves invited all the cultivated minds about them to become judges of art, they were not allowed, when the fancy came over them later, to arrogate to themselves the right to be the sole judges of art. Public opinion, in return for the admiration and applause they solicited from it, felt constrained to ask of them certain definite concessions, — concessions which they consented to make; and doubtless they were right in so doing, after all, since they were thus enabled to give, not only to French literature, but to the French language, that social character which it possesses in so high a degree.

It was in this wise, in fact, that there found its way into our literature — or if the reader prefers, into our rhetoric — that tenet which Buffon summed up at the end of the classic period in the recommendation never to name things except by " the most general terms." [1] Those who have ridiculed this phrase have misunderstood it; they have quibbled about the words; they have feigned to believe, and possibly they really have believed, that the most general terms are the most abstract, the vaguest, the most colorless, the opposite of the exact, appropriate, and special term. Yet it would have been enough for them to read more carefully Buffon himself, and Voltaire, and Racine, and Molière, and Bossuet, and Pascal! They would then have seen that the most general terms are the terms of ordinary usage, those in everybody's vocabulary, — terms that are intelligible without any need of going to the dictionary, that are not the peculiar dialect of a trade or the jargon of a coterie.   " If in talking of savages or of the ancient Franks," Taine writes somewhere, " I say the ' battle-axe,' everyone understands at once; if I say the ' tomahawk ' or the ' francisca,' a great many people will fancy I am talking Teutonic or Iroquois." And this strikes him as extremely amusing. It is natural that it should, harboring, as he does, the superstition of " local color " and of the " technical term." But he is wrong, and to prove it I need only seven lines of Boileau from the tenth Satire : —

" Le doux charme pour toi de voir, chaque journée,
De nobles champions ta femme environnée,

*   *   *   *   *

S'en aller méditer une vole au jeu d'hombre,
S'écrier sur un as mal à propos jeté,
Se plaindre d'un gâno qu'on n'a point écouté,
Ou querellant tout bas le ciel qu'elle regarde,
A la bête gémir d'un roi venu sans garde."

Whereby, it seems to me, two things are made plain: the
one, that upon occasion Boileau — Boileau himself!— called
things by their names, did not shrink from technical terms;
and the other, that in thus using technical terms in his verse,
and because he did use them, he has rendered himself unintelligible to everyone who is not acquainted with the game
of *ombre*. Is a cultivated man required to know the game of
ombre? Therein lies the danger of technical terms. In the
first place, few persons understand them; and when it happens
that everybody does understand them, they are no longer
technical. This is what Buffon meant: Use general terms,
because if you do not use them, you condemn yourself by
your own act to be understood by only a small number of
readers; because technical terms, in so far as they are technical,
are a stumbling-block in the way of expressing general truths,
which alone constitute the domain of literature.[2] Nay, more:
try by means of general terms to bring into this very domain
as much as possible of what is technical; do what Descartes
did for philosophy, Pascal for theology, Montesquieu for
politics, or what I myself, Buffon, have done for natural history. — Such has been the practice of our great writers; and
doubtless nothing has contributed more to the success of the
French language than its having become, thanks to them,
the best fitted for the expression of general ideas.

It has likewise become the most " oratorical "; and by this
word I do not mean at all the most eloquent or the most

grandiloquent, — Spanish might claim this honor, — but, on the contrary, the nearest to conversation and to the spoken language. We are sometimes told that we must not write as we talk. This is a mistake, against which, in case of need, our whole classic literature would protest. To write as we talk is precisely what we should do, with the proviso, of course, that we talk correctly. Vaugelas, who, as everybody knows, was the great French grammarian of the classic period, has said so expressly: " The spoken word is the first in order *and in dignity*, inasmuch as the written word is only its image, as the other is the image of thought." Possibly this may seem an odd bit of reasoning; it may even strike one as an amusing application of the law of primogeniture to criticism; and one is quite free to deny that the dignity of the different kinds of composition and literary forms is to be measured by their age. But what, on the other hand, is certain, and what I recollect to have pointed out more than once, in conformity with Vaugelas's suggestion, is that all the blunders with which puristical and pedantic grammarians are fond of reproaching Molière and La Fontaine, Pascal and Bossuet, are not even irregularities; on the contrary, they are seen to be the most natural and expressive form of their thought, as soon as we " speak " their comedies or sermons instead of " reading " them. In verse, as in prose, the grand style of the seventeenth century was a spoken style. Its merits are the merits of the conversation of well-bred people.

Or again, to use the language of experimental psychology of the present day, if it is true that writers are to be divided into " hearers " (*auditifs*) who hear themselves speak, and " visualizers " (*visuels*) who see themselves write, the greater part of the French writers of the seventeenth century belong to the first class. The ear, and not the eye, was their guide. It was not of their paper that they thought in writing, but of a body of hearers; and just as they use the most general terms to make themselves better understood by these hearers, so they strive to give to their " discourse," as they call it, the swing, the flexibility, and, it would not be too much to say, the familiar tone of conversation. Their way of arranging this discourse, which seems artificial to us, is, on the contrary, the most natural, since it follows the very movement of the thought. Their long periods, which we suppose to be premeditated and balanced by dint of laborious application, are, in truth, only the necessary form of sustained improvisation. If they happen to raise their voices, as do Pascal in his Thoughts and Bossuet in his Sermons, it is because the grandeur or the seriousness of the subject calls for it; and as a matter of fact, neither God nor death is to be spoken of lightly. But Molière in his great comedies and La Fontaine in his Fables give us the illusion of what is least set and formal in daily conversation. " You might think that you were there yourself; " you will see, too, if you scrutinize them closely, that their sentence structure does not differ from that of Bossuet and Pascal. That is what is meant when French is said to be of all modern languages the most " oratorical," the most similar when written — I mean, of course, when well written — to what it is when spoken, and consequently the most natural.

It is also " the most exact and the clearest ": the clearest, because what is obscure is precisely what is peculiar, special, or technical, the speech of the artilleryman or that of the sailor, the dialect of the factory or workshop; the most exact, because conversation would become a monologue if its finest shades of meaning were not caught, understood, and taken up immediately and as fast as the words fall from the lips. We cannot wait a quarter of an hour to laugh at a joke, and an epigram or a madrigal should have no need of commentary.

This clearness, moreover, is a result of the oratorical character of the French language as it has just been defined. We must think of other men, since we are speaking to them or for them, and spare no effort to give them ready access to our thought. This, again, is thoroughly French. Great writers, especially poets and philosophers, Carlyle and Browning in English, Schelling and even Goethe in German, have thought less of being intelligible to others than to themselves. " I have just finished reading Sordello," wrote Carlyle to his wife, " without being able to find out whether Sordello was a poem, a city, or a man; " and who will deny that there is some obscurity — willful and deliberate obscurity, it is true — in Sartor Resartus and in the famous lectures on Hero Worship ? But a French writer always speaks to his reader as he would to a hearer, or to one with whom he is conversing. He believes with Boileau that " the mind of man teems with a host of confused ideas and vague half-glimpses of the truth," and also that " we like nothing better than to have one of these ideas *well elucidated and clearly presented* to us." His endeavor is, not to veil his thought, but, on the contrary, to lay it bare. He does not try to screen it, as it were, from the eyes of the profane, but, on the contrary, he takes every pains to render it accessible to them. He does not keep his secret jealously to himself, but he desires rather to impart it to everybody, — to his countrymen, to foreigners, to the world. "The only good works," Voltaire has said, " are those that *find their way into foreign countries* and are translated there." Is it surprising, then, that French, the one modern language having this ambition, has succeeded, so far as it has realized its purpose, only by divesting itself of all ambiguity; only by filtering its ideas, so to speak, and ridding them of all impurities which would sully their transparent clearness; and sometimes, too, by sacrificing everything which calls for too close reflection? That is why, as I said, its precision and clearness did not come to it from any special or innate property, from any virtue which it brought with it as a natural dower, but from the application, the toil, the conscious effort, of its great writers. I may add that in this particular, the greatest of these writers, reserving for themselves other means of originality, have followed rather than guided public opinion.

What is indeed remarkable about these characteristics, which have come with time to belong to the French language, is that the demands of public opinion, its watchfulness and persistency, have done no less than the talent or even the genius of the individual writer in fixing and establishing them. Who took the first step, the public or the writer? It would be difficult to find an answer for the question stated thus barely: at one time it has chanced to be the public, at another time the writer, who has taken the lead. Yet it will be observed that nearly all the literary revolutions in France have been anticipated, desired, and encouraged before a Ronsard, a Pascal, or a Hugo has appeared to bring them about. The revolution once begun, the public has always taken pains to see that the writer did not indulge his idiosyncrasies too far. Free to choose their thought, — this our writers have rarely been; they have rarely even been more than half free in their manner of expressing this thought. They have been brought back, as often as they showed signs of wishing to depart from it, to the respect of an ideal, or rather to the working out of a design which was that of a whole race. To use the fine expression of Bossuet, praising this very feature in Greek literature, and admiring it there above all others, they have been forced to labor to " the perfecting of civil life." They have not been forced to confound art with morality, but they have not been allowed to forget that in a highly organized civilization literature is in some sort a social institution. They have even been rather sharply reminded of the fact, at times, when they have seemed to forget it. What they may have lost by being forced to bend to these requirements is not at present for me to say, concerned as I am with what they have gained: this is to have made of French literature a literature eminently human.

III

"Men's passions," it has been truly said, "everywhere originally the same, live amidst the ices of the pole as well as under the tropical sun. The Cossack Poogatchef was ambitious, like the Italian Masaniello, and the fever of love burns the Kamschatkan no less than the African." These are the " original " passions which the greatest of the French writers have studied in man. Other writers may have portrayed them more energetically, but surely no one has penetrated more thoroughly their innermost workings, or has had a closer knowledge of their psychology. This, we venture to say, is what foreigners like or value in our great writers. They are vaguely grateful to them, almost unconsciously so, for this effort to observe and note in man what is most general and most permanent. For in this way a particular literature has passed beyond its own boundaries, not in order to encroach on the boundaries of other literatures, or to appropriate qualities which did not belong to it, but to adapt them to its uses, and thereby establish itself, as it were, outside of space and time. It has not specially affected either its own ideas or those of others; but with the ideas of others and with its own mingled, fused together, and made to correct one another, freed from what was transitory in some of them and in some local, and consequently in either case accidental, French literature has tried to attain to a universal ideal which should be as lasting as the form in which it was clothed. Is not this very much what Italian painting of the Renaissance and Greek sculpture of the great period had done before? And is not that why the tragedies of Racine and the sermons of Bossuet, like the marbles of Phidias and the paintings of Raphael, speak very nearly the same language to everybody? Andromaque is for the drama what the Madonnas of Raphael are in the history of painting; and in like manner, the Funeral Oration of Henrietta of England holds a position in oratory not unlike that of the Daughters of Niobe in sculpture.

The result has been a tendency in French literature, and secondarily a special fitness in the language, to discuss what are called nowadays " social problems." Whether the rights of man in general, or those of woman in particular, are being debated, we have in French a large vocabulary more suitable than any other, more precise and more extensive, to plead for them; we have what the ancients called *loci*, — a store of ready-made phrases on which the orator and the publicist have only to draw. If we must turn to the English for arguments and even for words to discuss the " rights of the individual," and to the Germans for reasons to uphold the " rights of association," no literature has found more generous accents than ours, nor any language words more capable of expressing the rights of man so far as he is a subject for justice and charity. No loftier strains of eloquence have ever been uttered, to remind men of their equality in the presence of pain and death, than by our great preachers, Bossuet, Bourdaloue, Massillon; and this in language of marvelous strength, simplicity, and harmony. And where has all that can be said to make the powers of this world tremble for the validity of their claims been expressed in a keener or more impassioned form than in some of the pamphlets of Voltaire or in the fiery discourses of Rousseau?

Nothing, again, was more characteristic of the French press for many years, — I say " was," for of late things have changed somewhat, — as compared with the English or American press, for example, than the satisfaction, the copiousness, and the perfect clearness with which it treated those doctrinal questions which are the point of contact, or, if I may be allowed the expression, the point of intersection of morals and politics. The reason is that French journalism found in the language an instrument ready for its use, and had only to draw on the common stock of literary tradition. If it wanted, for instance, to show the iniquity of slavery, it had only to remember the Philosophic History of the two Indias or the Spirit of Laws. If it wished to remind wealth of its duties, it could consult, not Rousseau merely, but Massillon in his sermon on Dives, or Bossuet in his sermon on the Eminent Dignity of the Poor. Rather, it had no need of consulting the latter or remembering the former; the dictionary of every-day speech was sufficient. Two hundred years of literature had made social problems circulate in the very veins of the language; it had embodied them in its words. It had made of French the conspiracy spoken of by Joseph de Maistre: "Omnia quæ loquitur populus iste conjuratio est." Even to-day no other language has a power of propaganda like French, and so long as it keeps this power we need have no fear of its being neglected. To assure its position in the world, we have only to guard against giving up lightly the qualities it still retains; the abandonment of them, so far from being a progress, as some of the " symbolists " have supposed, would be a retrogression toward the origins.

Need I add here, to reassure those who may possibly see in the French language only an instrument of socialistic propaganda, that it is possible to give a good meaning to the word " socialism "; or should I not say rather that nothing is more dangerous than to leave the monopoly of the word to those who abuse it? This is to do violence to its etymology! It would be better to point out that social problems, comprising as they do all that is of interest or concern to society, include in their number the problems of the "polite world." And so, for the same reasons that have ·made French the language of social discussion, it has become, in the hands of our great writers, the language of polite conversation. This is one of the rare services we owe to the salons, — not to those most in repute, the salon of Madame Geoffrin or that of Madame Tencin, but, on the contrary, to those most ridiculed, especially to the salon of the Marquise de Rambouillet. Now, inasmuch as "society," or what passes under that name, has no other object than the putting in common of all that is deemed agreeable, elegant, and noble in life in order to enjoy it more fully, we can readily imagine what vivacity, flexibility, and ease two hundred years of society must have given to the French language. It was there, in society, and in the salons where women held sway, that a literature till then too pedantic and too masculine was forced to bend and yield, to learn to have respect for their modesty or for their delicacy, and to adorn itself, so to speak, with some, at least, of the virtues of their sex. It was there that due stress, and at times a little more than due stress, was laid on the art of enhancing what one says by the way of saying it. It was there that the plan was formed to make of French a universal language in place of the classics, and to this end to give it the qualities it still lacked. It was there, too, that the fact was realized that, language being a human product, it was the duty of men to rescue it from the fatality of its natural development, and to subordinate it not only to the requirements of art, but also to the necessities of social progress.

2 F

In conclusion, it is well to remember that Horace's line is
only half true: —

"Usus
Quem penes arbitrium est, et jus, et norma loquendi."[3]

No! Usage is not wholly this master or this capricious tyrant
of language. Granting that it were, its fluctuations or its
peculiarities would still have their history, this history its
reasons, and these reasons their explanation; or rather, usage
is only a name which serves to hide our ignorance of the
causes, and if, instead of taking it for granted, we analyze it,
languages are found to be the work of those who write them.
The example of French would be enough to prove this. It
was not naturally clearer than any other language; it has become so. It was no better fitted than any other language for
the expression of general ideas; it has become so. It was not
a work of art in the time of the Strasburg Oaths or the Canticle
of St. Eulalia, and yet it has become so. I have tried to show
how, by what means, in virtue of what united effort, and I
hope I have made it clear. Americans, I fancy, will not be
sorry to see thus restored to the domain of the will what
philologians or linguists had unjustly taken away from it, —
if indeed this be not, in their eyes, an additional reason for
valuing our language. They are supposed to prize nothing
more highly than the victories of the will: the diffusion of the
French language in the world is one of these victories; and
may I not say that what renders it more precious is the fact
— evident, I trust, from the foregoing — that our writers have
won it only by identifying the interests of their self-love with
the interests of art and of humanity?

[1] Compare Buffon, above, p. 176.
[2] Compare Swift, above, p. 162.
[3] Horace, *Art of Poetry*, ll. 71, 72.

XVIII

FREDERIC HARRISON (1831–)

On English Prose (1898)

[From *Tennyson, Ruskin, Mill, and Other Literary Estimates*, New York and London (Macmillan), 1902 (pp. 149–165).

Mr. Harrison's slightly bantering address " to the Bodley Literary Society, Oxford," was delivered in response to an invitation from the " President, C. René Harrison " — the author's son. It was subsequently printed in the *Nineteenth Century* for June, 1898 (Vol. 43, pp. 932–942), with the title *On Style in English Prose*, a caption which some readers may still prefer. The article was copied from the *Nineteenth Century* by the *Eclectic Magazine* (Vol. 131, pp. 327 ff.), by *Living Age* (Vol. 218, pp. 230 ff.), and by the *Writer* (Vol. 11, pp. 113 ff.). Still later it received a few verbal corrections for inclusion as Chapter VII in the first imprint (London, 1899) of Mr. Harrison's volume, cited above. In his review of that volume (*Forum*, Vol. 30, September, 1900) Professor W. P. Trent discusses Chapter VII in some detail (pp. 120–121).

Mr. Harrison's coloring of playful overstatement is not likely to obscure the rich fund of good sense and long experience which his address discloses; yet the tinge must not be disregarded.]

Fili mi dilectissime (if, sir, I may borrow the words of the late Lord Derby when, as Chancellor of the University, he conferred the degree of D.C.L. on Lord Stanley, his son) — I fear that I am about to do an unwise thing. When, in an hour of paternal weakness, I accepted your invitation to address the Bodley Society on *Style*, it escaped me that it was a subject with which undergraduates have but small concern. And now I find myself talking on a matter whereof I know very little, and could do you no good even if I knew much, in presence of an illustrious historian, to say nothing of your own Head, who was an acknowledged master of English when my own literary style aspired to nothing more elegant than the dry forms of pleadings and deeds.

Everyone knows how futile for any actual result are those elaborate disquisitions on Style which some of the most consummate masters have amused themselves in compiling, but which serve at best to show how quite hackneyed truisms can be graced by an almost miraculous neatness of phrase. It is in vain to enjoin on us " propriety," " justness of expression," " suitability of our language to the subject we treat," and all the commonplaces which the schools of Addison and of Johnson in the last century promulgated as canons of good style. " Proper words in proper places," says Swift, " make the true definition of a style."[1] "Each phrase in its right place," says Voltaire. Well! Swift and Voltaire knew how to do this with supreme skill; but it does not help us, if they cannot teach their art. *How* are we to know what is the *proper* word? *How* are we to find the *right* place? And even a greater than Swift or Voltaire is not much more practical as a teacher. " Suit the action to the word, and the word to the action," says Hamlet. " Be not too tame neither. Let your own discretion be your tutor." Can you trust your own discretion? Have undergraduates this discretion? And how could I, in presence of your College authority, suggest that you should have no tutor but your own discretion?

All this is as if a music-master were to say to a pupil, Sing always in tune and with the *right* intonation, and whatever you do, produce your voice in the *proper* way! Or, to make myself more intelligible to you here, it is as if W. G. Grace were to tell you, Play a " yorker " in the *right* way, and place the ball in the *proper* spot with reference to the field! We know that neither the art of acting, nor of singing, nor of cricket can be taught by general commonplaces of this sort. And good prose is so far like cricket that the W. G.'s of literature, after ten or twenty "centuries," can tell you nothing more than this — to place your words in the right spot, and to choose the proper word, according to the " field " that you have before you.

The most famous essay on Style, I suppose, is that by one of the greatest wizards who ever used language — I mean the *Ars Poetica* [2] of Horace, almost every line of which has become a household word in the educated world. But what avail his inimitable epigrams in practice? Who is helped by being told not to draw a man's head on a horse's neck, or a beautiful woman with the tail end of a fish? " Do not let brevity become obscurity; do not let your mountain in labor bring forth a mouse; turn over your Greek models night and day; your compositions must be not only correct, but must give delight, touch the heart," and so forth, and so forth. All these imperishable maxims, as clean cut as a sardonyx gem — these " chestnuts," as you call them in the slang of the day — serve as hard nuts for a translator to crack, and as handy mottoes at the head of an essay; but they are barren of any solid food as the shell of a walnut.

Then Voltaire, perhaps the greatest master of prose in any modern language, wrote an essay on Style, in the same vein of epigrammatic platitude. No declamation, says he, in a work on physics. No jesting in a treatise on mathematics.[3] Well! but did Douglas Jerrold himself ever try to compose a Comic Trigonometry; and could another Charles Lamb find any fun in Spencer's First Principles? A fine style, says Voltaire, makes anything delightful; but it is exceedingly difficult to acquire, and very rarely found. And all he has to say is, " Avoid grandiloquence, confusion, vulgarity, cheap wit, and colloquial slang in a tragedy." He

might as well say, Take care to be as strong as Sandow, and
as active as Prince Ranjitsinhji, and whatever you do, take
care not to grow a nose like Cyrano de Bergerac in the new
play!

An ingenious professor of literature has lately ventured
to commit himself to an entire treatise on Style, wherein
he has propounded everything that can usefully be said about
this art, in a style which illustrates things that you should
avoid.   At the end of his book he declares that style cannot
be taught.   This is true enough; but if this had been the first,
instead of the last, sentence of his piece, the book would not
have been written at all.   I remember that, when I stood for
the Hertford Scholarship, we had to write a Latin epigram on
the thesis —

Omnia liberius nullo poscente —
— *fatemur*, (I replied —)
Carmina cur poscas, carmine si sit opus?

And so I say now.   Style cannot be taught.[4]   And this
perhaps puts out of court the professor's essay, and no doubt
my own also.   Nothing practical can be said about Style.
And no good can come to a young student by being anxious
about Style.   None of you by taking thought can add one
cubit to his stature; no!   nor one gem to his English prose,
unless nature has endowed him with that rare gift — a subtle
ear for the melody of words, a fastidious instinct for the
connotations of a phrase.

You will, of course, understand that I am speaking of
Style in that higher sense as it was used by Horace, Swift,
Voltaire, and great writers, that is, Style as an element of
permanent literature.   It is no doubt very easy by practice
and good advice to gain a moderate facility in writing current language, and even to get the trick of turning out lively

articles and smart reviews. " 'Tis as easy as lying; govern these ventages with your finger and thumb, give it breath with your mouth, and it will discourse most eloquent music " — quite up to the pitch of the journals and the magazines of our day, of which we are all proud. But this is a poor trade; and it would be a pity to waste your precious years of young study by learning to play on the literary " recorders." You may be taught to fret them. You will not learn to make them speak!

There are a few negative precepts, quite familiar common form, easy to remember, and not difficult to observe. These are all that any manual can lay down. The trouble comes in when we seek to apply them. What is it that is artificial, incongruous, obscure? How are we to be simple? Whence comes the music of language? What is the magic that can charm into life the apt and inevitable word that lies hidden somewhere at hand — so near and yet so far — so willing and yet so coy — did we only know the talisman which can awaken it? This is what no teaching can give us — what skilful tuition and assiduous practice can but improve in part, and even that only for the chosen few.

About Style, in the higher sense of the term, I think the young student should trouble himself as little as possible. When he does, it too often becomes the art of clothing thin ideas in well-made garments. To gain skill in expression before he has got thoughts or knowledge to express, is somewhat premature; and to waste in the study of form those irrevocable years which should be absorbed in the study of things, is mere decadence and fraud. The young student — *ex hypothesi* — has to learn, not to teach. His duty is to digest knowledge, not to popularize it and carry it abroad. It is a grave mental defect to parade an external polish far more mature than the essential matter within. Where the learner is called on to express his thoughts in formal compositions — and the less he does this the better — it is enough that he put his ideas or his knowledge (if he has any) in clear and natural terms.   But the less he labors the flow of his periods the more truly is he the honest learner, the less is his risk of being the smug purveyor of the crudities with which he has been crammed, the further is he from becoming one of those voluble charlatans whom the idle study of language so often breeds.

I look with sorrow on the habit which has grown up in the university since my day (in the far-off fifties) — the habit of making a considerable part of the education of the place to turn on the art of serving up gobbets of prepared information in essays more or less smooth and correct — more or less successful imitations of the viands that are cooked for us daily in the press.   I have heard that a student has been asked to write as many as seven essays in a week, a task which would exhaust the fertility of a Swift. The bare art of writing readable paragraphs in passable English is easy enough to master; one that steady practice and good coaching can teach the average man.   But it is a poor art, which readily lends itself to harm.[5]   It leads the shallow ones to suppose themselves to be deep, the raw ones to fancy they are cultured, and it burdens the world with a deluge of facile commonplace.   It is the business of a university to train the mind to think and to impart solid knowledge, not to turn out nimble penmen who may earn a living as the clerks and salesmen of literature.

Almost all that can be laid down as law about Style is contained in a sentence of Madame de Sévigné in her twentieth letter to her daughter.   " Ne quittez jamais le naturel," she says; " votre tour s'y est formé, et cela compose un style parfait."   I suppose I must translate this; for Madame de Sévigné is no subject for modern research, and our *Alma*

Mater is concerned only with dead languages and remote epochs. " Never forsake what is natural," she writes; " you have moulded yourself in that vein, and this produces a perfect style." There is nothing more to be said. Be natural, be simple, be yourself: shun artifices, tricks, fashions. Gain the tone of ease, plainness, self-respect. To thine own self be true.[6] Speak out frankly that which you have thought out in your own brain and have felt within your own soul. This, and this alone, creates a perfect style, as she says who wrote the most exquisite letters the world has known.

And so Molière, a consummate master of language and one of the soundest critics of any age, in that immortal scene of his *Misanthrope*, declares the euphuistic sonnets of the Court to be mere play of words, pure affectation, not worth a snatch from a peasant's song. That is not the way in which nature speaks, cries Alceste — *J'aime mieux ma mie* — that is how the heart gives utterance, without *colifichets*, with no quips and cranks of speech, very dear to fancy, and of very liberal conceit. And Sainte-Beuve cites an admirable saying: " All peasants have style." They speak as nature prompts. They have never learned to play with words; they have picked up no tricks, mannerisms, and affectation like Osric and Oronte in the plays. They were not trained to write essays, and never got veterans to discourse to them on Style. Yet, as Sainte-Beuve says, they have style, because they have human nature, and they have never tried to get outside the natural, the simple, the homely. It is the secret of Wordsworth, as it was of Goldsmith, as it was of Homer.

Those masters of style of whom I have spoken were almost all French — Molière, Madame de Sévigné, Voltaire, Sainte-Beuve. Style, in truth, is a French art; there is hardly any other style in prose. I doubt if any English prose, when judged by the canons of perfect style, can be matched with the highest triumphs of French prose. The note of the purest French is a serene harmony of tone, an infallible nicety of keeping, a brightness and point never spasmodic, never careless, never ruffled, like the unvarying manner of a gentleman who is a thorough man of the world. Even our best English will sometimes grow impetuous, impatient, or slack, as if it were too much trouble to maintain an imperturbable air of quite inviolable good-breeding. In real life no people on earth, or perhaps we ought to say in Europe, in this surpass the English gentleman. In prose literature it is a French gift, and seems given as yet to the French alone. Italians, Spaniards, and Russians have an uncertain, casual, and fitful style, and Germans since Heine have no style at all.[7]

Whilst we have hundreds of men and women to-day who write good English, and one or two who have a style of their own, our French critics will hardly admit that we show any example of the purest style when judged by their own standard of perfection. They require a combination of simplicity, ease, charm, precision, and serenity of tone, together with the memorable phrase and inimitable felicity which stamp the individual writer, and yet are obvious and delightful to every reader. Renan had this; Pierre Loti has it; Anatole France has it. But it is seldom that we read a piece of current English and feel it to be exquisite in form, apart from its substance, refreshing as a work of art, and yet hall-marked from the mint of the one particular author. We have hall-marks enough, it is true, only too noisily conspicuous on the plate; but are they refreshing and inspiring? are they works of art? How is it that our poetry, even our minor poetry of the day, has its own felicitous harmony of tone, whilst our prose is notoriously wanting in that mellow refinement of form which the French call Style?

If I hazard a few words about some famous masters of

language, I must warn you that judgments of this kind amount to little more than the likes and dislikes of the critic himself. There are no settled canons, and no accepted arbiter, of the elegances of prose. It is more or less a matter of personal taste, even more than it is in verse. I never doubt that the greatest master of prose in recorded history is Plato. He alone (like Homer in poetry) is perfect. He has every mood, and all are faultless.[8] He is easy, lucid, graceful, witty, pathetic, imaginative by turns; but in all kinds he is natural and inimitably sweet. He is never obscure, never abrupt, never tedious, never affected. He shows us as it were his own Athene, wisdom incarnate in immortal radiance of form.

Plato alone is faultless. I will not allow any Roman to be perfect. Cicero even in his letters is wordy, rhetorical, academic. Livy is too consciously painting in words, too sonorous and diffuse for perfection; as Tacitus carries conciseness into obscurity and epigram into paradox. Of Latin prose, for my own part, I value most the soldierly simplicity of Cæsar, though we can hardly tell if he could be witty, graceful, pathetic, and fantastic as we see these gifts in Plato.

One of the most suggestive points in the history of prose is Boccaccio's *Decamerone*, where a style of strange fascination suddenly starts into life with hardly any earlier models, nay, two or three centuries earlier than organic prose in any of the tongues of Europe. For many generations the exquisite ease and melody of Boccaccio's language found no rival in any modern nation, nor had it any rival in Italy, and we have no evidence that anything in Italy had prepared the way for it. It is far from a perfect style, for it is often too fluid, loose, and voluminous for mature prose; but as a first effort towards an orderly array of lucid narrative, it is an amazing triumph of the Italian genius for art.

Prose, as you all know, is always and everywhere a plant of much later growth than poetry.[9] Plato came four or five centuries after Homer; Tacitus came two centuries later than Lucretius; Machiavelli came two centuries after Dante; Voltaire a century after Corneille; Addison a century after Shakespeare. And while the prose of Boccaccio, with all its native charm, can hardly be called an organic, mature, and mellow style, in poetry, for nearly a century before Boccaccio, Dante and the minor lyrists of Italy had reached absolute perfection of rhythmical form.

Although fairly good prose is much more common than fairly good verse, yet I hold that truly fine prose is more rare than truly fine poetry. I trust that it will be counted neither a whim nor a paradox if I give it as a reason that mastery in prose is an art more difficult than mastery in verse. The very freedom of prose, its want of conventions, of settled prosody, of musical inspiration, give wider scope for failure and afford no beaten paths. Poetry glides swiftly down the stream of a flowing and familiar river, where the banks are always the helmsman's guide. Prose puts forth its lonely skiff upon a boundless sea, where a multitude of strange and different crafts are cutting about in contrary directions. At any rate, the higher triumphs of prose come later and come to fewer than do the great triumphs of verse.

When I lately had to study a body of despatches and State papers of the latter half of the sixteenth century, written in six modern languages of Europe, I observed that the Italian alone in that age was a formed and literary language, at the command of all educated men and women, possessed of organic canons and a perfectly mature type. The French, German, Dutch, English, and Spanish of that age, as used for practical ends, were still in the state of a language held in solution before it assumes a crystallized form. Even the men who wrote correct Latin could not write their own language with any real command. At the death of Tennyson, we may remember, it was said that no less than sixty-two poets were thought worthy of the wreath of bay. Were there six writers of prose whom even a log-rolling confederate would venture to hail as a possible claimant of the crown? Assiduous practice in composing neat essays has turned out of late ten thousand men and women who can put together very pleasant prose. It has not turned out one living master in prose as Tennyson was master in verse.

I have spoken of Voltaire as perhaps the greatest master of prose in any modern language, but this does not mean that he is perfect, and without qualification or want. His limpid clearness, ease, sparkle, and inexhaustible self-possession have no rival in modern tongues, and are almost those of Plato himself. But he is no Plato; he never rises into the pathos, imagination, upper air of the empyrean, to which the mighty Athenian can soar at will. Voltaire is never tedious, wordy, rhetorical, or obscure; and this can be said of hardly any other modern but Heine and Swift. My edition of Voltaire is in sixty volumes, of which some forty are prose; and in all those twenty thousand pages of prose not one is dull or labored. We could not say this of the verse. But I take *Candide* or *Zadig* to be the high-water mark of easy French prose, wanting no doubt in the finer elements of pathos, dignity, and power. And for this reason many have preferred the prose of Rousseau, of George Sand, of Renan, though all of these are apt at times to degenerate into garrulity and gush. There was no French prose, says Voltaire, before Pascal; and there has been none of the highest flight since Renan. In the rest of Europe perfect prose has long been as rare as the egg of the great auk.

In spite of the splendor of Bacon and of Milton, of Jeremy

Taylor, and of Hooker, and whatever be the virility of Bunyan and Dryden, I cannot hold that the age of mature English prose had been reached until we come to Defoe, Swift, Addison, Berkeley, and Goldsmith. These are the highest types we have attained. Many good judges hold Swift to be our Voltaire, without defect or equal. I should certainly advise the ambitious essayist to study Swift for instruction, by reason of the unfailing clearness, simplicity, and directness of his style. But when we come to weigh him by the highest standard of all, we find Swift too uniformly pedestrian, too dry; wanting in variety, in charm, in melody, in thunder, and in flash. The grandest prose must be like the vault of heaven itself, passing from the freshness of dawn to the warmth of a serene noon, and anon breaking forth into a crashing storm. Swift sees the sun in one uniform radiance of cool light, but it never fills the air with warmth, nor does it ever light the welkin with fire.[10]

Addison, with all his mastery of tone, seems afraid to give his spirit rein. *Il s'écoute quand il parle:* and this, by the way, is the favorite sin of our best moderns. We see him pause at the end of each felicitous sentence to ask himself if he has satisfied all the canons as to propriety of diction. Even in the *Spectator* we never altogether forget the author of *Cato*. Now, we perceive no canons of good taste, no tragic buskin, no laborious modulations in the *Vicar of Wakefield*, which in its own vein is the most perfect type of eighteenth-century prose. Dear old Goldie! There is ease, pellucid simplicity, wit, pathos. I doubt if English prose has ever gone further, or will go further or higher.

After all I have said, I need not labor the grounds on which I feel Johnson, Burke, Gibbon, Macaulay, and Carlyle to be far from perfect as writers and positively fatal if taken as models. Old Samuel's Ciceronian pomp has actually dimmed our respect for his good sense and innate robustness of soul. Burke was too great an orator to be a consummate writer, as he was too profound a writer to be a perfect orator. Gibbon's imperial eagles pass on in one unending triumph, with the resounding blare of brazen trumpets, till we weary of the serried legions and grow dizzy with the show. And as to Macaulay and Carlyle, they carry emphasis to the point of exhaustion; for the peer bangs down his fist to clinch every sentence, and " Sartor " never ceases his uncouth gesticulations and grimace.

In our own century, Charles Lamb and Thackeray, I think, come nearest to Voltaire and Madame de Sévigné in purity of diction, in clearness, ease, grace, and wit. But a living writer — now long silent and awaiting his summons to the eternal silence — had powers which, had he cared to train them before he set about to reform the world, would have made him the noblest master who ever used the tongue of Milton. Need I name the versatile genius who labored here in Oxford so long and with such success? In the mass of his writings John Ruskin has struck the lyre of prose in every one of its infinite notes. He has been lucid, distinct, natural, fanciful, humorous, satiric, majestic, mystical, and prophetic by turns as the spirit moved within him. No Englishman — hardly Milton himself — has ever so completely mastered the tonic resources of English prose, its majesty and wealth of rhythm, the flexibility, mystery, and infinitude of its mighty diapason.[11]

Alas! the pity of it. These incomparable descants are but moments and interludes, and are too often chanted forth in mere wantonness of emotion. Too often they lead us on to formless verbosity and a passionate rhetoric, such as blind even temperate critics to the fact, that it is possible to pick out of the books of John Ruskin whole pages which in harmony, power, and glow have no match in the whole range of our prose.

And now I know I must not end without hazarding a few practical hints — what betting men and undergraduates call " tips " — for general remarks upon literature have little interest for those whose mind runs on sports, and perhaps even less for those whose mind is absorbed in the schools. But as there are always some who dream of a life of " letters," an occupation already too crowded and far from inviting at the best, they will expect me to tell them how I think they may acquire a command of Style. I know no reason why they should, and I know no way they could set about it. But, supposing one has something to say — something that it concerns the world to know — and this, for a young student, is a considerable claim, " a large order," I think he calls it in the current dialect, all I have to tell him is this: Think it out quite clearly in your own mind, and then put it down in the simplest words that offer, just as if you were telling it to a friend, but dropping the tags of the day with which your spoken discourse would naturally be garnished. Be familiar, but by no means vulgar. At any rate, be easy, colloquial if you like, but shun those vocables which come to us across the Atlantic, or from Newmarket and Whitechapel, with which the gilded youth and journalists " up-to-date " love to salt their language. Do not make us " sit up " too much, or always " take a back seat "; do not ask us to " ride for a fall," to " hurry up," or " boom it all we know." Nothing is more irritating in print than the iteration of slang, and those stale phrases with which " the half-baked " seek to convince us that they are " in the swim" and "going strong" — if I may borrow the language of the day — that Volapük of the smart and knowing world. It offends me like the reek of last night's tobacco.

It is a good rule for a young writer to avoid more than twenty or thirty words without a full stop, and not to put more than two commas in each sentence, so that its clauses should not exceed three. This, of course, only in practice. There is no positive law. A fine writer can easily place in a sentence one hundred words, and five or six minor clauses with their proper commas and colons. Ruskin was wont to toss off two or three hundred words and five-and-twenty commas without a pause. But even in the hand of such a magician this ends in failure, and is really grotesque in effect, for no such sentence can be spoken aloud. A beginner can seldom manage more than twenty-five words in one sentence with perfect ease. Nearly all young writers, just as men did in the early ages of prose composition, drift into ragged, preposterous, inorganic sentences, without beginning, middle, or end, which they ought to break into two or three.

And then they hunt up terms that are fit for science, poetry, or devotion. They affect " evolution " and " factors," " the interaction of forces," " the coördination of organs " ; or else everything is " weird," or " opalescent," " debonair," and " enamelled," so that they will not call a spade a spade. I do not say, stick to Saxon words and avoid Latin words as a law of language, because English now consists of both: good and plain English prose needs both. We seldom get the highest poetry without a large use of Saxon, and we hardly reach precise and elaborate explanation without Latin terms. Try to turn *precise and elaborate explanation* into strict Saxon ; and then try to turn " Our Father, which art in heaven " into pure Latin words. No! current English prose — not the language of poetry or of prayer — must be of both kinds, Saxon and Latin. But wherever a Saxon word is enough, use it; because if it have all the fulness and the precision you need, it is the more simple, the more direct, the more homely.

2 G

Never quote anything that is not apt and new. Those stale citations of well-worn lines give us a cold shudder, as does a pun at a dinner-party. A familiar phrase from poetry or Scripture may pass when imbedded in your sentence. But to show it round as a nugget which you have just picked up is the innocent freshman's snare. Never imitate any writer, however good. All imitation in literature is a mischief, as it is in art. A great and popular writer ruins his followers and mimics as did Raffaelle and Michelangelo; and when he founds a school of style, he impoverishes literature more than he enriches it. Johnson, Macaulay, Carlyle, Dickens, Ruskin have been the cause of flooding us with cheap copies of their special manner. And even now Meredith, Stevenson, Swinburne, and Pater lead the weak to ape their airs and graces. All imitation in literature is an evil. I say to you, as Mat Arnold said to me (who surely needed no such warning), " Flee Carlylese as the very devil ! " Yes, flee Carlylese, Ruskinese, Meredithese, and every other *ese*, past, present, and to come. A writer whose style invites imitation so far falls short of being a true master. He becomes the parent of caricature, and frequently he gives lessons in caricature himself.

Though you must never imitate any writer, you may study the best writers with care. And for study choose those who have founded no school, who have no special and imitable style. Read Pascal and Voltaire in French; Swift, Hume, and Goldsmith in English; and of the moderns, I think, Thackeray and Froude. Ruskin is often too rhapsodical for a student; Meredith too whimsical; Stevenson too " precious," as they love to call it; George Eliot too laboriously enamelled and erudite. When you cannot quietly enjoy a picture for the curiosity aroused by its so-called " brushwork," the painting may be a surprising sleight-of-hand, but is not a masterpiece.

Read Voltaire, Defoe, Swift, Goldsmith, and you will come to understand how the highest charm of words is reached without your being able to trace any special element of charm. The moment you begin to pick out this or that felicity of phrase, this or that sound of music in the words, and directly it strikes you as eloquent, lyrical, pictorial — then the charm is snapped. The style may be fascinating, brilliant, impressive; but it is not perfect.

Of melody in style I have said nothing; nor indeed can anything practical be said. It is a thing infinitely subtle, inexplicable, and rare.[12] If your ear does not hear the false note, the tautophony or the cacophony in the written sentence, as you read it or frame it silently to yourself, and hear it thus inaudibly long before your eye can pick it forth out of the written words, nay, even when the eye fails to localize it by analysis at all — then you have no inborn sense of the melody of words, and be quite sure that you can never acquire it. One living Englishman has it in the highest form; for the melody of Ruskin's prose may be matched with that of Milton and Shelley. I hardly know any other English prose which retains the ring of that ethereal music — echoes of which are more often heard in our poetry than in our prose. Nay, since it is beyond our reach, wholly incommunicable, defiant of analysis and rule, it may be more wise to say no more.

Read Swift, Defoe, Goldsmith, if you care to know what is pure English. I need hardly tell you to read another and a greater Book. The Book which begot English prose still remains its supreme type. The English Bible is the true school of English literature.[13] It possesses every quality of our language in its highest form — except for scientific precision, practical affairs, and philosophic analysis. It would be ridiculous to write an essay on metaphysics, a political article, or a novel in the language of the Bible.

Indeed, it would be ridiculous to write anything at all in the language of the Bible. But if you care to know the best that our literature can give in simple noble prose—mark, learn, and inwardly digest the Holy Scriptures in the English tongue.

[1] Compare above, pp. 160, 161.

[2] Strictly speaking, you cannot call Horace's *Ars Poetica* an "essay on Style"; though of course an epistle on the art of poetry would have to consider style, that is, *poetical* style, as an important side of the craft. — Compare Wackernagel, above, p. 3.

[3] See above, p. 181.

[4] Yet observe what Mr. Harrison says of style among the French (p. 442), and compare Brunetière's opinion of the way in which that style has been attained (above, pp. 417 ff.).

[5] Mr. Harrison is in accord with Mr. John Morley on this point. See the latter's *Studies in Literature*, p. 222: "I will even venture, with all respect to those who are teachers of literature, to doubt the excellence and utility of the practice of over-much essay-writing and composition. I have very little faith in rules of style, though I have an unbounded faith in the virtue of cultivating direct and precise expression. But you must carry on the operation inside the mind, and not merely by practising literary deportment on paper."

[6] "To thine own self be true." This is said by Polonius in *Hamlet*. Is the rest of Polonius's speech sound wisdom? How do these six words agree with the third Beatitude, or with Mark viii. 34?

[7] Compare Schopenhauer, above, p. 256. Is Schopenhauer addicted to exaggeration?

[8] Compare Longinus, above, pp. 103, 137, 142.

[9] Compare Wackernagel, above, pp. 6–7.

[10] Compare Coleridge, above, pp. 205–207.

[11] Chapter II of Mr. Harrison's volume is a fine appreciation of *Ruskin as Master of Prose*, the last paragraph beginning: "If, then, John Ruskin be not in actual achievement the greatest master who ever wrote in English prose, it is only because he refused to chasten his passion and his imagination until the prime of life was past."

[12] Yet Mr. Harrison attempts an explanation of "the quality of musical assonance" in Ruskin (Chap. II, pp. 57 ff.). His remarks there offer an interesting parallel to Stevenson's essay (above, pp. 379 ff.); compare also Coventry Patmore as quoted in his *Life*, by Basil Champneys, Vol. 1, p. 106.

[13] See Professor Albert S. Cook's *The Bible and English Prose Style*. Boston, Heath, 1892, and Professor C. S. Baldwin's *How to Write: A Handbook Based on the English Bible*, New York, Macmillan, 1905.

INDEX OF PROPER NAMES

453